Information Technology

and the Networked Economy

Information Technology

and the Networked Economy

Patrick G. McKeown
University of Georgia

Harcourt College Publishers

Fort Worth   Philadelphia   San Diego   New York   Orlando   Austin   San Antonio
Toronto   Montreal   London   Sydney   Tokyo

Publisher	Mike Roche
Executive Editor	Christina A. Martin
Market Strategist	Bill Bernys
Developmental Editor	Larry Crowder
Project Editor	Louise Slominsky
Art Director	Scott Baker
Production Manager	James McDonald

Cover Design   Bill Brammer Design
Cover Images   EyeWire, Inc.

ISBN: 0-03-020832-7

Address for Domestic Orders
Harcourt, Inc., 6277 Sea Harbor Drive, Orlando, FL 32887-6777
800-782-4479

Address for International Orders
International Customer Service
Harcourt, Inc., 6277 Sea Harbor Drive, Orlando, FL 32887-6777
407-345-3800
(fax) 407-345-4060
(e-mail) hbint@harcourtbrace.com

Address for Editorial Correspondence
Harcourt College Publishers, 301 Commerce Street, Suite 3700, Fort Worth, TX 76102

Web Site Address
http://www.harcourtcollege.com

Printed in the United States of America

0 1 2 3 4 5 6 7 8 9   048   9 8 7 6 5 4 3 2 1

Harcourt College Publishers

ⓟ r e f a c e

As we move into the twenty-first century, we also are moving quickly into the networked economy. Whereas the industrial economy was built on producing goods by leveraging human strength with machines, the networked economy will be built on producing services by leveraging human knowledge with computers and connectivity. The networked economy will be characterized by rapidly changing market conditions and methods of commerce. It will also require that organizations concentrate on improving their organizational productivity rather than worrying about personal productivity. As a result, colleges and universities must immediately begin to prepare their students to work in the networked economy. This textbook, *Information Technology and the Networked Economy*, is aimed at helping educators do just that by providing today's business students with the knowledge of the networked economy necessary to be successful employees and managers in the twenty-first century.

Every economy has needed an infrastructure to support the flow of goods and services between buyers and sellers. For the networked economy, information technology (IT) provides that infrastructure in the form of computers and connectivity that can process data into information and share data, information, and resources with others. Companies that want to survive and flourish in the networked economy must understand how that infrastructure works and how to take advantage of it. Learning how to use electronic commerce and the Internet to their advantage will be essential, as virtually all commerce becomes electronic. *Information Technology and the Networked Economy* uses this idea of information technology as the infrastructure of the networked economy to link the two concepts together.

When information technology is applied to organizations to help managers and employees make decisions, the result is usually referred to as information systems. These information systems must enable organizations to handle the present, remember the past, and prepare for the future. Handling the present requires organizations to have some way of processing transactions. Remembering the past requires that organizations find ways to use computers and networks to manage data, information, and knowledge resulting from handling the present. Preparing for the future requires that organizations use the stored data, information, and knowledge to make decisions that will enable them to be successful in the future. It also requires organizations to understand the use of electronic commerce to market and distribute products and services over the Internet. *Information Technology and the Networked Economy* covers the use of information systems and electronic commerce to handle the present, remember the past, and prepare for the future as a part of the preparation of the student to work in the networked economy.

Learning Objectives   *Information Technology and the Networked Economy* is built around achieving the following five key learning objectives. In so doing, it ensures that students will be prepared to be successful employees and managers in the networked economy. After reading this book, the student will be able to:

v

1. Understand the networked economy and how information technology provides the infrastructure for this new economy.

2. Describe how information technology is used to process data into information and to share data, information, and resources.

3. Discuss how information systems are used in organizations to handle the present, remember the past, prepare for the future, and to use electronic commerce.

4. Discuss the issues involved in the selection, acquisition, and development of information systems.

5. Understand the effect that information technology and the networked economy will have on crime, security, privacy, ethics, and society.

Achieving these learning objectives will go a long way toward providing the student with an understanding of the networked economy, information technology, information systems, and their effect on society.

Organization

To achieve the learning objectives, *Information Technology and the Networked Economy* is divided into four parts, as shown in the table below. In general, these parts should be covered in the order in which they appear, as should the chapters within each part. The one exception to this is part 4, which can be covered immediately after parts 1 or 2 have been covered if so desired. Because part 3, the design and development of information systems, is dependent on an understanding of the material on information systems in part 2, parts 2 and 3 should be covered in sequential order.

Part	Topical Coverage
1	Introduction to Information Technology and the Networked Economy
2	Information Systems in Organizations
3	Design and Development of Information Systems
4	Issues in the Networked Economy

Part 1 provides information about the networked economy and information technology. This part includes chapters on the networked economy, elements of information technology, and networks for sharing data, information, and resources.

Part 2 covers the effects of information technology on organizations and includes chapters on transaction processing systems for handling the present, organizational memory for remembering the past, decision support systems for preparing for the future, and electronic commerce as a way of transforming organizations. This section provides the student with a complete discussion of information systems as they enable organizations in the networked economy not just to survive, but to grow.

Part 3 considers the issues involved in developing or acquiring information systems. This includes topics on designing new information systems and making the decision whether to acquire, outsource, or develop the new system. This section also covers the process of developing an information system. These chapters provide the student with an understanding of the systems development process including the structured approach, RAD, outsourcing, and acquisition.

Finally, part 4 covers the impact of information technology and the networked economy on society in the areas of security, crime, privacy, ethics, health, and lifestyle. This includes a chapter on crime and security in organizations, a chapter on privacy and ethical issues, and a chapter on the societal issues associated with information technology and the networked economy.

Approach to Topics

To prepare readers to work in the networked economy using information technology and information systems, *Information Technology and the Networked Economy* uses a variety of pedagogical elements. An important element is a case, fareastfoods.com, that runs through all of the chapters. Involving a small distributor of oriental foods via the Internet, this case provides students with a look at the ways in which companies use information technology and information systems to transact business in the networked economy. Fareastfoods.com takes orders over the Internet that it fulfills by ordering individual items from wholesalers. The individual food items are combined to create a shipment that is picked up by a package delivery company and delivered to the customer. As we move through the book, the various aspects of information technology and information systems are applied to the company. For example, in the chapters on systems development (chapters 8 and 9), a new information system is created for the company.

Other pedagogical elements in this book include Quick Review questions after each major section, sixty boxed inserts, review questions, discussion questions, and a case at the end of each chapter. The Quick Review questions enable students to check their understanding of the material immediately after reading it. Answers to these questions are available on the Web site associated with the book so students can gauge their comprehension of the material.

There are five boxed inserts in each chapter covering six different focus areas: management, society, technology, the Internet, and people. They provide interesting information about elements of the networked economy beyond the material covered in the body of the chapter. The Focus on Management boxes discuss companies or situations that illustrate business situations or problems in the networked economy. For example, the Focus on Management box in chapter 1 describes the transition of General Electric to the use of electronic commerce. The Focus on Society boxes present scenarios or problems associated with the onset of the networked economy. For example, the Focus on Society box in chapter 12 covers the problems facing people living in "Internet time." The technology focus boxes describe, in greater detail, technologies associated with the chapter topic. For example, the Focus on Technology box in chapter 3 describes the latest technology for wireless access to the Internet. The Focus on the Internet boxes describe Internet applications or companies that use or support the chapter topic. For example, in the chapter on security and crime (chapter 10), the Internet focus box describes a new Internet application that enables users to securely save electronic documents in Safe-DepositBox.com. Finally, the Focus on People boxes provide an inside look at people closely associate with the growth of the networked economy. For example, the Focus on People box in chapter 6, on decision support systems, describes Bill Inmon, the father of the data warehouse.

The review and discussion questions at the end of the chapter provide the reader with an opportunity to review what they have learned from the chapter and to research and discuss issues associated with the material. The end-of-chapter case, WildOutfitters.com, is a continuing case that introduces the reader to Alex and Claire Campagne, owners of a small shop specializing in equipment and provisions for outdoor recreation located near the New River Gorge of West Virginia. The Campagnes are moving their business onto the Internet and the case asks students to apply what they have learned in the chapter to the development of the company. The WildOutfitters.com cases also requests that readers use Microsoft Office (or equivalent software) to solve problems associated with the situation described in the case.

Ancillary Materials

In addition to this textbook, there are a variety of ancillary items that are a part of the *Information Technology and the Networked Economy* package. These include a complete set of slides in Microsoft PowerPoint format, created by Norman Hollingsworth of Georgia Perimeter College; and a Test Bank, in electronic format, that includes more than fifteen hundred test questions, created by Mark Huber of the University of Georgia. Both of these are available to adopters of the textbook. In addition, there will be two Web sites associated with this book, one that provides information and data files to both instructors and students and one that is associated with the running case on fareastfoods.com.

The Web site for the textbook, at http://www.harcourtcollege.com/infosys/mckeown, will provide students with data files necessary to work with the WildOutfitters.com case as well as answers to the Quick Review questions in the text. For instructors, this Web site provides a wealth of material, including an online Instructor's Manual, additional boxed inserts, and Microsoft Excel projects. The online Instructor's Manual contains a variety of items for each chapter, including: teaching objectives, learning objectives, chapter outlines, chapter reviews, list of teaching suggestions, annotated list of boxed inserts, suggested readings and Web sites, answers to review and discussion questions, and suggested solutions to the WildOutfitters cases.

The Web site, http://www.fareastfoods.com, corresponds to the case that runs throughout the textbook and allows students to interact with a simulated electronic commerce company. Although students cannot actually receive goods from fareastfoods.com, they can carry out all of the other activities described in the text.

A special ancillary available only to adopters of *Information Technology and the Networked Economy* are a group of Microsoft Excel projects and associated spreadsheet grading software. These Excel projects can be assigned independently of the textbook, to provide the students with opportunities to practice their spreadsheet skills. The spreadsheet grading software can grade spreadsheet projects stored on a local or network drive, create a class roll spreadsheet of student names and ID numbers and copy the grading results to it, and send the graded spreadsheets back to the student. All of this is accomplished automatically without requiring the instructor to be involved in the process.

Acknowledgments

Anyone familiar with writing a textbook such as this knows that the final product is not just the work of the author, but the result of a team effort. The team for *Information Technology and the Networked Economy* included many talented people, and I am thankful for their efforts. First, I want to thank Richard T. Watson of the Terry College of Business at the University of Georgia for his work as Consulting Editor on the text. In this role, Rick worked with me to define the key ideas in the text, discussed the topical coverage of each chapter with me, and acted as first reviewer of each chapter. I certainly could not have written this book without his help. I also want to thank Craig Piercy of Towson University for writing the WildOutfitters.com cases that appear at the end of each chapter. He brought to this part of the book a special talent for making the cases interesting as well as useful in the learning process. The health section of chapter 12 is primarily the result of work carried out by my wife, Carolyn McKeown, RN, BSN, and I want to express special thanks to her for that effort.

I also want to express my appreciation for those who reviewed one or more chapters of the manuscript. The final text reflects many of their ideas.

I would like to thank those at Harcourt College Publishers who were involved in editing and producing this textbook. Larry Crowder did an outstanding job as Developmental Editor in working with me to create the project. Louise Slominsky worked as Project Editor and I appreciate her efforts. Thanks also go to the Production Manager, James McDonald; to the Permissions Editor, Linda Blundell; to Mike Nichols who copyedited the manuscript; and to the Art Director, Scott Baker, who designed the book. I also want to express my sincere appreciation to Christina Martin, Executive Editor for Computer Technologies, for doing an outstanding job of seeing this project to completion and for being patient with me.

Finally, my acknowledgements would be incomplete without again mentioning my wife, Carolyn. Without her love, support, and work on the project, I would not have been able to complete it on time.

Reviewers

Stephen Barclay *Southwest Texas State University*

Harry Benham *Montana State University*

Melinda Cline *University of North Texas*

Lauren Eder *Rider University*

Dale Goodhue *University of Georgia*

Susan Helms *Metropolitan State College of Denver*

Dolly Samson *Weber State University*

Richard Watson *University of Georgia*

*To my family—my wife, Carolyn; my daughter,
Ashley and her husband, Todd; and my son, Christopher*

Contents

⊙ Part 2   INFORMATION SYSTEMS IN ORGANIZATIONS 95

CHAPTER 4   HANDLING THE PRESENT WITH TRANSACTION PROCESSING SYSTEMS 97

Introduction to Information Technology and the Networked Economy

The dramatic growth of electronic commerce over the Internet and the World Wide Web is changing the way we live, work, and play in many ways. One important change is the transition from the industrial economy to the new networked economy. The networked economy is based on computers, connectivity, and human knowledge and will involve changes in the way goods and services are created, produced, sold, and distributed. Like the industrial and agricultural economies, the networked economy must have an underlying infrastructure. In the case of the networked economy, the infrastructure is known as information technology (IT). IT includes computer hardware and software as well as the computer networks that make connectivity possible.

Part one will introduce you to the networked economy and information technology. This introduction will begin with a broad discussion of both areas followed by chapters on computer hardware and software and computer networks. After reading this first part, you should have a good idea about the networked economy and information technology.

The Networked Economy: A New Way of Doing Business

> Learning Objectives

After reading this chapter, you should be able to answer the following questions:

> In what ways is our world moving into a networked economy?

> How is the networked economy "changing the rules"?

> What are the key elements of the networked economy?

> What is the infrastructure of the networked economy?

> What is the role of information technology in organizations?

Ⓕocus on Management

Selling Tickets at AirTran

Today, the airline industry is highly competitive, with a heavy emphasis on customer service and low ticket prices. Customers give (or withhold) loyalty to an airline based on their perception of a wide range of issues. Because it competes in the same market as Atlanta-based Delta Airline, AirTran Airlines must be able to provide services that exceed those offered by Delta if it hopes to survive. Although AirTran is a pioneer in low fares and ticketless travel, Delta has been able to match AirTran's fares on the same routes and has also gone to electronic tickets on many routes.

In early 1998, faced with competing with an industry giant like Delta, AirTran made the move to the World Wide Web as a way of increasing ticket sales. This enabled it to sell tickets on a 24–7 basis while keeping costs down. Unlike many other airline Web sites, the AirTran site developed by Intellimedia Commerce is designed to show the customer the *least* expensive flights and routes.

Even with a great Web site, AirTran felt that there were other ways to market tickets that otherwise might go unsold. This led AirTran to use e-mail as a marketing tool to sell what it calls *e-fares* to customers who sign up to receive announcements of special fares, new routes, and other information. These e-mailings build loyalty, increase sales, and allow AirTran to send messages to its Internet-savvy customers. When AirTran sent out the first e-mail offer, Internet-based sales *tripled*. Now, if they are interested in special deals, customers know to wait for these e-mailings before purchasing their tickets.

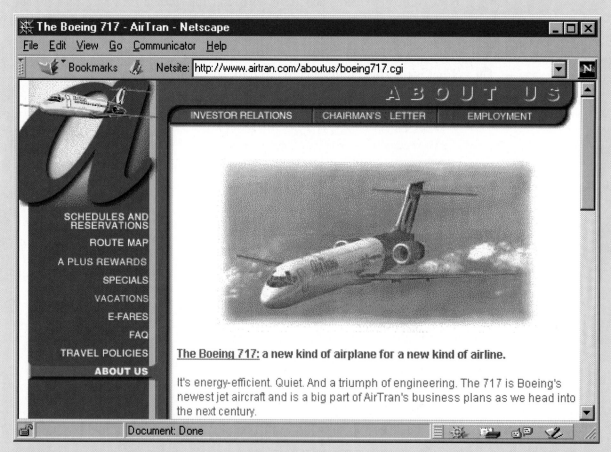

Customers can make reservations and purchase tickets at the AirTran Web site.

Our Changing World

Depending on when you are reading this text, the twenty-first century either will arrive soon or has already come on January 1, 2001. Although we do not yet have the spaceships and artificially intelligent computers portrayed in the movie *2001: A Space Odyssey,* we do have many other dramatic innovations not even considered in the wildest dreams by the creators of this movie. Specifically, computers combined with connectivity in the form of high-speed communications media form **computer networks** that are dramatically changing the way we live, work, and shop. For example, as noted in the previous Focus on Management box, you can visit Web sites to purchase airline tickets or just wait until an e-mail message offers you a special low fare. Similarly, almost all television advertisements now have a subtitle that gives the advertiser's Web page that it wants you to visit to purchase items. It is also becoming quite common for your business card to have both an e-mail address and your personal Web page address in addition to your name, affiliation, telephone number, fax number, and postal address.

It would be impossible to try to discuss the many ways that computer networks, specifically the **Internet** and the **World Wide Web,** have changed our lives. In fact, these networks are having far greater effects on our lives than any other event since the invention of the printing press. Just as the printing press made books available to a large proportion of the population, leading to widespread education, computer networks are making it possible to carry out a virtually unlimited number of activities from our home or office. For example, we can find information on automobile features and prices before actually buying a car, communicate with friends and relatives with e-mail on a virtually instantaneous basis, join a chat group discussing problem cats, listen to distant radio stations live, and buy gifts and have them shipped without ever going to the mall. Surely you can think of many more ways to use computer networks.

By the middle of 1999, it was estimated that 165 million people were using the Internet around the world, up from only 26 million in 1995. Approximately half of these users are in the United States, and another 37 million are in Europe. This number is expected to grow to at least 320 million by the end of 2000 and 720 million worldwide by the end of 2005. You should remember, however, that most estimates of Internet growth have fallen far short of the actual results.

With the Internet, business is changing as more and more people "go online" to make purchases from businesses on a basis of twenty-four hours a day, seven days a week (24-7). **Electronic commerce,** which is the term used for carrying out business transactions on the Web, like those discussed in the opening Focus on Management box, is growing at a rapid rate, with over $10 billion in U.S. sales for the 1999 holiday sales season alone—three times the amount in 1998. During the 1998 holiday period, it is estimated that over thirty-two million adults in the United States used the Web to research purchases and that eight million actually made a purchase. Total consumer online sales are predicted to reach $920 billion by 2002, but as with predictions of the number of people using the Internet, predictions of the volume of electronic commerce are probably too conservative. Even more important will be the transactions between businesses, which are predicted to grow from $48 billion in 1998 to $1.3 *trillion* by 2003. Figure 1-1 shows the projected growth for both business-to-consumer and business-to-business electronic commerce.

The Networked Economy

Electronic commerce is not just a new way of handling business transactions—it is part of a new economy that is rapidly replacing the industrial economy in which the world has lived and worked for two hundred years. The industrial economy was built on the existence of capital, in the form of factories and machines, and labor, in the

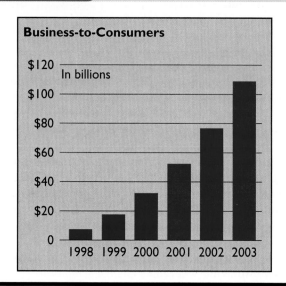

Business-to-Consumers

$120
In billions
$100
$80
$60
$40
$20
0
1998 1999 2000 2001 2002 2003

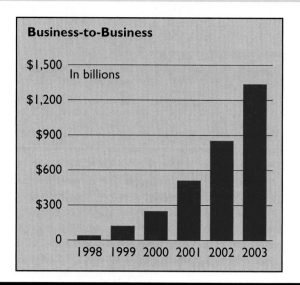

Business-to-Business

$1,500
In billions
$1,200
$900
$600
$300
0
1998 1999 2000 2001 2002 2003

form of employees. The new economy, which we term the **networked economy** (also known as the Internet economy or the digital economy), is a combination of enhanced, transformed, or new economic relationships based on computer networks and human knowledge. Because all economies are built on meeting the needs and desires of humans, they encompass a wide variety of economic relationships between people, including those between firms and customers, between firms and employees, and so on. Although electronic commerce is just a small portion of the total economy today, in the near future it is quite possible that the vast majority of all commerce will be electronic in some way. A report from the University of Texas in mid-1999 estimated that the networked economy generated $507 billion in 1999 and created 2.3 million jobs.[1] The size of the networked economy is doubling every nine months and includes infrastructure (computer hardware), applications (computer software), and intermediaries, in addition to electronic commerce. Workers in networked economy companies were found to be twice as productive as other workers and to earn 78 percent more. Finally, the report predicted that almost half of all U.S. workers will be employed by networked economy companies by the year 2006.

Although you may not buy an automobile over the Internet, you will probably conduct research, prior to making a purchase, that way. To see how our economy has changed over the last one hundred years, in 1900, 35 percent of Americans worked in farming, 35 percent worked in manufacturing, and 30 percent worked in service industries. In 1999, only 2 percent worked in farming, and 75 percent worked in service industries! A primary result of the movement to the networked economy is that organizations of all types will need to learn how to use the combination of computers, connectivity, and human knowledge to remain competitive and to survive. No longer can organizations hope to do the same thing they have been doing for years; instead, they must change or else risk being driven out of business by competitors they did not know existed. The essence of the networked economy is not just change; it is change at an accelerating rate of *speed*. Speed is such an important element of the networked economy that it is not uncommon to hear executives speak of working in *Web time*, in which one *Web year* equals about three months of a normal year. Companies must continually

1. http://www.internetindicators.com

scan the environment for new ways to serve their customers or else another company will serve their customers instead. This may mean radically changing the way these companies have done business or actually may spur companies to move into a new business.

The transition to the networked economy will affect you both as an individual and as an employee of a business or nonprofit organization. As an individual, you will need to learn how to take advantage of the new opportunities for information, employment, and entertainment that are becoming constantly available in this new economy. As an employee, you will need to look for ways to help your organization take advantage of the opportunities for new markets afforded by the networked economy. You will need to do this regardless of the type of position you hold in the organization—it will not be restricted to those elements of the company normally associated with technology. This textbook is aimed at helping you, the business student, who must be prepared to take advantage of the almost unlimited possibilities associated with this new economy.

As an example of a company that was able to make the transition to the networked economy, consider the publisher of *Encyclopedia Britannica*. For over two hundred years, the *Encyclopedia Britannica* company was an extremely successful business, publishing and selling twenty-volume sets of books that summarized the known knowledge of humankind. However, in 1994, it slipped from number one to number three in this market behind two CD-ROM-based encyclopedias. These CD-ROMs provided audio and video that could be updated every three months rather than every ten years like a text encyclopedia. When the Britannica company looked at this situation, it made a dramatic decision; rather than copy the CD-ROM market, which, after all, provided only a "snapshot" of the knowledge, Britannica decided to put its encyclopedia online on the Internet and to charge subscriptions for access to the Web site. With this approach, information can be updated on an hour-by-hour basis instead of waiting for a new CD-ROM version to come out in three months.

Old versus New: Purchasing a Camera

To help you understand the many ways the networked economy is changing our lives and our ways of doing business, we will compare the process of purchasing a camera before the introduction of the World Wide Web with that of purchasing a camera using the Web. In making this comparison, we will use the ownership model shown in Figure 1-2. In this model, there are four stages of ownership:

Figure 1-2   The Ownership Process

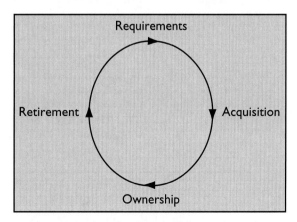

Source: B. Ives and G. P. Learmouth, "The Information System as a Competitive Weapon," *Communications of the ACM*, 27 (12) (1984), pp. 1193–1201.

requirements, acquisition, ownership, and retirement. In the requirements stage, the customers determine their needs, and in the acquisition stage, they actually acquire (purchase, rent, or lease) the product or service. In the ownership stage, the customers use the product or service, whereas in the retirement stage, they dispose of it.

The methods of carrying out the four stages of the ownership process are compared in Table 1-1 for the "old" (pre-Web) way of doing things and for the "new" (using the Web) way. The addresses for some example Web sites are also included in this table.

Looking at Table 1-1, we can see that before the introduction of the World Wide Web, the potential owner was forced to spend a great deal of time carrying out the various activities on the telephone, corresponding by mail, or in person as compared to the capability to handle all the activities over the Web, including researching types of cameras, finding the best prices and purchasing a camera, learning better ways to use it, and later disposing of the camera by selling it.

For example, consider the requirements process; instead of purchasing magazines and looking through the advertisements searching for information on cameras, or calling a camera company requesting a paper brochure, the would-be camera owners simply point their Web browser at any of a multitude of Web sites that provide a wealth of information on specific brands or that compare types of cameras. This saves the purchasers a great deal of time and effort while providing them with much more useful information. The same can be said about the other three stages of this ownership model.

As an aside, it is worth noting that the type of camera being purchased in this example may be different also. Instead of a traditional film camera (35mm or otherwise), a digital camera that can be used to download pictures directly into a computer may be purchased.

Quick Review

1. Discuss examples of the networked economy with which you are familiar.
2. Compare some activity or purchase as it would have been handled before the Web with how it can be handled now using the Web.

Table 1-1	Comparing the Ownership Process	
Ownership Stage	**Old (pre-Web)**	**New (using the Web)**
Requirements	Go to the library or purchase magazines to review camera types; request brochures from camera companies	Visit Web sites of camera companies to learn about cameras (www.minolta.com); visit independent Web sites to compare cameras (www.photoshopper.com)
Acquisition	Call or visit camera stores to determine the availability and prices of cameras; purchase camera from store	Compare camera prices at online camera suppliers or online retail stores (www.thecameraclub.com); purchase camera online (www.wolfcamera.com)
Ownership	To learn photographic techniques, check out or purchase books on photography; also, attend classes	Visit Web sites to learn photographic techniques (www.shortcourses.com or www.photo-seminars.com)
Retirement	Advertise camera for sale in newspaper classified section	Sell camera on auction Web sites (www.ebay.com)

The purchase of a camera can be researched and carried out easily using the Web.

Changing the Rules

As noted in a comparison of the old (pre-Web) and the new (using the Web) ownership process shown in Table 1-1, things are being done differently in the networked economy. Not only are events occurring at a much faster rate in the new economy, but many other basic changes also are occurring, as shown in Table 1-2. This table compares five key areas of change in the industrial and networked economy: scarcity, searching strategies, transactions, communications, and information storage.

Scarcity

In terms of scarcity, the most precious commodity in the networked economy will not necessarily be land or capital (money), as has been the case in the industrial economies; instead, it likely will be time. Although it usually is possible to find another place to build a factory or office building or to borrow additional funds to start a business, everybody is limited to the same amount of time each day—exactly twenty-four hours, of which some time must be set aside for sleep. With the world moving at a faster and faster pace, any way to reduce the time necessary to carry out

Table 1-2 Areas of Change in Economies

Areas of Change	Industrial Economy	Networked Economy
Scarcity	Land, capital (money)	Time
Searching strategies	Paper-based, in person or by telephone	Web-based
Transactions	Face-to-face, telephone, or postal mail using coins, paper money, checks, or credit cards	E-mail, Web, other electronic means using electronic payment methods
Communications	One-to-one, one-to-many	Many-to-many
Information storage	Analog	Digital

an activity will be valuable. Instead of being limited by so-called business hours, during which traditional merchants are open, in the networked economy, banks, stores, and other providers will be open on a 24-7 basis, meeting customer needs rather than their own needs. This does not mean that people will stop sleeping, only that Internet technology will provide services around the clock.

As further evidence of changes that the networked economy is bringing to the concept of scarcity, consider the fact that every computer added to the Internet or other computer network *increases* rather than decreases the value of computers already on the network. This contradicts one of the major tenets of the industrial economy: that value is derived from fewer rather than more of some item. To understand how adding a new device to a network can *increase* the value of the other devices on the network, think about the first fax machine. No matter how much money was spent creating the first fax machine, when it was first built, it was useless until a second fax machine was built, at which time it became valuable. The same was true of the first telephone, first modem, and so on. Today, as each new fax machine is added in a home or office, it makes your fax machine more valuable because there is a new person with whom to exchange faxes.

Known as **network externalities,** this relationship states that as the number of devices added to a network goes up linearly, the power (or value) of the network goes up as the square of the number of devices on the network. Each person who joins the Internet or adds a Web page to the World Wide Web makes your connection to the Internet more valuable. For example, every person who joins the very popular eBay auction network adds value to current members because of additional opportunities to buy and sell items. This relationship was first realized by Bob Metcalf (and named after him), the inventor of Ethernet, the most popular network for local sharing of data and information. The result of Metcalf's Law is demonstrated in Figure 1-3.

Metcalf's Law can cause seemingly strange tactics from companies. For example, why do mobile phone companies give away (or sell at a much reduced price) their phones, or why do both Microsoft and Netscape give away very valuable Web browser software? In both cases, it is to expand the network from which the companies may receive greater returns. For the mobile phone companies, it is the airtime used by their customers from which returns are received. Microsoft and Netscape hope to make a profit to cover the free browsers from the other software they market that is required to support the Web. There are many other examples of this principle at work as the networked economy supplants the industrial economy.

Figure 1-3 Metcalf's Law

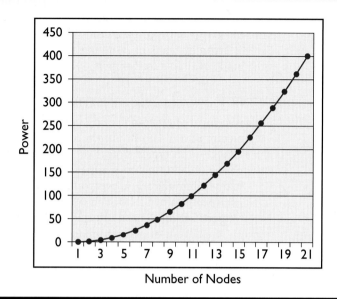

Number of Nodes

Searching Strategies

Regardless of whether a consumer or a business is making a purchase, finding the right product or service for the best price is an important part of the process. This requires a search strategy and is another area in which the networked economy has changed from the industrial economy. No longer is it necessary to search in person, over the telephone, or by mail; instead, the entire process can be handled using the World Wide Web. The Web's many search engines can bring enormous amounts of information to your desktop in a matter of seconds. For example, this book was researched almost entirely over the Web using a variety of news sources and searching techniques. If we accept the concept that time is *the* scarce commodity in the networked economy, then a Web-based searching strategy is the most valuable tool available.

Although the convenience of a Web-based searching strategy often translates into a few saved hours for consumers, for businesses it can mean the difference between prospering in the networked economy or going out of business. Instead of searching manually for a supplier to obtain a needed part or service at the lowest price, Internet technology makes it possible for businesses to do this search electronically from their offices. There are even computer programs, known as **intelligent agents,** that can be trained to carry out this search for the businessperson. Companies that find ways to deliver products and services while saving the customer time will be the ones that prosper in the networked economy.

Transactions

Instead of dealing with merchants on a face-to-face basis in their store or place of business, over the telephone, or through the postal mail, it is now possible for customers to access a much wider array of goods and services from the Web. Once selected, these goods and services can be purchased in much less time with a few clicks of the mouse. Items for sale over the Web cover the full spectrum of goods and services, from groceries to automobiles to computer software. In the case of physical goods, package delivery services deliver the goods to your door in a matter of days, whereas for computer software, you can usually download the software and use it for a period of time (usually up to thirty days) *before* you actually pay for it.

In the industrial economy, payment was usually in the form of coins, paper money, checks, or some form of credit. Today, it is possible to use a wide variety of electronic payment options to purchase goods and services over the Web. Although the credit card is still the most widely used payment method, other, more flexible electronic means of handling this part of the transaction are being developed and made available to shoppers.

Communications

One of the key results of the World Wide Web is **many-to-many communication,** that is, a form of communication in which any person on the Internet can easily communicate with a large number of people also using the Internet. This is a dramatic change from typical forms of communication that have been one-to-one (e.g., telephone calls) or one-to-many (e.g., newspapers, radio, and television). With many-to-many communication, everyone on the network can be a writer, a publisher, an artist, or an entertainer. Although not everybody is a good writer or artist, there is still a tremendous amount of information that flows around the Web each day.

The advent of many-to-many communication is creating **electronic communities,** that is, exciting communities that are real in the sense that there are actual people but electronic in the sense that community members communicate with other members without regard to who they are, where they live, or what time of day or night it is. In a sense, the tyranny of time and distance has been defeated.

Information Storage

Since the introduction of the printing press, the most common form of information storage has been paper. However, in the networked economy, information is being stored in a **digital form,** that is, as strings of zeros and ones in computers. As we shall discuss shortly, computers are based totally on digital technology.

Focus on Technology

Downloading Digital Music

In the fall of 1998, a company named Diamond Multimedia changed the face of music when they released a device called the Rio PMP 300, or as it is commonly called, Diamond Rio. As you may know, the Diamond Rio was the first of many devices that can play MP3 files. An **MP3 file** is a digital file that has been compressed to one-twelfth its original size with little loss of sound quality. MP3 stands for MPEG-1, Audio Layer 3 where MPEG is a standard compression method sponsored by the Motion Picture Experts Group and is one of several standards for compressing audio and video. Compression was necessary since one second of music stored digitally takes the equivalent of 175,000 characters (about 87.5 typewritten pages). This means that one three-minute song could require 31.5 million characters of memory. By using MP3 compression, this is reduced to about 2.5 million characters—a far more manageable amount.

The reason that MP3 changed the face of music is that the huge files on music CDs can be com-pressed down to a size that allows them to be stored internally on the players or on a computer hard disk. This means that almost anybody can make pirated copies of music CDs and distribute them over the Internet. This brought a very strong reaction from the Recording Industry Association of America (RIAA), which unsuccessfully sued to stop the release of the original Diamond Rio playback device. There are many sites on the Web where music can be illegally downloaded. To combat this music piracy, several other digital systems have been created including some that have been approved by RIAA. One such competitor to MP3 is Liquid Audio, which markets a compression system that does not allow songs to be copied. A variety of artists and record labels are testing this market by allowing songs to be downloaded in MP3 and Liquid Audio formats in hopes of increasing sales for the associated album.

Analog cassette tapes now are widely available in a digital form for both music and videos.

Digital storage of information is much more compact than paper storage and is less subject to deterioration. In addition, it is possible to create backup versions of the information. To understand the use of digital storage, let's compare it to **analog** devices that convert conditions, such as movement, temperature, and sound, into analogous electronic or mechanical patterns. You may have used both analog and digital devices to play music. For example, an analog audiocassette uses physical changes in the magnetic field on the tape to represent the music or other sounds that have been recorded. On the other hand, a compact disk or minidisk contains all sounds in a digital form that is played using a laser light. Although analog machines can capture the subtle nature of the real world, they cannot make repeated copies of output without marked signs of deterioration. On the other hand, digital devices provide consistency in manipulation, storage, and transmission that is not possible with analog devices. Also, the compact disk or minidisk can be played thousands of times without loss of quality, something that is not possible with an audiocassette tape.

In addition to information storage, there is a rapid movement from analog to digital technology in communications and in cameras as we see the market for digital cameras increasing. Table 1-3 compares analog and digital services for the same needs.

Table 1-3	Comparing Analog and Digital Services	
Purpose	**Analog**	**Digital**
Reproduce music or speech	Cassette tapes or vinyl records	Compact disk, minidisk, or Diamond REO
Reproduce video	Analog video tape	Digital video tape and DVD
Send audio	Plain old telephone service (POTS) and analog mobile phones	Digital cellular telephone service, ADSL service
Send audio and video	Broadcast and analog television	Direct broadcast satellite service, digital cable service
Photography	Film cameras	Digital cameras

Impact on Business and Industry

What does this change from an industrial economy to a networked economy mean to business and industry? In the industrial economy, every production worker's job was to find out how to do his or her job better, thereby increasing the productivity of the factory. Entire fields of study have been built around the concept of optimizing the known. In the networked economy, most repetitive production tasks will be handled by robots controlled by chips, freeing humans to use their unique knowledge to find the task that should be accomplished next. Instead of worrying about solving a current problem, organizations should explore ways to use their current knowledge base to take advantage of new opportunities. Although many of these explorations may turn out to be failures, it takes only one success to generate far more revenue than does solving all existing problems. As noted management author Peter Drucker said, "Don't solve problems, seek opportunities."

It is important to remember that *success in a networked economy is nonlinear*—by the time you realize something is a success, it has probably gone beyond the point where you can take advantage of it. This means that both individuals and organizations must constantly scan their environment to find new ideas and technologies *before* they become successes. By so doing, they will be able to benefit from the oncoming success. Unlike the industrial economy, where companies had the luxury of taking a "wait-and-see" attitude about new technology, companies in the networked economy cannot afford to delay.

The speed of change in the networked economy means that organizations must constantly reinvent themselves if they are to survive. Termed **creative destruction** by the European-born U.S. economist Peter Schumpeter (1883–1950), this concept emphasizes that the most important part of the change process for a business is not what *remains* after the change but rather what has been *destroyed*. Without a destruction of the old ways of carrying out business, we cannot create the new. Creative destruction often requires an entirely new way of thinking about the problems facing a business. Executives may need to redefine the problems or reframe the questions; simply doing business as usual will not suffice. For example, Reuben Mattus decided that he needed to creatively destroy his existing Bronx ice cream product in order to be successful. Rather than change the ingredients or the formula, he changed the product name to Haagen-Dazs and raised the price. It did not matter that the name had no meaning in any language or that the same product now cost more, he had successfully redefined his approach to business.

The need to carry out creative destruction is never more important or more difficult than when a company is at the top of its industry. Often, there is a feeling of having done well and little desire to rock the boat. However, it is at this time that looking for new opportunities becomes critical; otherwise, the company can easily be surpassed by competitors as they take advantage of opportunities. There are numerous examples of companies that were industry leaders one year only to find themselves outstripped by competition the next. Lotus, with its 1-2-3 spreadsheet product, and WordPerfect, with its word processing software, were two companies that failed to take full advantage of the transition to the Windows operating system and quickly lost much of their market share to the Microsoft Office Suite. Similarly, Hayes Microcomputers, at one time the dominant force in computer modems, went bankrupt in 1998 because other companies found better and cheaper ways to manufacture modems. On the other hand, Apple Computers is a company that went through a painful process of creative destruction only to survive as a stronger company with new products and ideas.

Quick Review

1. List the five ways in which the rules are being changed.

2. What are *network externalities,* and what do they have to do with the networked economy?

Elements of the Networked Economy

By now, you should be convinced that the networked economy is bringing about great changes in our personal lives as well as in business and industry. Let's now take a closer look at the elements of the networked economy: computers, connectivity, and knowledge. These three elements work together so that each element *multiplies* the effect of the other elements, thereby enhancing, transforming, and creating new economic relationships in the networked economy. This can be represented as a triangle, as shown in Figure 1-4.

Economic Relationships

Traditionally, management primarily has been concerned with three economic relationships: relationships with customers, relationships with employees, and relationship with suppliers. However, in the networked economy, a whole host of different relationships is now possible. Consumers are not always just customers; in some cases, they take on the role of employees. For example, over one million consumers acted as testers for advance copies of Windows 95. While performing the testing, were these testers considered customers or unpaid employees of Microsoft who benefited from being among the first to use the new operating system? In addition to modified existing relationships, new relationships can come into being. For example, relationships between customers are now important to firms when those customers form user groups that provide important feedback to the firms about their products. In some cases, employees within the firms actually form direct relationships between themselves and customers, as they become special service representatives. The firms that will benefit most from these changes will be those that take the greatest advantage of the new and different relationships by thinking "outside of the box" about ways to improve customer service. Figure 1-5 shows the various relationships that are possible in the networked economy.

Computers

Computers provide the processing and communications capabilities for the networked economy. That is, they are the element that can process raw data into useful information and then send this information over the network to other computers. When you think of a computer, you probably immediately think of a personal computer as either a desktop or laptop computer. However, there are many other types of computers that are an important part of the networked economy, including computers that handle the millions of transactions that occur on a daily basis either over the Internet or at the local grocery store or at a shop in the mall. The computers that keep track of inventory at all stages of production and distribution are included in the networked economy, as are the computers that are used to design products or to run the network. Today, there are between 400 and 500 million computers in use.

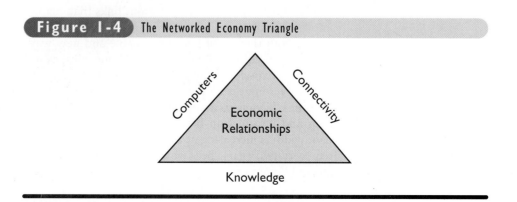

Figure 1-4 The Networked Economy Triangle

Figure 1-5 Possible Relationships in the Networked Economy

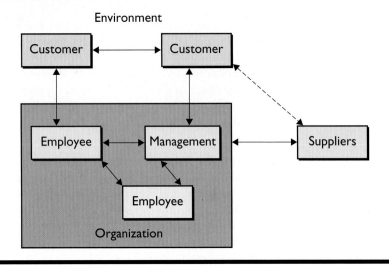

All of these computers are built around the **chip,** the ever-shrinking marvel of miniaturized electronic circuitry that carries out instructions from the user or the manufacturer. A chip can contain as many as twenty million transistors—electronic on–off switches—that are connected on the chip in such a way as to carry out an almost infinite variety of operations. It may be obvious to you that, in addition to computers, fax machines, cellular phones, pagers, handheld games, digital clocks, and other electronic devices also have at least one chip in them, but its use is far more widespread than that. Chips are used in many other devices to measure and report data to computers, where the data are processed or used to control operations of some machine. For example, there are more chips in today's automobile than there are in a personal computer.

Since the invention of the chip in the early 1970s, chips that power today's computers and other information technology have followed Moore's Law, which states that they will double in power every eighteen months. This has resulted in faster, easier-to-use computers as well as in cheaper, more useful machines of all types. Chips are becoming so cheap to manufacture that they are a part of our "throwaway" economy. For example, we have already seen the introduction of chips on one-time usage smart cards.

Connectivity

Although computers are a key element in our changing world, another development—connectivity—has magnified their potential. **Connectivity** refers to the availability of high-speed communications links that enable the transmission of data and information between computers and conversations between people. This has involved both the use of fiber optic cable and new ways of using traditional copper wire to send voice and data over telephone lines, as well as the increasing use of TV cable as a two-way communications medium.

The ever-increasing power of chips has also had a significant impact on communications, leading to dramatically increased capacity, or **bandwidth,** for transmitting data and information between computers. Author George Gilder has noted that bandwidth is increasing at a much faster rate than computer power—by a power of ten every two years. Because communication is the basis for our entire culture, increased communications capabilities will have far-reaching implications for all of us. In the year 2000, the volume of data (computer-to-computer) traffic over our telecommunications networks surpassed that of voice traffic. It is predicted that by

ⓕocus on People

Ted Hoff

With chips being the technological driving force behind the networked economy, it is useful to look at their origins. In 1959, Jack Kilby of Texas Instruments and Robert Noyce of Fairchild Semiconductor simultaneously developed the first integrated circuit (IC), which combined a transistor and the required electrical connections on a single piece of silicon. Noyce and another scientist, Gordon Moore, formed the Intel (for INTegrated ELectronics) Corporation in 1968. In 1971, Marcian (Ted) Hoff, an employee of Intel Corporation, invented the first microprocessor chip, which was named the Intel 4004. This breakthrough invention powered a calculator and paved the way for embedding intelligence in inanimate objects as well as the personal computer.

The 4004 was followed in 1974 by the 8080 chip, which was used to power the first commercially available personal computer, the Altair. The 8080 was, in turn, followed by the 8086 and 8088 chips, with the 8088 being used in the first IBM PC in 1981. Even though the 4004's processing capabilities were puny compared to those of today's pro-

cessing chips, it was revolutionary in design and gave rise to Intel chips (and those of other companies) that are the processing "brain" of the vast majority of personal computers in use today.

Ted Hoff invented the first microprocessor chip—the Intel 4004.

2003, voice traffic will make up only 2 percent of the total traffic volume.[2] In a sense, the era of computers as computational devices may soon be over with their greatest use being that of communication devices.

Knowledge

To fully understand the concept of knowledge, two other terms need to be defined: *data* and *information*. Together with *knowledge,* these two terms are widely used in discussing the networked economy. **Data** are facts, numbers, or symbols that can be processed by humans or computers into information. Data on its own has no meaning and must be interpreted in some way before it can be useful. While this interpretation can be accomplished by a human, today this is more commonly accomplished by inputting the data into a computer and processing it into a meaningful form known as **information.** Information comes in many forms including documents, reports, tables, charts, and so on, all of which are meaningful to humans. For example, 1247.93 is one piece of data that has no meaning by itself, but when this is combined with other numbers on your bank statement, it becomes information. Processing data into information takes on many forms. Figure 1-6 shows the process of converting data into information.

Figure 1-6 Converting Data to Information

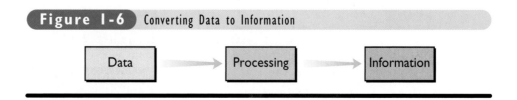

---

2. Frances Cairncross, *The Death of Distance* (Boston: Harvard Business School Press, 1997).

A few examples of transforming data into information include:

- Combining grade reports from many professors, each of which submits grades for numerous students, to be processed into an individual grade report for each student
- Transforming the numbers and formulas in a spreadsheet into a chart
- Creating a model of a hurricane from observations, assumptions, and formulas

There are literally millions of other situations where data are processed into information; you can probably come up with quite a few with just a moment's reflection.

In thinking about data, you should realize that the difference between data and information is in the eye of the beholder; that is, what are data to one person or organization is information to another. For example, an employee's payroll statement is information to the employee but is a data item when the departmental manager must combine it with payroll values for all other employees in the department to determine the departmental payroll. The departmental payroll is information to the department manager but to the comptroller of the company this departmental payroll is data that must be combined with payrolls for all other departments to determine the overall company payroll. This idea is shown in Figure 1-7.

At one time, converting data into information was the primary purpose of computers, and the term *data processing* came about to describe this use of computers. Early thinking in the use of computers was that if sufficient data were processed into information this would almost automatically improve the management of organizations. However, it has become quite clear that information by itself is almost as useless as data and that a uniquely human capability known as knowledge is necessary to improve the management of organizations. **Knowledge** can be defined as the capacity to request, structure, and use information. For example, it takes knowledge to understand the meaning of the numbers in the departmental payroll and if these numbers are within acceptable values. Although a variety of computer programs have attempted to incorporate human knowledge, they cannot make the decisions that require hunches, intuition, and leaps into totally unrelated areas, which humans make every day without a second thought.

Figure 1-7   Data and Information

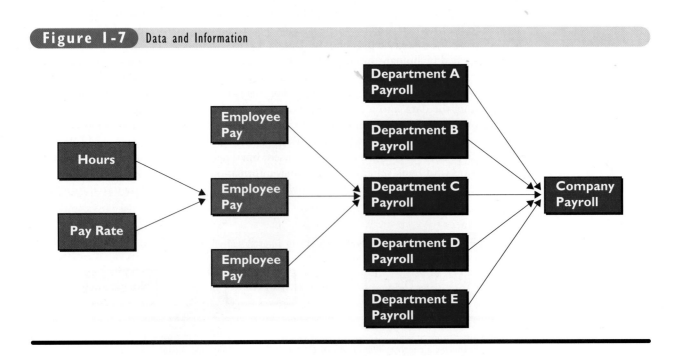

The networked economy is often referred to in the popular media by a variety of terms, including *information age* and *digital economy*. However, the use of the terms *information* and *digital* do not clearly describe the importance of knowledge used by people in the networked economy. Workers in organizations who use their knowledge to work with information have been referred to as **knowledge workers.** Many of the 75 percent of American workers in the service sector are actually knowledge workers rather than being in industries typically associated with *service*. In fact, in addition to the traditional economic sectors (manufacturing, agriculture, and service) there should probably be a fourth sector of the economy to reflect this emphasis on knowledge.

To understand the importance of knowledge workers, consider Microsoft Corporation. In 1998, Microsoft became the most valuable company in the world, surpassing General Electric. In this case, company value is measured by multiplying the number of shares of stock outstanding times the value of a single share of stock. In looking at Microsoft, it is important to note that what makes it valuable is not the small amount of land that it owns or the few factories that make copies of its software. It is far from the biggest firm in the world, with less than thirty thousand employees. However, each of these employees has a great deal of knowledge that goes into the software created and distributed by Microsoft, and it is this knowledge that makes Microsoft so valuable.

This textbook is aimed at making you a better knowledge worker by providing you with an understanding of the necessary skills and capabilities. It is only a beginning—the networked economy is changing so fast that you will need to constantly scan the environment to update these skills.

Quick Review

1. Point out at least three devices in your surrounding environment that contain chips. How many of these devices are connected in some way?
2. Give an example of a type of knowledge that is unique to you or to a member of your family.

Infrastructure of the Networked Economy

The industrial economy was supported by an infrastructure. **Infrastructure** can be defined as the underlying foundation or basic framework of a system or organization. The infrastructure of the industrial economy included canals, roads, railroads, power plants, factories, and so on that enabled companies to bring in raw materials, produce finished goods, and transport them to the customer. For the networked economy, the infrastructure is based on chip-based technology and communication networks. This infrastructure is commonly referred to as information technology. Specifically, **information technology (IT)** refers to all forms of technology used to create, store, exchange, and use information in its various forms.[3] The most obvious form of IT is the computer found on millions of desks in offices around the world.

Because the computer is such an important part of the infrastructure for the networked economy, let's look at the computer more closely. A **computer** is a digital machine that stores, manipulates, and transmits numbers and symbols based on instructions from human users. The operations of storing, manipulating, and transmitting information are carried out using chips.

All computers are a combination of two elements: hardware and software. The computer's machinery is referred to as **hardware** and is made up of chips and other electronic devices. Typical hardware includes system boxes, disk drives, monitors, keyboards, printers, and so on. Although computer hardware has continuously become smaller, faster, and cheaper, it can do *nothing* without the instructions commonly referred to as **software.** A common saying that helps to differentiate hardware from

---

3. www.whatis.com.

software is: "If you bump into it, then it's hardware!" Software is composed of one or more sets of instructions called **programs.** The many different types of computer systems in use in modern organizations are composed of a multitude of programs that work alone or in groups to meet the needs of the organization. All of the machines in everyday use with embedded chips have programs already built into a chip.

In considering the use of computers, it is worth noting that two features have strongly contributed to the rapid growth in their use: *speed* and *value*. In terms of speed, a computer is limited only by the speed at which electrical signals can be transmitted between chips, enabling desired operations to be carried out in a fraction of the time needed to do them manually. This enables even personal computers to execute millions of operations per second in carrying out the software instructions. In terms of value, the price of computers has dropped dramatically at the same time as their power and speed have increased. Computers are more valuable because there are more of them connected via networks.

The Effect of Personal Computers

With the introduction of the personal computer (PC) in the early 1980s, individuals were able to use the PC to carry out their work using word-processing, spreadsheet, database, and presentation software without sharing the computer with other users. Often referred to as **personal productivity software,** software for PCs allows an individual to become more productive than before their introduction. Although PCs are more powerful today than older, large computers, by themselves they do not necessarily lead to greater **organizational productivity.** For this to occur, they must be linked via a network so that the result of individual work can be *shared*. It is for this reason that the stand-alone computer is such a rarity in a networked economy organization. Louis Gerstner, CEO of IBM, noted that "...what the computer industry has been spending its time on for fifteen years was upgrading the spreadsheets and word processors of clerical workers, which is as far away from a CEO's agenda as you can get."[4]

Computing has moved from shared computing, in which you and your coworkers would use the same computer, to personal computing, in which you would work on an individual machine, to the present—shared information and resources—in which you work on your own computer but are able to share information and resources with others via the network. Shared information and resources lead to improved productivity for all members of the organization. Figure 1-8 shows the movement from shared computing to shared information.

Computers have moved from mainframes in a special environment to PCs in the home and office.

---

4. William J. Cook, "Men in Blue," *U.S. News & World Report*, February 16, 1998, pp. 45–49.

Figure 1-8 Transition from Shared Processing to Shared Information

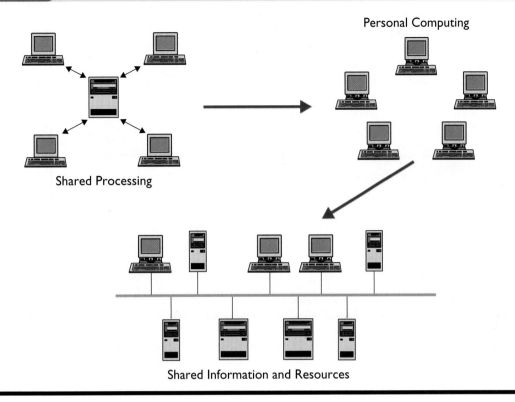

Personal Computing

Shared Processing

Shared Information and Resources

The Role of Information Technology

We have termed information technology as the *infrastructure* of the networked economy because it enables companies to carry on their business using computers and connectivity. As with the industrial economy, the key event is the **transaction** between buyer and seller. The buyer may be the end consumer, another company, or another unit within the same company, but without a transaction, no economy would work. Included in the transaction process are ordering the product, transferring the funds between buyer and seller to pay for the product, and delivering the product to the buyer. As previously noted in Table 1-2, the transaction process in the networked economy is quite different from that in the industrial economy, with the capability for electronic searching, purchase, and payment.

fareastfoods.com

As an example of a networked economy company, we will use a fictitious distributor of Oriental food items named fareastfoods.com. This company specializes in marketing Oriental food items but is not involved in their production, storage, or distribution other than to combine orders from wholesalers to be picked up by the package delivery company. It has a Web site at www.fareastfoods.com where prospective buyers can view and order the wide variety of Far Eastern foods, paying by credit card, as shown in Figure 1-9. Note that there are five elements in the process: fareastfoods.com, the food wholesalers, the bank, the package delivery company, and the customer. Note also that there are a variety of electronic and physical flows between the objects. We will be using fareastfoods.com in all of the chapters of this book as a continuing example of a networked economy company.

Quick Review

1. What types of computers have you used or come in contact with?

2. Have you shared data or information with anyone over a computer network? If so, how?

Figure I-9 fareastfoods.com

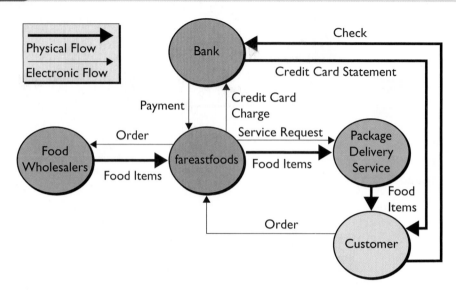

Source: Adapted from Richard T. Watson, *Object-Oriented Strategy*, 1999.

Focus on the Internet

Going Online for Textbooks

How did you buy this textbook? Did you go to the university bookstore or to one of the off-campus bookstores to search the stacks for it and your other textbooks and then stand in line for what seemed like hours to check out? Did you pay what seems like a lot for your textbooks this term? What will you do with them when the term is completed—sell them back to the same bookstore for a fraction of what you paid? While the majority of college students are still using this time-tested method for purchasing their textbooks, many others are using the Internet to search for and purchase textbooks at a reduced cost and then sell them to other students the same way. On the purchase side, there are many options including VarsityBooks.com (http://www.varsitybooks.com), Textbook Source (http://www.textbooksource.net), and Bigwords.com (http://bigwords.com). Varsity-Books.com claims to cut list prices by as much as 40 percent while Bigwords.com makes the same claim but does not charge shipping on orders over

$35. In a test search for a textbook (not this one), the author found a wide variation in prices, ranging from a low of $37.19 to a high of $51.30; therefore, it is definitely worth the small effort to look at more than one Web site as long as you have the time to wait two or three days for the book to arrive.

Once you are finished with the textbook, there are a variety of Web sites that enable you to dispose of it including TextDepot.com (http://www.textdepot.com) and BookSwap.com (http://www.bookswap.com). Both Web sites allow the users to either post books for sale or to search for books by author, name, or ISBN available for sale. In either case, the posting or search is done for a specific school. This avoids problems with virtual exchanges between individuals—paying for but not receiving the book or sending the book but never receiving payment. The BookSwap.com site even warns against meeting strangers in private settings!

Information Technology in Organizations

Organizations have used information technology (IT) for many years in an effort to reduce their labor costs by automating many of their operations. Many organizations have also used IT to ensure that the correct information is made available to the correct person so they can make better decisions. The most successful companies are those that have found that their goal must be to use IT to serve their customers better. This increasingly will become the case in the networked economy as prices and profit margins associated with manufactured goods drop.

The use of information technology to make organizations more competitive by helping them better serve their customers is an extremely important topic, so much so that it is the primary focus of this textbook. As a student of business, knowledge of information technology is critical to your success in the workplace. It may have been possible, as recently as ten years ago, to get by without knowledge of information technology if this was not your major area of interest; however, regardless of your major, today you will need to know how to use information technology to perform your job better and to provide better service to your customers.

Systems

While working with information technology, you will often hear the term *systems* used: A **system** is a group of elements (people, machines, cells, etc.) organized for the purpose of achieving a particular goal. Almost everything around you is a part of one type of system or another. Examples of systems include your college, a business, a computer

(F)ocus on Management

General Electric

For a 108-year-old company that sprang from the Industrial Revolution and whose chairman once described himself as a "Neanderthal" when it came to the Internet, the networked economy brought a need for changes. However, in early 1999, John Welch Jr., chairman of GE, was willing to admit his past failures relative to electronic commerce and to have his company embrace the new world business model. Welch calls the new strategy DestroyYourBusiness.com and the message is: "This is going to be the world business model and [GE] wants to be in front of that." He has made it clear to his top executives that if they don't have their unit of GE focused on the changes electronic commerce will bring to distribution, sales, and marketing, they're in trouble. To make this possible, Welch has brought in younger people who are more comfortable with technology and has put them to the task of reinventing business models, really shaking up the status quo at a company that has the second highest market valuation behind only Microsoft.

The message seems to be getting through: GE's plastics unit, which accounted for over 6 percent of GE's 1998 $100.5 billion revenue, put up its first Web site in February of 1999 and by May of that year it was generating $1.5 million in weekly revenue. Customers can order virtually any type of plastic from GE as well as plastics from other companies if they are not manufactured by GE. Most of GE's eleven main businesses are involved in electronic commerce in some way, ranging from providing software and systems for business-to-business trading to its joint venture with Micosoft: MSNBC. By early May of 1999, GE Capital, the world's largest nonbank finance company, had investments in dozens of Internet companies and GE Information Services unit provided electronic trading systems for 50,000 businesses with 15,000 of them through the Internet. These numbers are undoubtedly larger by now.

Source: Bloomberg News, "No Longer a 'Neanderthal,' GE Chief Embraces Internet." *The Atlanta Journal-Constitution,* May 11, 1999, p. E8.

system, and even your body. Your college is a system composed of all the faculty, staff, and students, in addition to the buildings and equipment that are organized for the goal of providing a college-level education to the students. A business is composed of a variety of elements, including production, marketing, distribution, accounting, and so on. The goal of a business is to make a sufficient profit to remain in existence. A computer system is composed of input, output, processing, and secondary storage elements. The goal of a computer system is to process data into information. Finally, your body is composed of cells that are organized into subsystems. The body's goal is to convert oxygen and food into energy that your body uses.

All systems have input, processing, output, and feedback. Anything that enters the system is classified as **input,** which is transformed in some way by **processing** and is then **output** in some form. **Feedback** is information about the output that may cause the system to change its operation. As an example of a system, consider a business like fareastfoods.com. This business has numerous types of input, processing, output, and feedback going on simultaneously. One important type of input is the orders from customers. These orders must be processed, resulting in output in the form of shipments to the customers. An important type of feedback is in the form of complaints from customers regarding the timeliness of deliveries or quality of food. If the food items are delivered late, a different package delivery company may be chosen. Similarly, poor food quality should result in a change to different suppliers. If feedback is ignored, the company could quickly go out of business. Obviously, virtually all businesses have many other systems besides those of just fulfilling orders, but this gives you an idea of how a business can be viewed as a system. Figure 1-10 shows fareastfoods.com viewed as a system.

Information Systems

You will often hear the terms *information technology* and *information systems* used interchangeably, sometimes leading to some confusion. In this context, we will use the term **information systems (IS)** to refer to systems that are combined to develop the information and knowledge needed by managers and other employees of organizations to make decisions. Basically, information systems can be thought of as information technology applied to organizations. The relationship between data, knowledge, information, and decisions in information systems is shown in Figure 1-11, where data are processed into information that is requested and interpreted by knowledge, leading to decisions.

Information systems are used in organizations for three primary purposes: handling the present, remembering the past, and preparing for the future. Handling the present means that the organization must be able to take care of its day-to-day business, primarily through processing transactions that involve customers, suppliers, and employees. The transactions must be stored in order for the organization to remember its past. Data on transactions are then used to prepare for the future, which results in decisions that determine the way transactions are handled in the

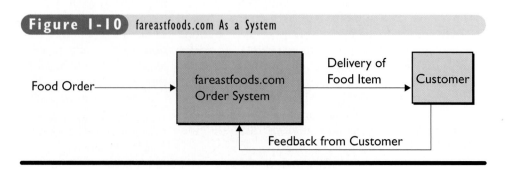

Figure 1-10 fareastfoods.com As a System

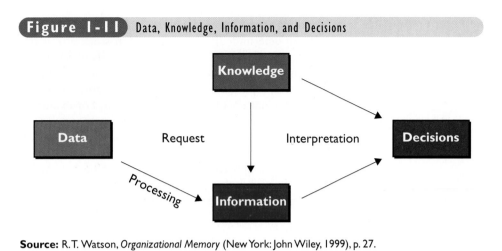

Figure 1-11 Data, Knowledge, Information, and Decisions

Source: R. T. Watson, *Organizational Memory* (New York: John Wiley, 1999), p. 27.

future. These three purposes are represented in Figure 1-12. We will discuss them briefly now and expand on these three purposes in much greater detail in later chapters.

Handling the Present

In many cases, the original purpose of many types of IT was to process data into information. This operation continues to be extremely important for all organizations because it handles the present by processing transactions. If the organization fails to process transactions accurately and in a timely manner, it will not continue to exist for very long. If customer transactions are not handled, revenue will not come in, and the organization will cease to exist. If transactions involving suppliers are not handled appropriately by the organization ordering and paying for raw materials, the organization will have nothing to offer its customers. Finally, the organization must ensure that its employees are paid in a timely manner or else they will cease to work for that organization. Today, many transactions today involve a customer "swiping" a credit card to pay for groceries or other goods. This is an example of transaction processing that must be handled appropriately.

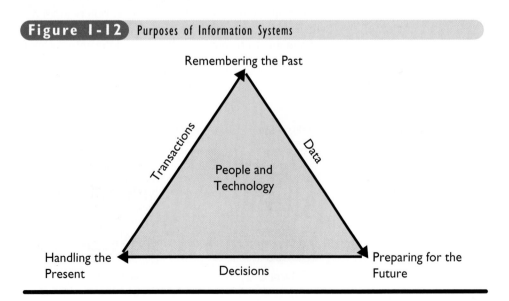

Figure 1-12 Purposes of Information Systems

Remembering the Past

Handling the present through transaction processing involves checking existing data (e.g., to determine if the product is in stock and if the buyer has good credit) and storing new data (e.g., the number of units of what item were sold to whom and for how much). This requires that the past be remembered through an extensive amount of **organizational memory** in the form of databases, data warehouses, information management systems, and so on. For example, when you purchase a product from Land's End (www.landsend.com), the transaction processing includes looking up information on you such as your address, your credit card number, and your previous purchases. It also includes checking the availability of the items you are ordering and checking if they must be backordered and sent at a later date. When the transaction is completed, all of these data must be updated or, if you are a new customer, new data created. Figure 1-13 shows the relationship between transaction processing and organizational memory.

Preparing for the Future

Although handling the present and storing the data and information generated by this process are critical to the efficient operation of almost any type of organization, another important operation is extracting the data and information and combining it with human knowledge to prepare the organization for the future. Preparing for the future involves using information technology to improve the capability of employees to understand, respond to, manage, and create value from information. Often this involves using a variety of types of information systems to help employees make better decisions. Examples of the use of information systems include using data mining to find needed data in the data warehouses, combining the data with models of the firm to predict the result of various courses of action, or presenting information to executives in a form that they can use to make decisions. These **decision support systems** have been in use for almost a quarter of a century and have become important to the financial health of today's firms.

In addition to helping employees make better decisions, information technology is having another effect on organizations—it is *transforming* them into new types of organizations. As we noted in our discussion of the networked economy, organizations must constantly undergo the process of creative destruction in order to remain in existence. One way to do this is for an organization to use electronic commerce to take advantage of the opportunities offered by the networked economy. For example, many firms, such as the Britannica company discussed earlier, are transforming the way that they serve their customers by using the Internet and World Wide Web to engage in electronic commerce. Whereas many firms are simply replicating their traditional methods of doing business, others are actually changing the process by which they do business. Britannica did not try merely to replicate its paper encyclopedia in an electronic form; it changed the entire way it approached the distribution

Figure 1-13 Transaction Processing

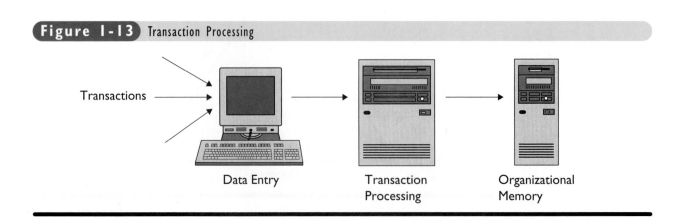

Transactions → Data Entry → Transaction Processing → Organizational Memory

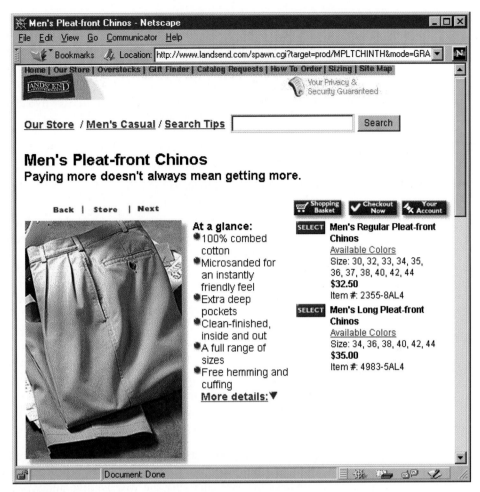

Customers can visit the Land's End Web site to purchase clothes and other items.

of information. Companies that are changing the way they do business will be able to take full advantage of the new information technology by transforming themselves into different entities.

Quick Review

1. Give some examples of the use of information technology by organizations to handle the present.
2. Is a company that converts its mail order catalog into a Web page with a toll-free number that you can call to order its products transforming itself using information technology? Why or why not?

A Look Ahead

Chapter 1 has provided you with an introduction to the networked economy and information technology. This textbook is divided into four parts, with this chapter opening the first part. The remaining chapters in part 1 provide additional information about the information technology infrastructure for the networked economy and includes a chapter on the hardware and software components of information technology and networks for sharing data and information. The second part includes chapters on the use of information systems in organizations to handle the present, remember the past, prepare for the future, and transform themselves using electronic commerce. Part 3 addresses the problems that organizations face in designing and then developing or acquiring information technology. Finally, the fourth part addresses the impact of the networked economy and information technology on crime, security, and privacy as well as discussing issues arising from the growth of the networked economy.

Learning Objectives

This textbook will develop your skills to master five learning objectives. After reading this book, you will be able to:

1. Understand how information technology has created the networked economy and discuss the implications of this transformation
2. Describe how information technology is used to process data into information and share data and information
3. Discuss how information technology can be used in organizations to handle the present, remember the past, and prepare for the future as well as transforming organizations
4. Discuss the processes involved in the development and acquisition of information systems
5. Understand the effect that information technology and the networked economy are having on crime, security, and ethics and the issues created by the networked economy and information technology

⊗ Summary

To summarize this chapter, let's answer the Learning Objectives questions posed at the beginning of the chapter.

In what ways is our world moving into a networked economy? Electronic machines combined with high-speed communications media form electronic networks that are changing the way we live and work. These electronic networks enable individuals, organizations, and businesses to transmit huge amounts of voice and data anywhere in the world almost instantaneously. They are rapidly changing the way we do business as more and more people "go online" to make purchases from businesses on a basis of twenty-four hours a day, seven days a week (24–7). The networked economy is an economy based on enhanced, transformed, or new economic relationships resulting from a combination of computers, connectivity, and human knowledge. A result of the movement to the networked economy is that organizations of all types will need to learn how to use the combination of computers, connectivity, and knowledge to remain competitive if they want to remain in business. The essence of the networked economy is not just change; rather, it is change at an accelerating rate of speed.

How is the networked economy "changing the rules"? The networked economy is changing the rules in five important areas: the definitions of scarcity, searching strategies, transactions, communications, and information storage. In a networked economy, time is becoming a scarce commodity, and searching will be handled over the World Wide Web rather than on paper or in person. Transactions will also be handled over the Web with electronic forms of currency. Communications will become many-to-many, creating electronic communities. Information storage will become digital on computers rather than on paper or other analog devices. As a result of these changes, companies need to search constantly for new opportunities, and actively to practice creative destruction.

What are the key elements of the networked economy? The networked economy is built on economic relationships based on computers, connectivity, and knowledge. Relationships are changing in the networked economy to include not just business to customer but also customer to business, employee to customer, and customer to customer. Computers are essential to the networked economy because they provide the required processing capabilities. Connectivity is required to share the data and information between the computers. Human knowledge is necessary to use the information that results from processing raw data into information.

What is the infrastructure of the networked economy? Information technology (IT) provides the infrastructure of the networked economy. The essence of IT is the computer. All computers are a combination of two elements: hardware and software. Two features have made the computer an essential part of the infrastructure—speed and value. The use of computers has moved from shared processing to personal computing to today's shared information. IT makes it possible for transactions to be handled much differently than in previous economies and to save and use the result of these transactions in the organizational memory.

What is the role of information technology in organizations? Information technology in organizations is often referred to as information systems (IS). IS involves organizations handling the present, remembering the past, and preparing for the future. *Handling the present* refers to taking care of all the transactions that an organization must deal with. *Remembering the past* refers to creating and using organizational memory using the results of handling the present. *Preparing for the future* refers to extracting data and information and combining it with human knowledge to help make better decisions that will determine the future of the firm. Information technology is also important in transforming organizations into new ones. In so doing, it meets the need for creative destruction.

⊙ Review Questions

1. Give three examples of electronic networks other than those mentioned in the text.

2. In what ways does the networked economy differ from the industrial economy?

3. How has scarcity changed in the networked economy?

4. What is Moore's Law, and what does it have to do with the networked economy?

5. How does knowledge differ from information?

6. What is the infrastructure of the networked economy? How does it relate to information systems?

7. How does information technology handle the present in an organization?

8. How does information technology remember the past in an organization?

9. How does information technology help an organization prepare for the future?

10. What is creative destruction, and how does it relate to transforming organizations with information technology?

⊙ Discussion Questions

1. Research a company and discuss how it uses information technology to handle the present.

2. Discuss the degree to which the company you researched in question 1 is affected by the movement to a networked economy.

3. Take a product other than a camera and discuss how purchasing it differs in the networked economy.

❯ CASE

WildOutfitters.com

Alex stomped the mud off of his boots and shrugged off his backpack before entering through the screen door to the kitchen. The odor of the stew cooking on the stove had made the walk up the hill to the house seem longer than any of the mountain trails he had hiked over the last three days. A warm shower and one of Claire's homecooked meals would be the perfect way to wind down, he thought.

Turning from the stove, Claire greeted him with a kiss: "Hi dear, I didn't expect you so soon. How was your adventure?"

"Not bad at all. I caught a glimpse of a black bear on the bald above Panther Creek Falls," Alex replied. "And the trip was just long enough to give the new equipment a good field test. The new *Featherlite 2000* performed better than most other backpacking tents I've tried. I'll be touting it's virtues in my next review."

Claire and Alex Campagne are the owners of a small shop specializing in equipment and provisions for outdoor recreation. Their location near the New River Gorge of West Virginia places them in the heart of an area rich with the possibility of outdoor adventure. Hiking, camping, rock climbing, and whitewater rafting combine with the rugged beauty of the region to entice visitors from all over the east coast. Having arrived in the area to sample the world class whitewater of the Gauley and New Rivers six years ago, the couple fell in love with the place and decided that here they could begin their dream of owning their own business. They left two fairly lucrative jobs, pulled up stakes, and found a home/store just off the main highway near the New River bridge.

Since starting their shop almost five years ago, the couple has become well known for their knowledge of the region and the equipment that they sell. Spending most of their personal time in the outdoors, they try to personally use most of the equipment that they sell. This well-earned reputation has spread slowly and mostly by word of mouth. In addition to the often sought after information, the hot muffins that Claire bakes on weekend mornings help to provide a homey ambience and has made the shop a favorite starting point for many adventurers who stop by for provisions and a chat with the owners.

Despite the small success that they have had in starting and maintaining Wild Outfitters, Alex has been interested in finding some way to increase sales. Due to their location near the action and the nature of their business, most transactions occur on the weekend. Thus, they feel that some business is lost to the big sports stores in the city such as Dick's and REI. One problem that they foresee with increased sales would be the need

to maintain more and longer hours at the store. Currently, they have been opening from Thursday to Sunday. This schedule leaves the rest of the week to enjoy the outdoors and test equipment. More hours serving customers would leave less time for these pursuits.

Another idea that they have been toying with is to develop their own line of products under the Wild Outfitters brand name. While they haven't yet worked out the details, the product line could include anything from guide books to outdoor clothing to camp cuisine. They have tried a few items in the store that sold well. To be successful, the product line would need to have better advertising than the word-of-mouth process that they have relied on so far.

Lately, Alex has been playing around with the Internet and posting a personal home page. Besides a brief background of the store, the site is basically composed of reports describing the outdoor sports that he and his wife have enjoyed. These are complete with photos, maps, descriptions of the area, and brief reviews of the equipment used. The two have been wondering how they might turn this new hobby into an asset for their business.

As he began to wash for dinner, Alex thought more about what he would write about the equipment in his next trip report. Yes, he thought, the tent worked wonderfully but the ache in his shoulders told him that the review of the backpack would not be so kind. Perhaps a few well-timed moans and groans will convince Claire to help him with a nice backrub while he types.

1. How could electronic commerce benefit the Campagnes?

2. What special knowledge do the Campagnes have that may help them to succeed in the networked economy?

3. What features would you include on WildOutfitters.com to help customers with each stage of ownership?

4. Can Wild Outfitters be thought of as a system? If so, identify the inputs, outputs, processes, and feedback of its current business.

5. What steps of creative destruction might you take with Wild Outfitters?

6. *(Hands on)* Think about the type of site you would like to start on the Web. Provide a general description of your site. What product or service would you sell? What would you call it? Check one of the domain registration sites on the Web to see if your name is available. Research domain registration and briefly describe what you would need to do to register your site's name.

CHAPTER ②

Information Technology: The Infrastructure of the Networked Economy

> Learning Objectives

After reading this chapter, you should be able to answer the following questions:

> What does information technology have to do with the networked economy?

> What are the four major hardware elements of the computer, and how do they process data into information?

> Why is software necessary to use a computer?

> How has computer processing evolved over time, and what are the three types in use today?

> What role does information technology play in a transaction in the networked economy?

Focus on Management

Problems at eBay

The Internet auction site eBay.com[1] has been extremely successful by enabling its members to buy and sell items over the Internet. eBay has developed a trading site in an auction format on the Web that is available twenty-four hours a day, seven days a week. By mid-1999, eBay had more than 3.8 million registered users bidding for over two million items listed for sale and the Web site registered over 1.5 *billion* visits per month. Items are sold in more than sixteen hundred categories ranging from antiques, books, movies, and music to coins, stamps, and other collectibles. It is also possible to bid on computers, dolls and figures, jewelry and gemstones, photo and electronics, pottery and glass, sports memorabilia, and toys. However, several times during the summer of 1999, eBay experienced service outages totaling over thirty-six hours. Although we have all experienced power outages, with some lasting as long as a couple of days, only in rare cases did those power outages cut off as many people from business opportunities as did the outages at eBay.

Like all electronic commerce Web sites, eBay depends on a variety of computer hardware and software to respond to the bids of its members, and this information technology must run at all times to make the Web site available to its members. In the summer of 1999, service outages and several problems with the technology combined to keep the site down for over twenty-four hours at one time. The primary problem was traced to a failure of the company that supplied the operating system to alert eBay to a software correction that needed to be installed to avoid known problems with the system. Although eBay was only days away from having a backup computer ready that would have kept the system up when the primary computer failed, it had spent six months working on this project. Previous problems in May of 1999 had been traced to problems in other computers. Although eBay hopes it has solved its information technology problems, electronic commerce Web sites that are *always open* are so new that outages are going to continue to be a problem.

1. www.ebay.com.

eBay is the most popular auction site on the Web today.

Elements of Information Technology

To begin, let's review the concept of information technology as it was described in the previous chapter. **Information technology (IT)** is the *infrastructure* of the networked economy (i.e., the elements necessary for the networked economy to exist and for transactions to take place by processing raw data into information). It is also necessary for accessing data and information and for sharing data, information, and knowledge with other people in the networked economy. Without information technology, it is not possible to handle the present, remember the past, and prepare for the future.

In addition, you may recall that information technology has two parts—hardware and software—that work together to provide the infrastructure to the networked economy. **Hardware** is the electronic part of information technology that carries out various operations under the direction of **software**. The preceding Focus on Management box discussed the importance of having the information technology behind a popular electronic commerce auction site, eBay, constantly up and running.

A brief overview of computer hardware and software introduces this chapter and is followed by the discussion of an example that demonstrates the use of both hardware and software. This example follows a single transaction from its origination on a personal computer (PC) to its culmination with the delivery of the product. The various information technology elements involved in this process will be discussed in detail.

Hardware: The Physical Side of Information Technology

Most operations performed by hardware are electronic—that is, there are few moving parts. Instead, the operations are accomplished by millions of transistors acting as electronic switches. Because the operations are electronic, hardware is both fast and accurate when carrying out the instructions of the software. The speed of many operations performed within the computer is only limited; by the speed at which transistors can change from "on" to "off" and is measured in *billionths of a second*. These operations also obey physical laws that do not change from operation to operation and are therefore accurate; however, if the instructions are incorrect—even in a single place, incorrect results can occur.

All IT hardware, whether in a large computer, PC, handheld game, or other chip-based device, is composed of three elements: *input, processing,* and *output*. In addition, most computers have some form of secondary storage. Figure 2-1 shows a

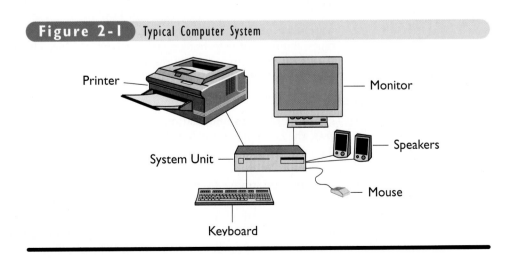

Figure 2-1   Typical Computer System

Printer

Monitor

System Unit

Speakers

Mouse

Keyboard

typical computer with a system unit, a keyboard and mouse for input and a monitor, printer, and speakers for output. Housed within the **system unit** (and therefore unable to be seen) are the secondary storage disk drives, the processing unit that processes data into information, and a modem for telecommunications input and output. You have probably used a computer system similar to that shown in the figure and are aware of the terminology used to describe it; however, for completeness, let's review the various hardware elements found in the typical computer system.

Input

Input enables the hardware to receive the data to be processed and the software instructions for processing those data. As shown in Figure 2-1, the most common input devices are a **keyboard** for entering data and instructions, a **mouse** for pointing to elements of the computer screen, a modem, and some form of secondary storage. Although bar codes are far and away the most common (and accurate) form of data input for transactions in business and industry, keyboard input is a widely used form of data input for individuals and for documents. It is also the primary method of entering the instructions to create the programs that make up software. Although not shown in Figure 2-1, a microphone, scanner, or digital camera may also be connected to the computer for input.

The **modem** is an essential input (and output) element for connecting the computer to the networked economy since it links the computer to the Internet. Different types of modems can be used to connect the computer to a telephone line or to a broadband television cable. The cable modem is capable of much faster speed than the ordinary modem with a telephone hookup but is not available in nearly as many locations. We will discuss modems in more detail in a later section.

Processing

Once input has taken place, the hardware must process the data into information using software instructions. This is accomplished using two types of chips: processing chips and memory chips. The actual processing of data into information takes place on the processing chips. Because the instructions to process data items must be carried out sequentially, it is necessary to store the instructions and data as well as the resulting information internally on memory chips. In computers, the processing chip or chips are referred to as the **central processing unit (CPU)**, and the internal storage is carried out on **random access memory (RAM)** chips. Over 90 percent of CPU chips in use today are based on a standard created by Intel. Although not all such machines use Intel chips, they use chips that use the same software as Intel chips.

In addition to CPU chips and RAM chips, there is an important type of memory chip known as **read-only memory (ROM)**. ROM chips have instructions built into them at the factory and are an important component of many types of information technology. In computers, ROM chips carry out many operations such as starting the computer and storing information on how the computer interfaces with other hardware elements—keyboard, monitor, printer, secondary storage, and so on. In other types of information technology where there is no need for RAM or secondary storage; the ROM chips contain all of the software needed by the device to operate. Software stored on ROM chips in devices like mobile phones is often referred to as **firmware**.

Output

Because processed information is of no use unless it is provided to the user in some way, the computer must have an **output unit.** Once again, as shown in Figure 2-1, the most common forms of computer output are information displayed on a **monitor,** output on paper by a **printer,** or audio from speakers. Output often is also sent to secondary storage for permanent storage or sent over a network using a modem.

A monitor is required for almost any computer system for two reasons. First, the data or instructions input from the keyboard or other input device are shown on the monitor. Second, the monitor is an almost instantaneous outlet for the result of the processing. Printers are necessary to obtain a "hard copy" of a document or the

The Pentium III processing chip from Intel, shown here, is used in many computers found in organizations.

screen contents. Two types of printers commonly used with PCs are ink-jet printers and laser printers. The **ink-jet printer** sprays tiny droplets of ink to create letters and graphic images. The **laser printer** is much like a copier except that instead of photocopying an existing document, it converts output from a computer into a printed form. The **speakers** are a relatively new addition to PCs and are useful for watching movies on DVDs or over the Internet, for providing sound to games, or for listening to audio CDs.

Secondary Storage

Because the internal memory of a computer is both limited and nonpermanent, most computers have some form of secondary storage. This is permanent storage, usually on a magnetic disk or an optical disk device. With either of these devices, stored data, information, or instructions are accessed by internal memory when the CPU decides it is needed. Because the secondary storage unit must locate the needed material, read it, and then transfer it to internal memory, secondary storage is a much slower form of memory than internal memory; however, this slow transfer of information is balanced by the virtually unlimited storage capacity.

Magnetic-disk secondary storage is composed of metal or plastic that is covered with an iron oxide whose magnetic direction can be arranged to represent symbols. This magnetic arrangement is carried out on a **disk drive,** which spins the disk while reading from it and writing information to it. Magnetic disks can be either fixed (also known as **hard disks**) or portable.

Optical-disk secondary storage comes as **CD-ROM disks** (compact disk-read only memory) and **DVDs** (digital versatile disks), both of which are portable and primarily *read-only* storage devices. However, versions of both types of optical disk storage on which data and information can be written are now also in widespread use.

Conceptual Computer

To understand how the three hardware elements work together with secondary storage to process data into information, consider the conceptual computer shown in Figure 2-2. In addition to the hardware elements mentioned earlier, this conceptual computer shows the flows into, within, and out of the computer. In Figure 2-2, note that processing data into information begins with the input unit sending data and

Figure 2-2 Conceptual Computer

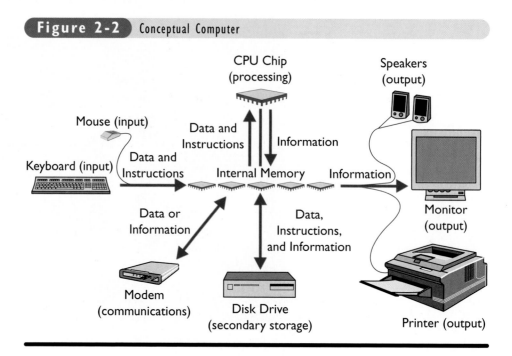

instructions to the internal memory unit. Next, the instructions and data are sent to the processing unit as they are needed. The processing unit may also request that additional data or instructions be retrieved from secondary storage. Once the processing is completed, the resulting information is sent to internal memory from the processing unit. The internal memory unit then transfers the information to the output unit for display, printing, or listening. The information may also be stored in secondary storage for later use or additional processing. Although this is a simplified account of the processing of data into information, it does depict the way a computer works.

Bits, Bytes, and Binary Numbers

Because humans have ten fingers, we use a base-10 number system to perform calculations. Similarly, we use written symbols to communicate ideas to other people. Instead of using written characters, information technology hardware uses transistorized on–off switches on chips to work with numbers and symbols. These switches can be used to carry out calculations using the base-2, or **binary number system** instead of the base-10 system that humans use. Each transistorized switch corresponds to one **bit** (**BI**nary digi**T**) of storage. For example, the number 20 in binary is 10100. Just as base-10 numbers can be added, subtracted, multiplied, divided, and so on, so, too, can binary numbers.

On the other hand, to represent letters, punctuation marks, and special symbols internally and on secondary storage, standardized representations were created. A standard representation involves using a group of eight bits, called a **byte,** where each bit pattern represents a given symbol. Why was eight bits chosen? Possibly because 256 characters can be achieved with this number, and this was thought to be a sufficient number. Several patterns of bits have been suggested, but the standard code for personal computers is **ASCII** (pronounced "as-key"), which is an acronym for *American Standard Code for Information Interchange*. For example, the letter *A* is coded as 01000001 in ASCII. Because each character can be represented by one byte in ASCII, the terms *byte* and *character* are commonly used interchangeably.

The ASCII codes are used to transmit information between the keyboard and the internal memory and between the internal memory and the display screen and for storing information in internal memory and secondary storage on personal computers. Table 2-1 shows the ASCII code for several letters and symbols.

Table 2-1	ASCII Code		
Character	**ASCII Code**	**Character**	**ASCII Code**
0	00110000	a	01100001
1	00110001	b	01100010
2	00110010	y	01111001
A	01000001	z	01111010
B	01000010	!	00100001
Y	01011001	;	00111011
Z	01011010			

As discussed earlier, data, information, and instructions must be stored in both a computer's internal memory and secondary storage. The amount of storage in both is measured in **kbytes** (kilobytes), **mbytes** (megabytes), and **gbytes** (gigabytes). A kbyte is approximately one thousand bytes, a mbyte is approximately one million bytes, and a gbyte is approximately one billion bytes. Table 2-2 shows the relationships between bits, bytes, and the various amounts of memory and secondary storage, and Table 2-3 shows the typical amounts of storage in internal memory and secondary storage devices for personal computers.

Table 2-2	Memory Relationships	
Memory Term	**Amount of Memory**	**Amount Represented**
1 bit	1 transistor on–off switch	1 binary digit
1 byte	8 bits	1 character
1 kbyte	2^{10} or 1,024 bytes	Approximately one-half double-spaced printed page
1 mbyte	1,024 kbytes (2^{20} or 1,048,576 bytes)	Approximately 500 printed pages
1 gbyte	1,024 mbytes (2^{30} or 1,073,741,824 bytes)	Approximately 500,000 printed pages

Table 2-3	Typical Amounts of Storage
Storage Media	**Typical Amount Stored**
Internal memory	32 mbytes to more than 128 mbytes
Hard drive	1 gbytes to more than 10 gbytes
Floppy disk	1.44 mbytes
Portable disks	100 mbytes up to 1 gbyte
CD-ROM	650 mbytes
DVD	4.7 gbytes up to 17 gbytes

*Quick
Review*

1. List the hardware elements of a conceptual computer.

2. Why are a byte and a character essentially the same thing? How much internal memory does your computer have? How much secondary storage does your computer have?

Software: The Instructions for Information Technology

Although the hardware advances in recent years have been mind-boggling in terms of increased speed and storage and decreased cost, without software, information technology would be nothing more than a well-constructed combination of silicon chips and electronic circuitry. Recall that **software** is the general term for all of the instructions given to the computer or other chip-based device by the user or the manufacturer. The idea of an information technology without software has been described as everything from a car without a driver to a camera without film. Using any analogy you wish, hardware must have software to direct it.

Software has been developed for virtually every application imaginable, including those necessary to handle the present, remember the past, and prepare for the future in an organization. This section introduces the various types of software and software terminology. The fareastfoods.com example, mentioned in chapter 1, will be used in a later section to provide more details on actual software in use today. Later chapters will elaborate on the ways that software can be combined with hardware to create information systems in organizations. Other chapters will discuss many of the issues involved in designing and creating or selecting and acquiring software in organizations.

Types of Software

The two major types of software are *operating systems software* and *application software*. Except in special situations, both software types are at work in the computer at the same time, each serving a different purpose. Figure 2-3 shows the relationship between the various types of software within the computer.

As seen in Figure 2-3, the software that controls the hardware is the **operating system software**. This type of software is extremely important because it controls the operations of all other software, as well as controlling the computer itself. In the opening Focus on Technology box, a failure to update the operating system of the primary computer at eBay resulted in over twenty-four hours of downtime for this popular Web site. Running under the control of the operating system is the **application software** that actually performs the specialized tasks that we hear so much about. Calculating payrolls, generating grade reports, running electronic commerce Web sites like eBay, creating documents using word processing, forecasting sales

Figure 2-3 Relationship between Types of Software

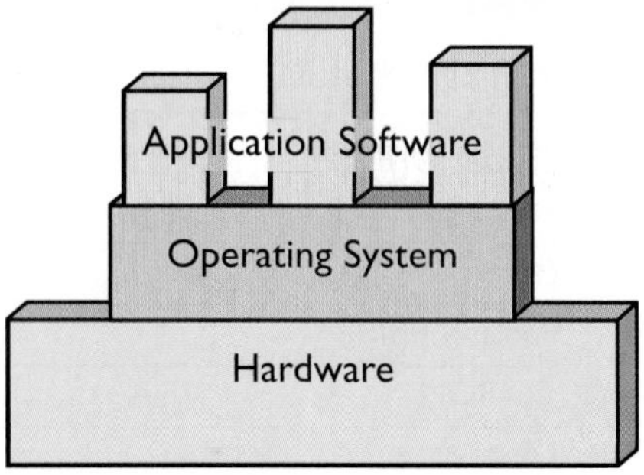

demand, running the Internet, controlling robots, and many more tasks now can be accomplished with application software.

Operating System Software

Operating system software manages the many tasks going on concurrently within a computer. These tasks include launching application software, supervising multiple applications running concurrently, allocating memory to the applications, and managing the storage of programs, data, and information on secondary storage. This software also must manage various input and output devices as well as the frequent transfer of data and programs between internal memory and secondary storage. On computers that serve multiple users (i.e., mainframes and network servers) the operating system may also manage the allocation of memory and processing time to each of the multiple users as well as providing security to each user and to the system as a whole.

In order for the operating system to manage the storage of programs, data, and information on secondary storage and the many transfers from secondary storage to internal memory, files must be used. **Files** are programs, data, or information to which the user or software assigns a name. Both the operating system and application software work with files, with the operating system responsible for making the files available when needed by the application software.

On personal computers, the types of files generated by application software have become interchangeable through standardization. For example, all word-processing, spreadsheet, database, and presentation graphics software can now read files created by other packages. The standard for each of these is the type of file generated by Microsoft Office Suite (i.e., .doc files for word processing, .xls files for spreadsheets, .mdb files for database software, and .ppt files for presentation graphics software). In addition, Web files use an htm or html extension and can be read from any browser regardless of the type of computer.

For PCs, the most widely used operating system is Windows (3.1, 95, or 98) from Microsoft. Well over 90 percent of all PCs use some form of this operating system. Macintosh computers use their own operating system. For business computers, the most popular operating systems are Windows NT or 2000, UNIX, and Linux. Windows NT and 2000 are similar in operation to Windows 98, but with increased security features and the capability to manage multiple computers on a network. UNIX was originally developed by AT&T in the early 1970s for its internal computers and is the oldest operating system, widely used for directing networks with many Internet computers running it. As discussed in the following Focus on Management box, a version of UNIX, called *Linux,* has enjoyed increasing popularity recently as an operating system for both home and business computers.

Application Software

By far, the largest amount of software available to the computer user is in the area of application software. The applications for which software has been written cover the entire range of human activities. In fact, it is quite difficult to think of a single area of human endeavor for which application software has *not* been developed. This is especially true in business, industry, government, and personal uses. Just as our daily lives would be changed dramatically if there were no chips, most organizations would quickly grind to a halt if their application software were to cease working. We have already mentioned application software for many situations, and you can probably think of many others.

Application software for organizations comes in two primary forms: that which is developed commercially and that which is developed within an organization. Also sometimes referred to as **shrink-wrapped software** because it usually comes in a package containing the disk, instructions, and documentation all wrapped together, commercially developed software is widely used for many clerical and personal productivity tasks. This software is also widely available over the Internet as a download from a Web site.

Focus on Management

Big Blue Selects Linux

Every computer must have an operating system that directs the many activities that are simultaneously occuring in the computer. For most personal computers and many business computers, this operating system is Microsoft Windows. Controlling the operating system market has long been a mainstay of Microsoft's software empire. However, this may be changing as IBM and other computer manufacturers are now loading an operating system called Linux on their business computers. Created by a Finnish graduate student, Linus Torvald in 1991, Linux is a version of a much older operating system (UNIX). By 1998, Linux comprised 17 percent of the business computer operating system market. With the 1999 announcement by IBM, this could grow significantly. Linux is considered by many computer professionals to be more stable than any of the versions of Windows now available. A major difference between Windows and Linux is that Linux is an *open* standard for which the programming code is available to anyone who wishes to modify it. Linux can be downloaded for *free* from the Internet for use by individuals, or it can be purchased from companies like Red Hat Software. This growth of Linux, and the delays in the release of the newest version of Windows for business computers, may cause companies to rethink their operating system decisions.

You might ask: What does Linux have to do with the networked economy? The answer is that Linux is a *product* of the networked economy because, without the Internet, it would have been impossible for Linux to have grown to the extent that it has. The Internet has made it possible for programmers around the world to participate in the continued improvement of Linux. As a result, other software companies are making their product's source code available in the hope that it also will be improved by the electronic community. Even Microsoft is talking about making the code for Windows freely available.

Source: "IBM Deal a Boost for Windows Competitor," *The Atlanta Journal/Constitution,* February 19, 1999, p. F1.

Linus Torvald created the initial version of the Linux operating system.

As mentioned in chapter 1, commercially developed personal productivity software are used in both personal and corporate situations. The most widely used of such software are word processing programs to create documents, spreadsheets to carry out financial and other quantitative analyses, database programs to manage lists and tables of data, and presentation programs to create presentations. There exists a virtually endless variety of other application software, including Web browsers for accessing the World Wide Web, utilities (e.g., software to detect viruses or software to automatically back up a hard disk), games, and so on.

Software developed by a company specifically for its own use often has important competitive implications for the company. Although companies could buy commercially developed software like word processing programs or spreadsheets to run their businesses, in most cases software must be custom developed to meet their particular needs. This means that no matter how good off-the-shelf software may become, the demand for programmers to work in organizations to develop software for the organizations' special needs will always exist and almost certainly grow as we move further into the networked economy.

Figure 2-4	Use of Command-Driven Software

```
[andy@ludwig andy]$ ls *.jpg
Mvc-044f.jpg        whole_screen.jpg
[andy@ludwig andy]$ xv whole_screen.jpg
[andy@ludwig andy]$ ls -l *.jpg
-rw-r--r--    1 andy       users           86920 Oct 11 12:40 Mvc-044f.jpg
-rw-r--r--    1 andy       users          143667 Nov 25 11:36 whole_screen.jpg
[andy@ludwig andy]$ xv
```

Software Terminology

Every type of software has its own method for entering data and commands called its **user interface.** The two most common user interfaces are command driven and graphical. In software with a **command-driven interface,** the software responds when the user enters the appropriate command or data. There is usually a **prompt** to indicate to the user where on the screen a command or data is expected, and the user must enter that based on their knowledge of the software. The most widely used example of command-driven software is the UNIX operating system. In Figure 2-4, the first line shows the LS command entered at a prompt (the $ symbol) to provide a listing of the files on the disk with a .jpg extension.

The type of user interface that is standard for personal computers is the **graphical user interface,** or **GUI** (pronounced "gooey"). The GUI interface is also standard for almost all Web browsers regardless of the type of computer. In a GUI, **icons** (pictures) on the monitor are used to represent the functions to be performed. A function is executed by positioning the pointer over the corresponding icon with a mouse and clicking a mouse button. Selecting an icon can cause a command to be executed or a new screen of icons representing other options to be displayed. For example, if an icon of a file folder represents a file and an icon of a trashcan represents the erasure of a file, the user can erase a file by pointing to the file folder icon and then "dragging" it to the trashcan icon. This type of operating system interface was pioneered by the Apple Macintosh in 1984 and was brought to Intel-based PCs in 1990 with the introduction of Microsoft Windows 3.0. Since that time, Windows 3.1, 95, and 98 have been the standard for operating systems. Similarly, all software written to run with the Macintosh and Windows operating systems use the GUI interface. There is even a GUI interface for Linux-based computers. Figure 2-5 shows the use of a GUI on a Windows-based machine and a Linux system.

Computer Programs and Languages

Earlier in this chapter, we discussed the idea that a computer manipulates and stores symbols by turning switches on and off. For the computer to know which switches should be "on" or "off," it must be given a very specific set of rules called a **program.** All software, whether built into the machine by the manufacturer, purchased from a software development firm, or developed within the organization, is created by one or more persons using a process known as **programming.** Because the hardware knows nothing other than what it is told by the program, the program must be quite specific about the process that converts data into information. This requires a step-by-step approach to be created by the development team in such a way that no steps are assumed to be known by the computer. These steps are then converted into a program that is written in some **computer language.**

Figure 2-5 Examples of GUI

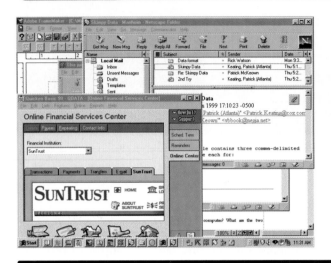

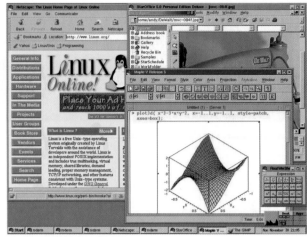

ⓕocus on People

Douglas Engelbart

To find the origins of many of the GUI and network concepts that we are accustomed to using, we have to go back to the almost prehistoric (in computer terms) year of 1963, when Douglas Engelbart published a paper on how to augment human intellect through the use of the computer. This paper was almost thirty years ahead of its time in its description of such unknown concepts as personal workstations, networks of users communicating with one another, and word processing. Based on this paper, Engelbart received a grant to try out some of his ideas for using computers.

With this grant, Engelbart and his colleagues at the Stanford Research Institute (SRI) worked on implementing his ideas. Five years later, on December 5, 1968, he made a ninety-minute presentation to the American Federation of Information Processing Societies' Fall Joint Computer Conference that stunned the computing world. In this presentation, Engelbart and his team of visionaries from SRI demonstrated a mouse-driven interface (his rolling pointer prototype was made of wood), hypermedia like that used with the World Wide Web, multiple windows, outline processing, display editing, context-sensitive help, and many of the other computing functions now at users' fingertips. Considering that computing in 1968 was completely command-driven and text-based on mainframes, this presentation was one of those world-changing events that occurs infrequently.

Thirty years later on December 9, 1998, Engelbart, at seventy-three, was honored at a symposium at Stanford University. Called "Engelbart's Unfinished Revolution," the symposium recalled that fateful day in 1968 when Engelbart gave what is now referred to as the "greatest demo of all time." Although personal computers have implemented his ideas on GUI, the networking of computers is what he believes will have the greatest impact.

Douglas Engelbart was a visionary who first created much of the information technology in use today.

Table 2-4 Commonly Used Computer Languages

Language	Full Name	Common Use
COBOL	**CO**mmon **B**usiness **O**riented **L**anguage	Writing business software (usually for mainframes)
Fortran	**FOR**mula **TRAN**slator	Writing scientific and engineering software
VB	**V**isual **B**asic	Writing software for PCs
C++-	Same	Writing software for PCs or network servers
Java	Same	Writing software to run on any computer or operating system using a Web browser

Programs are written in a number of computer languages. Some of the more commonly used languages and their uses are listed in Table 2-4 along with their full names (if different from the commonly used name). Each computer language, like a human language, has its own vocabulary and grammatical rules, but most share a similar logical approach to communication with the computer.

As an example of a popular computer language, we have created an application in Visual Basic for a video store. Figure 2-6 shows the interface for this application and some of the corresponding programming instructions (code) necessary to implement the logic behind it.

Quick Review

1. Why is software an essential element of every computer? What are the two main types of software?
2. Why is programming necessary for software development?

Figure 2-6 Visual Basic Interface and Code

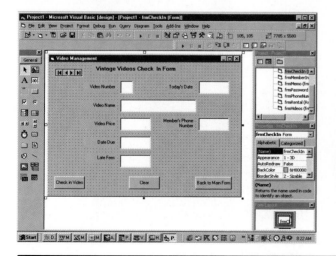

Organizational Computing

In order to understand computing in the organizational environment, you must look at the three types of computing that coexist within the corporate world—mainframes, PCs on a LAN, and client/server computing. Mainframes are the large computers that have been around since the dawn of computing in the 1950s and are aimed at providing the heavy-duty processing required by many corporate activities. On the other hand, PCs are relatively newer, smaller computers that have been around for a little over twenty years and are responsible for bringing computing to the desktop. In organizations, they are typically connected over an internal network called a **local area network (LAN)**. Finally, client/server computing is the newest form of corporate computing; it attempts to combine the best features of mainframes and PCs. In this section, we will discuss each type of organizational computing in more detail.

Servers and Mainframes

Mainframes were originally huge machines that took up entire buildings or large rooms; however, today they have shrunk in size to the point that some of the smaller ones resemble a larger version of a PC. For years, there have been predictions that larger computers would go the way of dinosaurs, but this has not been the case—in fact, just the reverse is occurring. For example, in late 1998, IBM announced that it had shipped the first one thousand of its latest line of large computers faster than any other new line of mainframes in history. Customers of these

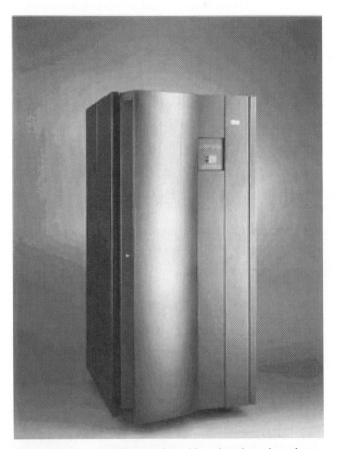

IBM mainframes, such as the one pictured here, have been the mainstay of corporate computing since the 1950s.

large computers include any organization that requires large-scale transaction processing; production processing; or scientific computations; including airlines, manufacturers, retailers, finance, banking and insurance companies, telecommunications and travel service providers, and energy companies, many of which are upgrading from older mainframe systems. Although mainframes are larger and more powerful than desktop PCs, they work on exactly the same principles as the smaller computers with operating systems running application software to accomplish the tasks required of them. As mentioned earlier, the operating systems for these machines must be able to handle requests from multiple users to accomplish multiple tasks.

Users typically interface with the larger computers through dumb terminals or PCs. A **dumb terminal** is a low-cost device that consists of a keyboard, a monitor, and a connection to the mainframe but no processing chip, internal memory, or secondary storage. It is restricted to character input and output with no GUI or pointing devices. Even when a PC is used as an interface to a mainframe, it typically emulates a dumb terminal and uses only a fraction of its computing power. Figure 2-7 shows the use of a mainframe with dumb terminals.

In this type of computing, the mainframe—or, as it is often called, the **host**—handles all of the processing and storage leading to centralized massive computing power. This gives the mainframe the capability to run applications that are critical to the continued profitability and existence of the organization—so-called **business critical applications**. Any individual that wishes to use a mainframe must have a user identification number and a password to access it, resulting in a high level of security. On the other hand, mainframes are usually restricted to command-driven applications that involve only text and numbers, are very expensive to purchase and maintain, can stop all processing when they fail ("go down"), and can be a bottleneck to processing when the demand is extremely high. Table 2-5 shows a summary of the advantages and disadvantages of mainframe computing.

Personal Computers

The primary reason for the dramatic growth in the use of computers over the last twenty years has been the **personal computer (PC)**. The PC has become a fixture in homes, offices, factories, and colleges and schools around the world. In addition,

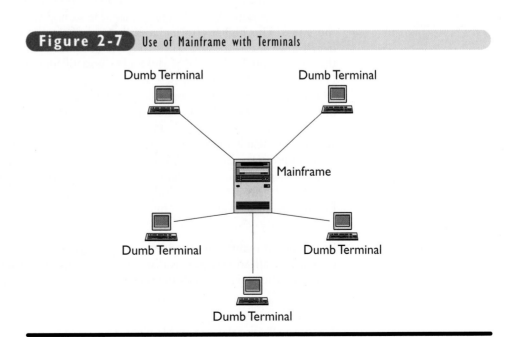

Figure 2-7 Use of Mainframe with Terminals

Table 2-5 Advantages and Disadvantages of Mainframe Computing	
Advantages	**Disadvantages**
Centralized computing power, including management and backup	Command-driven application displaying only text and numbers
High levels of security	High initial cost and cost of upgrades to existing systems
Capability to run enterprise applications	Problems with failure of centralized computing Inability to keep up with high demand

the PC introduced the GUI in the workplace, leading to increased employee productivity in a user-friendly environment. It also introduced distributed computing to the workplace (i.e., an organization's computing power is extended out from the machine room, where the mainframe "lives," to the desktops of the employees). No longer is the user restricted to a text-based dumb terminal or dependent on the availability or load on the mainframe because many of its functions can now be handled on the PC. An additional benefit is that the cost of computing power and storage is much less on PCs compared to on mainframes, with PC computing power being one thousand times cheaper. In a word, the PC has *revolutionized* the world of organizational computing.

Most PCs in the organization are now connected via a local area network (LAN) to facilitate sharing of data, information, and resources. In fact, it is very rare to find an unconnected computer in an organization today.

Much of this tremendous growth of the PC can be attributed to the standardization of both hardware and software. By having a single operating system (Windows) in over 90 percent of all PCs and a standard CPU chip (the Intel standard) in 95 percent of the machines, users and developers can depend on a single **Wintel (Windows + Intel)** standard. In addition, the standardization of Web browsers has added to the popularity of PCs because it is possible to visit almost any Web site regardless of the browser you are using.

Although an individual PC is initially *much* less expensive to purchase than a mainframe, taken collectively, the total cost of ownership of PCs in an organization is much *more* than that of a mainframe due to higher cost to manage and support those PCs. This higher cost includes the cost of a technical staff that is available to install new hardware and software as it becomes available or to repair machines that fail. Another element of the higher cost of management and maintenance of PCs is the purchase cost of new software or new versions of existing software. In fact, support for an organization's personal computers makes up about 70 percent of the cost of owning them. According to the Gartner Group, this means that when a company pays $2,100 for a PC, it will pay an additional $4,900 over the three-year life of the machine.[2]

In addition to these costs, PCs present other problems, including a lack of centralized management and backup and security risks (i.e., physical security, data security, and virus protection). Table 2-6 shows the advantages and disadvantages of PCs in organizational computing.

Client/Server Computing

In looking at mainframes and PCs, we see the two extremes of corporate computing—a centralized host versus distributed computing. However, there are obviously many situations where both the power of a mainframe and the ease of use of a PC

---

2. Elizabeth Waise, "Slaves to the Machine," *USA Today*, February 17, 1999, p. 5D.

| Table 2-6 | Advantages and Disadvantages of PCs |

Advantages	Disadvantages
Standardized hardware and software with ease of use (GUI)	High cost of management and support (total cost of ownership)
High user productivity	Lack of centralized control
Low initial processing costs	Security risks
Distributed computing	Cost of software upgrades

are needed. Even when PCs are connected via a LAN, they still may not meet the needs of many business critical applications. To meet these needs, **client/server computing** was developed. With client/server computing, processing is shared between multiple small computers known as **clients** that are connected via a network to a host computer known as a **server.** It is important to note that although the terms *client* and *server* often are used to refer to the machines being used, it is actually the *client software* and *server software* that carry out the processing. In fact, it is possible to run several different types of client or server software on the same machine. For example, you probably have both Web browser and e-mail client software simultaneously running on your computer.

Clients on the network are typically PCs, a type of high-powered small computer built for specialized applications called a **workstation,** or a new type of computer called a **network computer (NC).** Workstations are often used for tasks that require processing capabilities beyond those available on a standard PC, such as simulating complex business situations. On the other hand, a network computer looks much like a PC without a hard drive or CD-ROM or DVD drives, or internal sockets for expanding the capabilities of the computer. The NC is dedicated to working on a network rather than working as a stand-alone computer. NCs offer a number of advantages over PCs in organizations, mainly in terms of the total cost of ownership due to lower purchase, setup, and software installation costs. In a client/server environment, NCs are often referred to as **thin clients** as compared to PCs and workstations, which are referred to as **fat clients,** with *thin* and *fat* referring to client capabilities. In the evolution of computing, we have gone from a strictly host-based system with dumb terminals (extremely thin clients) to a system of distributed computing with fat clients to a client/server system with either fat or thin clients.

The server in a client/server network is typically dedicated to a specific type of processing, like providing files with a file server, responding to database queries with a database server, or handling high-speed processing with an application server. Because both the client and the server are capable of processing, processing is shared between the two computers depending on the capability of each. The simplest form of client/server computing involves a **file server** that manages the network. The file server does not handle any of the computing load—its primary role is to control access to the network, manage communications between PCs, and make data and program files available to the individual PCs. The computing load is still distributed among the individual PCs.

Three-Tiered Architecture

A widely used client/server setup involves the use of a client, an application server, and a database server. In this client/server environment, a user working at a GUI-based client PC or workstation sends a request for data or processing to an application server, which decides what data are needed and sends a query to the database server to retrieve those data. The database server processes the query and returns the matching data to the application server, which processes the data into the form required by the

Figure 2-8 Three-Tiered Client/Server Architecture

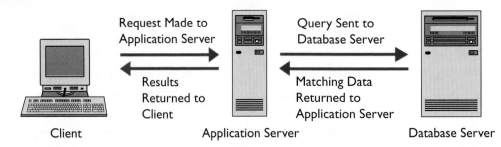

Client   Application Server   Database Server

Request Made to Application Server

Results Returned to Client

Query Sent to Database Server

Matching Data Returned to Application Server

user. Because one client and two servers are involved in this process, this is commonly referred to as a **three-tiered client/server architecture.** Note that this is different from a file server that supplies the entire database file, with the local PC still handling all of the processing. Figure 2-8 shows a three-tiered client/server architecture.

Today, a variety of servers are in use in a client/server environment. In addition to file, database, and application servers there are Web, e-mail, fax, and modem servers, as shown in Table 2-7. Each of these servers has application software that is specialized for the task that the server carries out on the network. For example, Web server software is specialized to handle requests for Web pages, whereas e-mail server software is specialized to send and receive e-mail. It is worth noting that in many organizations the application server shown in Table 2-7 is replacing mainframes for handling large-scale processing tasks. In fact, IBM refers to its large computers as *enterprise servers* to emphasize their use in client/server computing as application servers.

As shown in the three-tiered client/server architecture, requests for processing on a server often come from another server, which in turn may be processing a request from a client. For example, a client may make a request to a Web server that in turn makes a request to an application server that then makes a request to a database server. One of the strengths of client/server computing is the capability to string a series of servers together to respond to a client's request. Figure 2-9 shows a typical client/server network with the various servers and clients.

Like the other types of computing, client/server computing has its advantages and disadvantages, as shown in Table 2-8.

Quick Review

1. List the various types of computing that are in use in organizations.

2. List the various types of servers that one might find in an organization.

Table 2-7 Servers on a Client/Server Network

Server Type	Purpose
File	Provides both software and data files to users
Database	Handles queries to a large database and returns matching records
Application	Handles high-speed processing for an application
Web	Handles requests for Web pages
E-mail	Sends and receives e-mail for entire organization
Fax	Sends and receives faxes for entire organization
Modem	Enables users in organization to access other networks through a telephone line

Figure 2-9 Client/Server Network

File
Server

Fax/Modem
Server

PC

PC

Mail Server

NC

Database
Server

Application
Server

Web
Server

Table 2-8 Advantages and Disadvantages of Client/Server Systems

Advantages	Disadvantages
Computing burden can be shared between clients and servers	Programming relationship between clients and servers is more complex
Servers can be specialized to one particular type of task	Updating system requires that all clients and servers be updated regardless of location
Upgrading system can be done in small steps	
Loss of a client does not stop other clients from accessing server	

Sun is a large supplier of servers and network computers such as the Sun Ray 1.

Follow the Transaction at fareastfoods.com

In chapter 1, we discussed an example of a company in the networked economy: fareastfoods.com. This company markets nonperishable Oriental foods over the Internet. In this chapter, that scenario continues to demonstrate the types of information technology typically used in transactions in the networked economy. This same scenario will be revisited in subsequent chapters.

To demonstrate the use of information technology in the networked economy, we will follow a transaction from its beginning with the purchaser's PC through the network to fareastfoods.com, where it is processed and the food products are shipped to the purchaser. Figure 2-10 provides an overview of this process, starting with the generation of an electronic order form on a PC.

We concentrate on following the transaction because it is the heart of the networked economy. Without transactions, there would be no economy, so understanding how transactions occur and are processed is essential to your understanding. Transactions are usually handled by a type of information system called a **transaction processing system (TPS),** which is the basis for all data collection in an organization and between organizations. A TPS performs functions that include recording sales, hiring and paying employees, purchasing goods, and the like. Although transaction processing systems will be covered in detail in chapter 4, we will use them here to discuss the use of hardware and software to purchase food items from fareastfoods.com.

As seen in Figure 2-10, there are four primary steps in the food order and fulfillment process, each of which will be discussed in detail from the hardware and software perspectives. The four steps are:

Step 1: The purchaser uses a PC to generate the order.

Step 2: The order is sent from the PC via telephone lines or cable along the Internet to the proper address.

Step 3: The order arrives at fareastfoods.com, where it is processed.

Step 4: The food is sent to the purchaser.

Figure 2-10 Overview of Steps in Food Order

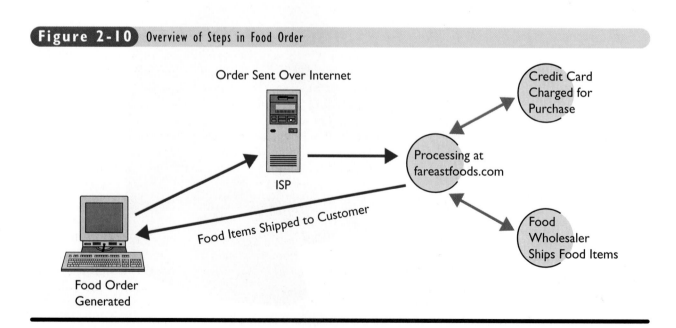

Ⓕocus on the Internet

Dave's Guides

Unfortunately, there was not room in this chapter on information technology as the infrastructure of the networked economy to provide more than a cursory overview of hardware and software. Topics on buying a PC, setting it up, and troubleshooting had to be left out in favor of other information technology topics. Fortunately, there are numerous Web sites that do provide a wealth of information on these topics. One of the most complete sources of such information is that found at the Web site created by Dave Strauss of Michigan State University, which can be found at www.css.msu.edu/PC-Guide.html. Actually, this site provides access to a series of guides as well as to two Web-based courses that Dave teaches. The guides include Buying a Home PC, Buying a Used PC, Setup and Upgrade, Troubleshooting, and Frequently Asked Questions.

In the section on buying a home PC, the Web site includes a great deal of information and advice on a variety of topics including operating systems, processing chips, internal memory, modems, and graphics. For example, if you are unsure of what is meant by some term, such as "USB", you can look it up in Dave's Guides to Buying a Home PC. There you will find that it means Universal Serial Bus and also that it is a fairly new way of connecting devices to your computer that provides a much higher degree of flexibility than previous methods. If you want to know more, Dave provides a link to Intel's Web site as a part of the discussion. This site provides one of the best discussions around on processing chips under the heading "Processor Paranoia" in which types and speeds of chips are compared. In summary, this a good site to bookmark for future reference on anything to do with Windows-based PCs. Its only shortcoming is that Apple Macintosh computers are not discussed.

Student PC Hardware and Software

In this scenario, we will assume that the purchaser has a PC that is connected to the Internet via a telephone line or cable. We will assume that the PC is an Intel-standard PC, but it could just as well be an Apple Macintosh. The hardware elements are just like those discussed earlier in the chapter.

In order for a purchaser to order Oriental food over the Internet, two key pieces of software are necessary—an operating system and a **Web browser.** In our case, we will assume that the student is running Windows 98 as the operating system and one of two popular Web browsers—Navigator from Netscape or Internet Explorer from Microsoft. Although there are differences between the two browsers, in principle they work the same, so we won't worry about which one is being used.

The Windows 98 operating system enables the student to start the computer and to select the application software to run, which, in this case, is a Web browser used to access fareastfoods.com's Web site over the Internet at www.fareastfoods.com.

Once the Web browser is used to access fareastfood.com's Web site, a variety of nonperishable Oriental foods can be viewed on an electronic catalog. Desired food items can be ordered by filling out an online order form and submitting it back to the company over the Internet. Payment can be made by using a credit card. Figure 2-11 shows a browser screen with an order form for fareastfoods.com.

Follow the Transaction: Submitting the Order

Once the order has been completed using a browser, the next step is to submit the order over the Internet to fareastfoods.com. This is initiated from within the browser by clicking the *Submit* button on fareastfoods.com's Web site. This command accomplishes two things: First, the browser software **encrypts** the order information in such a way that criminals will not be able to intercept it and use the credit card number. Second, the order information is converted into a stream of

Figure 2-11 Completed Food Order Form on Browser

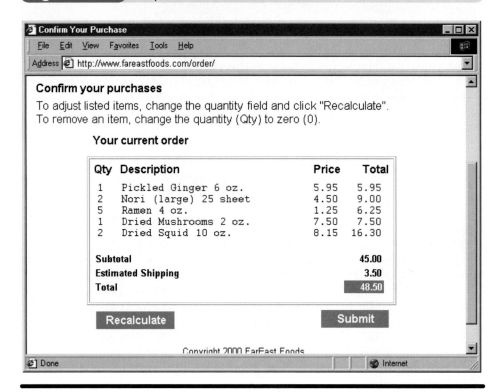

data bits that is sent from the browser to the PC's modem for actual transmittal over the Internet.

As mentioned earlier, the modem is a device for sending and receiving data or information over a telephone line. To do this, it converts the digital form of computer data and information into either the analog form sent over telephones or the digital form sent over cable TV networks. In the case of the telephone modem, at the sender's end, the modem **mo**dulates the digital computer data or information into an analog form that can be sent over standard telephone lines. At the other end, the modem **dem**odulates the analog signal back into a digital form that can be understood by the receiver's computer. For a telephone modem, the transfer rate is measured in kilobytes per second (kbps), with 56 kbps being the standard today. This process is shown in Figure 2-12.

Just as telephone modems are necessary to connect two computers over a telephone line, making the cable-to-PC connection requires a cable modem to modulate and demodulate the cable signal into a stream of data. In addition, cable modems incorporate a variety of other functions to allow the PC to be linked to a network.

Figure 2-12 Use of Telephone Modem

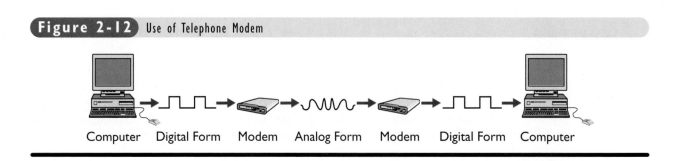

Computer   Digital Form   Modem   Analog Form   Modem   Digital Form   Computer

ⓕ o c u s   o n   T e c h n o l o g y

Customers Talking to Your Computers

Even before the first *Star Wars* movie was released in 1977, there was interest in being able to talk to computers rather than having to type commands from a keyboard. Today, businesses are turning to speech recognition systems to avoid having their customers deal with frustrating touchtone mazes while at the same time reducing the cost of twenty-four hour customer service. The financial service and travel industries are leading the way in this movement as they look for better ways to enable their customers to input stock symbols and flight numbers.

Customers of financial services companies want access to their portfolio information from any place and at any time of day and they don't want to try to deal with a twelve-digit telephone keypad in an airport while also carrying their luggage. Discount brokers E*trade and Schwab started using voice-based telephone systems in early 1998 and Fidelity intro-

duced their own system in December of that year. These systems allow users to say things, such as "get my account balance" or "sell all of my XYZ stock" using *natural language understanding* systems.

In the travel industry, Northwest Airlines and Anderson Consulting are using a voice recognition system that enables customers or employees to change travel reservations by being able to jump around in computerized reservations systems in a way that would not be possible with a touchtone system or even a human reservation agent. With customer service being an essential element to remaining competitive in both the financial services and travel industry, voice recognition is giving these companies an advantage.

Source: Brad Stone, "Look Who's Talking Now." *Newsweek,* February 22, 1999, pp. 48–49.

Regardless of the type of modem being used to access the Internet, **data communications** software is necessary to direct the data or information flow over the telephone line or cable. This software once was sold separately from the operating system or other application software, but most PC operating system software now incorporates the data communications software in it. This software is concerned with grouping the data bits (0's and 1's) into **packets** and transmitting the packets over the telephone line.

In the case of the food order, the data about the food items being ordered, the mailing address of the person ordering it, and the credit card information are converted to data bits by the data communications software and directed to the modem, where they are then transmitted over the telephone line or cable.

Sending Data on the Internet

In order for data (or information) to be sent over the Internet from a PC using a telephone line, the data must first be sent to an **Internet service provider (ISP)** that has at least one high-speed server computer and a high-speed connection to the Internet.

Quick Review

1. List the steps necessary to create and send an order from a PC to a company like fareastfoods.com.
2. What is the role of a *modem* in the process of sending data or information on the Internet?

Follow the Transaction: Processing the Food Order

So far, the process of ordering food products over the Internet has involved using a PC to generate and submit the order. We won't worry about how the order is transmitted to the computers at fareastfoods.com—that will be explained in chapter 3. For now, we will worry about what happens to the order once it arrives over the Internet at the company. At fareastfoods.com, the order arrives through a computer called a **gateway** that connects the corporate network (which looks like that shown in Figure 2-9) into the Internet. This gateway is connected to a cable that allows transmission of data at speeds at least three hundred times that of a voice telephone line and modem.

Fareastfoods.com is like many other networked economy companies in that it is a **virtual company**, (i.e., one that does not have a physical presence other than for a small marketing and administration staff). In this case, fareastfoods.com uses computers to take orders for food products over the Internet, charge the buyer's credit card for the amount of the order, order the food items from wholesalers, combine the orders from wholesalers into a single package, and have a package delivery company pick them up and deliver them to the buyer. The only way that fareastfoods.com actually handles the food items is to combine orders from multiple wholesalers into a single package, and this is accomplished by temporary employees who work for an outside firm with which fareastfoods.com has contracted. For example, this allows orders for Thai and Korean foods that come from different wholesalers to be sent out together.

Order Fulfillment Operations

Once the order has arrived at the Web server, a series of five operations must be carried out to result in the order being fulfilled and the food items shipped to the customer. These five operations are:

Operation 1: The data stream from the gateway is decrypted and split into the various fields of the order (i.e., data on the person ordering the food items, the order number of the products being ordered, and the credit card number being used to pay for the order). The order is then sent to the application server for processing.

Operation 2: The application server computes the total bill for the order. It also requests that the customer record in the database be updated.

Operation 3: The application server also sends a query to the credit card company to ensure that the card number is valid and that the available balance is larger than the amount of the order. If it is, the card is charged for the amount of the purchase, and a message is sent back to fareastfoods.com validating the card.

Operation 4: The application server sends a message to the Oriental food wholesalers that will actually fill the order requesting them to pull the item(s) from their warehouse(s) and to ship them to fareastfoods.com.

Operation 5: When the orders arrive from the wholesalers, they are combined into a single package with a bar code that is scanned into the application server and matched with the original order from the customer. A message is then sent to a package delivery company to pick up the combined food items for delivery to the customer. A message is also sent over the e-mail server to the customer indicating that the order has been processed and is on its way.

Note that the first and second operations are handled within the company by the servers on the corporate network The third, fourth, and fifth operations involve connecting with other corporate networks, in this case, those of the credit card company, food wholesaler, and the package delivery company. Let's now take a brief look at these operations. Many of them will be covered in more detail in succeeding chapters.

Operation 1: Web Server Processing

The data on the food order arrive over the Internet to the gateway, from which they are sent to the Web server. Software is then used to decrypt the data stream using a reverse of the encryption method used by the browser. Finally, the data stream must be decoded into the fields of the order form and sent to the application server. Although standard PCs can be used as Web servers for low-traffic Web sites, for high-volume sites like fareastfoods.com, computers with higher-speed or multiple processing chips and extra amounts of internal memory are usually required.

Operation 2: Application Server Processing

From the Web server, the order is transmitted to the application server for actual processing. This includes computing the total amount of the bill, including the cost of the food items, taxes (if any), and shipping charges. Of all the servers, application servers are most like mainframes in both size and purpose. They must be high-speed machines capable of handling thousands of transactions per hour, twenty-four hours a day, seven days a week, 365 days a year on a **real-time basis,** that is, as they are received instead of waiting until multiple orders are received and processed together. The large number of high-speed computers sold by IBM in late 1998 can be attributed directly to the need for application servers that can accomplish these tasks.

In addition to processing the transactions, the application server at fareast-foods.com will typically send a query to the database server regarding this customer. If this is a new customer, he and his current purchase are added to the customer database. Otherwise, his purchase history is updated for marketing purposes. The use of Web, application, and database servers is shown in Figure 2-13. Note that with the introduction of the Web server in the process, we actually have a *four-tiered client/server system* in use here.

Operation 3: Querying the Credit Card Company

Because the purchaser is using his credit card to pay for the food, the card must be validated, the available balance checked against the amount of the purchases, and, if it is a valid card with a sufficient balance, the total amount of the purchase charged against the card. This is handled by the application and database servers at the credit card company, and a message is sent back to fareastfoods.com. This process is shown in Figure 2-14.

Operation 4: Filling the Order

When the credit card authorization is received, orders for the food items are placed with the food wholesalers over a network connection between application servers using a process similar to that used to check the credit card. At each wholesaler, the orders are picked from their warehouses and shipped to fareastfoods.com.

To deliver the food order to fareastfoods.com, a wholesaler must have a way of picking the items from its warehouse. Often this involves special application software that groups or *batches* orders of food items in similar locations and then prepares a plan for employees to follow in finding and retrieving the necessary food items. Once the items are retrieved, they are packed for shipment to fareastfoods.com along with other orders that have arrived that day.

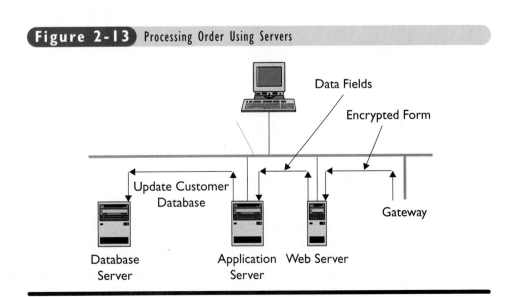

Figure 2-13 Processing Order Using Servers

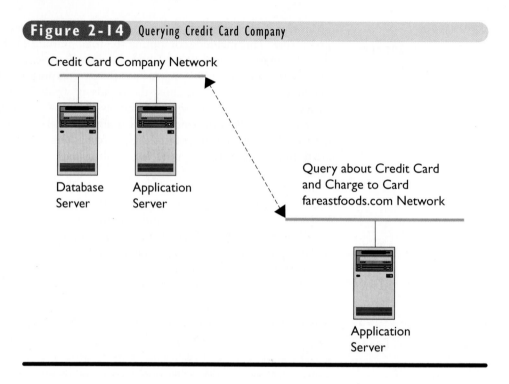

Figure 2-14 Querying Credit Card Company

When these orders arrive at fareastfoods.com from the wholesalers, they must be quickly combined into a shipment to be sent to the customer. This is actually handled by employees of a firm that fareastfoods.com engages expressly for this purpose. This is another example of the company's virtualness because it does not become involved in this manual process of creating packages to be sent out. When the packages are ready to go out, bar codes will be used on the packaging slip and address label to identify each one. These bar codes will be scanned and the information entered into the application server, which updates the database server.

Operation 5: Requesting Delivery

When fareastfoods.com's application server receives data that a package is ready, it sends a message to the package delivery company to pick up the package. This process is very similar to that for the credit card and food wholesaler companies. In addition, a message is sent through fareastfoods.com's e-mail server to the buyer that the food order has been filled with his credit card being charged for the amount of the order.

Quick Review

1. List the operations that typically take place when an order is processed at a virtual company like fareastfoods.com. How would these operations differ in a company that manufactures and/or warehouses the goods its sells?
2. Take a company from which you or someone you know has ordered goods either over the telephone or on the Internet and speculate at the steps that the company followed to deliver the order.

Follow the Transaction: Delivery of Order

After the package is picked up by the delivery company, every time the package is handled, the address label bar code is read with a **bar code reader** to generate data on time, location, and status of the package. These data are transmitted to the package delivery company's application server to be incorporated into the delivery company's database and Web server to generate a Web page. Now, the history and

It is now possible to track the delivery process for a UPS package using the Web.

current status of the package can be checked from the package delivery company's Web site. A chip that stores this information also may be included on the outside of the package to expedite this process.

When the package is delivered, the purchaser is requested to sign an electronic tablet that digitizes the signature and transmits it to the delivery company's application server and database server as proof of receipt. It can also be displayed on the package delivery company's Web page.

Quick Review

1. What does the term *batching* refer to in the process of delivering an order?

2. How are bar codes used in the delivery process?

⊘ Summary

To summarize this chapter, let's answer the Learning Objectives questions posed at the beginning of the chapter.

What does information technology have to do with the networked economy? Information technology is the infrastructure of the networked economy—that is, the elements necessary for the networked economy to exist. This infrastructure is necessary for transactions to take place in the networked economy by processing raw data into information. It is also necessary for accessing existing data and information and sharing data, information, and knowledge with other people in the networked economy. Hardware is the electronic part of information technology that carries out various operations under the direction of the software.

What are the four major hardware elements of the computer, and how do they process data into information? Information technology hardware is composed of three elements: input, processing, and output; secondary storage is also included with most computers. The input element enables the hardware to receive the data to be processed and the software instructions for processing those data.

Once the data are input, the hardware must be able to process the data into information using software instructions. This is accomplished using two types of chips: processing chips and memory chips. The actual processing of data into information takes place on the processing chips. Because the processed information is of no use unless it is provided to the user in some way, the computer has an output unit. Secondary storage units are necessary because memory chips are both limited in space and nonpermanent. Letters, punctuation marks, and special symbols are stored internally and on secondary storage using a standardized representation that uses groups of eight bits, called bytes, where each bit pattern represents a given symbol.

Why is software necessary to use a computer? Without software, information technology would be nothing more than a well-constructed combination of silicon chips and electronic circuitry. *Software* is the general term for all of the instructions given to the computer or other chip-based device by the user or the manufacturer. The two major types of software are operating systems software and application software. Both software types are at work in the computer at the same time, each serving a different purpose. The operating systems software controls the operations of application software, as well as controlling the computer itself. Application software actually performs the specialized tasks that we hear so much about.

The two most common user interfaces are command driven and graphical. In software with a command-driven interface, the software simply waits for the user to enter the appropriate command or data. The interface that is standard for personal computers is the graphical user interface, or GUI. In a GUI, icons are used to represent the functions to be performed, which are selected with a pointer.

All software, whether built into the machine, purchased from a software development firm, or developed within an organization, is created by one or more people who use a process known as programming, using a computer language, of which there are many.

How has computer processing evolved over time, and what are the three types in use today? The three types of computing that coexist within the corporate world are mainframes, PCs on a LAN, and client/server computing. Mainframes are the large computers aimed at providing the heavy-duty processing required by many corporation activities. They handle all of the processing and storage, leading to centralized massive computing power and the capability to run enterprise-level business critical applications.

PCs are small computers that have been responsible for bringing computing to the desktop. In general, they are cheaper to purchase, easier to use, and result in more user productivity than mainframe computers. In organizations, they are typically connected over an internal network called a local area network (LAN).

Client/server computing is the newest form of corporate computing; it attempts to combine the best features of mainframes and PCs. With client/server computing, processing is shared between multiple small computers known as clients and a type of host computer known as a server. Clients are typically PCs, workstations, or network computers. The server is typically dedicated to a specific type of processing. There are a variety of servers in use today in a client/server environment, including database servers, application servers, Web servers, e-mail servers, fax servers, and modem servers. Requests for processing often come from another server, which in turn may be processing a request from a client.

What role does information technology play in a transaction in the networked economy? Information technology makes it possible for a customer sitting at a personal computer to use the Internet to find information on products, order those products, and have them delivered directly to the customer's home or office. The company uses information technology to receive the order, check on the customer's credit, request shipment of products from wholesalers, request a pickup from a package delivery company, and notify the customer that the order is on its way.

> Review Questions

1. Why is information technology a necessary element of the networked economy?

2. What are the two elements of information technology? What is the purpose of each element?

3. What are the three parts of information technology hardware? What is another part of hardware that is found on most computers?

4. Of the two types of software discussed in the text, which is used to actually process transactions in the networked economy? Which type of software is used to manage the operations of the hardware and software?

5. List the operations carried out by the operating system. How are data, information, and instructions organized?

6. What are the two types of user interfaces in common use today? Which user interface uses icons, toolbars, and menu bars to carry out operations?

7. What are the three types of computing used in the corporate or organizational environment? Which is the oldest type of computing used in the corporate or organizational environment? Which is the newest type of computing used in the corporate or organizational environment?

8. What is the difference between a client and a server? What is the difference between a fat client and a thin client?

9. List five types of servers and give their purpose.

10. Which type of server has taken over many of the tasks previously handled by mainframes?

> Discussion Questions

1. Give two examples of application software with which you are familiar and discuss them briefly.

2. Discuss the strengths and weaknesses of mainframes and PCs in a corporate or organizational environment. How does the client/server system address some of the weaknesses of both systems?

3. Assume you are purchasing computer game software over the Internet. Discuss the steps that might be required for this purchase, including the hardware and software that are required.

> CASE

WildOutfitters.com

"I forgot. Is this rock the Web server or the printer?" asked Claire.

Alex replied, "That's the server, this stick is the printer."

After a long day of paddling, Alex and Claire were discussing their plans for WildOutfitters.com at their campsite by the river. Alex was attempting to explain the system with a diagram made up of whatever was at hand. By the light of the campfire, he had placed a few stones and sticks to represent various hardware and he had drawn lines in the dirt to represent the connections between them. If left as it was, future archaelogists might be puzzled by the strange patterns but Alex seemed to know exactly what they meant. Now, he only hoped that he could explain it adequately to Claire.

The Campagnes have decided to set up a Web storefront to sell outdoor sport products—of their own design and others—over the Internet. For this purpose, they have obtained the license for the URL WildOutfitters.com, named after their current business. They hope that a Web storefront not only will increase their sales with orders from the Web but also will serve as a form of advertising for their physical location.

They plan to start small with a minimum of features but with the flexibility to add more functionality as desired. The initial site will consist primarily of a catalog of products along with product reviews. A shopping cart feature will be provided for accumulating items to purchase. Payment for online orders will be by credit card only. Shipping and handling charges will be calculated automatically and added, based on the total cost of the products ordered.

To this end, Claire and Alex figure that their site, while small compared to other Web stores, will require a number of pages. A purchaser will enter the site through a home page with background information about the store and its products. This page will include contact information, location, and hours for the store as well as the appropriate links to the online catalog. In addition to links to the catalog, there also will be links to pages describing the shipping and privacy policies.

The online catalog will allow the user to search in several modes. One mode will allow customers to browse the products by category. A second will allow them to use a search engine to search by keyword. For either mode, pages will be returned with listings of matching products, photos, and the price. A customer may then click on the photo of a product to get more information and a review of the product written by Claire or Alex. Various form and message pages will be needed to process a customer's order and notify them of any problems that occur.

A customer will visit the Web site and search the catalog. When a desired product is found, the customer may add it to the shopping cart. When the customer finishes shopping, she can then complete the purchase. A form page will be presented showing the total cost calculations, including shipping and handling. If this is acceptable to the buyer, she may then continue on to a payment form and enter her credit card information. The customer also will be able to remove individual items or cancel the order altogether.

While the initial storefront is limited primarily to the catalog, Alex and Claire wish to purchase hardware and software for the system that will allow them to expand their Web offerings in the future.

The couple discussed these plans over a warm meal and late into the night by the fire. After moving a stone here and a stick there, they brewed a pot of coffee and looked on their system design with satisfaction.

Finally, after surveying the crude diagram laid out before her, Claire announced in her best caveman voice: "Ugh, computer good! Tomorrow make wheel."

With a groan, Alex decided to call it a night and headed for the tent.

1. Carry out some research into what ISP services are available for a small business such as Wild Outfitters. Compare each service that you discover and discuss which would be best for WildOutfitters.com. Be sure to back up your argument by discussing the criteria that you used to rate the services and how well each service performed.

2. What are the procedures for obtaining and using a Web address such as WildOutfitters.com?

3. What hardware devices should be purchased for WildOutfitters.com? Why?

4. What application software should be purchased for the system? Why?

5. *(Hands on)* Search through newspaper and magazine advertisements or Web sites for vendors of the hardware and sofware that you discussed in questions 3 and 4. Prepare a spreadsheet listing the desired items and their price from each vendor. Calculate the total cost of the systems from each vendor. Be sure to include any extra charges such as shipping and maintenance or technical support contracts.

Appendix to Chapter 2

A Short History of Computers

The development of computers is usually described as occurring in generations. The first generation is considered to span the period 1946–1959. This generation of computers is characterized by the use of vacuum tubes in the CPU and internal memory units, the first commercial computers, and many fundamental advances in computing. The first commercial computer was the UNIVAC 1 (**UNIV**ersal **A**utomatic **C**omputer), which was sold to the Census Bureau in 1951.

In the second generation of computers, during the period 1959–1964, the vacuum tube was replaced by the transistor. The transistor, a solid-state device, was the major breakthrough that allowed computers to have reasonable size and power. A solid-state device is made of minerals so that it can be instructed to allow or not allow a flow of current. Because solid-state devices did not use the hot filament that was in vacuum tubes, the use of transistors reduced the computer's heat output and power requirement. Transistors also increased the reliability of the computer because they did not burn out the way vacuum tubes did. This breakthrough in turn reduced the cost of owning and operating a computer. This period saw tremendous growth in the use of computers by government, business, and industry.

The introduction of the integrated circuit in 1965 was the beginning of the third generation of computers. With this technological advance, an entire circuit board containing transistors and connecting wires could be placed on a single chip. This advance meant greater reliability and compactness combined with lower cost and power requirements. During this period, IBM controlled the mainframe market with its 360 (later to be 370) series of computers. This series was so well designed and built that its successors are still in heavy use today.

The fourth and current generation of computers began in 1971 with the introduction of the microprocessor—a central processing unit on a chip. This generation includes the introduction of supercomputers. These "monster computers" are in heavy demand for military and meteorological applications that require a high speed of operation. Another important advance of this generation has been the introduction of the personal computer, making the power of the computer available to anybody who wishes to use one.

The Evolution of the PC

The term *PC* was coined by a computer scientist, Alan Kay, in a 1972 paper entitled "A PC for Children of All Ages." As a result of Kay's work in this area, Xerox built a PC called the Alto, though Xerox never put it on the market. Other established computer companies also considered the concept of a PC but decided that there was no market for such a machine. As a result, it was not until 1975 that an Albuquerque, New Mexico, company called MITS released the first PC in kit form. This machine, named "Altair" after a planet in the *Star Trek* TV series, had just 1K of memory and was very slow by today's standards. MITS had five thousand orders for the Altair after it was pictured on the cover of *Popular Electronics*. A pioneer in the field, the current computer science publisher Rodney Zaks, remarked that "never before had such a powerful tool been invented and so few people realized what it could do."

Although MITS was the first to come out with a PC, it was up to Apple, Radio Shack, and Commodore to popularize its use. These were among almost one hundred companies that rushed to put out PCs in the years immediately after MITS offered the first one. An amazing success story of this period is that of the Apple Company, formed by two young Californians, Steve Jobs and Steve Wozniak, when they built the first Apple computer in their garage.

With all of these infant companies competing for the emerging computer market, Apple made a real breakthrough in 1978 when it offered a disk drive to go along with the original Apple II. This was the key addition that, along with the VisiCalc spreadsheet software package offered only on the Apple, allowed Apple to leapfrog over Radio Shack and Commodore into first place among the pioneer companies.

The next breakthrough came when in 1981 IBM offered its PC, which used an Intel CPU chip. Although not an innovation technologically, the IBM PC almost immediately became an industry standard and legitimized the concept of a PC. It was followed by the Apple Macintosh in 1984 and the short-lived IBM PS/2 line in 1987.

Over the last twenty years, there has been a continued movement toward faster and less-expensive computers to the point that the under-$500 PC is a reality. Today, although the vast majority of all PCs follow the Wintel standard, Apple has made recent inroads with its iMac line of computers. At the mainframe level, the introduction of air-cooled instead of water-cooled computers has lead to a reduction in their size to the point that they are often indistinguishable from a standard personal computer.

CHAPTER ③

Sharing Information and Resources through Networks

❯ Learning Objectives

After reading this chapter, you should be able to answer the following questions:

❯ What are computer networks, and what is their role in the networked economy?

❯ What is the network layer model, and how does it work?

❯ What are the parts of a local area network?

❯ What is the Internet, and how is it used?

❯ What is the World Wide Web, and how does it work?

Focus on Management

Charging Ahead at Square D

Although computers and electronics are key elements in the networked economy, some manufacturers and distributors in the $77.7 billion wholesale electrical equipment business have been slow to join them. Part of the problem has been the reticence of their customers to leave behind paper-based information. However, if Square D Company, a manufacturer of electrical products based in Palatine, Illinois, has its way, its customers will soon look first to the Internet to get product and shipment information, training, and to place orders. The $2.6 billion subsidiary of Paris-based Schneider Electric is using the Web not just to make itself faster and more efficient, but also to move this large and mature industry onto the networked economy.

To do this, Square D created eBusiness, a group that will run its electronic commerce push. The eBusiness group consists of both business and IT experts who can solicit input companywide in putting together Web projects. This group has already put in place Web technology that it is using to push product information and training materials out to its two thousand distributors. It has also created a service called E-Way that allows distributors to check order status, verify price and stock availability, and place orders for uncomplicated products online. Plans include E-Way enabling distributors to track shipments by hooking into UPS and Federal Express. Future plans include such initiatives as helping customers map out electrical diagrams on the Web.

For its innovation in using Web technology, Square D was awarded the 1999 number one ranking in using Web technology by *PC Week*.

Source: Lisa Vaas, *PC Week Online,* May 10, 1999. http://www.zdnet.com/pcweek.

Square D is a leader in the wholesale electrical equipment business.

Computer Networks

In chapter 2, we discussed the use of hardware and software for processing data into information. For this information to be useful, it must be shared with others over a computer network. A **computer network,** like the Internet, exists whenever two or more computers are linked together through some type of communications medium. In the preceding Focus on Management box, the Square D company has found ways to use Internet technology to better serve its customers.

Computer networks have many uses in addition to sharing information. For example, when you go to an ATM either at home or in another part of the world, information technology reads the magnetic strip on your card, compares it to the personal identification number (PIN) keyed in, and decides if you are a valid user of that card. When you attempt to withdraw cash from the ATM, it makes a connection with a local computer, which in turn connects to your home bank's computer to verify that your account balance is sufficient to cover the amount to be withdrawn. If you are in a foreign country, this involves a currency conversion between your home currency and that of the country in which you are withdrawing the money. Through computer networks, this entire process usually takes less than a minute.

Computer networks are also important for sharing resources, usually other computers. As presented in chapter 2, computing is moving toward a client/server model in which client computers make requests of server computers for files, database records processing results, or Web pages. In the client/server model, sharing resources is as important as sharing information.

The previous chapter also discussed the role of information technology as the infrastructure for the networked economy. In this chapter, that discussion will be extended to relate specifically to the role of networks in supporting the networked economy. Because networks are so important, this entire chapter will be devoted to networks and how they work. Although networks can link a variety of information technology devices, we will concentrate on those that connect computers. Such computer networks can be classified in several ways, but we will restrict ourselves to the most common classification scheme, which is based on size. Networks can be defined according to their size as *local area networks* or *wide area networks*.

Network Size

A **local area network (LAN)** is a computer network that is confined to a single geographical area (e.g., an office, a building, or a group of buildings). LANs are a very important part of business information systems because they allow workers to communicate with one another and to share information, software, and hardware. Because even a small organization can have multiple LANs, it is necessary to link them together. The most common way of linking multiple LANs is through a **backbone,** which typically is a transmission medium created to connect networks. Backbones for connecting LANs typically span several miles and offer high-speed communications between the LANs. Backbones can also connect wide area networks into the Internet.

When computers are connected over a region, country, or the world, this is referred to as a **wide area network (WAN).** WANs are typically connected together by high-speed communication links that enable the sending of messages and files between geographically distant computers. The Internet is a WAN to which computer networks are connected. This connection can be through a mainframe computer, a LAN, or a private Internet service provider to which you connect your computer over a telephone line. You are probably able to access the Internet from your school computer lab over a LAN.

As an example of this hierarchy of networks, consider the Terry College of Business at the University of Georgia in Athens, Georgia. Terry College, home to over six thousand undergraduate and graduate business students, has several LANs, all of which are connected to the campus backbone, which connects all LANs at the University of Georgia. Finally, all of these networks are also connected into a regional wide area network called *Peachnet* and then into the Internet backbone—so-named because it connects many regional networks. Figure 3-1 shows the networks that involve the Terry College of Business.

Individuals working from a computer that does not have a direct link to the Internet must go through an **Internet service provider (ISP)**. The ISP has a server that is linked to a regional network that is, in turn, linked to the Internet. For example, a college student, who is linked to her college's LAN, wishes to send an e-mail to her parents (the connection is shown in Figure 3-2); the e-mail goes from the college LAN to a regional network, then onto the Internet, to another regional network, to the parent's ISP, and, finally, to the parents.

Each network or ISP that connects to the Internet pays for this privilege, not to the Internet but rather to some organization that has created a communication link to the Internet. If you access the Internet through your school computer connected to a LAN, then the college has paid for this link to the Internet. This is typically a flat rate per month rather than a fee based on usage. For individuals, the Internet is usually accessed through a local or national ISP or a national information service for which you may pay a flat fee or an hourly fee. The ISP or information provider then pays a telecommunications company for its connection to the Internet.

In the next sections, we will cover WANs first and then LANs. We cover WANs first because of their importance to electronic commerce. Finally, we will cover the Internet and World Wide Web as applications of WANs.

Quick
Review

1. In what ways can a computer network be classified according to size?
2. What is the difference between a backbone and a wide area network?

Figure 3-1　Networks Involving the Terry College of Business

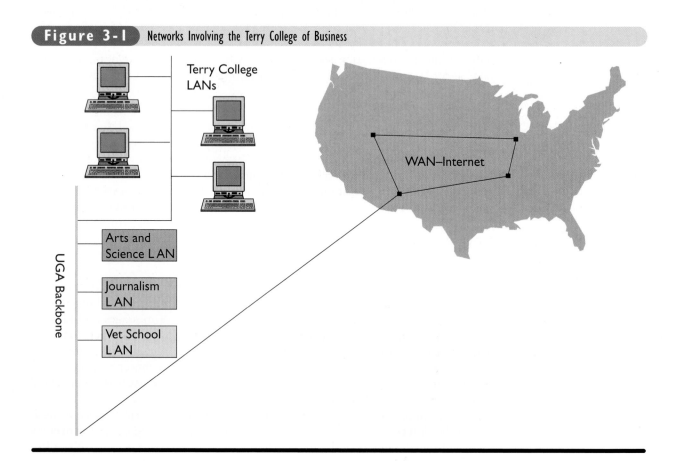

Figure 3-2 Use of ISP to Link to Internet

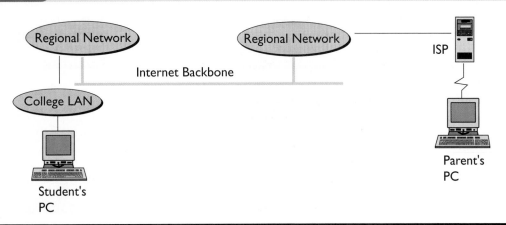

The computers in this *server farm* work as a unit to respond to client requests.

Understanding Wide Area Networks

Wide area networks (WANs) provide the infrastructure for the networked economy by making it possible for individuals, companies, and organizations to form economic relationships without regard to place or time. With a WAN, it is possible for a company in Charlotte, North Carolina, to deal with customers in Hong Kong and vendors in Paris and Beijing without anyone leaving the home office. Because having a basic understanding of how networks operate is important, a simple model is provided here.

To help you understand how a WAN operates, let's use a model that involves *network layers*, where each layer handles part of the communications between computers. The original version of this model was created by the International Standards Organization (ISO) and consisted of seven layers. Our simplified version of this model contains only three layers: the *application software layer*, the *networking*

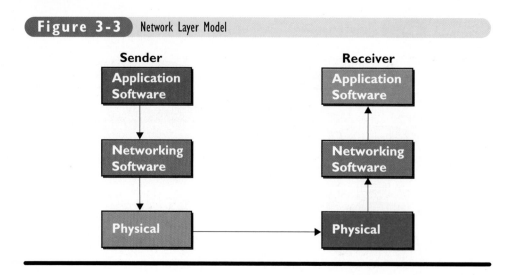

Figure 3-3   Network Layer Model

software layer, and the *physical layer,* as shown in Figure 3-3. To help you understand the layers of this model, an example is used from chapter 2, where a customer sends a food order to an Oriental food retailer, fareastfoods.com, over the Internet. In essence, the following transaction will fill in the missing steps from chapter 2.

Application Software Layer

At the top of the network layer model, as shown in Figure 3-3, is the application software layer. This is the software on each computer on the network that the user sees and uses to send and receive messages and data between computers. At the sender end, the application layer includes such well-known software applications as Web browsers and e-mail. This software *formats* (places in a special form) the message by adding important information to make it conform to a specific standard or **protocol,** which is a special set of rules for communicating. Typical protocols for the application layer of the Internet are **simple mail transfer protocol (SMTP)** for e-mail, **hypertext transfer protocol (HTTP)** for Web pages, and **electronic data interchange (EDI)** for large-scale exchange of data between organizations. The resulting message is a combination of the message generated by the application software and the protocol. The message may also be *encrypted* (placed in an unreadable form) to protect it from unauthorized readers. For our fareastfoods.com example, the customer is responding to a Web page by filling out a form (refer to Figure 2-11) and submitting that form. In this case, the application is a Web browser, the message is the contents of the food order, and the protocol is HTTP. In addition, the message is encrypted. The combination of protocol and encrypted message is shown below.

> Encryption / HTTP / Food Order

Networking Software Layer

In the networking software layer, the message from the application software layer is formatted according to whatever protocol will actually be used to send it over the network. Commonly used protocols for WANs are **Transmission Control Protocol/Internet Protocol (TCP/IP)** for the Internet and **Ansi X 12** or **EDIFACT** for **EDI.** For the time being, we will restrict our discussion to the Internet and discuss EDI later.

With the TCP/IP Internet protocol, the networking software layer carries out a series of operations to prepare the message to be sent across the Internet to a destination computer. It must first convert the address of the destination computer from a text form (name@computer.com) to an **IP address,** which consists of four groups of decimal numbers in the range 0 to 255. This is accomplished using a conversion table stored either on the user's computer or on a computer with which the local

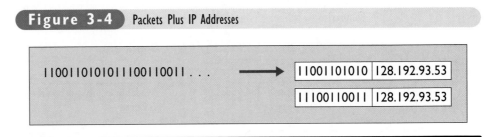

Figure 3-4   Packets Plus IP Addresses

```
11001101010111001100111 . . .  ──────▶   │11001101010│128.192.93.53│
                                          │11100110011│128.192.93.53│
```

computer can communicate. For example, if you were sending an e-mail message to the president of the United States, whose address is President@Whitehouse.gov, then Whitehouse.gov is the name of the e-mail server at the White House, which is converted into an IP address of 198.137.241.30.

Next, the message is divided into smaller digital units called **packets,** each of which contains a specific number of bytes. At this step, each packet is given a sequence number, and the destination address is added to it. This process is shown in Figure 3-4, where a series of binary digits has been converted to packets and the IP address is added to them.

Physical Layer

Once the message has passed through the preceding two software layers (i.e., the application software layer and the networking software layer), it is ready to be sent out over the *hardware* (i.e., a modem, a telephone line, cable, etc.) by the physical layer of the network model. Data and information transmitted over networks travel over various media, including *twisted pairs, coaxial cable, fiber optics, microwaves,* and *satellite transmission.* **Twisted pairs,** which consists of twisted pairs of copper wires, are like those used in much of the existing telephone system and are used widely in many types of networks.

Coaxial cable is used to transmit cable television signals into your home. It is also widely used in networks. In many areas, television cable is being converted to a type capable of handling two-way signals instead of one-way signals associated with television transmissions. This two-way cable enables the connection of home computers to ISPs at much faster speeds than those available with traditional telephone connections.

Fiber optic cable is the newest medium and consists of thousands of glass fiber strands that can transmit a large number of signals at extremely high rates of speed. The glass fiber strands also reduce the size of the cable required; however, individual computers are not set up to connect directly to fiber optic cable, so it is often necessary to use twisted pairs or coaxial cable for the last few feet to the computer. Figure 3-5 shows a comparison of copper wire and fiber optic cables for transmitting the same volume of information.

Figure 3-5   Comparison of Coaxial and Fiber Optic Cables

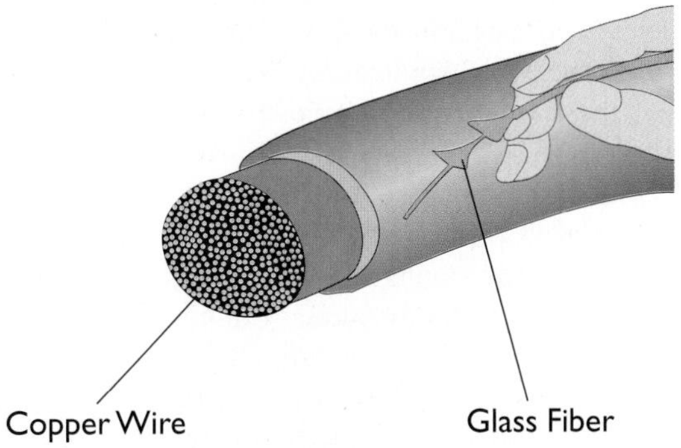

Copper Wire   Glass Fiber

Table 3-1 Comparison of Transmission Rates

Media	Speeds	Comments
Standard telephone service	56 kbps	Widely available
Integrated digital services network (ISDN)	128 kbps or 384 kbps (compressed)	Available in most urban areas but requires special adapters in home
Digital subscriber line (DSL)	1.544 mbps in; 128 mbps out	Becoming more available; does not require special equipment
TV cable	5 mbps	Cable must support two-way communication; available in many locations
T-1 to T-4	1.544 mbps to 275 mbps	Used for commercial purposes with a single T-1 line costing over $1,000 per month

Microwaves are high-frequency radio transmissions that can be sent between two earth stations or between earth stations and communications satellites, which is the method commonly used to transmit television signals. The use of direct broadcast satellites, which use microwaves for one-way downloads of data to homes and offices, is a new way of carrying out this operation, especially where land lines do not exist or are difficult to install.

In terms of speed, the transmission rates are measured in kilobits per second (Kbps) or megabits (Mbps). Table 3-1 shows a comparison of the various transmission alternatives.

Copper wire, in the form of twisted pairs, has typically been used for slow, **baseband transmissions** that include text and numerical data. On the other hand, other

Focus on Technology

Wireless Internet Access

With Internet access via telephone lines becoming common in most developed nations, it was only a matter of time before wireless Internet access became available. The surprising feature of it, though, is that it is primarily aimed at wireless telephones and personal digital assistants (PDAs) rather than at laptops. Started by a small U.S. company, but quickly picked up by Symbian—a joint venture between leading makers of wireless phones including Motorola, Britain's Psion, Sweden's Ericsson, Finland's Nokia, and Japan's Matsushita, this technology allows wireless phones to display Internet information through the Web Application Protocol (WAP). Because of the leading role of Ericsson and Nokia, this technology has been in use in Europe for a few years, but only appeared in the United States in 1999 on Sprint PCS phones. With this system, the content of specially configured Web sites can be displayed using a minibrowser on the phone's screen.

This movement was enhanced in late 1999 by an agreement between Symbian and Palm Computing, the maker of the very popular Palm series of personal digital assistants that will allow the Palm interface and applications to be used in smart wireless phones and personal digital assistants with Internet access. The devices will use an operating system developed by Psion rather than Windows CE from Microsoft and will combine wireless voice and data access with mobile information management and PDA capabilities. The new devices will support Palm's Web-clipping technology that "clips" key information from Web sites that support the technology and displays it on the PDA screen, with the capability to write on the screen with Palm's Graffiti system. According to Palm Computing, this is just the start of a projected huge market for wireless Internet access.

Source: Sandeep Junnarkar and Stephanie Miles, "Nokia, Palm Tackle Wireless Net." *CNET News.com,* October 13, 1999. http://news.cnet.com/news.

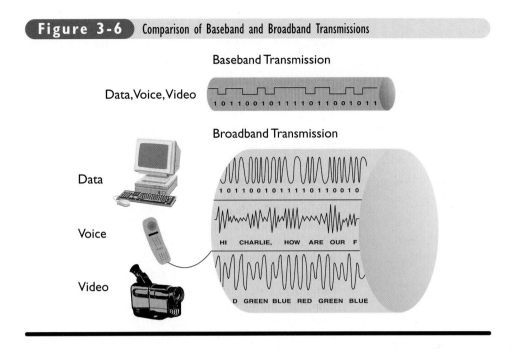

Figure 3-6   Comparison of Baseband and Broadband Transmissions

media have traditionally been used for much higher-speed **broadband transmissions,** which can simultaneously transmit large amounts and types of data, including audio, video, and other multimedia using different frequencies. However, recent advances in the technology of twisted pairs have made twisted pairs a viable option for broadband transmissions. Figure 3-6 shows the difference between baseband transmissions and broadband transmissions.

In the case of the food order to fareastfoods.com, the physical layer includes the customer's modem and telephone line or cable modem and cable link. When the message reaches the ISP, it is handled by its modem and hardware connections. Figure 3-7 shows the process of the food order leaving the customer's computer via a modem and telephone line.

Receiving the Message

At the receiving end, the process used in sending a message is reversed. That is, the message enters the physical layer and is passed up through the networking software layer, where the packets are put back together using their sequence numbers. The

Figure 3-7   Food Order Leaving Customer's Computer

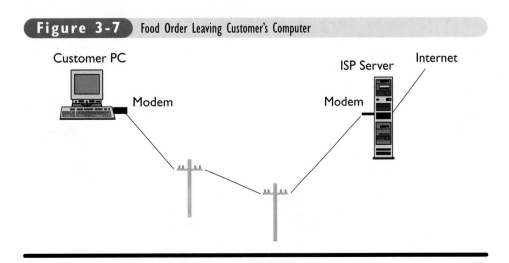

complete message is then sent to the application software layer of the receiving computer, where software decrypts the message and interprets it. If it is an e-mail message, it is displayed by the e-mail software. On the other hand, for the food order to fareastfoods.com, the message is delivered to a Web server, where software interprets the order and starts the process of fulfilling the order.

Packet Switching

As mentioned in the description of network operations, the networking software layer divides an Internet message into groups of bytes called *packets*. When the physical layer sends these packets over telephone lines, it uses a different approach from voice and fax telephone calls. For these types of calls, a complete path from the caller to the receiver is created and kept open during the duration of the call. Because computers send large amounts of data quickly and then do not send any data for a while, such an approach would be very inefficient, tying up telephone lines when none are needed. Instead, using a technology called **packet switching,** individual packets are routed through the network based on the destination address contained in each packet. With packet switching, the same data path can be shared among many computers in the network, and if a computer on the network is inoperable, the packet finds another way to reach its destination. Packet switching has been the key technology that has made the Internet work as well as it does.

When a group of data packets, like the food order, is sent to a computer with an IP address, software on the sending computer sends the packets to the *nearest* router for retransmission to other routers on the network. A **router** is a special type of computer that has the sole purpose of accepting packets and determining the *best* way to send them to the destination computer—that is, *switching the packets.* Note that in this context, the terms *nearest* and *best* do not have the same meanings as they would for someone taking a trip from Charleston, South Carolina to Seattle, Washington. Instead, they refer to the least-congested network path to the eventual goal. Very sophisticated software has been written to carry out this process on the routers and speed the data packets to their destination. Figure 3-8 shows the process of sending data from one computer to another on the Internet.

Figure 3-8 Sending Data between Computers on the Internet

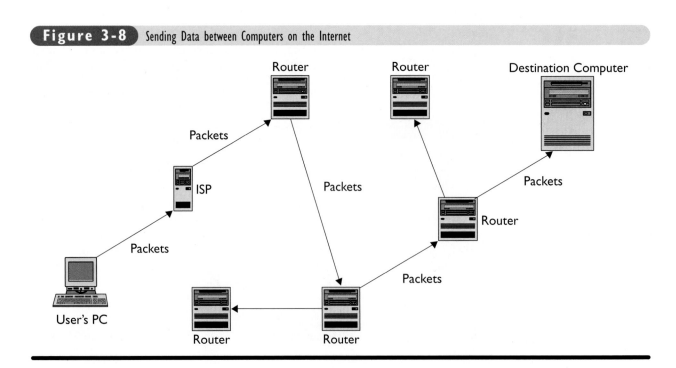

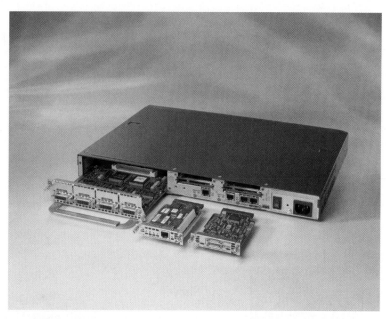

Routers, such as the one shown here, are crucial for sending data over the Internet.

Because a packetized message can be reconstructed using the sequence order that is attached to each packet, the packets do not necessarily need to follow the same path through the network and do not need to arrive in the order in which they were sent. If packets are missing, the destination computer can send a message to the sending computer requesting that the missing packets be resent.

Electronic Data Interchange

Although we have discussed networks largely in the context of the Internet, it is important to be aware that EDI is a heavily used protocol when businesses are exchanging data and information, automating much routine business between retail stores, distributors, and manufacturers. Instead of sending paper documents (e.g., purchase orders, invoices, bills of lading, shipping slips, etc.) back and forth through traditional communication channels, EDI allows companies to transmit the same information electronically between their computers. By combining EDI with point-of-sale inventory systems, a computer at a retail store can automatically order goods, based on units sold, from its supplier. The supplier, in turn, can automatically ship the goods to the retail store and electronically transmit the appropriate document. EDI greatly reduces human involvement in the ordering and shipping process, thereby reducing costs and speeding service. Figure 3-9 compares the use of EDI to traditional methods of handling transactions.

EDI and other non-Internet protocols are typically sent over **value-added networks (VANs)**. These VANs are networks that are available by subscription and provide clients with data communications facilities. The company that runs the VAN assumes complete responsibility for managing the network, including providing conversion between different systems. In a sense, a VAN adds value to the data by ensuring that it reaches its destination with little effort on the part of the subscriber. Now that you have an understanding of WANs and the network layer model, you are ready to look at local area networks.

Quick Review

1. What are the three layers of the simplified network layer model?
2. In which layer is the message encrypted? In which layer is the message packetized?

Figure 3-9 Use of EDI

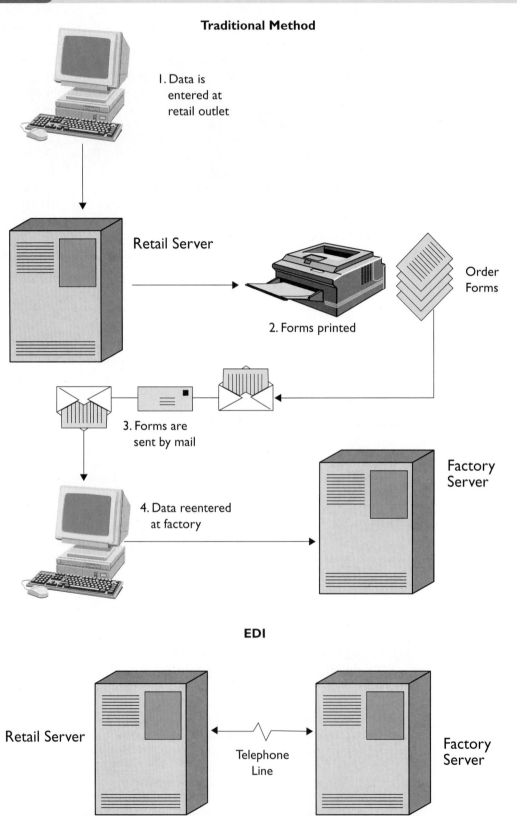

Understanding Local Area Networks

As we discussed in chapter 2, most organizations today use local area networks (LANs) to share information and resources among employees or members and to link to the Internet. Sharing information enables users to work with the same data or information files, to send messages and files via e-mail, and to carry out Internet operations on a local level. Sharing resources involves the users ability to share software and hardware. Sharing software means that the organization will not need to purchase a copy of a software package for every computer in the organization. Instead, a number of software licenses sufficient to meet most needs can be purchased and shared. (It is illegal for multiple persons to simultaneously use a software package unless a sufficient number of licenses have been purchased.) Sharing hardware means that users can use printers, disk storage, scanners, and so on through the network rather than the necessity of everyone having every possible piece of hardware. Hardware that is available from the LAN, especially highly specialized types of hardware, can significantly reduce the hardware cost to the organization.

Most LANs are **dedicated server networks** in which at least one of the computers linked to the network acts as a server that is accessed by the **client** computers on the network. Recall from chapter 2 that a **server** is a computer that carries out one of many specialized tasks enabling sharing of information and hardware. Types of servers include file servers, database servers, Web servers, application servers, communication servers, and so on. There are also **peer-to-peer networks,** which are used for smaller networks where the emphasis is on sharing files between computers, with each computer functioning as both a server and a workstation. This configuration is significantly cheaper than the dedicated server configuration, but it is not well suited for heavy-duty transaction processing. Both configurations are shown in Figure 3-10.

LAN Components

Local area networks are composed of five basic elements: servers, clients, network cabling and hubs, a network interface card, and network operating system. Because servers and clients were discussed in chapter 2, we will concentrate on the other three elements here.

Network cabling physically connects each computer on the network and also connect the hardware peripherals through a hub. Although all of the types of communications media discussed earlier for the physical layer of the network model are used for network cabling, copper twisted pairs are the most widely used medium due to their low cost. Coaxial cable and fiber optics are also used when high-speed

Figure 3-10 Dedicated Server and Peer-to-Peer Network Configurations

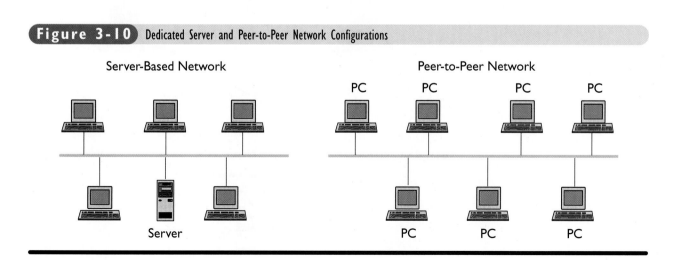

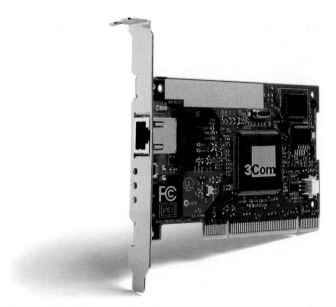

A network interface card such as this connects computers on a network.

networks are required. A **hub** is a device that allows cables to be connected together. Hubs also can be used as amplifiers or repeaters to extend the range of the network.

The network cabling is connected to the computers on the network through a **network interface card (NIC)** within each computer. The NIC handles all the electronic functions of connecting a computer to the network (i.e., receiving information that is intended for this computer and sending information from it over the network as needed). Figure 3-11 shows clients connected to the network cabling through NICs and then to a server through a hub.

The **network operating system (NOS)** is the software that controls the network. It is primarily located on the server, but a component of the network operating system resides on each client's computer. The server portion of the NOS runs the

Figure 3-11 Connecting Computers on a Network

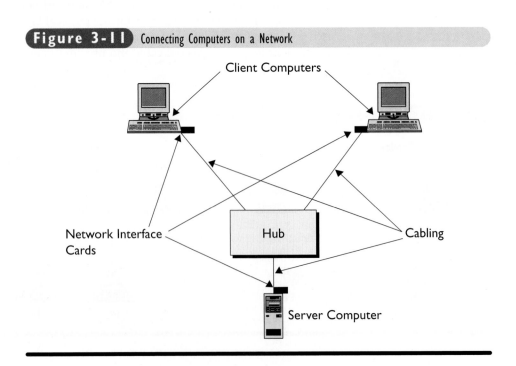

server and handles operations associated with supervising the network. The client portion of the NOS handles the connection of the client to the network and its communication with the server. By creating different versions of the client NOS software, it is possible to connect dissimilar computers (e.g., Apple Macintosh and Windows-based PCs) to the same LAN. The most popular LAN operating systems are those from Novell (Netware) and Microsoft (Windows NT).

Ethernet LANs

In the past, a number of different ways were used to connect LANs and to move data and information between computers on the network; but today, the vast majority of LANs use the **Ethernet protocol.** This protocol is used to transmit packets on a **bus network,** which uses a **bus** (a main cable) to which all clients and servers on the network are connected. With the Ethernet protocol, a computer on the network transmits a message that contains the address of the destination computer. Because all computers are free to transmit at any time, collision-detecting software must be in place to control those cases in which two or more computers are trying to transmit at the same time. When a collision is detected, each computer is directed to stop transmitting and wait a random length of time before retransmitting their message. This system works quite well and is the basis for at least 85 percent of all LANs.

If you looked at a bus network, it would appear to be in the form of a star because the actual bus is located in a central hub to which all clients are connected. Figure 3-12 shows the logical setup and the physical setup for a bus network.

A client on a LAN not only can share information and software with other PCs on the same LAN but also can communicate through gateways and bridges with other types of computers and with other LANs. A **gateway** is the combination of hardware and software that connects two dissimilar computer networks. The gateway allows a LAN user to access a mainframe network without leaving his or her PC. Similarly, a gateway between a LAN and a WAN enables a LAN user to send e-mail over the WAN. On the other hand, a **bridge** connects two similar networks. For example, if two LANs are connected with a bridge, computers on each LAN can access the other network's file server without making any physical changes to the data.

LANs at fareastfoods.com

At fareastfoods.com, there are two Ethernet LANs—one for performing administration and one for handling orders that are connected via a bridge. The bridge enables users on one LAN to access a server on the other LAN without making special connections. The administration LAN connects the various units of the company so they can communicate about issues facing the company. On the other hand, the order-handling LAN connects the temporary employees who make up and ship the

---

Figure 3-12 Bus Network (logical setup on left and physical on right)

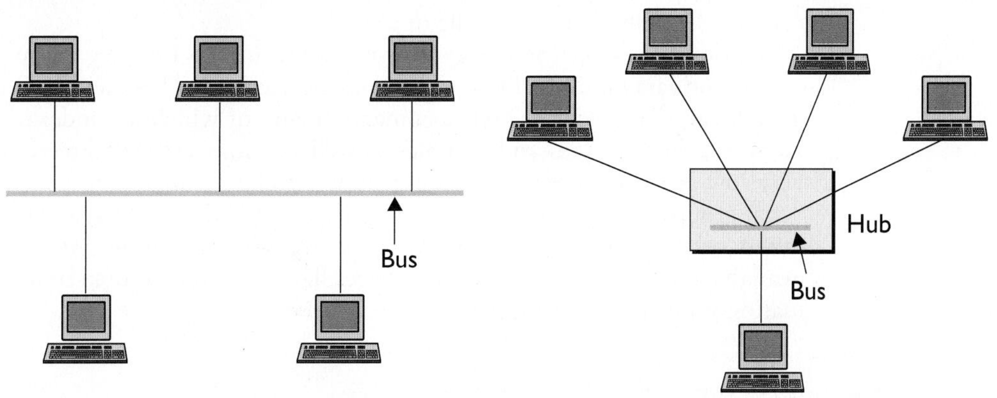

orders with the application server that generates the instructions on the orders to be filled. When the packages are ready to go out, the bar code on the packaging slip is scanned and the information returned via the LAN to the application server, which updates the database server.

Wireless LANs

The newest trend in networks is toward **wireless LANs (WLANs),** in which the cabling is replaced with either radio or infrared transmissions between computers. WLANs can be very useful for a variety of situations including eliminating the need for cable in areas that are difficult to access, providing an inexpensive alternative to shared printing, and connecting two networks separated by some obstacle, such as a highway or wall, through which cable cannot be run.

WLANs make it possible to take computers almost anywhere while remaining linked to the network. Applications of WLANs include a company that used a wireless approach to linking two networks that were separated by a large parking lot and a television station that used a wireless approach to enable reporters to set up an office wherever necessary and still have a working network.

Computers are more mobile as a result of the implementation of WLANs. Users are no longer tied to an office network because they can contact the network from almost anywhere. This has led to the new and rapidly growing field of **mobile computing,** which combines laptop computers, wireless fax/modems, cellular phones, and pagers.

Quick Review

1. What are the five basic elements of a LAN?
2. How does the Ethernet protocol work?

The Internet: A Network of Networks

Because of its tremendous growth over the last decade, the Internet is the subject of much discussion in newspapers, books, magazines, movies, and so on. As with many companies like Square D, discussed in the opening Focus on Management box, the Internet is the basis for the widespread use of electronic commerce that eventually will lead to a truly networked economy. Without a doubt, the Internet is the biggest technology innovation to come along since the invention of the computer itself over fifty years ago.

Originally developed in the 1960s and 1970s as a way of sharing information and resources among universities and research institutions, the Internet began its dramatic growth in 1991 when the U.S. government, which had been subsidizing it, opened the Internet for commercial use. This growth was further accelerated by the introduction of the World Wide Web in 1994. Today, the Internet is growing so fast that no one can say exactly how many people are using it, with estimates ranging as high as 215 million at the middle of 1999.[1]

A primary reason for the explosive growth of the Internet is the tremendous amount of data and information that may be accessed. These data and information include large numbers of text documents (many of which are indexed by topic or keyword), both images and graphics as well as audio and video recordings, free or very low-cost software, discussion groups on almost any subject imaginable, live "chat groups" that discuss a variety of issues, e-mail newsletters, and access to computers other than your own, to name a few. Although some information is also available on national information services like AOL, the volume of data and information is much greater on the Internet.

---

1. http://www.euromktg.com/globstats/

ⓕ ocus on the Internet

On the Road to Abilene

The Internet has undoubtedly changed our lives in many ways. However, as amazing as the Internet's impact has been, it cannot continue in the same way with the many demands that are being placed on it. Originally created to facilitate the transmission of text data, it is now being asked to transmit live audio and video as well as ever increasing amounts of data. To ensure that the Internet will be able to meet these demands in the future, a group of universities, government agencies, and industry partners have been working on a new version of the Internet named Internet2. The first step in creating Internet2 already has been created by the University Corporation for Advanced Internet Development in the form of the Abilene Network. Abilene is a national high-performance network using advanced fiber optics that spans over ten thousand miles across the United States. Abilene runs at 2.4 gigabits per second, over 1,600 times faster than T-1 lines that are the most common connection to the Internet and *45,000 times* faster than the widely used 56K modem.

Currently, many universities, individual and in regional groups, are being connected to Abilene. For example, the University of Georgia (UGA) was recently connected to Abilene through an OC3 connection that carries data at the rate of 155 million bits per second. This connection is now available to UGA users in connecting to other Internet2 institutions. When fully implemented, Internet2 will make possible applications such as high quality videoconferencing, telemedicine, digital libraries, sharing of very large databases, and virtual laboratories that are not possible now with current Internet technology. For example, a physician in a rural area could use Internet2 to send images of a patient's condition to a specialist anywhere in the world and receive back almost instantaneous recommendations for treatment. For more information on Internet2, visit the Web site at www.internet2.edu.

Source: Ruthann Benyshek, "UGA Heads to Abilene." *The University of Georgia Columns,* September 20, 1999, pp. 1, 8.

What Is the Internet?

The Internet is not a single network, but rather a *network of networks.* In fact, the name *Internet* is a shortened version of the term *inter-networking* because you can work between multiple networks. As shown earlier, to connect to the Internet, your computer will usually be connected to a LAN through a network interface card (NIC) or to an ISP through a modem and telephone line. The LAN, mainframe, or ISP is, in turn, connected to a regional network via a high-speed telephone line. The regional network in turn links into the backbone of the Internet.

Each computer, LAN, and regional network that connects to the Internet agrees to use TCP/IP for assigning addresses and packet switching for exchanging information. By having all networks following the same TCP/IP protocol, users on any network can exchange information with users on other networks with little or no knowledge of their physical location. An important part of this set of rules is the way in which e-mail and other Internet addresses are assigned. For e-mail addresses, the address is composed of two parts: the user name and the **server address.** The user name is assigned to a person or organization that is connected to a server, and it is separated from the server address by the "at" symbol (@). The server address (also known as the **domain name**) is composed of groups of letters separated by periods. This address goes from the most general (country name or organization type) to the most specific (computer name) moving from the right to the left. Addresses are controlled by the Internet Corporation for Assigned Names and Numbers (ICANN), a not-for-profit company set up specifically for this purpose. For the sales department at fareastfoods.com, the e-mail address is shown in Figure 3-13.

In this example, the user name is *sales* and the server name is *fareastfoods.com.* Even though the country (the United States) is not shown, by default it is known to be located in the United States. For servers located in another country, a two

Figure 3-13 E-Mail Address

sales @ fareastfoods.com

User Name   Server Address

letter suffix is required at the end of the server name (e.g., uminho.pt for the University of Minho in Portugal). Because the Internet originated in the United States, an Internet country suffix is not required for that country. Because this is the general e-mail server for fareastfoods.com, it has just the company name (fareastfoods) as the server address. Others may have additional "names" to distinguish them from this server, say, returns.fareastfoods.com for the e-mail server for the returns department or www.fareastfoods.com for the Web server. Table 3-2 shows the most commonly used designations for types of organizations. (You should be aware that a new set of organization designations has been proposed and may be in use by the time you read this text. If this is the case, you may find them at http://www.harcourtcollege.com/infosys/mckeown.) It is important to note that these Internet addresses are easy-to-remember versions of the numeric addresses that actually identify computers on the Internet.

Using the Internet

The Internet is a client/server network with each server on the network providing data and information to client computers connected to the network. The client computer that you are using must run two types of software to take advantage of the Internet: Internet conversion software and client software. The Internet conversion software enables your computer to work with the Internet packets. Windows 95 and 98 come with this software built into the operating system; therefore, it is not necessary to run the application software to access the Internet.

Once you have accessed the Internet, you also need client software to actually carry out the desired operation, such as sending e-mail, downloading files from a server, participating in a discussion group, working on someone else's computer, or accessing the World Wide Web. For example, with e-mail, you would use an e-mail client to generate the message, which then goes to the Internet conversion software that translates it into a form that can be sent over the Internet. Table 3-3 shows the five most widely used Internet operations, which will be discussed in more detail shortly.

At one time, you needed a separate client software package for each of the Internet operations. For example, to send e-mail you needed a separate e-mail client software package. Similarly, to retrieve software or documents using FTP, you needed a separate FTP client software package. However, today's client software for the World Wide Web in the form of the Web browser has the capability to carry out *all*

Table 3-2 Designations for Organizations

Type of Organization	Designation
Educational	edu
Military	mil
Commercial	com
Nonprofit	org
Network	net
Government	gov

Table 3-3	Internet Operations

Internet Operation	Purpose
E-Mail (electronic mail)	Exchange electronic messages with other Internet users
FTP (file transfer protocol)	Retrieve software, documents, or data files from a server located on the Internet
Telnet	Work on a computer elsewhere on the Internet
Newsgroups	Participate in a wide variety of online discussion groups
World Wide Web	Transfer text, images, video, and audio to your computer; search for information on the Internet

of the operations, so you do not need separate Internet client software packages for each operation unless you especially want them. Let's now take a brief look at each of these applications.

E-Mail

E-mail over the Internet is a very popular operation, coming in a close second to the Web in terms of Internet traffic. As we mentioned earlier, e-mail typically uses the simple mail transfer protocol (SMTP) for sending plain text files. Mail with graphics, animation, and so on is actually using the Web protocol, which we will discuss shortly. To send an Internet e-mail message, you simply start your e-mail client (often a part of a Web browser), enter the Internet address, type a message, and then tell the e-mail client to send it. You can also send a file by *attaching* it to the message. Reading your e-mail is even easier: Just click the message line in your "New Mail" window, and the text of the message will appear on the screen for you to read. You can also reply to the message, forward it to someone else, or save it for future reference. If the message has a file attached to it, the software will either start the software program associated with the file or ask you where to save it.

A special use of e-mail is for listservs. A **listserv** is server software that can broadcast an e-mail message from one member of a group to all other members. Group members simply *subscribe* to a listserv, and any messages sent to the listserv are automatically broadcast to the group members. Depending on how the listserv is set up, a member may be able to send messages to the listserv or may be able only to receive messages.

In terms of commercial e-mail applications, many companies are finding that e-mail is becoming a very important marketing tool. Incoming e-mail can provide them with information about problems with products, suggestions on better ways to serve their customers, or just helpful ideas. On the other hand, customers expect the companies to respond to e-mail queries, complaints, or comments generated by clicking a link on a commercial Web page. Failure to respond can result in very unhappy customers. Companies are finding it necessary to develop systems of responding to incoming e-mail, in addition to sending an automated response that acknowledges the customer's e-mail message.

In addition, companies are discovering that outbound e-mail can generate revenue in ways never before considered. This includes sending special offers to customers who have purchased items online or who have sent a question via e-mail. For example, as mentioned in chapter 1, AirTran Airline regularly sends notices of special *e-fares,* which are specially priced tickets that can be purchased only online. This has resulted in a significant increase in ticket sales with almost no additional cost to the company. Fareastfoods.com could very easily use outbound e-mail to alert customers to the availability of special Oriental food products or to sales on certain combinations of products.

FTP

Companies and individuals frequently need to make software, data, or document files available to a wide audience over the Internet. A software company may want to distribute an upgrade of a software package to current users that it markets, or to make a new piece of software available for a trial period (usually thirty days) and then sell it to the user at the end of the trial period, or to make a utility software package or data files freely available. In most cases, the best way to distribute files to a large audience is to place them on a **file transfer protocol (FTP)** server and have the users download them over the Internet.

Using an FTP site to download files is straightforward. You run your FTP client software, enter the address of the FTP server that you want to use, and enter your user ID and password. At this point, you will see a list of directories or folders on the FTP server from which you can select files to download. By selecting a file and entering or pointing to the download command, the file will be transmitted over the Internet to your local computer. You do not need a user ID and password to access an **anonymous FTP site.** Such sites are open to anyone who wants to download files. Some private sites do require a user ID and password as a security measure to prevent protected or personal files from getting into the wrong hands. Figure 3-14 shows the process of downloading a file from an FTP site using a popular FTP client.

A popular commercial use of FTP is for the software developers to deliver their products over the Internet. As software companies continue to discover the significantly lower costs of this form of distribution, FTP will become an even more important source of revenue. In addition, the distribution of upgrades, software fixes, and data files via FTP will continue to grow. For example, antivirus companies regularly distribute upgrades to their software via FTP to keep their product up to date, with protection against the latest viruses. Fareastfoods.com can use FTP to distribute software that enables its customers to convert between various units of measure, such as centiliters to ounces or vice versa.

Figure 3-14   Use of FTP Client Software

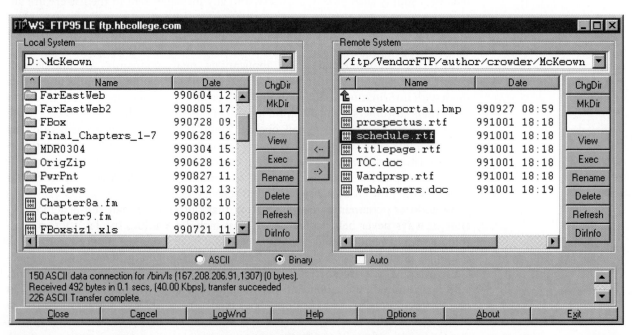

Focus on Management

Instant Messaging at WestSphere

When employees of WestSphere Equity Investors LP see Executive Vice President John Lugar's name appear on their instant messaging buddy lists, they know regardless of the time of day or day of the week or where he's located, he's online and can be contacted to discuss company business or answer a question. With offices in the United States, Argentina, Columbia, and Brazil, the use of instant messaging (IM), which is the capability to chat online with one or more other users in a real time mode, is believed to be saving the privately held equity management company more than 25 percent a year on telephone calls and postage. In addition, IM can increase employee efficiency by making internal expertise immediately available to employees and creating tighter bonds with customers.

Millions of individual users have already discovered the communications capabilities that instant messaging brings to them. American Online (AOL) has millions of IM users, and it is predicted that the number of instant messages sent each day will surpass e-mail messages by 2002. For instant messaging to be widely accepted by corporations, two problems must be solved: security and interoperability. In the first case, companies are adverse to sending messages that can be read by outsiders and not all IM systems provide encryption. In the second case, unlike e-mail, there is currently no common standard for IM messages. In fact, an argument arose in 1999 regarding Microsoft attempting to enable its IM to access AOL's system; however, some companies, like WestSphere, are not waiting for these problems to be solved before they use it to gain a competitive advantage.

Source: Anne Chen and Matt Hicks, "IM's Enterprise Powers." http://www.zdnet.com/pcweek, August 30, 1999.

Telnet

One of the original purposes of the Internet was to allow researchers at one university to use a computer at another university. This is done to spread the computing load around or to use a special program available only at a distant computer. To make this possible, the **telnet** protocol was made a part of the Internet from the beginning. With telnet, you actually log on to the other computer and run the application there, with your computer acting as a terminal. For example, the Arlington Public Library's online catalog runs on a mainframe that cannot be accessed as a Windows application. Instead, you must use telnet to run a text-based mainframe application in a Window on your PC, as shown in Figure 3-15.

Telnet has many uses for organizations that wish to provide a service to their clients by enabling them to use an application server or mainframe. Just as telnet enables students at the University of Georgia to register on a mainframe, it can be used to directly access library catalogs around the world. For example, the Library of Congress Web site (lcweb.loc.gov) has links to many libraries in the United States. Telnet can also be used to send and receive e-mail from a remote computer by telneting into your host computer and using an e-mail client there.

Newsgroups

The **newsgroups** Internet application is a vast number of discussion groups on a wide range of topics. The groups are organized in a tree structure of discussion topics and use the **network news transfer protocol (NNTP)**. A newsgroup is a discussion group about a particular subject and consists of messages written on a series of news servers, each of which transfers messages to each other so that all postings to one newsgroup are replicated on all the other news servers.

Newsgroups are organized into subject hierarchies, with the first few letters of each newsgroup name indicating the major subject category. Some of the more popular major headings (there are many more) are shown in Table 3-4. For each major heading, there are many subgroups with headings that are separated from the major heading by a period (e.g., soc.culture.australia).

Figure 3-15 Using Telnet to Access a Library Catalog

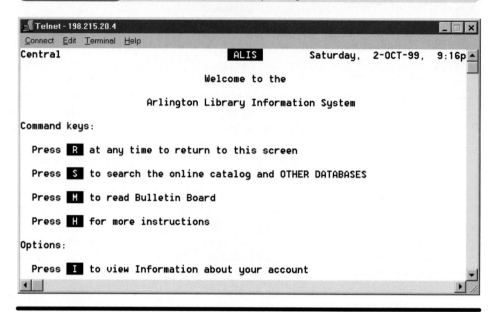

Newsgroup users can post questions or comments to existing newsgroups, respond to previous posts, and create new newsgroups. Messages on newsgroups are *threaded* so that answers or comments on a post appear beneath it in a list of messages, regardless of the data posted. This allows a reader to easily follow a discussion. Newcomers to newsgroups should learn basic "netiquette" and become familiar with a newsgroup before posting to it by reading the **frequently asked questions (FAQ)** list. Figure 3-16 shows the Microsoft Windows 98 newsgroup with an ongoing discussion on Web browsers.

Many companies have begun to monitor newsgroups that are devoted to their products to find out what their customers are saying about them. Because bad news travels fast on the Internet, it is important for companies to detect quickly any emerging problems and respond as needed. For example, you can participate in a variety of newsgroups on food and wine by visiting the Foodcom Web page at www.foodcom.com/newsgroups.html by clicking on *Usenet Newsgroups*. Fareastfoods.com would probably want to monitor newsgroups dedicated to Oriental foods to find

Table 3-4 Major Newsgroup Categories

Category	Description
alt	Alternative: Just about anything that's not mainstream
comp	Computers: Anything to do with computers in general, including hardware, software, and operating systems (e.g., comp.internet)
misc	Topics not covered by other categories (e.g., misc.forsale)
news	News network maintenance and software (e.g., news.admin.policy)
rec	Recreation and hobbies (e.g., rec.arts.cinema)
sci	Sciences (e.g., sci.astro.hubble)
soc	Social issues and social communications (e.g., soc.culture.australia)
talk	Discussion and debate on a variety of issues (e.g., talk.politics.gun)

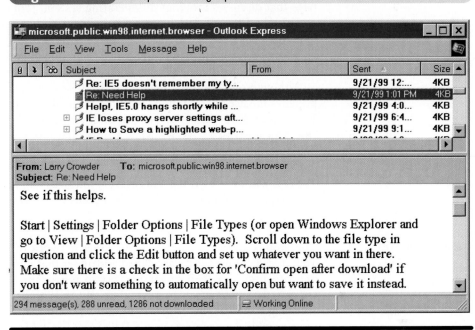

Figure 3-16 Example of a Newsgroup

new ideas for marketing its products as well as to watch for negative or erroneous postings about them. They might also want to start a newsgroup so customers can ask questions and exchange recipes with other customers.

Quick Review

1. What are the five operations used with the Internet?
2. If you need to log on to a distant computer to carry out some type of processing operation, which of the Internet operations would you use?

The World Wide Web

Of the five Internet operations listed earlier in Table 3-3, the newest is the World Wide Web or, as it is more commonly known, simply the Web. The **World Wide Web (WWW)** is a body of software and a set of protocols and conventions based on hypertext and multimedia that make the Internet easy to use and browse. Also commonly referred to as the **Web,** the World Wide Web and e-mail are the primary reasons for the tremendous growth of the Internet during the 1990s. Originally developed to enable scientists to easily exchange information, the Web is now the most popular application on the Internet as individuals and organizations find new and innovative ways to share information with others. It was developed in 1989 at the European Laboratory for Particle Physics (CERN) in Geneva, Switzerland, by Tim Berners-Lee, a computer scientist who saw a need for physicists to be able to communicate with colleagues about their work while it was ongoing rather than waiting until a project was finished. To make this *real-time* communication possible, he wanted to create an interconnected *web* of documents that would allow a reader to *jump* between documents virtually at will.

With hypertext, a user can navigate throughout the system, limited only by his or her mental connections. For example, if you were reading about information systems on the Web and came upon a hypertext reference to operating systems, you could click on this hypertext keyword and be shown another page that discusses operating systems in more detail. From there, you might be able to jump to another page that discusses Linux as an operating system. Jumps within a document or to a completely different document are possible with hypertext, dependent only on the hypertext links created by the author of the documents. The World Wide Web is based on this concept of hypertext by which documents are located on Web servers around the world.

Although only used since the early 1990's on most computers, hypertext actually predates the use of computers, with the original notion being proposed by President Franklin D. Roosevelt's science advisor, Vannevar Bush, in a 1945 *Atlantic* magazine article entitled "As We May Think." Twenty years later, computer visionary Ted Nelson coined the term *hypertext*; however, hypertext remained a largely hidden concept until Apple Computers released its Macintosh HyperCard software in 1987. If you have used the Microsoft Windows Help system, then you have already used hypertext to jump to other help screens by clicking on a highlighted keyword.

Using Browsers to Access the Web

The Web is a special type of **client/server network** discussed in chapter 2. For the Web, the client uses software called a **browser** that initiates the partnership by sending a request to a Web server for certain information. The server responds by retrieving the information from its disk and then transmitting it to the client. Upon receiving the data, the browser formats the information for display. Web browsers use a **graphical user interface (GUI)** like that available on Microsoft Windows or the Apple Macintosh. With a GUI-based Web browser, you can perform various operations simply by pointing at menu selections or icons representing operations and clicking the mouse button—so-called **point-and-click operations** (e.g., you can use a browser to navigate the Web by pointing at a hypertext link in the current document and clicking on it). This operation causes the linked document, image file, or audio file to be fetched from a distant computer and displayed or played on the local computer. Although it is not a point-and-click operation, you can also enter an address to retrieve a desired document or file.

When displaying information, the browser processes formatting instructions included in the text file retrieved from the server. For example, assume that the creator of a document stored on a Web server has decided that a certain phrase should appear in boldface when displayed. Instead of saving the file with a boldface font, the server stores the text with tags to indicate which text will be in bold when displayed. For instance, the following character string stored on a server as:

The <b>World Wide Web</b> is a <i>new</i> way of doing business

will be displayed by the client as:

The **World Wide Web** is a *new* way of doing business

because the browser interprets the tag <b> as turn *on* bolding and the tag </b> as turn *off* bolding and <i> and </i> as turning italics on and off.

The tags in the World Wide Web are part of a special publishing language called **hypertext markup language (HTML)**, and the documents on the Web all have an .html (or .htm) extension. Documents on the Web are referred to as **Web pages,** and their location is a **Web site.** Because HTML is standard for all computers, any Web browser can request an HTML document from any Web server. For instance, a browser running on a PC using Windows 98 can access files on a Macintosh or UNIX-based server with no problems.

A Web server can also store **multimedia files** (i.e., digitized text, images, video, and audio). The browser retrieves these files and displays them using appropriate software. The transfer of multimedia files from the Web server to the client browser is one of the key operations that sets the Web apart from the other Internet applications and is the major reason for the phenomenal growth of the Web. Figure 3-17

Figure 3-17 Typical Web Page

shows the Web page for FarEast Foods, where the underlined words at the bottom of the page are hypertext links. All of the items on the left side of the page are also hypertext links. Note the pointing finger cursor over the word "Korea" indicates a hypertext link beneath it.

Figure 3-18 shows a fairly simple Web page and the HTML source language necessary to display it. Tags used in this code enclosed in angle brackets (< >) include *h1* and *h3* for two sizes of headings, *center* to center the next, and *b* to boldface

Figure 3-18 Web Page and HTML Source Code

This is a sample page!

With different headings and

different sizes and locations of text.

Here is the logo for the University of Georgia

```
<html>
     <title>Example of HTML Source Code</title>
<body><center><h1>This is a sample page!</h1></center>
<h3>With different headings and</h3>
<div align=right>different sizes and locations of text.</div>
<center><img SRC="page-logo.gif" height=84 width=585>
<br><b>Here is the logo for the University of Georgia</b></center>
</body>
</html>
```

text. Although knowing HTML is a nice skill to have, you can now create Web pages with word processing-like software such as Microsoft FrontPage and Netscape Composer without knowing HTML.

It is also possible with a Web browser to fill out forms like that used to order food items from fareastfoods.com and submit them over the Internet back to the Web server. Before sending the form over the Internet, the browser encrypts the form. At the Web server, the form is decrypted and the contents interpreted to determine the necessary information on the customer, his or her credit card, and the order for items.

Browser Operations

The primary purpose of a Web browser is to retrieve Web pages from Web servers and to display them on a client computer. In addition to being electronic rather than physical, Web pages are different from pages in a book or magazine in other ways. For example, although the amount of information on a physical page is restricted to the size of the paper page, a Web page can extend beyond that shown on the screen. Table 3-5 shows the differences between Web pages and physical pages.

Many individuals, companies, and organizations have created Web sites that contain information about themselves and their activities, and more pages are added to the Web every day. In January 2000, a search service reported that there were over 87 million Web pages that begin with the three letters: "www."[2] Web pages are identified by their address. In Web terminology, the address of a home page is referred to as its **URL (uniform resource locator)**. It is so-named because a URL is a standard means of consistently locating Web pages or other resources no matter where they are stored on the Internet. For example, the URL of the welcome page for fareastfoods.com's Web site is:

http://www.fareastfoods.com/welcome.html

Like every URL, this one has four parts: the protocol, the Internet address of the server computer on which the desired resource is located, the port number (optional), and the path of the resource (sometimes hidden). The three parts of the fareastfoods.com welcome page address (which does not have a port number) are shown in Figure 3-19.

For Web resources, the protocol (also called the **service resource**) defines the type of resource being retrieved. The Web page resource is defined by the letters *http*,

Table 3-5 Differences between Web Pages and Physical Pages

Characteristic	Web Page	Physical Page
Form	Electronic	Ink on a paper page
Amount of information	Can extend beyond a single screen	Restricted to one piece of paper
Types of information	Can include text, images, audio, and video information	Restricted to text and images
Links to other pages	Can be linked to an unlimited number of Web pages through hypertext	Can be linked only through a separate index
Creation	Can be created with HTML or with software and saved to a server	Can be created using a word processor, desktop publishing, and laser printer

2. http://www.altavista.digital.com/

Figure 3-19 Three Parts of a Web Address

http://www.fareastfoods.com/welcome.html

Protocol   Web Server Address   Path Name

which, as we discussed earlier, stand for *hypertext transfer protocol.* In addition to home page documents, some of the other allowable protocols include file, telnet, FTP, mailto, and news. Table 3-6 shows these protocols (service resources) and their purposes. A very important aspect of these protocols is that they are *all* in lowercase. For example, *FTP,* when included in a URL, must be entered in lowercase.

We have already discussed the server address (or domain name) that gives the address of the computer on which the resource is stored. The third part of the URL is the **port number,** which indicates an internal address within the server. It is shown as a colon (:) followed by a number immediately after the organization or country code. For example, an address that does have a port number is the URL for the Terry College of Business:

http://www.terry.uga.edu:8080/

where the protocol is *http,* the server name is *www.terry.uga.edu,* and the port number is *8080.*

The fourth part of the URL is the **path** of the Web resource, which includes the name of the home page file plus any directories or folders in which it is located. In the fareastfoods.com example, the path of the Web page document is simply the file name, *welcome.html.* In many cases, the path name will be much longer, including the folder(s) in which the Web page is stored. For example, the URL for the Web site for computer projects in marketing at the University of Georgia is:

http://www.cba.uga.edu/~pmckeown/mark3000/

In this case, the tilde (~) symbol is shorthand for the home directory of the computer on which this file is stored. This is done for security reasons by the person managing the Web server. In this URL, mark3000 is a subfolder in the pmckeown folder. Note also that this URL ends with a slash (mark3000/). This indicates that a **default HTML file,** usually either index.html or default.html, will be accessed. In the case of marketing projects, the complete path is interpreted as ~pmckeown/mark3000/index.html. The use of index.html or default.html files is quite common and saves unnecessary typing. It also means that you can often guess the URL of an organization's home page. For

Table 3-6 Web Protocols

Protocol	Purpose
http	Retrieve Web pages
file	Retrieve files on local disk
telnet	Log on to a computer connected to Internet
ftp	Retrieve files from an Internet FTP server
mailto	Send outgoing e-mail
news	Open a news program and display a newsgroup

Ⓕocus on People

Len Kleinrock and Bob Metcalfe

Both the Internet and Ethernet protocols use packet switching. This approach to sending data and information over networks was developed theoretically in 1962 by a graduate student at MIT named Len Kleinrock. His theory was put into practice by the BBN consulting company when it created ARPANet in 1969. This was the predecessor to the Internet and originally linked UCLA (where Kleinrock was a professor), Stanford University, the University of California at Santa Barbara, and the BBN offices in Boston. At each location, a minicomputer was used to accept the packets and convert them to a form that the local host computer could accept. In 1972, both e-mail and FTP capabilities were added to the network.

This network grew slowly, there being only 583 hosts on the network in 1983, when it officially became the Internet and the National Science Foundation took it over. At this time it began to grow at an explosive rate that only increased with the inclusion

of the World Wide Web in 1993. Today, Len Kleinrock continues to work as a professor of computer science at UCLA and is president of a firm called Nomdix dedicated to meeting the needs of technological "nomads."

As part of his Ph.D. thesis in 1973, Bob Metcalfe (of Metcalfe's Law) studied the only two packet-switching networks in existence at that time: ARPANet and a radio-based network in Hawaii called AlohaNet. When he finished his doctoral research, Xerox offered him a position. In thinking about networks, Metcalfe came upon the idea behind the Ethernet protocol and developed it at Xerox. However, Xerox was not sure what to make of it and allowed Metcalfe to take it with him in 1979 when he founded 3Com corporation. Today, most LANs in the world use his idea, and the company he founded has annual revenues in excess of $6 billion.

Len Kleinrock (left) and Bob Metcalfe are two networking pioneers with their work on the Internet and LANs, respectively.

example, you would guess correctly if you tried http://www.dell.com/ to access Dell Computer's home page. In fact, most browsers now have built-in search engines that will search for the *home* Web site for a well-known corporation if you simply enter the company name. For example, simply entering *Dell* will result in the preceding Web site being found and displayed.

Once a valid address for a resource has been entered, the next step is automatic: The browser software attempts to connect to the server computer at that address and to find the page referenced in the address. If this operation is successful, then the page is displayed on the screen.

It is quite common now to refer to the process of moving from one Web site or page to another Web site or page and then to another ad infinitum as *surfing the Web*. This quickly can become a time-consuming process as you follow links looking for information or a product to purchase. This process can be short-circuited to some extent by using the numerous search engines into which you can enter a query word or term and find pages or sites that match your query; however, a problem with this approach is the large number of Web pages that can be returned, many of which have nothing to do with the query you entered.

The Web and Electronic Commerce

As discussed earlier, the other four Internet operations—e-mail, FTP, telnet, and newsgroups—all have commercial uses. However, together they do not come close to having the economic impact of the Web. In fact, the Web can be said to have created electronic commerce. Virtually all of the volume of sales mentioned in chapter 1 can be attributed to the Web as companies find ways to make their products available to both consumers and other companies. Similarly, individuals are finding that shopping over the Web is much more convenient than fighting traffic, finding a parking place, and searching from store to store for a particular item. Instead, the search can take place in the comfort of their home or office with a browser and a search engine. As this trend continues to grow, we will indeed be moving into a networked economy.

Intranets and Extranets

Two specialized versions of the Internet have been created specifically to facilitate electronic commerce—intranets and extranets. An **intranet** is a LAN that uses Internet protocols but restricts the access to employees of the organization. For example, an intranet Web server could allow only certain people to have access to the information stored there. On the other hand, an **extranet** is a business-to-business network that uses Internet protocols instead of EDI or other private protocols for transmitting data and information between trading partners. Once again, it is a restricted form of the Internet that is not open to the general public (e.g., a company might want only its wholesale customers to see pricing information on an extranet Web server). We will return to the topic of the Internet as well as intranets and extranets as they relate to handling the present, remembering the past, and preparing for the future in part 2.

Quick Review

1. What is the role of hypertext in the World Wide Web?
2. What is a URL? What are its parts?

⊙ Summary

To summarize this chapter, let's answer the Learning Objectives questions posed at the beginning of the chapter.

What are computer networks, and what is their role in the networked economy? A computer network exists whenever two or more computers or other information technology devices are linked through some type of media.

Computer networks have many uses in addition to sharing information and resources. Because the networked economy cannot exist without networks, understanding networks is essential to your understanding of this new economy.

Networks can be defined according to their size as local area networks and wide area networks. A local area network (LAN) is a computer network that is confined to a single geographical area, such as an office, a building, or a group of buildings. When computers are connected over a region, country, or the world, this is a wide area network (WAN). Networks are often connected via a backbone.

What is the network layer model, and how does it work? The network layer model is used to understand the way networks operate. In the model used here, there are three layers: application software layer, networking software layer, and physical layer. The application software layer contains the software on each computer on the network that the user sees and uses to send and receive messages and data between computers, as well as that necessary to encrypt the message or data streams. In the networking software layer, the message from the application software layer is formatted according to whatever protocol will actually be used to send it over the network. The Internet protocols (TCP/IP) and EDI protocols are important protocols in the network layer model. This includes converting the address into a numeric form, dividing the message into smaller units called packets, and determining the first stop on the message's route to the destination. The physical layer sends the message out over the hardware (i.e., modem, telephone line, cable, etc.). Data and information transmitted over networks travel over various media, including twisted pairs, coaxial cable, fiber optics, microwaves, and satellite transmission. Packets are transmitted over the Internet using a packet switching methodology that uses routers.

What are the parts of a local area network? The parts of a local area network include the server, the clients, the cabling and hubs, the network operating system (NOS), and the network interface card (NIC). The cabling and hubs tie the server and client computers together. The network operating system directs the operations of the LAN with parts in both the server and the clients. Finally, the network interface card handles the electronic interface between the servers or clients and the rest of the network. The Ethernet protocol is used in the vast majority of LANs. These LANs have a bus physical setup that is usually handled within a hub.

What is the Internet, and how is it used? The Internet is a network of networks that uses the TCP/IP protocols for addressing computers and sending packets over the network. There is no governing authority or central computer; only the agreement to use TCP/IP ties the networks of the Internet together. The five primary operations on the Internet are the World Wide Web, e-mail, FTP, telnet, and newsgroups. E-mail uses the simple mail transfer protocol (SMTP) to send messages over the Internet to individuals and groups. A listserv is a method of easily sending e-mail messages to a group. FTP uses the file transfer protocol to transfer files between computers over the Internet. Telnet allows users to log on to a distant computer and use software on that computer. Finally, newsgroups enable users to engage in discussions on a global network of news servers.

What is the World Wide Web, and how does it work? The World Wide Web (WWW), often referred to as the Web, is a body of software and a set of protocols and conventions based on hypertext and multimedia that make the Internet easy to use and browse. It is a client/server network by which the client browser software requests Web pages created in hypertext markup language (HTML) from the Web server. Multimedia files are retrieved separately from the text page. Hypertext allows the user to jump within pages or from page to page. The address of the Web site is called a uniform resource locator (URL) and is composed of a protocol, Web server address, port number, and path of Web page.

⊙ Review Questions

1. Give an example of a computer network other than those listed in the text.

2. How does access to the Internet from a home or small business computer differ from access over a LAN?

3. What is a value-added network, and how does it differ from the Internet?

4. Take an e-mail message that is not encrypted and is sent from a PC linked to an Ethernet LAN over the Internet and show the three layers of the network model.

5. For the physical layer, list three types of media used to transmit messages. Which can be used for broadband transmissions?

6. Why is packet switching used to send data between computers over the Internet?

7. What is EDI, and why will businesses continue to use it instead of the Internet?

8. Why do we say that LANs use a star physical topology but a bus logical topology? What is the difference between a gateway and a bridge?

9. Of the five Internet operations, which would you use to request information on the Linux operating system? Which operation would you use to download updates to antivirus software?

10. What is HTML, and what does it have to do with the Web? List three protocols that would be used in a URL.

⊙ Discussion Questions

1. Research the way in which your college's LAN is linked to the Internet. Is there a backbone and a regional network at your college like at the University of Georgia?

2. Find out the physical and logical topologies and access control methods used in your LAN.

3. List other examples of commercial uses for non-Web Internet operations.

⊙ CASE

WildOutfitters.com

Claire rubbed her eyes and stared at the vision before her as the light flickered across her face. This time, however, she wasn't gazing at a campfire with Alex. She was staring aghast at the flaming logo that he had put on the home page they were designing for the store.

"What are you trying to say...that the store burnt down?" Claire inquired.

"No," Alex replied. "I just want to have something to get people's attention."

"You're right, the site will need to attract customers, but remember the Web site is an extension of our brick-and-mortar store," Claire explained for the umpteenth time. "It needs to reflect the same style and ambiance that we try to give to our store customers."

"So the flaming logo is out, I guess I can still use it on my personal home page," admitted Alex grumpily.

"Given your success with the store, I'll bow to your wisdom regarding the design elements of the store's page. But I do have a few more ideas about jazzing up both the store and the Web page to run by you."

While waiting for their new hardware for the Wild Outfitters store to arrive, the Campagnes have decided to use Alex's old Pentium II computer to start designing their new Web site. Having only a standard page editor available, they have decided to work on mainly the "look and feel" of the site. They will add various transaction capabilities to the site later as they obtain the software and expertise.

After some initial research into what seems to work and what doesn't seem to work for commercial Web sites, Claire and Alex have decided that there are no standard answers. The field is so new that the multitudes of possible Web design elements have not had the chance to stand the test of time. They did find that there is at least common agreement about the elements that must be considered when designing their pages and they came up with a list of their own criteria for these elements.

Navigation: Customers tend to shy away from sites that are difficult to navigate. The Campagnes have decided that the layout of their pages should not be too complex so that customers know where they are and where they are going. They would like to make access to any page as quick and easy as possible. To accomplish this, all links should be clearly labeled on all of their pages. In addition, they hope to use a "three click" rule of thumb by which any page on the site can be obtained in a maximum of three clicks.

Content: The primary purpose of WildOufitters.com is to sell Wild Outfitter products. With this in mind, Claire and Alex have decided on several types of content to include. First, information will be designed to inform customers about their products and to help them make buying decisions. Second, they also want content designed to draw people to their brick-and-mortar store. Finally, they would include fun content designed to draw customers back to the Web site.

Graphics: Along with product photos, the Campagnes also would like to include graphics that reflect a consistent and stylish theme for WildOutfitters.com. The graphics should bring color to the site while not causing too much distraction. Also, the use of graphics should be managed so that the overall size of each page is not too large, therefore causing long download delays for the customer.

Other Elements: The Campagnes also discussed other design elements that they will need to decide. They would like to choose a text font that looks good in various sizes, for use throughout the site. They prefer a white background but might change their minds as long as they find an overall color scheme for the site that is both attractive and legible. Finally, they have not yet decided on the addition of links to other sites. If used, they will closely monitor the links to ensure that their site is not associated with anything that would tarnish their image.

Claire couldn't resist needling Alex a little more about his sense of style, saying: "I suppose that next

you're going to light up the front of the store with neon and strobes."

"Hey, that's a great idea," Alex replied. "And how about one of those spinning mirror balls over the counter?"

Laughing, Claire exclaimed: "Then we'd have to change our name to Wild Disco Outfitters. Couldn't you just see us in bell-bottomed cargo pants?"

After several more minutes of laughter over silly disco jokes, the pair was able to settle down and get back to work.

1. Compare and contrast the design elements of a Web page with those of a physical printed page of information. What criteria should one consider for both? What should be considered differently when designing a Web page? Are there other criteria for Web design that you can add to the WildOutfitter.com list?

2. One of the main strengths of the Web is the use of hyperlinks that allows a netizen to jump quickly from one Web site to another related site. Many commercial Web sites include hyperlinks to other sites within their pages. What are the advantages and disadvantages of including links to other sites in a commercial Web page? Should the Campagnes include some on their site? If so, what procedures should they put in place to monitor and maintain the links?

3. There is more to designing a Web page than writing HTML. Conduct some research on the Web for the various opinions about what constitutes a good design for a commercial site. A few interesting sources to get you started can be found at:
   Yale Style Manual:
   http://info.med.yale.edu/caim/manual/
   C-Net—Elements of Web Design:
   http://www.builder.com/Graphics/Design/
   Web Pages that Suck.com:
   http://www.webpagesthatsuck.com/
   Web Design Group: http://www.htmlhelp.com/

4. *(Hands on)* Using a Web editor or a Web-enabled word processor such as Word, create a set of Web pages for WildOutfitters.com. Try to incorporate as many of the criteria discussed in the case as possible. You can find graphic elements to go with the Web page at http://www.harcourtcollege.com/infosys/mckeown.

P A R T ② Information Systems in Organizations

When information technology is used in organizations it often goes by the name of *information systems*. Information systems help organizations carry out three key operations: handling the present, remembering the past, and preparing for the future. Organizations handle the present with transaction processing systems that enable them to sell goods and services as well as to order and pay for raw materials. Remembering the past is accomplished with organizational memory in the form of database management systems, information management systems, and knowledge management systems. Preparing for the future involves organizations using decision support systems to make good decisions. Decision support systems are information-based, data-based, and model-based systems. Preparing for the future also involves using electronic commerce to tranform the organization.

In part 2, we will cover information systems, in general, in the first chapter within this part. Transaction processing systems, organizational memory, and decision support systems are also covered in detail in chapters 4 through 6, and electronic commerce is covered in chapter 7. After reading this part, you should have a good idea how information systems ensure that organizations thrive in the networked economy.

CHAPTER ④

Handling the Present with Transaction Processing Systems

❯ Learning Objectives

After reading this chapter, you should be able to answer the following questions:

❯ What roles do information systems play in organizations?

❯ How do information systems help reduce risks to the organization?

❯ List and discuss the business processes that exist in organizations.

❯ What is a transaction processing system, and what functions does it accomplish in an organization?

❯ List and discuss the various transaction processing methods and activities.

❯ How do business-to-business transactions in a networked economy differ from traditional methods?

Focus on Management

Manheim Auctions

With worldwide sales of over $1 trillion, the automobile market is a significant part of the global economy, and, in the United States, 78 percent of all automobiles sold are previously owned. Many of these used cars are supplied to local dealers by Manheim Auctions, the world's largest auto auction company, which wholesales more than three million vehicles annually to dealerships in the United States and Europe. One particular type of vehicle that it handles is the *program car*—an automobile that has been used by an auto company executive, that has a lease that is complete, or that has been returned by an automobile rental company. This segment of the used car market has grown tremendously over the last five years.

Traditionally, dealer representatives attend auctions to purchase vehicles that they believe are in demand in their locale. To reduce dealers' cost of sending representatives to purchase program cars at auctions, in 1996 Manheim began to use a restricted form of the Internet called an **extranet** to wholesale cars to certified dealers. With this system, a dealer with a user name and password can search for program cars by accessing the Manheim Web site at www.manheim.com. The Web page returned to the dealer contains information on vehicles that meet his or her needs, including pictures both of the vehicle and of any problems (dents, scratches, etc.). If the dealer decides to order a vehicle, Manheim will arrange transportation to the dealer's location. Dealers know that Manheim stands behind the vehicles it sells and feel confident that they will match the pictures and description on the Web page. Since the inception of Manheim's Web site, sales over the Internet by Manheim have grown from zero to more than 5 percent of its total sales.

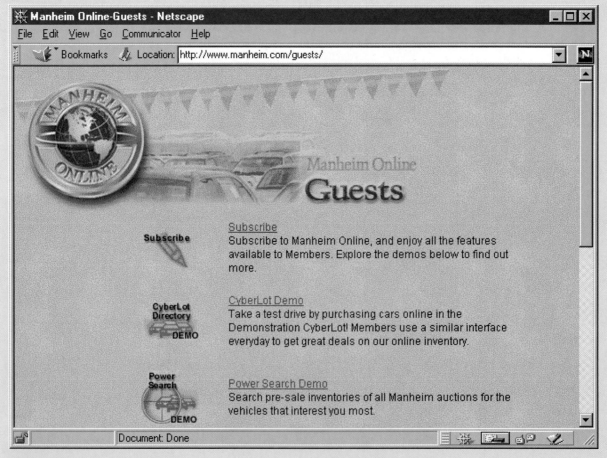

Manheim Auction's Web site has allowed the auto auction company to increase sales over the Internet.

Information Systems in Organizations

The term, **information technology (IT)**, previously was defined as the *infrastructure* of the networked economy and information systems as the information technology applied to organizations. Specifically, **information systems (IS)** are the systems that are combined to develop the information and knowledge needed by managers and other employees of organizations to make decisions. Because organizations are the elements of the networked economy that supply the wants and needs to the economy's consumers, they are of great interest to us. Virtually all of you who are reading this textbook will go to work in some type of organization—business, government, nonprofit, military, and so on. As a result, it is important that you understand the types of information systems used in organizations and how they work to enable organizations to handle the present, remember the past, and prepare for the future. In this chapter, the various types of information systems will be introduced as well as how they relate to managerial decision making, to organizational memory, and to each other. We will then consider one type of information system in some detail. Later chapters in part 2 will introduce organizational memory and other types of information systems.

Recall that information systems are systems that have input in the form of data that are processed into information that is output. If the appropriateness, frequency, or accuracy of the information is wrong, then feedback to the information system will cause change to correct the problem.

Types of Information Systems

Let's briefly look at the various types of information systems that coexist to carry out three tasks for any organization: handling the present, remembering the past, and preparing for the future. Handling the present means that the organization must be able to take care of its day-to-day business, primarily through processing transactions involving customers, suppliers, and employees. The transactions must be stored in order for the organization to be able to remember its past. These data on transactions are used by information systems to help employees and managers make decisions that will determine the future of an organization through the way the present is handled. To illustrate the purposes of information systems, the resulting **information system cycle** is shown in Figure 4-1 (where the topic of this chapter—handling the present—is highlighted).

Figure 4-1 Information System Cycle

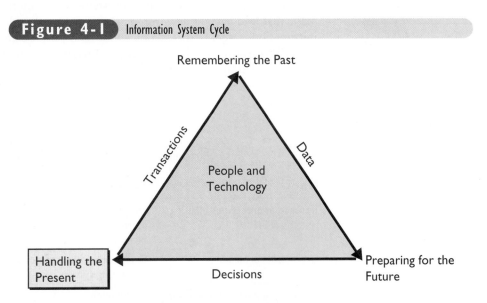

Source: Adapted from Richard T. Watson, *Data Management*, 2nd ed. (New York: John Wiley, 1999), p. 11.

The organization's failure to process transactions in an accurate and timely manner quickly could result in problems with customers, suppliers, and employees. If customer transactions are not handled, no revenue will come in and the organization will cease to exist. If transactions involving suppliers are not handled appropriately by the organization, ordering and paying for raw materials, the organization will have nothing to offer its customers. Finally, the organization must ensure that its employees are paid in a timely manner or else they will cease to work for it. All of these operations are typically handled by the organization's **transaction processing system (TPS).** In the opening box, you saw the use of a form of the Internet called an *extranet* to allow automobile dealers to purchase used cars for resale at their local stores. This is an example of a transaction processing system that handles the present for organizations. Because it is the basis for all internal data stored in organizational memory and then used in the various information systems, the transaction processing system is covered in this chapter.

Understanding and using the data generated by handling the present are essential to the future survival of any organization. In order for the organization to be able to do this, those data must be first stored in **organizational memory,** usually a database or data warehouse. In addition to storing the transaction processing data, organizational memory stores the large volume of documents created by the transaction processing system and other operations in any organization through some form of information management system. It also stores the knowledge that the organization uses to run its operations, solve problems, and seek new opportunities in a knowledge management system. Organizational memory will be discussed in detail in chapter 5.

Regardless of how well transactions are processed or the resulting data stored in organizational memory, if good decisions are not made by employees and managers, the survival of the organization can be in doubt. Information systems that aid in decision making are commonly referred to as **decision support systems (DSS).** Three broad categories of decision support systems are available: information-based DSS, data-based DSS, and model-based DSS. All three of these systems will be discussed in detail in chapter 6.

These information systems are interdependent, ongoing, and fit into the information systems cycle shown in Figure 4-1, beginning with handling the present through transaction processing and then remembering the past by storing these transactions in organizational memory. Based on the stored data, the organization can prepare for the future through decision support systems. Based on this preparation, decisions are made that lead back to new transactions to be processed. Table 4-1 shows all of these information system elements along with their purpose and their roles, that is, to handle the present, remember the past, or prepare for the future. These same elements are also added to the information systems cycle as shown in Figure 4-2.

Table 4-1 Information Systems

Type	Purpose	Role
Transaction processing system (TPS)	Handles transactions and stores result in organizational memory	Handle the present
Organizational memory	Stores data from transaction processing system	Remember the past
Decision support systems (DSS)	Aids employees and managers in making decisions	Prepare for the future

Figure 4-2 IS Cycle with Information Systems Included

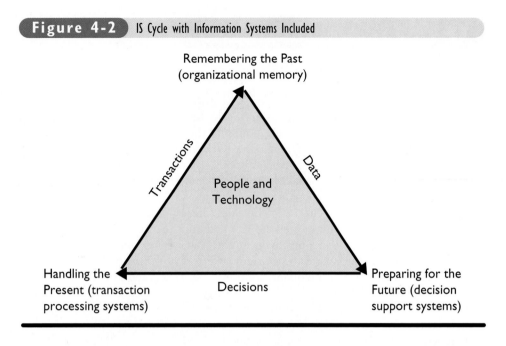

Information Systems and Risk

All businesses face risks, and this even truer in the networked economy. Businesses that successfully deal with these risks by turning them into opportunities are the ones that will survive. In looking at risks, there are basically three types: demand risk, innovation risk, and inefficiency risk. **Demand risk** means that fewer customers want to buy a firm's wares. The globalization of the world market and increasing deregulation expose firms to greater levels of competition and magnify the threat of demand risk. To counter it, firms need to be flexible, adaptive, and continually searching for new markets and stimulating demand for their products and services.

Failure to be as innovative as competitors—**innovation risk**—is a second challenge. In an era of accelerating technological development, the firm that fails to continually improve its products and services is likely to lose market share to competitors and maybe even disappear. To remain alert to potential innovations, among other things, firms need an open flow of concepts and ideas. Customers are one particular source of innovative ideas because firms adapt and redesign products and services to meet their evolving needs. Thus, firms need to find efficient and effective means of continual communication with customers.

Finally, failing to match competitors' unit costs—**inefficiency risk**—is the third strategic challenge. Companies must find ways to reduce inefficiencies or else they will not be competitive. In the networked economy, because business moves so quickly, inefficient companies will go out of business much more quickly than in the traditional economy.

Information systems are one important way by which companies can deal with demand, innovation, and inefficiency risks. For example, they can deal with demand risk by choosing to engage in **electronic commerce** to go global over the World Wide Web. The Web is global; millions of people have Web access, and this number is growing rapidly. Furthermore, many Web users are well-educated, affluent consumers—an ideal target for consumer marketing. Any firm establishing a Web presence, no matter how small or localized, instantly enters global marketing. Similarly, they can deal with innovation risk by using e-mail to create open communication links with a wide range of customers. E-mail can facilitate frequent communication with the most innovative customers. Inefficiency risk can be handled by reducing the cost of handling orders by using interactive forms of input to capture customer and order information. Processing an order via the Web, compared to processing an

Focus on Technology

Virtually Clipping Coupons

On any trip to the supermarket, you will notice shoppers with handfuls of coupons trying to find a product that matches one of the coupons they clipped from a newspaper or magazine. Or, you may see shoppers pulling paper coupons that match products in their basket from red dispensers. In both cases, the paper coupons must then be submitted at the checkout counter, where the bar code on each coupon must be scanned and compared with the appropriate product. The coupon market is huge as is the amount of effort involved in a transaction involving coupons. Each paper coupon must be handled an average of thirty-six times, an expense that must be borne by retailers and manufacturers. Fraud is also a problem with paper coupons, sapping as much as $1 billion a year.

All of the effort and fraud associated with paper coupons may soon be a thing of the past, with the introduction of the SoftCard in 2000. This card does not rely on paper at all; instead, a shopper selects a product and then swipes the card through a card reader located near the product to save information about the product on the card. At the checkout register, a processor sorts the coupon information from the card and matches it with the products purchased. The discount amount is calculated and automatically deducted from the total cost of the purchase. The SoftCard is a form of smart card with a computer chip built into the plastic card. While widely used in Europe, smart cards have not caught on in the United States. However, the developers of the SoftCard and its investors think it will change all of that. It is interesting to note that the company that controls fully 50 percent of the paper coupon market, Rupert Murdoch's News Corporation, has a significant investment in the company creating the SoftCard.

Source: Stephen Gurr, "The Smart Card Way to Cut Back." *The Athens Daily News/Banner Herald,* July 25, 1999, pp. 1C, 4C.

order via a toll-free number, is estimated to be about a third of the cost. This saving results from the customers' directly entering all data. Also, the firm can balance its workforce because it no longer has to staff for peak phone ordering periods. Electronic commerce will be discussed in detail in chapter 7 as a way for organizations to survive in the networked economy.

Quick Review

1. What are the three operations that information systems must carry out for any organization?
2. What is the difference between a transaction processing system and a decision support system?

Understanding Business Processes

Before beginning our discussion of transaction processing systems, we need to consider the business process—that is, what activities must an organization carry out in order to thrive and stay in existence? On the surface, all organizations, whether they be for-profit or not-for-profit, must provide a product or service for which there is a demand. For this product or service, an organization receives revenue from which it must pay the direct costs of providing the product or service as well as covering the overhead costs that are not directly associated with providing the product or service. If the revenue is consistently less than the direct and overhead costs, without additional funds, the organization will eventually cease it operations. This process is typically called the **revenue process** and involves many types of transactions. In

Figure 4-3 Revenue Process

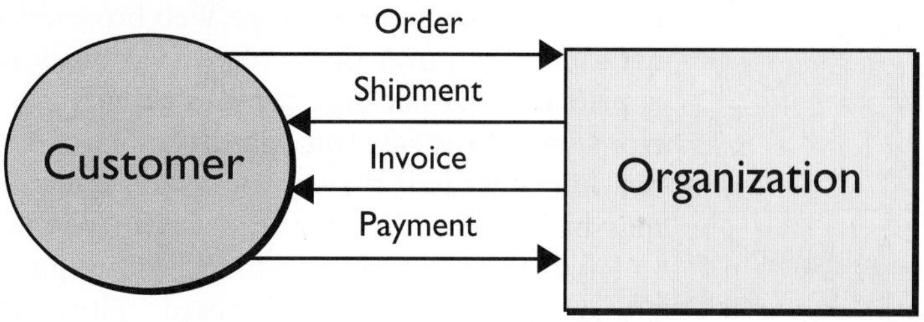

general, revenue process transactions include making a sale or accepting an order, shipping goods or providing services, sending invoices (bills) to the customer or accepting payment at the time of the sale. Finally, in any case, a transaction occurs in which the revenue is collected. The revenue process is shown in simplified form in Figure 4-3, where some or all of the transactions are now electronic.

In addition to the revenue process, other processes in an organization that involve transactions include the expenditure process and the conversion process. The **expenditure process** handles the transactions associated with the payment of expenses of running the organization, and the **conversion process** handles the transactions associated with the production of goods and services. The major transactions in the expenditure process include purchasing, receiving, and payment, whereas transactions in the conversion process include work order preparation, material requisition, manufacturing and cost allocation, payroll, and inventory. It should be obvious that the conversion process is associated only with companies that actually produce a product or service, in comparison to companies like fareastfoods.com that specialize in merchandising products they purchase from other companies. In addition to the revenue, expenditure, and conversion processes, the **financial process** summarizes all of the transactions in accounting terms. Table 4-2 shows the four business processes, the purpose of each, and the various activities associated with each one.

Table 4-2 Business Processes

Business Process	Purpose	Activities
Revenue process	Generate revenue for organization	Making a sale or accepting an order, shipping goods or providing services, sending invoices (bills) to the customer, or accepting payment at the time of the sale
Expenditure process	Handle the transactions associated with the payment of expenses associated with running the organization	Purchasing, receiving, and paying
Conversion process	Handle the transactions associated with the production of goods	Performing work order preparation, material requisition, manufacturing and cost allocation, payroll, and inventory
Financial process	Keep track of all transactions	Posting to general ledger and journals

Business Processes in the Networked Economy

Like everything else, the networked economy will change the way business processes are handled. On the revenue side, we are already seeing the widespread introduction of electronic commerce where Web browsers are used to order goods over the Internet rather than over the phone or via the postal service. Shipment of physical goods is primarily via package delivery services. In those cases where the product is electronic in nature, say, software or computer game, the *shipment* itself is via the Internet. In many cases, the shipment may occur prior to the billing because the customer may have the product for a test period of thirty days prior to payment.

Payment for goods, whether they are physical or electronic, is currently handled primarily by credit and debit cards. However, in the future it is expected that payment methods will also include smart cards and various forms of electronic *cybercash*. The movement to smart cards or cybercash will be driven by the need to handle payments that are too *small* for a credit or debit card. For example, you may want to make a copy of a single article in an electronic magazine (a *Webzine*) without subscribing to multiple issues. Or, you may want to *rent* a piece of software for seven days. In either case, the cost of the transaction may be significantly less than $1, making the use of a credit or debit card too expensive. In cases like this (of which there will be many in the networked economy), a smart card or other form of electronic payment will be an absolute necessity. We will discuss electronic payment methods in more detail in chapter 7.

On the expenditure side, **electronic data interchange (EDI)** is already used by many large companies to order and pay for products. As noted in chapter 3, EDI enables companies to order, receive, and pay for products electronically. However, less than 2 percent of the over six million companies in the United States currently use EDI due to the expense of setting up linkages with their trading partners. In the future, it is possible that many more companies will be able to use extranets to carry out the same operations as EDI without the expense. Extranets will be discussed in more detail in a later section of this chapter.

The conversion process is also being dramatically changed by the introduction of information technology. A great deal of the work involved with design and production of products has been carried out electronically for a number of years with **computer-aided**

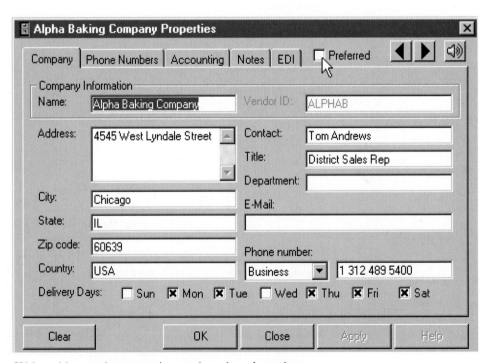

EDI is used by many large companies to order and pay for products.

design (CAD), **computer-aided manufacturing (CAM)**, and the use of robotics in the manufacturing process. At the extreme, the whole conversion operation can be computerized via a **computer integrated manufacturing (CIM)** system. In these situations not only are all of these operations performed electronically but also they automatically trigger the next step.

In the networked economy, the capability to share data, information, and resources globally will be improved through the use of intranets, which will be discussed in more detail later in this chapter.

Finally, the financial process has become almost entirely computerized with the use of accounting software to post transactions to the general ledger and various journals.

Business Processes at fareastfoods.com

To help you understand the business processes for fareastfoods.com, consider the interactions between the customer, the company, the food wholesalers, the customer's bank or credit card company, and the package delivery company in Figure 4-4, where the revenue and expenditure process transactions are shown.

In looking at Figure 4-4, you should note that the revenue process involves the customer using her Web browser to submit an order to the company for various Oriental food items. The order includes a credit card number that is checked by the company, and then, if it is valid, the order is shipped to the customer by the package delivery company. It also involves the billing of the customer's bank (or credit card company) and the payment by the bank. The expenditure process includes ordering the food items from the food wholesalers, receiving them, requesting a shipment to the customer by the delivery company, and receiving and paying invoices from the food wholesalers and delivery company.

At fareastfoods.com, there is no conversion process other than combining food items purchased from suppliers, but there is a financial process for posting and summarizing all of the transactions.

Improving Business Processes

Because these business processes are of such importance to the organization, a great deal of thought has been given to finding ways to improve upon them, thereby reducing inefficiency risk. Most organizations have automated those business processes

Figure 4-4 Business Process at fareastfoods.com

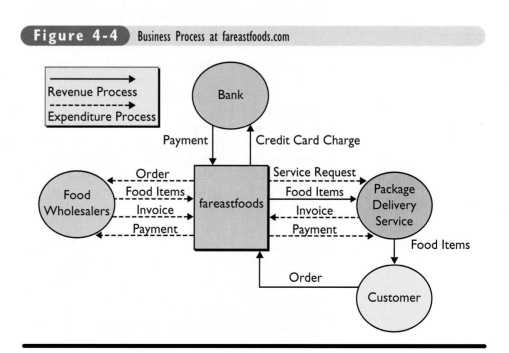

that easily lend themselves to this, that is, computers have been used to replace humans for business processes that involve a great deal of repetition like writing payroll checks or tracking inventory. This is the easy work of improving business processes because it does not involve changing the processes—just computerizing them. Many organizations have gone a step further to use **business process improvement (BPI)** to take advantage of the opportunities for improved operations offered by information technology. This has required them to make changes to the way in which they operate. BPI has been found to improve both efficiency and effectiveness by *doing the right things.*

However, for many companies, just automating operations or making incremental changes with BPI is not enough to remain competitive. Instead, these companies have had to change the very way they operate using **business process reengineering (BPR)**. In so doing, they have creatively destroyed their current way of doing business in favor of new ideas and new technology. For example, when the Britannica company (discussed in chapter 1) considered its situation with the *Encyclopedia Britannica,* it realized that automating the process of publishing a paper encyclopedia would not solve its problems and that making incremental changes by switching to CD-ROMs would only postpone the inevitable demise of the company. However, the company effectively reengineered the entire company to make a constantly current version of the encyclopedia available on the Web for a subscription fee.

Although BPR can bring about the most improvements in the organization's business processes, it is also the riskiest. Most reengineering projects are not as successful as the one at the Britannica company and fail to deliver the benefits they promise.

Quick Review

1. Which four business processes are found in organizations?
2. For each business process, give its purpose.

Transaction Processing Fundamentals

The transaction processing system (TPS) is the system that handles the present by compiling an accurate and current record of the organization's activities while also generating data that are stored in organizational memory. To do this, transaction processing systems should be able to provide fast and efficient processing of large numbers of transactions, resulting in reports that aid in the management of the organization. Because the transactions must be correct to have any meaning, a TPS must be able to closely check the accuracy of the transactions and correct any that are in error. Also, because the transactions being processed involve the transfer of funds between consumers and businesses or between businesses, a TPS has a high potential for security-related problems. Finally, even though it is a very mundane activity that involves repeatedly carrying out similar activities, a TPS is the very basis for the ongoing well-being of the organization. If the TPS fails, it can have a very negative impact on the organization, potentially resulting in a cessation of operations. These characteristics of a transaction processing system are summarized in Table 4-3.

TPS Activities

To meet the needs of an organization, a TPS must carry out a series of transaction processing activities, including input (data collection, data validation, and data correction), processing (data manipulation and database update), storage, and output (document production). The transaction processing data are collected from cash registers, bar code readers, orders from Web browsers, and so on. The data can be internally or externally generated. Internally generated data include:

Table 4-3	Summary of TPS Characteristics
Characteristic	**Explanation**
Large number of transactions	TPS must quickly and efficiently handle a large number of transactions
Correct transactions	TPS must be able to validate correctness of transactions and correct invalid data
Security problems	Transactions involve transfer of funds, resulting in potential for security problems
Importance to organization	If TPS fails, the organization can quickly cease to operate

- Payroll statements
- Shipped orders
- Hours worked by employees

Externally generated data include:

- Customer orders
- Customer payments
- Bank transfers

These data are then *validated* for correctness. For example, if the date on a credit card purchase is entered as 2011 rather than 2001, this is obviously wrong and needs to be corrected. Although not all errors can be found in this manner, the most obvious or inconsistent errors can be found and corrected. Once corrected, the data are reentered into the data collection process.

Once the transactions are found to be correct, they are used to update the organizational database and to generate reports about the transactions. The database update includes modifying the following items:

- Inventory status
- Customer data
- Supplier data

Processing transactions can involve a simple count and summation of transactions or a complex analysis of sales by brand or other characteristic. The results of this processing are then stored in organizational memory, from which they can be output in the form of reports. Typical reports include:

- Overtime hours worked
- Payroll by department
- Time to ship product

The activities of a TPS are shown in Figure 4-5.

Transaction Processing Methods

Transactions may be input and processed using two primary methods: batch and online. In a **batch processing system,** similar transactions are accumulated in a group and periodically processed. For example, the time that each employee works during a day is input into payroll records at the end of each day as a batch for that day. At the end of the week, payroll checks are written in a batch mode for all the

Figure 4-5 Transaction Processing System

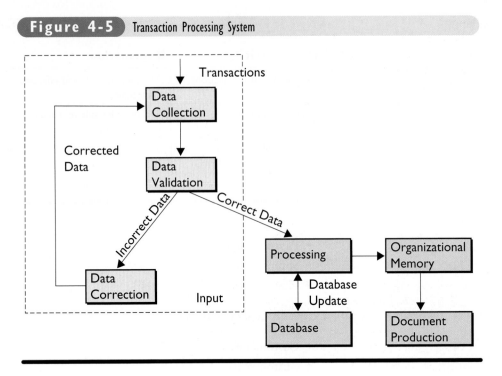

employees for all the work they did that week. Employees are not paid as they work on each work order when a batch mode is used. In contrast, in **online transaction processing (OLTP)** transactions are processed as they occur. An online transaction processing example is the use of **point-of-sale (POS) transaction processing** like that used to process grocery sales at a checkout station using a bar code reader linked to a computer. In this case, each sale is processed as it occurs.

Point-of-sale transaction processing systems are very common today.

In some cases of OLTP, especially those involving registration or reservations, the processing actually controls availability of the product or service being transacted. For example, as customers reserve airline seats using a travel agent or using their Web browser, the inventory of airline seats must first be checked to ensure that a seat is available before the transaction can be completed. If a seat is available and the transaction is completed, the inventory of seats is immediately updated to reflect the reservation. Other examples of this involve hotel/motel and automobile reservation systems.

In the networked economy, an important part of OLTP is checking credit cards and encumbering the amount of the sale prior to approving the transaction. Although this has been done for several years in many stores worldwide, the advent of electronic commerce has made the process of checking a credit card's validity and encumbering the amount of the sale even more important. This is especially true when a product like a game or software is being "shipped" by allowing the customer to immediately download the product over the Internet because once it has been transmitted, it cannot be recalled.

OLTP over the Internet usually involves the use of an application server, like those discussed in chapter 2, that has the necessary software to handle transactions. This server acts as an interface between the Web server and a larger computer (a server or legacy machine) that actually handles the transaction. The application server does this by sending sales requests as messages to the legacy machine, which processes them and returns a decision to the transaction server, which, in turn, sends it to the Web server for transmittal to the customers. This process is shown in Figure 4-6. Note that we are actually creating a *four-tiered* client/server system through the addition of the application server between the Web server and the legacy machine or server. Note also that even though we show two machines in this figure, because a *server* is actually a piece of software, both the Web server and the application server, although logically different, can physically reside on one machine.

Quick Review

1. What are the activities commonly associated with transaction processing?
2. How do online and real-time transaction processing differ? Which is most appropriate for airline and hotel reservations?

Figure 4-6 Use of Transaction Server

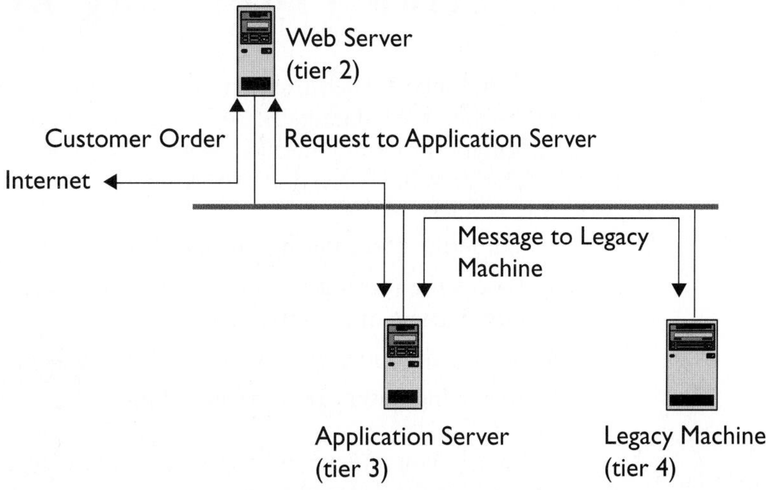

Web Server
(tier 2)

Customer Order   Request to Application Server

Internet ◀

Message to Legacy
Machine

Application Server   Legacy Machine
(tier 3)   (tier 4)

Focus on People

Herman Hollerith

The source of transaction processing on computers can be traced back to the end of the nineteenth century when the U.S. Census Bureau held a competition to find a better way to count the population of the fast growing country. The U.S. Constitution requires that a census be held every ten years, not just for bureaucratic or intellectual curiosity but to apportion seats in the House of Representatives. The 1880 census had not been completed until 1887, and the Census Bureau was very concerned with finishing the 1890 census before they had to start with the 1900 census. The winner of this competition was a young engineer by the name of Herman Hollerith.

Hollerith's idea was to use punched cards to tabulate the census data. The use of punched cards was not totally new, a French engineer named Joseph-Marie Jacquard had used them to control the pattern being woven on a loom in the early 1800s. However, Hollerith saw that the cards could be used to store data on individuals by punching holes in them. They could them be stacked in any desired order and tabulated by completing an electrical circuit through a hole. This completion of the circuit would cause the associated counter to increase by one. The use of stiff cards and electricity combined to create a very workable system. Early pioneers in computation, like Charles Babbage, tried to use mechanical gears with little success. Hollerith's approach to tabulating the census became the

forerunner of a method of computer input well into the 1970s.

Based on his work, in 1890, Hollerith founded a company called the Tabulating Machine Company. In 1911, his company merged with two other companies to create a company that would eventually become the International Business Machines company—IBM.

Source: Mark Russo, "Herman Hollerith: The World's First Statistical Engineer." http://www.history.rochester.edu/steam/hollerith/

Herman Hollerith is the "father" of today's transaction processing system.

More on Transaction Processing Activities

As mentioned earlier, transaction processing can be thought of as a series of steps proceeding from data gathering and entry to processing to storage to final output of information to users. Let's consider these steps or activities in more detail.

The steps in transaction processing include:

1. Gathering and entering the data that describe the activities of the organization
2. Processing (arranging and manipulating) the data so that they are usable for a large variety of potential users
3. Storing data so that they can easily be retrieved as they are needed
4. Reporting output information to users

To help you understand these four steps, consider the POS transaction processing systems mentioned earlier for a grocery (or other type) store. An example of such a system is shown in Figure 4-7.

Figure 4-7   POS Transaction Processing System

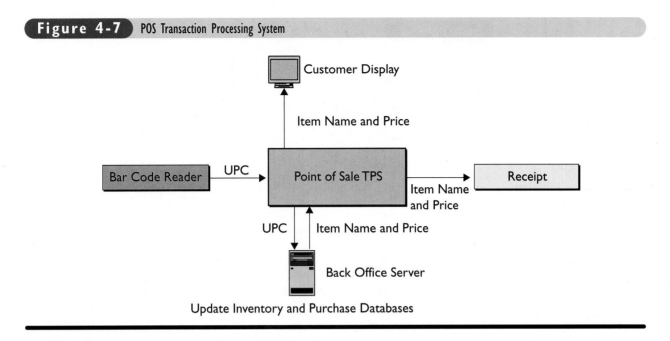

Data Gathering and Entry

In order for data to be used, they must first be gathered on the physical operations of the organization as it engages in its business activities. Management may then control the operations and make managerial and strategic decisions based on the information it is able to obtain from this data. Data are gathered from the input of resources, transformation of these resources into products and sales, and distribution of goods and services.

Data must be gathered from all of the physical input, processing, and output activities that an organization engages in as it markets and delivers its products and services. These activities involve a number of transactions with external parties as well as internal units within the organization, including sales, stock reduction, shipping, billing, cash receipts or collections, purchasing, receiving and stock increasing, and payment transactions. These transactions may also include the conversion of labor and materials into finished goods and services. Data can be gathered and processed in a number of ways. They may be grouped for future processing in a batch mode, or they may be processed as the transaction occurs using OLTP, depending on the situation.

Data may be entered into the computer system using any of a variety of input devices discussed in chapter 2, including dumb terminals, personal computers, network computers, bar code readers, or the Internet. Of these forms of input, bar code readers are currently the most widely used because of the speed and accuracy of input, with Web-based input being a fast-growing form of input.

In the bar code system like that used in the POS shown in Figure 4-7, each transaction is accomplished by passing the item over a bar code reader that bounces a laser light beam off the bar code and then measures the reflected light. The most common bar code is the universal product code (UPC), which is the standard for most transactions today. An example of a UPC code is shown in Figure 4-8 with the various elements pointed out. The measurements of the bars and spaces in the bar code are converted into binary data, which are transmitted to a back office server and used to query the product database for the name and price of the item. The product name and price are transmitted back to the checkout stand, displayed for the customer, and added to the customer's receipt.

Regardless of the form of input, all of this data entry requires validation and correction to ensure that the input is as accurate and as complete as possible. In terms

Figure 4-8 Example of UPC Bar Code

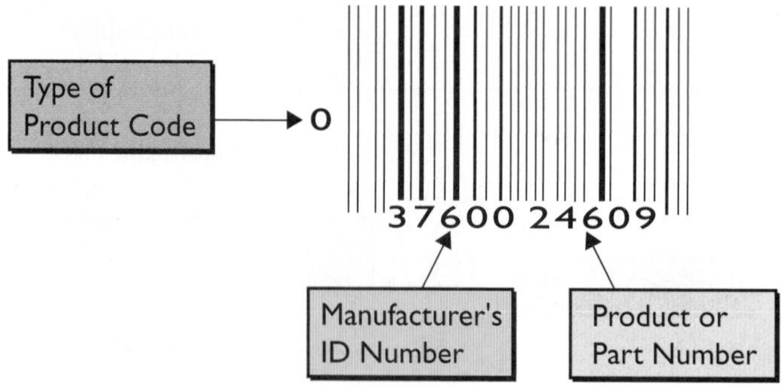

of accuracy, bar code and Web-based input are at the extremes. Bar codes have an input error rate of less than one in ten million. On the other hand, because consumers must use a keyboard to input much of the information on a Web-based order, it is subject to frequent errors, especially in the personal information and credit card fields. This means that editing and verifying are important parts of the data gathering step in a Web-based transaction processing system.

Processing and Data Manipulation

The processing of data into a form that is useful involves several activities, including calculating counts and sums of the transactions according to some classification, summarizing activities, and updating databases to reflect the transaction,. To carry out the calculations, transactions must be classified in such a way that they can be stored for effective use by operational and managerial personnel. For example, grocery store transactions can be classified in a number of ways, including groceries, meat, poultry, fish, fresh produce, and nonfood items. By classifying them in this way, the various managers at the grocery store can quickly look at the data that concern them. Continuing the example, the grocery manager may not be interested in the sales of nonfood items.

To be useful to management, data must often be manipulated before they are stored for use. This may involve combining the data with other data to arrive at subtotals or totals to arrive at such values as the number of units in stock, the total amount of an invoice, or the amount that a customer has due. On the other hand, all data need not be stored; sometimes it is sufficient to summarize data for future use. For example, sales summary data may be more useful to a sales manager than the details of every single sale for a period of time. Sales patterns that may be very evident when summary data are reviewed might never be seen if all that the manager ever saw was detailed data.

For the grocery store example, transactional data could be counted and summed by time period, thereby enabling managers to determine when additional employees need to be available to handle high-volume time periods or when fewer employees are needed. The transaction data could also be counted and summed by other criteria if management has questions that it needs to have answered. If the store has both in-store and Web-based sales, management would probably want to know the division of sales by each type.

Databases are both queried and updated as a part of the processing operation. We have already seen how the product database is queried in the grocery store example to determine the name and price of the product being scanned. In addition, databases must be updated to reflect the purchase and the corresponding reduction in inventory. The purchase database can be queried by store management at a later time to gather sales statistics for marketing and buying decisions. Similarly, the inventory database will be queried periodically to determine which items need to be ordered. Or, if the store is linked to distributors by EDI or other electronic collaboration technology, the back office server would order the needed items automatically based on rules built into its software. The processing and manipulating of data are shown in Figure 4-9.

Data Storage

The number of data elements that needs to be stored can become quite large for some types of transactions. In general, a transaction must be identified by number; the persons involved in the transaction, such as the customer number and the sales person number; what was transacted, such as the stock number and amount of merchandise sold; the date when the transaction took place; the department where the transaction took place; and the authorization, such as a supervisor's "OK" for overtime hours to authorize the transaction. In summary, the *who, what, when, where,* and *authorization* of each transaction must be gathered, classified, and stored for future use. The actual physical and logical structure used to store data for further use should be determined by the current and future user requirements for information needed to control and manage the organization. The volume of this transaction data is part of the reason for the growth in the use of data warehouses to store data for future analysis.

For example, each transaction in the grocery store situation needs to be temporarily stored locally on a purchase database on the back office server and then transmitted to the corporate database for more permanent storage. Periodically, the data will be added to the data warehouse at corporate headquarters.

Output and Reporting

Finally, the transaction processing system ends with the output of information for operational control. This output may take the form of printed periodic reports such as labor variance reports for the plant supervisors or online queries displayed on a monitor, such as the amount of components on hand by marketing personnel as they transact a sale. These reports may be internal documents or messages displayed on computer monitors, or they may be formal reports such as financial statements for outside parties. The output may be periodic and follow a set schedule, or it may be on demand as operational personnel in marketing, production, or financial services need data to carry on their respective activities.

For example, the grocery store management will look at daily reports on overall sales and sales by type. Management may also request periodic reports on sales by

Figure 4-9 Processing and Manipulating Transaction Data

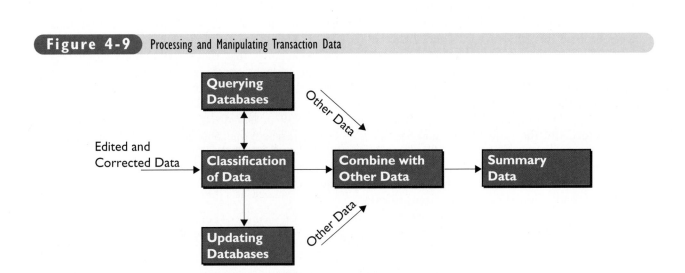

type of item or by brand to determine if shelf-space allocation should be revised. Managers may determine that a certain brand of wine is selling slowly, leading them to decide to sell the current stock at a reduced price and to cease carrying that brand in favor of another, more popular brand of wine.

Transaction Processing at fareastfoods.com

At fareastfoods.com, transaction processing begins at the Web server, which acts as the data collection device. As discussed in chapter 2, an order comes into the company's Web server. This order must be validated in a variety of ways. (Recall that some checking, say, to ensure that all fields are completed, was done at the customer's browser.) This includes a check to determine that the credit card number is valid, that is, it has the correct number of digits, the digits sum to an appropriate value, and the first four digits correspond to a valid credit card company, as well as a check on other input information that was not verified at the browser.

Once the data are input and verified at the Web server, they are sent to the application server, which has transaction processing software on it. (Recall that the Web and application server software can actually reside on the same machine.) The application server processes the transaction by creating order messages to each of the suppliers whose products are on the customer's order and transmitting them.

Ⓕocus on the Internet

Going Online instead of Getting in Line

To the old saying "Nothing is certain except death and taxes," a large number of other governmental transactions can be added. In addition to paying federal taxes, most individuals and organizations must pay a variety of state and local taxes (sales and property, as well as income). They must also deal with all levels of government regarding deeds, licenses, automobile tags, parking fines, speeding tickets, and so on. These transactions can be among the most time-consuming because they often require a personal appearance at the courthouse, city hall, or other governmental office. To make this process easier, more and more government agencies are making it possible for citizens to go online rather than standing in line. In addition to posting Web sites that provide information, these sites actually enable citizens to avoid a trip and include the cities of San Diego and Boston, and the state of Georgia. San Diego launched a system in March of 1999 that would enable it's residents to pay property taxes over the Internet. Boston began a similar system in May of 1999 that made it possible for its citizens to excise taxes and send complaints to the city government. In addition to making applications for various li-

censes available on the Web, the state of Georgia has made it possible to purchase automobile tags online.

To make these and many other governmental functions available to any city, county, or state agency that is interested in serving their customers better, an Internet start-up company has created a series of applications that handle common transactions between citizens and government. Ezgov.com (www.ezgov.com) has created applications for handling payments of taxes, fines, license fees, and registrations, as well as applications for searching deeds. The unique part of ezgov.com's approach to the problem is that these applications won't cost the government anything—the company is giving away the software in exchange for a small fee on each transaction. Their first installation was in August 1999 in Dekalb County, outside of Atlanta, Georgia, where the ezproperty and ezdeed applications were installed. You may soon see one of ezgov.com's applications available in your city, town, or state.

Source: Ben Smith III, "Tax Bills in Dekalb Payable on Web Site." *The Atlanta Journal/Constitution,* August 6, 1999.

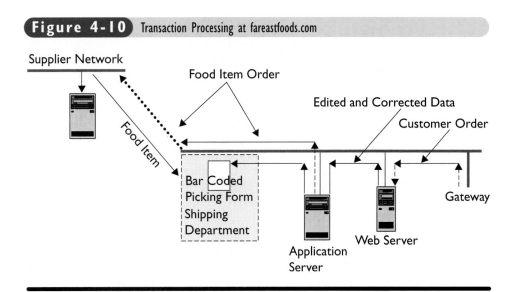

Figure 4-10 Transaction Processing at fareastfoods.com

(Because this is a business-to-business transaction, it will be covered in more detail in the next section.) The application server also includes the items ordered in its summary calculations by item and by supplier. For example, if the order includes lemongrass (a popular Thai item), then this is added to the number and value of lemongrass orders. In addition, the purchase database is updated to reflect this order.

Because fareastfoods.com does not keep any inventory, depending, instead, on *just-in-time* ordering from its suppliers to satisfy customer orders, there is no inventory database to update. On the other hand, because customer orders are typically satisfied by combining products from multiple suppliers, the application server must generate a *picking form,* which is sent to the shipping department. This picking form will have a bar code (not the UPC bar code, but one specific to this application) that will be used by the temporary employees to combine just the right items to satisfy the customer order. This transaction processing system for fareastfoods.com is shown in Figure 4-10.

 Quick Review

1. List the steps that take place each time an item is processed at your local grocery (assuming that a bar code scanner system is used).
2. Why do we say that data editing and verifying are more important in a Web-based transaction processing system than in a bar code-based system?

Business-to-Business TPS in the Networked Economy

In our discussions so far, we have concentrated on the relationship between the customer and an organization in the networked economy. Although this is the key relationship that must exist for any economy to function, the business-to-business relationship is as important. As noted previously, it is expected that business-to-business use of the Internet will grow from $48 billion in 1998 to $1.3 *trillion* by 2003. Whereas consumers will certainly continue to seek out local stores to do much of their shopping in order to deal with people they know in the community, businesses typically do not feel this need. Instead, they are interested in relationships with companies that supply their needs with high-quality products at a low cost regardless of where they exist on the globe. For this reason, doing business over the Internet is a natural for many companies around the world. They are able to reduce all three types of risks—demand, innovation, and inefficiency—through the use of the Internet. For example, Manheim Auctions in the box at the beginning of the chapter is just one example of many small companies—automobile dealerships—using the Internet to acquire used cars for resale quickly and easily from the auction company, thereby reducing inefficiency.[1]

Because of the potential widespread use of the Internet for business-to-business transactions, we will devote the remainder of this chapter to this topic. Whereas you individually are a consumer who may or may not choose to use the Internet to make purchases, the company or organization for which you will work will almost certainly use it to carry out its operations.

Interorganizational Systems

Business-to-business transactions are an important type of system known as an **interorganizational system (IOS)**. An IOS can be defined as a networked information system used by two or more separate organizations to perform a joint business function.[2] An IOS often involves electronically linking a production company to its suppliers or to its customers in such a way that raw materials are ordered, production takes place, and finished goods are sent to the customer to meet demands with little or no paper changing hands. The traditional IOS is based on EDI, which uses value-added networks (VANs) or private networks instead of the regular telephone system. As mentioned earlier, because EDI requires the use of expensive VANs or private networks, it has been found to be too expensive for all but the largest businesses. As a result, many businesses have not been able to participate in the benefits associated with IOS. However, the Internet enables smaller companies to take advantage of IOS and more efficiently carry out business-to-business transactions.

Using the Internet to Implement IOS

Internet technology has created a low-cost platform for linking computers. In addition to the global network of networks that is commonly referred to as the Internet, many organizations are creating internal versions of the Internet called intranets. Recall that an **intranet** is a LAN that uses Internet protocols but restricts the access to employees of the organization. For example, an intranet Web server could allow only certain people to have access to the information stored there. It is essentially a fenced-off mini-Internet within an organization. A **firewall** is used to restrict access so that people outside of an organization cannot access the intranet.

On the other hand, an **extranet** is a business-to-business network that uses Internet protocols instead of EDI or other private protocols for transmitting data and information between trading partners. Once again, it is a restricted form of the Internet that is not open to the general public. These three Internet technologies are shown in Figure 4-11.

These structures enable organizations to take advantage of low-cost Internet technology to communicate with and deliver information to different groups of stakeholders. The Internet can do this to all stakeholders in the organization, that is, investors, employees, customers, suppliers, and so on. An intranet, on the other hand, is restricted to sharing of information and computing resources among internal employees. Finally, an extranet is aimed at sharing information between trading partners. These three types of Internet-based systems can be classified

---

1. The discussion in this section is based on R. T. Watson and P. G. McKeown, "Manheim Auctions: The Power of the Extranet," *The International Journal of Electronic Commerce.*

2. J. I. J. Cash, F. W. McFarlan, J. L. McKenney, and L. M. Applegate, *Corporate Information Systems Management: Text and Case,* 4th ed. (Homewood, IL: Irwin, 1994).

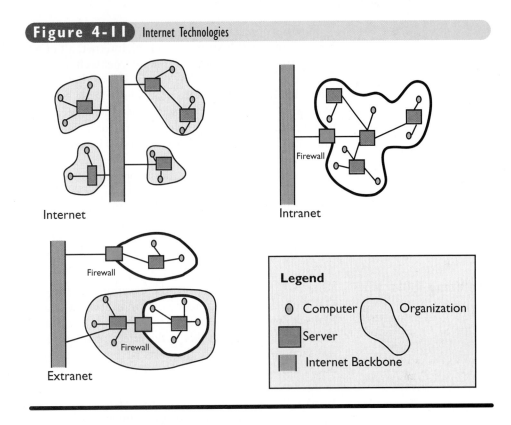

Figure 4-11 Internet Technologies

according to four characteristics: *breadth, focus, reach,* and *business processes,* as shown in Table 4-4.

In terms of breadth, EDI and extranets are restricted in their scope because they are aimed at business partnerships. On the other hand, the Internet has a global breadth because anybody with a computer and Internet access can read information on it. Intranets are also restricted in scope to users within the organization who are allowed access to them.

Considering the focus characteristic, both EDI and extranets are aimed at cooperation with trading partners in distribution channels, whereas the Internet is aimed at stakeholder relationships (anybody who has an interest in the organization). The focus of an intranet is communication and cooperation between groups of employees within the organization.

Table 4-4 Classification of Interorganizational Communications

IOS >>	EDI	Extranet	Internet	Intranet
Breadth	Business partnership	Business partnership	Global	Organizational
Focus	Distribution channel cooperation	Distribution channel cooperation	Stakeholder relationships	Employee communication and cooperation
Reach	Narrow	Broad	Broad	Broad
Business processes	Revenue and expenditure	Revenue and expenditure	Revenue	Expenditure and conversion

Source: Adapted from P. G. McKeown and R. T. Watson, *Metamorphosis: A Guide to the World Wide Web and Electronic Commerce,* 2nd ed. (New York: Wiley, 1997).

In terms of reach, an EDI is restricted by the high cost associated with it as compared to intranets, extranets, and the Internet, all of which have a potentially broad reach through the low cost of the Internet technology.

Finally, in terms of the business processes, both EDI and extranets can be used for the revenue and expenditure processes because they involve relationships with business partners—both suppliers and customers. Because of its openness, the Internet is used primarily to bring in revenue to the organization. Finally, intranets are used for the expenditure and conversion processes because they involve communications and cooperation between employees.

For example, as discussed in the opening box, an extranet is used by automobile dealers in their expenditure process to order used cars for resale. Similarly, as discussed, many companies are using the Internet for the revenue process. Intranets are being widely used for the conversion process when employees are able to easily share design documents or information about production issues.

Replacing EDIs with Extranets

Note in Table 4-4 that, with the exception of the reach dimension, extranets and EDI have the same characteristics, indicating that it may be possible to replace an EDI system with an extranet to carry out business-to-business transactions. The main reason for doing this is the effect of the Internet on the economies of these transactions. In general, the costs of business-to-business transactions can be reduced dramatically through the use of extranets. For example:

1. Extranet communication costs are significantly less than those of traditional EDI. Accessing the Internet though an Internet service provider (ISP) costs $20 *or less* per month. In fact, *free* access to the Internet by computer and telecommunications companies is a growing trend that started in the United Kingdom and with Gateway Computers in 1998. At the upper end, these costs are less than half those of using EDI over a VAN.

2. The software costs associated with an extranet are minimal because the most popular browsers are free.

3. Learning costs associated with extranets are likely to be lower than those with proprietary EDI software because the Web browser is a commonly used interface.

4. Hardware costs associated with using extranets are quite low because all that is required is a low-end personal computer system and modem (now considerably below $1,000).

Another factor that increases the potential replacement of EDI with extranets is the introduction of **extensible markup language (XML)**. One of the reasons why EDI is attractive to companies for exchanging purchasing and shipping information is the capability to format this information in a highly structured, standardized fashion. That is, it is clear that a particular field in the data stream is a part number and that another field is a price for that part. Currently, because the language of the Web, hypertext markup language (HTML), does not have a structure or tags for things like part numbers or prices, it is difficult to transmit large amounts of purchasing and shipping information over the Internet. However, XML solves this problem by allowing companies to define their own tags that their trading partners can understand. For example, the tag <PARTID> would indicate that the field that followed was a part number. This means that an XML file can be processed purely as data by a program or that it can be stored with similar data on another computer or, like an HTML file, that it can be displayed. For example, depending on how the application in the receiving computer wanted to handle the part number field, it could be stored or displayed or some other operation, depending on the contents of the field. Figure 4-12 shows an example of XML as applied to a classic

Figure 4-12 Example of XML

```
<oldjoke>
<burns>Say<quote>goodnight</quote>, Gracie.</burns>
<allen><quote>Goodnight, Gracie.</quote></allen>
<applause/>
</oldjoke>
```

Source: http://www.xml.com.

comic situation in which a variety of new tags, including <oldjoke>, <burns>, <allen>, and <applause>, have been defined.

An additional potential inhibitor of companies using electronic means for business-to-business transactions such as EDI is the threat of **switching costs.** By this, we mean that once a trading partnership is set up using EDI, the smaller of the two companies may not be able to afford to change to a different trading partner. Switching costs are far less likely to be a constraint on an business partnership when the total costs of installing hardware and software are an order of magnitude less than the traditional EDI. Furthermore, the cost of learning the supplier's system is reduced because it is based on standard Web browsing software. Thus, as in the Manheim Auction example, with an extranet model, the small business invests in highly flexible technology that can be easily adapted to other suppliers and other uses. In this case, switching costs should become significantly less important for an extranet compared to a traditional EDI.

Focus on Management

Filing Travel Expenses at Merrill Lynch

For any business traveler, possibly the only thing worse than spending time away from home on trips is having to submit your expenses and wait weeks for reimbursement. For the company, the problem is the expense associated with processing each transaction associated with a paper travel expense report. Merrill Lynch, a financial management company with over 56,000 employees in forty countries, estimates that it costs $30 to process each traditional paper expense form. In addition to the cost of processing the forms, Merrill Lynch felt that, with all of the sign-offs that were required, it was taking entirely too long for their employees to be reimbursed. This is not unusual with about 55 percent of all U.S. companies manually auditing every expense report before reimbursing the traveler.

To solve this problem, Merrill Lynch has gone to a Web-based expense reporting system developed by Captura, a Bothell, Washington-based software company. This system can be run entirely outside of corporate firewalls, alleviating any concerns with security for the company. In fact, a traveler can use their laptop in a hotel room to complete the process. The Web-based system obtains expense data each day from bank clearing houses or credit card issuers. This data is then made available to travelers to enter electronically in their expense report. The Captura software codes and charges each expense to the correct department and then connects with the company network. If everything meets company requirements, the traveler receives reimbursement through electronic funds transfer within three business days—a far cry from several weeks! Other well-known companies using the Captura software include GM, Ford, and Carson-Wagonlit Travel.

Source: David Field, "Travelers File Expense Reports Online." *USA Today,* September 14, 1999, p. 8B.

Extranets and Value Chains

Another way of thinking about an extranet is that it uses Internet technology to link partners in a value chain. The **value chain** model views the organization as a *chain* of activities, each of which adds value to the firm's products or services. It does this by dividing an organization's tasks into primary and support activities. Primary activities are directly related to the production and distribution of the firm's products and services that create value for the customer. Included as primary activities are inbound logistics, operations, outbound logistics, marketing and sales, and service. The inbound logistics for a firm is also known as the **supply chain** because it forms a chain of activities that brings supplies into the organization. On the other hand, support activities include administration and management, human resources, technology, and procurement. The value chain model is shown in Figure 4-13.

In terms of IOS, each organization's value chain is linked to the value chains of other organizations to create a **value system.** For example, the inbound logistics value chain activity of a firm must link to the marketing and sales, service, and outbound logistics activities of its suppliers. On the other side of the firm, its marketing and sales, service, and outbound logistics activities must match up with the inbound logistics activity of its distributors.

An extranet handles the linking of value chain activities by using the Internet to provide communications between the firm and its suppliers and distributors. With the exception of the operations activity, all primary activities are suited to an extranet. On the other hand, an intranet can generally handle all support activities other than procurement. Thus, we can see that extranets can support inbound logistics, outbound logistics, marketing and sales, service, and procurement.

The intention of an extranet is tighter integration and coordination of the activities of a supplier–buyer relationship. Consequently, an extranet should provide support for the logistical link between the two parties by enabling the flow of data (e.g., describing shipments and production plans). In other words, the outbound logistics of the seller should be chained to the inbound logistics of the buyer.

Application to fareastfoods.com

Because it is a fairly small company with yearly revenues of less than $5 million and because its suppliers are also small companies, fareastfoods.com is not among the less than 2 percent of U.S. companies that use EDI. Instead, fareastfoods.com has developed an extranet over which it shares information with its over fifty suppliers

Figure 4-13   Organizational Value Chain

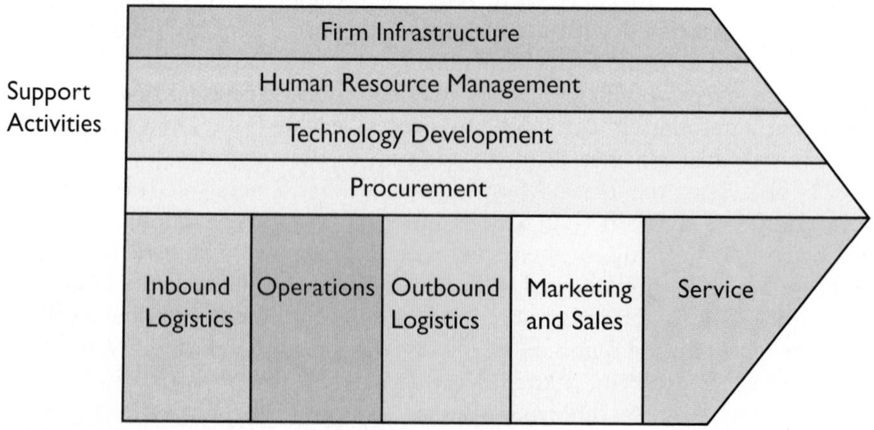

Source: M. E. Porter, *Competitive Advantage: Creating and Sustaining Superior Performance* (New York: The Free Press, 1985).

of Oriental food products. Orders processed by fareastfood.com's application server are automatically divided among the suppliers for specific items based on bids submitted each day over the extranet. The orders for individual items are sent to the appropriate supplier over the extranet. Along with the digital form of the bar code that has been assigned to the customer order, fareastfoods.com has developed XML tags with its suppliers that make this possible. Each supplier combines this item order with other items destined for fareastfoods.com and ships them via overnight package delivery. The bar code for each customer order ensures that there is no confusion between items.

Fareastfoods.com also uses the extranet to post information on its sales as spreadsheets, which suppliers can download and use to forecast future demand for Oriental food items that they sell to fareastfoods.com. This helps the suppliers avoid being out of stock on an item and having fareastfoods.com go to another supplier. The suppliers also act as market researchers for fareastfoods.com by keeping the company aware of special days or holidays for which it may want to run specials, for example, Chinese New Year.

Quick Review

1. What is the difference between an intranet and an extranet? Which is used for communications within an organization?

2. What is the difference between a value chain and a supply chain? What do they both have to do with business-to-business transactions?

⊘ Summary

To summarize this chapter, let's answer the Learning Objectives questions posed at the beginning of the chapter.

What roles do information systems play in organizations? Information systems (IS) are the systems that are combined to develop the information and knowledge needed by managers and other employees of organizations to make decisions. Information systems handle the present, remember the past, and prepare for the future. Types of information systems include transaction processing systems (TPS), organizational memory, and decision support systems (DSS). All of these systems have as their goal aiding managerial decision making.

How do information systems help reduce risks to the organization? All businesses face risks, and this is even truer in the networked economy. Businesses that successfully deal with these risks by turning them into opportunities are the ones that will survive. In looking at risks, there are basically three types: demand risk, inefficiency risk, and innovation risk. Demand risk means that fewer customers want to buy a firm's wares. Innovation risk is failing to be as innovative as competitors, and inefficiency risk is failing to match competitors' unit costs. Information systems are one important way by which companies can deal with demand, innovation, and inefficiency risk. Demand risk can be reduced by going global over the World Wide Web, and innovation risk by using e-mail to create open communication links with a wide range of customers. Inefficiency risk can be handled by reducing the cost of handling orders by using interactive forms to capture customer and order information.

List and discuss the business processes that exist in organizations. The business processes that all organizations must have are the revenue process, the expenditure process, and the financial process. The revenue process involves selling products and services, shipping them and billing the customer, and collecting the payment. The expenditure process handles the transactions associated with the payment of expenses associated with running the organization. The financial process summarizes all of the transactions in accounting terms. For organizations that convert raw materials into final products, the conversion process handles the transactions associated with the production of goods. Transactions in this process include work order preparation, material requisition, manufacturing and cost allocation, payroll, and inventory.

What is a transaction processing system, and what functions does it accomplish in an organization? The transaction processing system is the information system that handles the present by compiling an accurate and current record of the organization's activities while also generating data that are stored in organizational memory and used by other information systems to prepare for the future. Characteristics of a transaction processing system include the large number of transactions that it must handle, validation of the correctness of transactions, security problems because of the amount of money involved, and the potential injury to the organization if the system fails. A TPS must carry out a series of transaction processing activities, including input (data collection, data editing, and data correction), processing (data manipulation and database update), storage, and output (document production).

List and discuss the various transaction processing methods and activities. Transactions may be input and processed using batch or online methods. In a batch processing system, similar transactions are accumulated in a group and periodically processed. In online transaction processing (OLTP), transactions are processed as they occur. A point-of-sale (POS) transaction processing system is an example of OLTP. In some cases of OLTP, especially those involving registration or reservations, the processing actually controls availability of the product or service being transacted.

Transaction processing activities include:

1. Gathering and entering the data that describe the activities of the organization
2. Processing (arranging and manipulating) the data so that they are usable for a large variety of potential users
3. Storing data so that they can easily be retrieved as they are needed
4. Reporting output information to users

How do business-to-business transactions in a networked economy differ from traditional methods? Business-to-business transactions in the networked economy will continue to use EDI but will also use all three of the possible Internet technologies: the Internet, intranets, and extranets, with these technologies being differentiated by their breadth, focus, reach, and business processes served. Of the three, business-to-business transactions will primarily be handled over extranets because they serve the same purposes of EDI at a much lower cost, that is, their breadth is restricted to business partnerships, and their focus is on distribution channel cooperation.

⊘ Review Questions

1. Why are information systems important in an organization?
2. What three tasks must information systems carry out?
3. List the types of information systems used to carry out the three tasks you listed in exercise 2.
4. List the three types of risks that every organization faces today and discuss ways in which they can be handled in the networked economy.
5. List the business processes found in *all* organizations. In which type of organizations is the conversion process also found?
6. Which characteristics are common to most transaction processing systems?

7. What methods are commonly used to input and process data in transaction processing systems? Which method is used in most grocery store checkout systems?

8. What activities are carried out by transaction processing systems?

9. How do business-to-business transactions differ from consumer-to-business transactions?

10. What is an extranet, and what commonly used network protocol is it replacing?

⊙ Discussion Questions

1. For the college that you are attending, discuss the ways in which it may be handling the present, remembering the past, and preparing for the future.

2. For a business with which you are familiar, discuss the demand, innovation, and efficiency risks it is facing. Also discuss how it might address those risks in the networked economy.

3. Take a transaction processing system *other than* one like a grocery store's TPS and discuss it in terms of methods of data gathering and processing and how the TPS activities are carried out.

⊙ CASE

WildOutfitters.com

Claire pulled the slack out of the rope as Alex hauled himself up over the edge of the rock face. They were taking a break from the store to enjoy a morning climb.

"Man, I'm beat," Alex said, as he found a spot next to Claire to take in the view. "I'm glad you led today, I don't think I would have had the energy."

"I noticed that you were huffing and puffing," she replied, "even more than usual. Why were you up so late last night?"

Alex fashioned a crude pillow out of his sweater and laid back on the rock to rest his eyes. "It's all of those e-mails we're getting from the Web site. I was up half the night trying to figure out what they want to order," he said with a yawn.

"I noticed we're getting a lot of hits to the site. It looked like several hundred a day."

"Yes, and it seems that a lot of them are asking to buy something," he replied wearily.

"Well, nobody said that success is easy," Claire remarked as she watched an eagle drift over the valley below.

Since starting to put their business online, Alex and Claire have come a long way. They have designed, purchased, and set up the hardware infrastructure for their system. They have also developed Web pages to introduce their company to the online world.

The initial pages consist primarily of information about their store and product lines. They also included items designed to draw customers back, such as Alex's outdoor trip reports and Claire's "Wild Trail Recipes." In addition to links to further information about the products and their surrounding area, they also included an e-mail link so that the customers could easily contact them with questions or inquiries about purchasing their products. As an added touch, they included a counter in their page in order to get a feel for how many visitors that their site was attracting. The counter has shown that the site has been consistently gaining in popularity since its beginning.

Their current problem stems somewhat from the initial success of their site. While the pages have allowed customers to view and order products, it turns out that a simple e-mail link is not adequate for processing these orders. For one thing, the messages containing orders are mixed with those simply requesting information. This makes it difficult to organize and prioritize the messages. Also, Alex has found that each e-mail that contains an order is different because there is no standard format for the information. This requires them to search through the message for the relevant order information and record it for processing, a slow and tedious operation.

The Campagnes realize that they need to add user interaction and somehow automate the processing of transactions on their Web site. Their first goal is to temporarily provide order forms for each product line. While this may initially limit individual orders to a specific line, they feel that it would be the easiest to implement and would begin to standardize the order information. They would continue to use the e-mail link, but only for customer service-related items such as questions and complaints. Eventually, they hope to improve the site by providing a searchable catalog and shopping cart system for order transactions. Also, they would like to expand to electronic payment options.

After a short while, Claire began to gather the rope and prepare the equipment for their descent. Looking towards a noise from Alex's direction she saw that he had gotten quite comfortable despite the hardness of the rock they were on. Sitting down next to her husband, she thought to herself, I guess we can rest a little longer, the e-mail can wait. Better check for loose rocks though, wouldn't want an avalanche from the snoring.

1. Why would transaction processing be important to WildOutfitters.com? Explain.

2. What types of business processes and transaction activities do you think are needed at WildOutfitters.com? For the transactions in your list, describe the input and output, as well as what should be done to process the data.

3. Search through several commercial sites on the World Wide Web. What types of transactions can you find on these sites? How does each site handle these transactions? Identify the important information of each transaction. What interesting transactions and features did you see?

4. *(Hands on)* A Web page (WO.HTML) with a transaction form for one of WildOutfitters.com's product lines is available for downloading from the text's Web page at www.harcourtcollege.com/infosys/ mckeown. Obtain the page and create a link for it in the pages that you created for chapter 3. After you have incorporated the page into your site, try it out and describe the transaction that takes place. Have a look at the HTML source page. Can you understand the Javascript and HTML code behind this page? What changes would you make to improve this page?

CHAPTER 5

Remembering the Past with Organizational Memory

> Learning Objectives

After reading this chapter, you should be able to answer the following questions:

- > What is organizational memory?
- > What is a database, and how does it store data in a structured form?
- > What are the key elements of a relational database?
- > What methods are being used to improve the management of information?
- > What are the types of knowledge, and why is it so important to manage that knowledge?
- > What are two commonly used ways of sharing knowledge?

Ⓕocus on Management

Kompass International

With the rapid globalization of business has come the need to find products and services anywhere your company does business. For example, if your company does business in, say, Azerbaijan, then it may need to know of companies that provide computer products and services in that country. Although you could hope to ascertain this information from local authorities, it would be much better to have access to a database of companies that do business in that country and that have the products that your company needs. Such a database does exist in the form of Kompass Network. Founded in Switzerland in 1944, Kompass International set up a franchise system in which local publishers collect data on companies and publish this information in books (and now CD-ROMs). Beginning in 1996, Kompass International worked to move all of this information to the Internet at www.kompass.com as a searchable database. This includes detailed information on 1.5 million companies, 23 million key products and services, 2.7 million executives' names, and 400,000 trade and brand names for businesses located in sixty-six countries. In 1999, the Kompass Web site had more than 3 million pages served per month, 123,000 registered users, and 14,000 paying subscribers.

The centerpiece of Kompass International is its classification system, which is based on the type of technology used in various countries. This classification system covers close to fifty thousand products and services and has been translated into thirty-eight languages. This uniform classification system enables a user to find a needed product and supplier, regardless of where they are located in the world. A central classification unit at Kompass International works continuously to update this system to keep track of the fast-changing technological, industrial, and manufacturing developments in all countries. Truly a global combination of franchisees, Kompass International is headquartered in France, and its database server is located in Copenhagen, Internet project management in London, and Web development in Atlanta, Georgia.

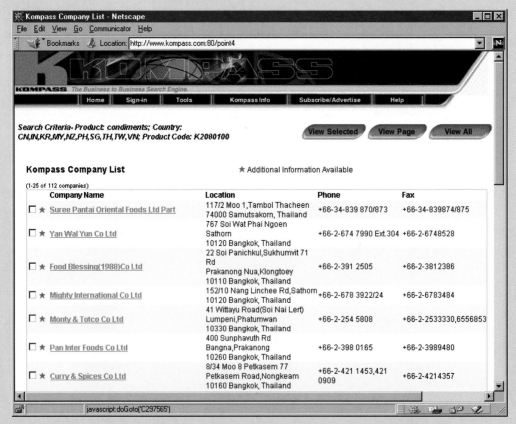

Kompass International provides users in over sixty countries data and information about parts and companies.
Copyright © Kompass International Neuenschwander SA 1999.

Organizational Memory

In chapter 4, various types of information systems that are used in organizations were discussed. These information systems provide management with information and answers to questions that help management make the decisions that will determine the future well-being of the organization. To review, the purpose of information systems is to handle the present, remember the past, and prepare for the future, as represented in the IS Cycle in Figure 5-1. The first of the three functions, handling the present through transaction processing, was discussed in the previous chapter. In the process of handling the present, these operations generate a great deal of data and information that must be stored in the organization's memory. In so doing, the organization is able to remember the past, thereby making it possible to prepare for the future. Remembering the past is the subject of this chapter.

Key to the process of remembering the past is organizational memory. **Organizational memory** is defined as an organization's electronic record of data, information, and knowledge that is necessary for transacting business and making decisions. Without memory, an organization (like humans) will not know how to carry out day-to-day activities or to make the many decisions that are necessary for continued existence. In this definition, we consider only *electronic* forms of organization memory because information systems have difficulty in using other forms of memory (e.g., paper, oral, etc.). As discussed in the opening Focus on Management box on Kompass International, in many cases organizational memory is moving from paper forms to electronic forms that can be accessed over the Internet.

Once data have been created by a transaction processing system, the next step is to store those data in a database or data warehouse. The stored data are then used in decision support systems to help the organization prepare for the future. In addition to data, organizational memory is composed of information and knowledge. The remainder of this chapter is dedicated to discussing organizational memory in its various forms.

Figure 5-1 Information System Cycle

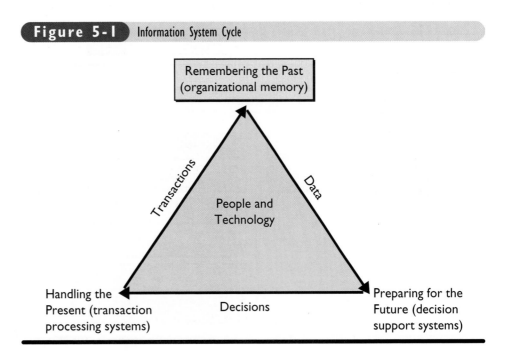

Components of Organizational Memory

As mentioned earlier, organizational memory is composed of three elements—data, information, and knowledge. Recall that **data** are raw facts, usually in a textual form (characters and numbers) and that **information** is the result of processing data into a usable form. Information can be in the form of text (tables and reports), hypertext, graphics (including charts), images, audio, and video. Text is all of the letters, digits, and symbols used in word processing packages, and hypertext is text and graphics that serve as linkages to other documents. Graphics differ from images in that they contain imbedded data (captions, dimensional data, etc.). Audio involves the storage of sounds, whereas video involves the storage of live-action pictures and sound. **Knowledge** is the human capacity to request, structure, and use information. Of these three elements of organizational memory—data, information, and knowledge—knowledge is the most difficult to store in an electronic form because it is a human capability. Knowledge usually is composed of such things as organizational culture (how things work in the organization), social networks (who can do what), and problem-solving models (how to solve problems) and, of the three, the only type of knowledge that can be stored is the models for solving problems. The components of organizational memory are shown in Figure 5-2.

Structured versus Semistructured Organizational Memory

Organizational memory can be either structured or semistructured. If it is easy to find something of interest, then that type of organizational memory is considered *structured*. If it is *not* easy to find something of interest, then the type of organizational memory is considered *semistructured*. For example, it is difficult to find a name in an unorganized (unalphabetized) list of names, so this would be considered semistructured data. On the other hand, it is easy to find a name in an alphabetized list, so this would be considered structured data. Data in a database are highly structured. Similarly, information stored in individually created and stored Web pages is semistructured information because finding the needed information is not easy; even the best search engines return many extraneous hits. On the other hand, it is much easier to find information in a properly managed and indexed Web site because it is structured information. Finally, it is difficult to find the answer to a question in semistructured knowledge stored on many different chat rooms or bulletin boards,

Figure 5-2   Components of Organizational Memory

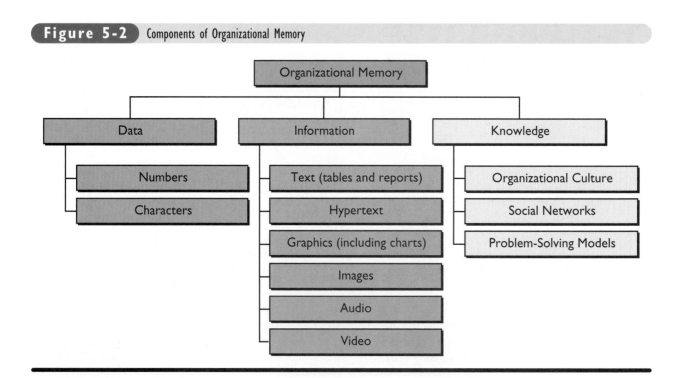

| **Table 5-1** | Structured and Semistructured Organizational Memory |

	Type of Organizational Memory		
Storage Type	**Data**	**Information**	**Knowledge**
Structured	Database, data warehouse	Indexed Web site, reports, charts, manuals	Groupware, expert system, FAQs, newsgroups
Semistructured	Unorganized list	Web pages, e-mail	Bulletin boards, chat groups

but it is relatively easy to find structured knowledge stored in an organized fashion using an expert system.

The key to structured versus semistructured organizational memory is the ease of searching. The easier the search, the more structured the organizational memory. Table 5-1 summarizes the concept of structured versus semistructured data, information, and knowledge.

The trend in organizational memory is moving from less-structured forms to more-structured forms because they are easier to search and more useful to management. For example, unorganized lists are converted into a database, and individual Web pages are converted into an indexed Web site. In each of the succeeding sections of this chapter, we will discuss the structured storage of the three elements of organizational memory and the ways by which each can be used to help management make better decisions.

Quick Review

1. What are the three elements of organizational memory?
2. What is the difference between structured and semistructured organizational memory?

Structured Storage of Data

Data are stored in a structured form in one of two ways: a database or a data warehouse. A **database** is a collection of different types of data organized in such a way as to make the data easy to be manipulated and retrieved. Although a database does not have to be stored on a computer, computerized databases quickly are becoming the norm, and when we make reference to a *database,* we are referring to a *computerized database.* Data must be readily available to the various information systems that aid the organization in preparing for the future; therefore, databases are essential to all information systems.

Because the computer can perform the manipulation and retrieval of information much faster than can manual methods, databases are replacing traditional methods of organizing information (e.g., books, paper lists, file cabinets, Rolodexes, index cards, etc.). In addition, databases can greatly reduce the space necessary to store information and can be used to access information from disparate sources. Database management software has been developed to work with databases by allowing the human user to create the database, enter information into the database, and then rearrange the database or retrieve desired information from the database. The information that is retrieved can then be output in a special report format if so desired. Without a database, many companies that depend on fast access to data would quickly go out of business.

When a transaction processing system generates large amounts of data, they are often stored in a **data warehouse,** which is a type of organizational memory. A data warehouse is a subject-oriented snapshot of the organization at a particular point in time. Data warehouses enable an organization to detect key facts or relationships within that data. Data mining and online analytical processing (OLAP) are typically used to extract and analyze the data stored in a data warehouse. Whereas data warehouses will be covered in this chapter, data mining and OLAP, along with other decision support tools, will be covered in chapter 6.

As an example of using a database and a data warehouse, consider fareast-foods.com. The company has a group of customers who are interested in special foods that are not normally carried by fareastfoods.com's supplier (e.g., a special type of bird pepper from Thailand is not always available, but when a supplier has some, these customers want to be notified by e-mail). To handle this problem, the company's database is essential. With fareastfoods.com's database, when a special order product arrives at the supplier, the database can be queried for the names and e-mail address of customers who have requested the product and an e-mail message can be sent to those customers, alerting them to the availability of the item.

The data generated by processing thousands of transactions each day at fareast-foods.com are stored in a data warehouse. Data mining or OLAP can then be used to learn more about the customers and their product preferences. This information can help fareastfoods.com prepare for the future by making decisions about what products to carry and what suppliers to use.

Development of Database Management Systems

When computers were first used for storing an organization's data, the data were stored in individual files. To manipulate the data and retrieve records of interest, a special type of software was developed. This software, called **file management systems,** was very useful for working with lists of records. The first so-called database software on personal computers was actually a file management system. As time went on and organizations found additional ways to use organizational memory, multiple files storing similar data were created in different locations within the organization. When data are stored on separate files in multiple locations, accessing the needed data is not an easy task, and fundamental questions about data redundancy, data integrity, and data dependence are raised.

Data redundancy is the repetition of data in different files. For example, college offices may have separate files containing much of the same information, such as names, Social Security numbers, addresses, and so on. Such redundancy is costly in terms of the money required to collect and process the data for computer storage and in terms of the computer storage itself.

Data integrity is the process of ensuring that data are accurate and reliable. Problems with data integrity occur when the same data are stored in multiple files throughout an organization and changes in the data are required. Obviously, any change in the data must be made in *all* files to maintain data integrity. For example, a student's change of address would be entered in all of the college files mentioned earlier. A change missed in only one file can lead to severe data integrity problems for the users of the data and for the person referred to by the incorrect data.

Whenever different departments in an organization collect, process, and store information, it is possible that they will use different software to perform this operation. When this occurs, there is a problem with **data dependence** between the software and the files. The files of one department are incompatible with the files of another department because the data storage is dependent on the programs or hardware used. As a result, it is often very difficult to combine data from the two files stored on different hardware or created with different software.

Taken together, the problems associated with data redundancy, data integrity, and data dependence mean that any effort to combine files from different departments can be a painstaking task. Consider again our example of a college. If a college administrator wished to write a report on the number of students accepted for admission who also requested financial aid and on-campus housing, the process of collecting the necessary data from three different files created by three different departments could be slow and awkward.

The solution to the problems resulting from the use of multiple files in different locations in an organization is the use of **integrated data management,** where all data for the organization are stored in a single database. With this approach, a single type of software is used by all units of the organization to access the database. This database software, termed a **database management system (DBMS),** is much more powerful than file-processing software and is capable of handling the data needs of a large, distributed organization.

Database Management Systems

To work with large amounts of data in a modern database, a number of approaches to database management systems have been developed for organizing and working with a database on large, centrally located mainframes or **legacy systems.** Today, the most popular approach to data is the **relational database management system (RDBMS),** in which two or more tables (files) related through common fields are used to store the data elements. Newer client/server systems make wide use of the RDBMS, as do older legacy systems and PC-based systems. Given its wide popularity, RDBMS will be discussed in more detail using the fareastfoods.com example; however, it is important to first understand some of the terminology commonly used in database management.

Database Terminology

Database management, like any field of study, has its own specific terminology that defines the various elements and operations used in working with databases. In this section, we provide an overview of this terminology. The first concept considered is the **data hierarchy,** which is the manner in which data are organized in organizational memory. Figure 5-3 shows the data hierarchy.

Looking at the data hierarchy, each item in the hierarchy is composed of the elements *below it* (i.e., a database is composed of files, a file is composed of records, etc.). Starting at the top, we have the database, which is a collection of related files

Figure 5-3 Data Hierarchy

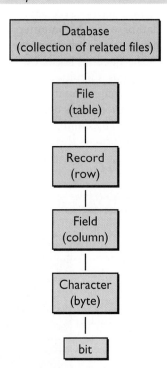

that are accessed together to generate needed information. Recall that a **file** is composed of programs, data, or information to which the user or software assigns a name. That these files are related means they have a common purpose (e.g., data about fareastfoods.com). The files that make up the database are also called **tables.** A table is composed of **records** (or rows), each of which pertains to a single person, place, or thing. For example, if a table contains data on fareastfoods.com's customers, then a record will contain data on one of those customers. Each record is composed of multiple **fields** (or columns) that store the specific details about each person, place, or thing described by the record (e.g., a customer's name, address, etc.). Fields are given **field names** to differentiate among them and **data types** that specify the type of data stored in the fields. The contents of each field are stored as **characters (bytes),** where each character is equal to eight bits. A **bit** is equivalent to a single electronic on–off switch in a computer chip.

As an example of the data hierarchy, consider the relational database at fareastfoods.com. This database consists of many tables covering all of the data that the company needs to serve its customers and to carry out its day-to-day operations. For example, there is a table with data on existing customers; a table with all of the items sold by the company; a table with data on products not normally available, and so on. The table with customer data will normally have many columns, including those for the customer ID, last name, first name, e-mail address, postal address, credit card information, and so on. The table will have one row for each customer, meaning that there could be many rows in the table. Both product tables (regular and special) will contain columns with product ID, product name, and price values.

Because we are interested in the special order situation in which only the table with customer data (Customer) and the table with special order data (Special) will be involved, the structures of these two tables are shown in Figure 5-4. For the Customer table, only the first four columns that we will need are shown, even though there are many others in the table. Figure 5-5 shows the first four columns of the Customer table in a relational database management package, MS Access (the e-mail addresses are not completely shown for privacy purposes). Although the fareastfoods.com database is much larger than just the two tables shown in Figure 5-4, these are the only tables with which we will be concerned. In addition, there are many more columns than those shown in the Customer table.

In a client/server environment, databases are typically stored on large, very fast database server computers that can handle queries requesting data. When the database is accessible from the Internet, as with the example of Kompass International in the opening Focus on Management box, the Web server must be able to accept questions submitted in the form of hypertext transfer protocol (HTTP) and pass them along to an application server that formulates these questions as queries. The application sends the queries to the database server that actually finds the matching values. The database server returns the matching values to the application server, which formats them in the form of a Web page and sends them to the Web server,

Figure 5-4 Tables for Special Orders at fareastfoods.com

Customer Table

Customer ID
Last Name
First Name
E-Mail Address
(other columns not shown)

Special Table

Product ID
Product Name
(other columns not shown)

Figure 5-5 Customer Table

Customer : Table

CustID	LastName	FirstName	Email
999-11-0012	Patrick	Chris	devildog@u
999-14-3143	Campbell	Lange	lcampbell@
999-19-1744	Devane	Samuel	samdev@1
999-23-4321	Smith	Joe	JoeGrunt@
999-31-9776	Mullins	Janice	griffingirl@1
999-73-8590	Watson	Betsy	aussie@xy
999-74-3343	Roth	Jerry	BullGuy@a
999-83-6682	Calstoy	Carol	7054cal@u
999-88-1532	Ronson	Suzy	SuzyLegs@
999-89-2269	Hyatt	Ashley	Volunteer@
999-99-1234	Randall	Roy	rrandall@u(

from which they are sent back to the user. This process is shown in Figure 5-6. Note that the introduction of the Web server creates a four-tiered client/server model, like that discussed in chapter 4.

Data Warehouses

Transaction processing systems typically generate a large amount of raw data about how the organization is dealing with its customers, suppliers, and employees—its stakeholders. For example, the over 600 million credit cards in use globally generate more than 100 billion transactions every year, and a popular Web site can easily

Figure 5-6 Querying Web Databases

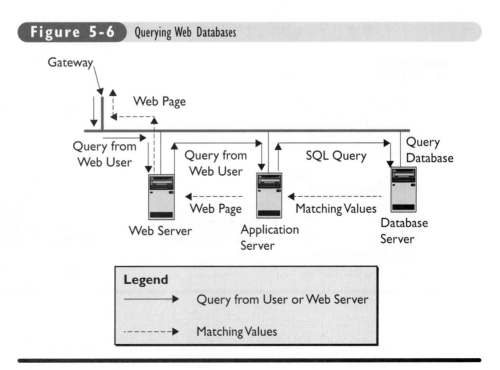

have thousands of hits per day. Often, these data are not as useful to the organization as one might think because they tend to be highly fragmented. The data may be stored on different databases (production and sales) at different locations and on different platforms (UNIX and proprietary mainframe). As a result, analysts find it difficult to access and use the data they need to understand what is happening in the organization. One solution to this problem is to use a data warehouse to organize these data into a logical collection from which specific data more easily can be found.

A data warehouse, discussed earlier, is a subject-oriented snapshot of an organization at a particular point in time. As defined by its inventor, a data warehouse is a subject-oriented, integrated, time invariant, and nonvolatile set of data that supports decision making.[1] This means that the data in the data warehouse are organized according to subject rather than applications and are consistently named and measured. *Time invariant* means that the data are accurate as of some point in time (i.e., it is a snapshot of the organizational data). Finally, the data are nonvolatile because they are not changed once they are loaded into the data warehouse.

Creating a data warehouse is a four-step process that involves extracting data from transaction processing systems; transforming the data into a form acceptable for the data warehouse, with all data using consistent naming conventions and units of measure; cleaning the data to remove errors, inconsistencies, and redundancies; and finally, loading the data into the data warehouse. The process of creating and using a data warehouse is shown in Figure 5-7. Due to the large amount of data typically stored in a data warehouse, the data are often stored on a mainframe-sized application or database server.

Because data warehousing emphasizes the capture of data from diverse sources for useful analysis and access, it does not always start from the point of view of the analyst or other knowledge worker who may need access to specialized databases. To meet these people's needs for a data source that emphasizes access and usability for a specific purpose, data marts have been created. The **data mart** is essentially a smaller form of the data warehouse with a more specialized purpose.

Quick Review

1. What problems arise when data are stored in multiple unrelated files in several locations?

2. What are the elements of the data hierachy?

Figure 5-7 Creating and Using Data Warehouses

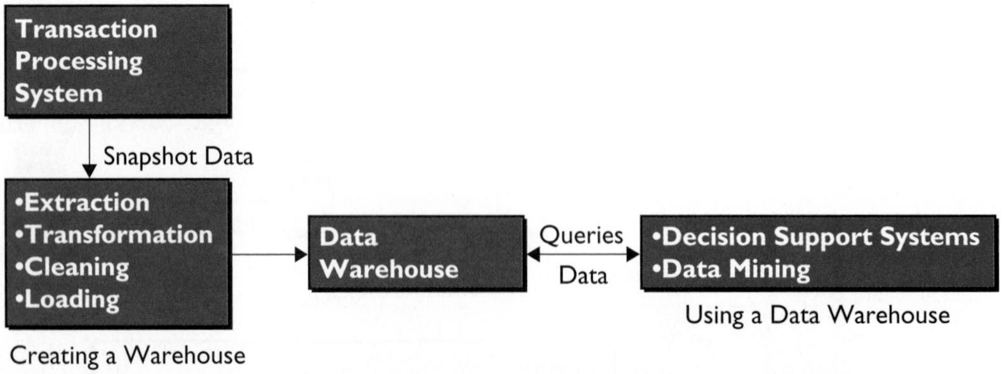

Transaction Processing System

↓ Snapshot Data

•Extraction
•Transformation
•Cleaning
•Loading

Creating a Warehouse

→

Data Warehouse

Queries ⟷ Data

•Decision Support Systems
•Data Mining

Using a Data Warehouse

---

1. W. H. Inmon, *Building the Data Warehouse,* 2nd ed. (New York: Wiley, 1996), p. 33.

Relational Database Management Systems

As noted earlier, the relational database uses a table structure where the rows correspond to records and the columns correspond to fields. In relational database terminology, the files (tables) are called **relations,** the records (rows) are called **tuples,** and the fields (columns) are called **attributes.** Each row must have the same number of columns, and the same specific format must be followed throughout. The word *relational* refers to the capability of a relational data model to relate the tables to each other to find the needed information.

The relational data model has become the most popular today, with most new database management systems using this model. It was developed in the 1970s by Edgar Codd, who was seeking a way to accommodate an end user's ad hoc request for data—something that prior database systems did not handle well. Relational database management systems are very flexible because it is possible to add tables as needed, providing certain conditions about the relationships are met to avoid redundancy while also ensuring integrity in the database.

As an example of a relational database, consider the two tables from the fareastfoods.com database shown in Figure 5-4 (e.g., the Customer table and the Special table). In addition to these two tables, there is also a Request table that contains information on each customer request, including fields for the customer ID number, the product ID number, and a number denoting the customer request. In this case, the Customer table is related to the Request table through the customer ID number that is common to both tables, and the Special table is related to the Request table through the product ID number that is common to both tables. Because both the Customer table and the Special table are related to the Request table, they are also related to each other. These relationships are shown in Figure 5-8.

Why are these particular columns related, rather than other columns? They were chosen for two reasons: First, each row in a table must be uniquely identified to distinguish it from all other rows. Second, it must be possible to link or relate a table to another table. In the first case, rows in a table are uniquely identified by a **primary key.** In the case of the fareastfoods.com Customer table, each row is identified by a customer ID number (either their Social Security number or an ID number assigned by the company) that is a unique identifier. Similarly, the product ID is the primary key for the Product table, and a request number is the primary key for the Request table, uniquely identifying each transaction. The Customer table is linked to the Request table by placing its primary key (the customer ID) in the Request table, where it is known as a **foreign key.** Similarly, the primary key for the Special table (the product ID) is a foreign key in the Request table.

The use of primary and foreign keys enables us to relate tables and find needed values. For example, we can now determine all customers who have requested a certain product or all of the products requested by a specific customer. In the first case, this will allow the company to send e-mail to interested customers when a certain product becomes available. In the second case, knowing what a customer likes enables the company to market similar products to that customer by e-mail.

Figure 5-8 Relationships in fareastfoods.com Database

Customer Table

- Customer ID
- Last Name
- First Name
- E-Mail Address

Request Table

- Request Number
- Customer ID
- Product ID

Special Table

- Product ID
- Product Name

Figure 5-9 Data Model

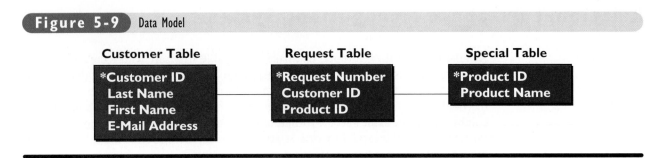

The tables, fields, and relationships that are being used to provide needed data are referred to as a **data model.** There are a variety of ways in which tables can be related, including one-to-one, many-to-one, and many-to-many relationships. In each case, the relationship denotes the rows from each table that can be related. For example, the special order data model is an example of a **many-to-many relationship** (each customer may want many special order products, and each special order product may be requested by many customers). However, to work with this data model, it needs to be converted to two **one-to-many relationships** through the use of the Request table (each customer can have many requests, and each product can be mentioned in many requests). These relationships are shown in Figure 5-9, where the three-pronged fork indicates a *many* relationship and a single line indicates a *one* relationship. The primary key fields in each table are also denoted with an asterisk (*).

Note that Figure 5-9 provides a succinct way of showing all of the necessary information about the data model the same way that various symbols are used to describe a mathematical model. Figure 5-10 shows the same data model in MS Access. Note that the three-pronged fork for the *many* side of the model is replaced with the infinity sign (∞). Finally, if values for the Request and Special tables are also entered in MS Access, the tables are as shown in Figure 5-11. Note that several food items and telephone numbers appear more than once in the Request table.

Because this is not a textbook on database design, we will not go any further into the very large and interesting topic of data modeling. For further information on this topic, you may wish to refer to a book on database management.[2]

Figure 5-10 Data Model in MS Access

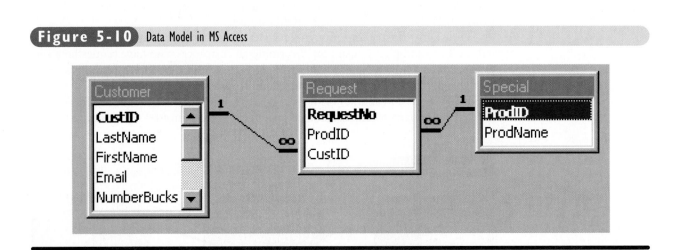

---

2. An excellent discussion of relational databases can be found in *Data Management*, 2nd ed., by Richard T. Watson (New York: John Wiley, 1999).

Figure 5-11 Special Order Product and Request Tables

Special : Table	
ProdID	**ProdName**
AM	Aka Miso
BBP	Black Bean Pas
DNM	Dashi-No-Moto
FS	Fish Sauce
HS	Hoisin Sauce
HSS	Hoi Sin Sauce
KLL	Kafir Lime Leave
KS	Kizami-Shoga
LG	Lemongrass
MP	Miso Paste
MS	Memmi Sauce
PS	Plum Sauce
SBS	Szchuan Bean !
SM	Straw Mushroor
ST	Shichimi Togara
TS	Tonkatsu Sauce
TYS	Tom Yam Soup
WS	Wakame Seawe

Request : Table		
RequestNo	**ProdID**	**CustID**
1	BBP	999-99-1234
2	MP	999-99-1234
3	DNM	999-14-3143
4	LG	999-11-0012
5	SBS	999-11-0012
6	LG	999-89-2269
7	TYS	999-31-9776
8	HSS	999-74-3343
9	KLL	999-74-3343
10	MP	999-88-1532
11	MS	999-88-1532

Focus on People

Edgar F. "Ted" Codd

There is no doubt that the single most important person in the development of organizational memory is Edgar F. "Ted" Codd, the creator of the first relational model for database management and the father of modern relational database technology. Born in England in 1923, Codd joined IBM in 1949 as a programming mathematician, participating in the design and development of several important IBM products including IBM's first manufactured and marketed computers (IBM 701 and 702), the IBM Stretch computer (IBM 7030), IBM's PL/1 programming language, and the first multiprogramming control system (STEM). Codd became interested in databases after seeing the enormous effect on the computing market of Fortran (the first computer language for modern computers). He realized that a language was needed for interacting with the information in databases. After considering a number of approaches, in 1969, he published a paper on the mathematical foundation for relational databases. Based on Codd's recommendations, IBM ultimately developed its DB2 relational database systems in 1983.

Codd retired from IBM in 1985 and formed a consulting firm with database author and lecturer, C. J. Date. He has continued to encourage the development, education, and standardization of relational systems. As a result of his work, relational databases are now the norm on all sizes of computers, from mainframes down to personal computers. However, Codd feels that no existing relational database fully meets the relational model he created in 1969. In 1981, Codd received the highest award given by the Association of Computing Machinery (ACM)—the Turing Award.

Source: Sharon Gamble Rae, "ICP Interviews: E. F. Codd." *Business Software Review,* October 1985, pp. 57–60.

Relational Database Operations with SQL

The primary use of a database is to obtain information from it in a usable form by constructing **queries** to the database. For example, a query might display the name and e-mail addresses for customers who are interested in a particular product (e.g., Tom Yan Soup) so that an announcement can be sent to those customers. Once a query has been used to find matching rows, it is then possible to **update** a row (i.e., to make changes to the contents of one or more columns) or to **delete** a row in a table if it is no longer needed in the database. It is also possible to **add** new rows to a table. For example, if a customer changed their e-mail address, it would be necessary to query the Customer table for this customer's row and update the e-mail address column to change it to the new one. Similarly, if a customer expresses an interest in a product not currently in the Special table, it would be necessary to add a row for that product. Finally, if a customer has not ordered a special product within some time period, the customer's name would need to be found in the table and deleted.

For a relational database, these queries are written in a special language known as **Structured Query Language (SQL)**, and they enable database users to find records in a database that meet some stated criterion. The general form of an SQL query is:

SELECT *fields* **FROM** *tables* **WHERE** *fields match query condition.*

For example, assume that the marketing department at fareastfoods.com wants to know the names and e-mail addresses of customers who have placed a special request so that it can send e-mail to those customers regarding new products that have recently become available on a regular basis. To find the last name, first name, and e-mail address for all customers who have made at least one request, the SQL command would be:

SELECT DISTINCT LastName, FirstName, Email

FROM Customer, Request

WHERE Customer.CustID = Request.CustID

ORDER BY LastName

In this query, the CustID column in the Customer table is compared to the corresponding column in the Request table, and all matching rows are shown. The SELECT DISTINCT command displays each name only once and the ORDER BY LastName command causes the names to be displayed in alphabetical order by last name. The result of this query is shown in Figure 5-12.

If a special order product becomes available (e.g., Lemongrass) then the database can be used to find the names and e-mail addresses of customers who have ordered that product. The query to do this is (where the product ID for Lemongrass is LG):

Figure 5-12   List of Customers Making at Least One Request

LastName	FirstName	Email
Campbell	Lange	lcampbell@
Hyatt	Ashley	Volunteer@
Mullins	Janice	griffingirl@1
Patrick	Chris	devildog@u
Randall	Roy	rrandall@ug
Ronson	Suzy	SuzyLegs@
Roth	Jerry	BullGuy@a

⊞ **Customer : Table**

Figure 5-13 List of Customers Requesting Lemongrass

	FirstName	LastName	EMail	ProdName
▶	Chris	Patrick	devildog@u	Lemongrass
	Ashley	Hyatt	Volunteer@	Lemongrass

SELECT FirstName, LastName, EMail, ProdName

FROM Customer, Request, Special

WHERE Request.CustID = Customer.CustID

AND Special.ProdID = Request.ProdID

AND Special.ProdName = "Lemongrass".

In this query, the CustID column in the Customer table is matched with the corresponding table in the Request table, and the ProdID column in the Special table is matched with the corresponding column in the Request table for the specific ProdName of LEMONGRASS. The customer's first name, last name, e-mail address, and the product name are displayed for each matching customer. The results of this query are shown in Figure 5-13, where Chris Patrick and Ashley Hyatt have requested Lemongrass.

The second query is an example of an important operation in relational database management systems: the JOIN operation. The JOIN operation creates a new table from two or more existing tables by combining columns from the tables for rows that match the criteria in the query.

A feature of SQL is its capability to provide access control and data sharing on multiuser database systems. **Access control** is a function that restricts access to the

Ⓕocus on the Internet

Changing the Rules for Buying a Car

Purchasing a new or used automobile can be a daunting task for anyone. First, you select the car you want, then negotiate a price with a salesperson, wait while they "check" with their supervisor, and then deal with the financing person at the dealership. If you have a trade-in, this only increases the complexity of the negotiation. Many people are very uncomfortable with this process, especially if they are not aware of the true price of the new car or the value of their trade-in and end up feeling they have been "taken."

To help the car-buying public feel better about this process, a very respected publisher of automobile magazines, Edmund's, created a Web site (www.edmunds.com) dedicated to providing all of the information anyone could need to purchase or lease a car. Based on a huge database of facts and fig-

ures about cars that is constantly being updated, Edmund's can provide the new car dealer invoice prices and holdbacks, as well as pricing for used cars, reviews of cars and competing models, and incentives or rebates. Together with a tutorial on buying or leasing cars, and a step-by-step buying process that are also available on the Web site, the pricing information at edmunds.com enables a consumer to walk into a dealership knowing more about a particular make and model of car than the salesperson!

Various success stories on the Web site attest to the value of this information when one becomes involved in price and trade-in negotiations. There are links on the Edmund's site to Web sites offering financing, low-cost cars, and car parts. By using Edmund's and other similar sites, the car-buying rules are changed in favor of the consumer.

data so that only authorized end users can retrieve, update, or delete data. On the other hand, **data sharing** is necessary to coordinate the sharing of the database by multiple end users. Data sharing must ensure that users do not interfere with one another while working on a common database.

Object-Oriented Databases

The newest form of database is the **object-oriented database,** which contains a new data type—called an *object*—that contains both the data and the rules for processing the data. Because any type of data can be stored in an object-oriented database, it provides maximum flexibility to store text, numbers, pictures, voice, and so on, either individually or in a myriad of combinations. Because the rules for processing the data are in the object, an object-oriented database management system is capable of handling complex queries that would be difficult in any of the traditional data models.

Quick Review

1. What is a data model?
2. What is SQL, and what does it have to do with relational database management systems?

Information Management

At the beginning of this chapter, we defined *organizational memory* as an organization's electronic record of data, information, and knowledge that is necessary for transacting business and making decisions. We discussed the structured storage of data in databases in the last section. In this section, we will address the information side of organizational memory. By *information* we mean the many different ways in which data stored in databases can be processed into a usable form, including text, hypertext, graphics, images, audio, and video formats. Information is typically stored in documents, books, reports, invoices, bills, and so on, in both paper and digital form. The newest forms of information are the millions of Web pages available on the World Wide Web that store all of the information formats mentioned earlier.

Whereas data are the basis for all computer processing, information is the result of this processing that humans combine with their special knowledge to make decisions. The information-based decision support systems mentioned in chapter 4 (and covered in more detail in chapter 6) are dedicated to automatically creating information in the form of reports, tables, charts, and so on to keep managers aware of the organization's operations.

It should be noted that in the cases of both information management and knowledge management, the approaches that we will discuss here are often used for handling the present and preparing for the future as much as they are for remembering the past. For example, an employee who wants to know the current status of a plant in a distant location will use information management to find that information and use it to make decisions or to respond to a question from their supervisor. Similarly, knowledge management is often used to help with questions about how to carry out some activity. Because of this, the distinction between organizational memory and handling the present or preparing for the future tends to be more blurred for information and knowledge than it is for data.

Paper-Based Information Storage

Information management has been around ever since the first person decided to organize their written documents, whatever the form—clay tablets, papyrus scrolls, handwritten or typeset books, and so on—into libraries in such a way that individuals could find the document for which they are searching. With the onset of widespread computer use, the need for information management has grown with the

Digital documents are much cheaper to store and retrieve than paper documents.

huge increase in the amount of information being generated in many forms—text, graphics, images, audio, and video. Although there has been quite a bit of publicity about the *paperless office,* and a great deal of information is now being stored in an electronic form on CD-ROMs or on the World Wide Web, the vast majority of the over three trillion items stored in U.S. organizations are still in the form of paper documents. In fact, the combination of networked personal computer and laser printer has actually *increased* the rate at which information is being stored on paper in folders in file cabinets.

Organizations of all types face this paperwork problem because of the many forms, letters, documents, and reports that must be filed away in preparation for the day (which may never come) when they will be needed for reference. It has been noted that a single document may be filed in numerous places in an organization (e.g., the originator keeps a copy, his or her office keeps a copy, the recipient has a copy made for his or her staff, etc.). It has been estimated that it costs $2 to store a single piece of paper. Even when documents are stored in a different form than paper, it is usually as microfilm or microfiche, each of which has its own problems.

In addition to the cost of storing paper documents, there are other costs, including time to find documents, lack of availability to multiple persons, delays in transmission, problems with manipulating information, and lack of backup. Regarding the time needed to find documents, there is the cost of time of walking to the filing cabinet to search through hundreds of documents anytime a document is needed. This is true even when the documents are stored on microfilm or microfiche because the user must still search through the documents. Regarding the lack of availability to multiple persons, if a document is needed by multiple people, then copies must be made, also adding to the flood of paper. Even after a document is found, sending it to another person or location can take time, and extracting information can require manual work. Finally, because of the volume of information, there are often no backups in case the originals are lost through fire or natural disaster. In the case of Kompass International, in the opening Focus on Management box, there was a need to publish versions of product lists in multiple languages. These problems with information stored in paper form are summarized in Table 5-2.

Table 5-2	Problems with Paper Storage of Information
Problem	**Explanation**
Storage costs	Paper documents are expensive to store in filing cabinets and storage boxes
Time costs	A large amount of time can be required to find documents
Multiple access (sharing)	Paper documents (or microfiche/microfilm) must be copied to be available to multiple people
Transmission delay	Paper documents can take a long time to be sent from one place to another
Information manipulation	Information on paper (or microfilm/microfiche) must be manually extracted; also, it is not easily searchable
Backups	Backups of paper documents are seldom kept due to space problems

Electronic Imaging

Today, because of the problems listed earlier, there is a movement to find a way to store and manage information electronically to reduce costs and speed access in most large organizations. To do this, there is an ongoing effort to find ways to convert much of this paper to a digital format using imaging. In **imaging,** paper versions of documents are converted to a digital form using some type of scanner and saved to optical or magnetic secondary storage. A **scanner** works like a copier to convert the document into a digital form. The results of imaging can be stored as images, in a special digital format, or converted into a textual format. In the first case, a digital photographic representation is created that can be stored, printed, or manipulated with various software packages. In the second case, a special digital file format known as **portable document format (.pdf)** is frequently being used to store the results of imaging. The advantage of a .pdf image is that it can be viewed and printed from any type of computer regardless of the type of computer on which it was created.

For a person to be able to manipulate the contents of a paper document, it must be converted into a textual form. Doing this requires that **optical character recognition (OCR)** be used. In OCR, a reader device is passed over a document to convert it into a digital form. Software is then used to determine the symbols present. This capability can greatly relieve the monotony and strain of keyboarding information from a document into the computer. The OCR software must try to identify the various letters and symbols by matching them to a predefined set of requirements or patterns. Many OCR packages will apply a spell-checker to find incorrect words or display a special symbol for the user to change to the correct character when it cannot make a match for a character.

Another popular use of OCR software is **fax conversion.** In fax conversion, the OCR software converts incoming fax documents into an ASCII text format. This is especially useful when a **fax modem** is being used to route fax documents directly to a computer. This allows fax documents to be saved electronically rather than as paper. They can also be edited or revised rather than just being read.

Even when documents are stored in a digital form, there can be problems. First, there must be a system capable of identifying and retrieving a given document. Second, once the document is found, there must be a way to search the contents of the document. Third, there must be adequate protection from loss of the document due to damage to the storage medium. Finally, there must be security against theft of or tampering with the document.

Structured versus Semistructured Information

In Table 5-1, which differentiated between structured and semistructured information, Web pages and e-mail messages were shown as examples of semistructured information, that is, they are difficult to search through to find needed information. Every one of us has had the frustration of entering a word or term in a Web search engine and receiving references to literally hundreds of extraneous Web pages that have nothing to do with our search. The reason for this problem with searching over the Web has to do with the way search engines interact with Web pages and the efforts often made by some Web developers to ensure that their Web page is included in your search results regardless of whether or not it actually matches your query.

Similarly, managers often receive each day tens or hundreds of e-mails that they must process and decide how to handle—write a response, ignore and discard, store for later action, and so on. Even when a message is processed, it and the response may need to be stored for later reference. Searching these stored e-mails at a later time to find one that is needed is often as difficult as searching the Web because many may match a query.

On the other hand, indexed Web sites, reports, charts, and manuals were included under the *structured information* heading. These forms of information are more easily searchable than are semistructured forms of information. The key word in structured information is *indexed* because **indexing** is the process of using data values or descriptors to search through documents. Many Web search engines go through every Web page they can find and index each word. This is why you find so many hits with a search engine when you enter a term like *management*—every page with this word somewhere in it is returned. However, many organizational **Web sites**, that is, collections of associated Web pages, use a more rational indexing scheme to search over only the pages in the Web site—avoiding unrelated pages or those outside the site. However, as we all know, this is still a hit-and-miss process, with extraneous Web pages still being returned.

The same problems exist with storage of electronic documents, that is, finding the document you need within the thousands or millions that may be stored on computer secondary storage at your location or at other locations. This is especially true as we move more into **multimedia** forms of information (i.e., images, graphics, audio, and video). Once again, structure is important in being able to search through this type of information because indexing allows us to use words to find the appropriate multimedia information item. There are several ways of indexing, including indexing just the name of the document, indexing on keywords, and full-text indexing. Although it would seem that full-text indexing would be the best, it is obviously not appropriate for nontext items and can lead to the problems we see with Web-based search engines. For example, it is not possible to use full-text indexing on a .pdf image, so another form must be used to access the many documents that are stored in this format. As with any other tool, indexing must be used with the end goal in mind—providing useful information to management, rather than assuming that one tool fits all situations.

Quick Review

1. What are some of the problems with paper forms of information?
2. What is indexing, and what does it have to do with information management?

Knowledge Management

We have tried to emphasize in this textbook the importance of that uniquely human capability we call knowledge to the long-term success of any organization. Regardless of the amount of data and information available to an organization, without the knowledge necessary to use them, the data and information will be of no use to the organization. There are a variety of ways to classify knowledge, depending on who has it, whether it is explicit or tacit knowledge, and whether it is semistructured or structured knowledge.

Ⓕocus on Technology

Personal Digital Assistants

After a number of failures, most notably the Apple Newton, reasonably priced personal digital assistants (PDAs) that are both useful and easy-to-use now exist. Pioneered by the Palm Pilot from 3Com, PDAs sold 5.7 million units in 1999, up 47 percent over 1998. To meet this demand, a number of competitors to the Palm PDA have entered the market. Regardless of which brand or model selected, they all provide a personal form of organizational memory including a calendar system, a to-do list, a telephone number/address list, and a note pad for creating memos. Even though the various lists are not related by a primary key, they still provide a very useful way to access data about appointments, friends and professional associates, tasks to be completed, as well as to write and store short memos. Newer versions have the capability to send faxes, send and receive e-mail, synchonize with calendaring systems like Lotus Notes, and access the Internet. All versions have a form of handwriting recognition that requires the user to write using a special alphabet.

Although the Palm series is the market leader today, a recent introduction by the developers of the original Palm organizer, called the Visor, may provide stiff competition. Marketed by Handspring, Inc., the Visor runs on the same operating system as the Palm organizers and, as a result, has access to the same software as the original device. In addition, it has a proprietary slot in the back that allows users to plug in an array of peripheral devices that will turn the Visor into a cell phone, pager, global-positioning system (GPS) device, MP3 music player, and universal remote, among other things. Imagine using the GPS add-on to interface with a database of ATMs so you can find the nearest cash machine in an unfamiliar city. With this and other devices from Palm, and other companies that are sure to appear to compete with it, the world of PDAs will provide individuals with all the personal organizational memory they can use. For example, Amazon.com has announced software that will enable PDA users to shop its Web site from just about anywhere.

Sources: Joshua Quittner, "All-In-One Gizmo?" *Time,* September 27, 1999.

Ernest Holsendolph, "Amazon.com Can Now Fit in the Palm of Your Hand." *The Atlanta Journal-Constitution,* October 4, 1999, p. A5.

Types of Knowledge

Earlier in this chapter, we mentioned three typical types of knowledge: organizational culture (how things work in the organization), social networks (who can do what), and models for handling problems (how to solve problems). Another name for a part of organizational culture is *policies and procedures*—that is, "This is the way we do things in our business." Other types of organizational culture cannot be codified into policies and procedures because they have to do with the ethics and core values of the organization. Organizational culture is an example of knowledge that is not generally associated with a single person or team and continues long after individuals have left the organization. Some of the knowledge of organizational culture can be transferred to new employees in orientation or training sessions, but other elements must be assimilated by working in the organization for a period of time.

On the other hand, the other two types of knowledge—social networks and problem solving—are often associated with a person or team and can walk out the door at anytime. The people who have this type of knowledge are often referred to as **human capital** because they are at least as important to the organization as the building in which they work (and often, much more important).

Another way of classifying knowledge is as explicit knowledge or tacit knowledge. **Explicit knowledge** is that knowledge that is codified and transferable, whereas **tacit knowledge** is personal knowledge, experience, and judgment that is difficult to codify. For example, knowledge about how to use a word processing package is explicit knowledge because it can be codified and transferred via books and other instructional material. On the other hand, the judgment regarding who to talk with in an organization about getting things accomplished is an example of tacit knowledge because it is not usually possible to codify this type of knowledge. In general, the part of organizational culture that is related to policies and procedures and problem solving knowledge are typically explicit. On the other hand, the part of organizational culture that is not included in formal policies and procedures as well as social network knowledge are both forms of tacit knowledge.

In Table 5-1, we included bulletin boards and chat rooms as examples of semistructured knowledge and newsgroups, groupware, expert systems, and frequently asked questions (FAQs) as examples of structured knowledge. As with data and information, we distinguish between semistructured and structured knowledge by the ease with which it can be searched. We suggest that bulletin boards and chat rooms are semi-structured forms of knowledge because they are difficult to search. For example, if you have a question about how to do something in Windows 98, you can go to a chat group on this subject and hope to find the answer to your questions, but due to the highly unstructured nature of a chat room, your search can be difficult.

On the other hand, with newsgroups, groupware, expert systems, and FAQs, structured methods exist for finding answers to questions. Newsgroups are **threaded** (i.e., answers or comments that relate to a previous question or comment are linked to it). This makes it possible to trace a discussion on a particular topic. You can also search newsgroups, but your success may not be any better (or worse) than searching the Web. With groupware, a structured method is used to enable collaboration between members of a team, organization, or interest group. Similarly, expert systems are a way of storing an expert's knowledge in a way that makes it easy to find answers to questions. Finally, **FAQs (frequently asked questions)** are a form of structured knowledge in which questions and answers are included for questions that are asked most often about a subject. They are often included with new software to make it easy for users to find solutions to their problems. We will discuss groupware and expert systems in more detail shortly.

Sharing Knowledge

Data and information are usually easy to share because they can be stored as files or documents and provided to other members of the team or organization. On the other hand, knowledge is often kept in a person's head and is much more difficult to share. The objective of knowledge management often is to simply find a way to share one person's or one team's knowledge with others in the organization.

Studies have found that most organizations are interested in sharing knowledge in order to improve operations or to embed them in products and services. Often this involves sharing what are called *best practices* (i.e., the best way of carrying out operations as discovered by individuals or groups within the organization). This includes ways to obtain, organize, restructure, and store knowledge. Companies have found that sharing knowledge can enable them to reduce the cost and time needed to produce a new product or service (cycle time), increase sales, and, in general, bring about increased customer satisfaction.

Sharing knowledge can be divided into two categories: group sharing and individual sharing. In group knowledge sharing, it is assumed that no one person or group has special knowledge that needs to be shared. In other words, everyone in the organization is assumed to be a potential source of knowledge that could help others in the organization. On the other hand, with individual knowledge sharing, almost every organization has one or more individuals (usually known as *experts*) who because of their knowledge (usually explicit) are essential to the successful operation of the organization. They are the people who can cut through superfluous details to get to the heart of a problem and are a large source of an organization's human capital. Finding ways to have these individuals share their knowledge with others in the organization is often essential to the continued success of the organization. Groupware systems are typically used for group sharing of knowledge, whereas expert systems are used for individual sharing.

Groupware

For group sharing of information, a new type of software has been developed over the last twenty years. Usually referred to as **groupware,** this software is aimed at helping groups of people structure, focus, and facilitate the transfer of information and knowledge among themselves. Although groupware can include many applications other than just sharing knowledge, we will concentrate our discussion on this important use of groupware.

Sharing knowledge with groupware can be done at the same time and place, the same time and a different place, a different time and the same place, and different times and places. Each situation has a special type of groupware associated with it. These categories of groupware are often displayed in a two-by-two table as shown in Figure 5-14.

Group support systems involve a wide range of technologies aimed at helping groups share knowledge in the same place. Usually, this involves a special-purpose meeting room outfitted with a computer for each member of the group and a large-screen video projection system that acts as an electronic blackboard. The associated software enables group members to carry out an *electronic brainstorm* by proposing ideas, reacting to ideas proposed by others, analyzing and evaluating alternatives, and, sometimes, trying to reach a consensus on a solution to a problem or decision on an issue facing the group. This system has advantages over a traditional meeting in that everyone can propose and react to ideas at the same time by typing rather than talking; members can make anonymous comments or suggestions without feeling pressure to please superiors; and alternatives can be easily ranked or voted upon. This same technique can be used on a delayed basis in which different groups use the same room but at different times. Each group can add ideas, respond to ideas, and so on over a set period.

Videoconferencing enables groups or individuals in different locations to meet at the same time through real-time transmission of audio and video signals between the different locations. The signals are picked up from cameras and special microphones in a specialized meeting room at each location and shown in the other room(s) on a large screen at the front of the room. The fastest-growing type of video conferencing is from one computer to another, enabling individuals to communicate with one another. This is often handled over the Internet using small, relatively inexpensive cameras and microphones.

Although group support systems and videoconferencing can certainly facilitate sharing of knowledge within an organization, they are often associated with collaborative decision making and problem solving. On the other hand, **document-based groupware** is most often used specifically for knowledge management through a document database. The most widely used software associated with this type of knowledge management is Lotus Notes from IBM. Lotus Notes is designed to store and manage large collections of text and graphics. Documents can be organized into

Figure 5-14 Different Types of Groupware

Time Place	Same Time	Different Time
Same Place	Group support systems	Group support systems
Different Place	Video conferencing	Document-based groupware

Using group decision support rooms such as this, groups can brainstorm solutions to problems facing the organization.

a hierarchical structure of sections, folders, and documents, thereby allowing easy searching for a needed document. A client/server network application, the Notes server is called *Domino* and operates on a variety of platforms and operating systems. The Notes clients are installed on the user's computer and can run independently of the server or can be connected to Domino.

In terms of knowledge management, Notes can be used as a question-and-answer bulletin board system that enables individuals to share their knowledge on a particular subject. For example, a topical area (e.g., relational databases) could be created in Notes to which users submit questions. If someone has an answer to the question, they submit the answer and Notes will link it to the question. Similarly, Notes can be used to organize reference material containing such things as policy and procedure manuals, organizational charts, telephone and e-mail address directories, and even software documentation. It is also possible to access some Notes functions through a Web browser.

The key to Notes is that it is a **document database** (i.e., instead of storing related tables, Notes stores related documents in a Notes file). The structure of the Notes document database is compared to a relational database in Table 5-3.

Table 5-3 Comparison of Relational and Notes Databases

Feature	Relational Database	Notes Database
Structure	Collection of related tables	Collection of related documents
Record	Row of a table	Document
Field	Column of a table	Field in a document
Access	SQL query	Tailored report
Replication	Ad hoc through file copying	Scheduled as part of Notes

Source: Richard T. Watson, *Data Management*, 2nd ed. (New York: John Wiley, 1999), p. 443.

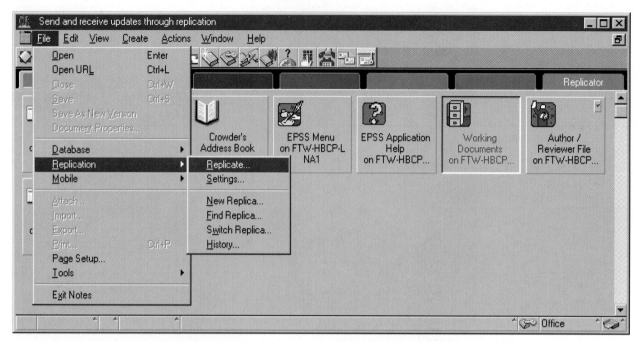

Lotus Notes is one way that many companies are using to share knowledge among their employees.

An important feature of Notes is its replication capability. By *replication,* we mean the capability of Notes to have copies of the Notes database replicated across multiple Notes servers on a set time schedule or whenever a user needs this to be done. Replication synchronizes the contents of the Notes databases on each server so all users are seeing the same documents regardless of where they are in the world.

Expert Systems

Individual sharing of information can be as important as group sharing, especially when the person doing the sharing is an *expert* on some subject that is key to the survival of the organization. Whether they are using their expertise to decide when a commercial soup is ready to be canned or to diagnose a pulmonary disease, experts use a body of knowledge and a set of "rules of thumb" to make recommendations to others who actually make decisions. Although such experts are obviously important to any organization, they can also be very expensive. In addition, when such experts retire or otherwise leave the company, their expertise and years of experience can be very difficult to replace.

Because of the importance of experts to all types of organizations, researchers began looking at ways to store years of knowledge in a computer. Early attempts to do this using databases proved problematic because the knowledge that an expert uses to reach a decision could not be stored in this fashion. Today, efforts to store individual knowledge are focused on expert systems. An **expert system** can be defined as a computer-based system that uses knowledge, facts, and reasoning techniques to solve problems that normally require the abilities of human experts.[3] Expert systems have enjoyed wide use in business, government, and industry as aids to sharing of an individual's knowledge. Expert systems differ from the decision support systems mentioned in chapter 4 and discussed in detail in chapter 6 because they actually suggest courses of action just as an human expert would, rather than just providing data, information, or solutions. Examples of productivity gains

---

3. James Martin and Steven Oxman, *Building Expert Systems—A Tutorial* (Englewood Cliffs, NJ: Prentice-Hall, 1988), p. 14.

ⓕocus on Management

Amazon.com

One of the biggest successes in e-commerce (if not the biggest) is Amazon.com, the online seller of books, music, and, fairly soon, just about everything else. The brainchild of Jeff Bezos, Amazon.com started out in 1995 as an online bookseller. Over time, it has added music, electronics, and toys. In the process, Amazon.com has become the biggest retailer of books and music on the Internet, and it plans to do the same for anything anyone wants to sell. Bezos's business model was simple—sell products directly to the consumer on the Web. Although Amazon.com has not yet shown a profit (revenues are being plowed back into the company to expand its market share), it has a valuation of $22 billion—more than twenty times that of Border's, which has 260 physical bookstores. In Bezos's model, once an online store gets past its fixed expenses of setting up its Web site and distribution channel, it can continue to expand sales without the requirement to build more brick-and-mortar stores and with very few additional expenses. As Bezo noted, "You can offer both the lowest prices and highest service level, which is impossible in the physical-world environment."

To make shopping at Amazon.com as interesting as going to the local mall bookstore, the company has taken the approach that it can be a place "to hang out." It does this through the concept that "information is entertainment." Providing more information to the customer is a way to encourage more purchases. Amazon repackages the huge amount of data it collects on sales to generate recommendations for a customer by ranking books by sales, identifying other books the buyer might like, and determining the best-seller among "purchase circles" in a given area code or company. Amazon also publishes *all* reader reviews; both the bad reviews as well as the good reviews. It does this because Amazon is not in the business of selling things, but, as Bezos says, "Our business is helping customers make purchasing decisions." For Amazon.com, organizational memory is not just for remembering the past, but also for handling the present.

Source: Steven Levy, "Wired for the Bottom Line." *Newsweek,* September 20, 1999, pp. 43–49.

---

resulting from using expert systems include a tenfold decrease in the time required to design a camera lens or a three hundredfold decrease in the time to organize a computer system to meet a customer's needs. Although not every user has benefited to this extent, expert systems are being used in many types of organizations.

You should note that in our definition of an expert system the emphasis is on problem solving using three elements: knowledge, facts, and reasoning techniques. The knowledge and facts are stored in the **knowledge base,** whereas the reasoning capabilities are handled by the **inference engine** of the expert system. These elements are shown in Figure 5-15.

The knowledge base includes all the facts and rules surrounding the problem at hand, and the inference engine works with the facts and rules in the knowledge base to make recommendations. It contains two databases: the **domain database** and the **rule database.** The domain database contains the facts about the problem being solved, and the rule database contains the rules to be used in the reasoning element of the expert system. These facts and rules try to include as much of the experience, intuition, and so on as possible in the form of IF–THEN rules. An **IF–THEN rule** states that, if a condition is true, then a conclusion is also true.

A unique aspect of expert systems is that they can answer queries from the user as to *why* a particular question is being asked and *how* a specific recommendation was made. This *justification* aspect of expert systems further sets them apart from conventional information systems that cannot provide information as to why and how they carry out their processing. The explanation facility of the expert system can provide the answers to "why" and "how" questions by keeping track of the rules that have been implemented to reach the current state of affairs. So, when a "why"

Figure 5-15 Elements of Expert System

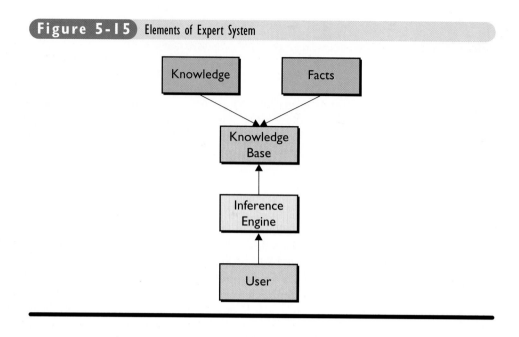

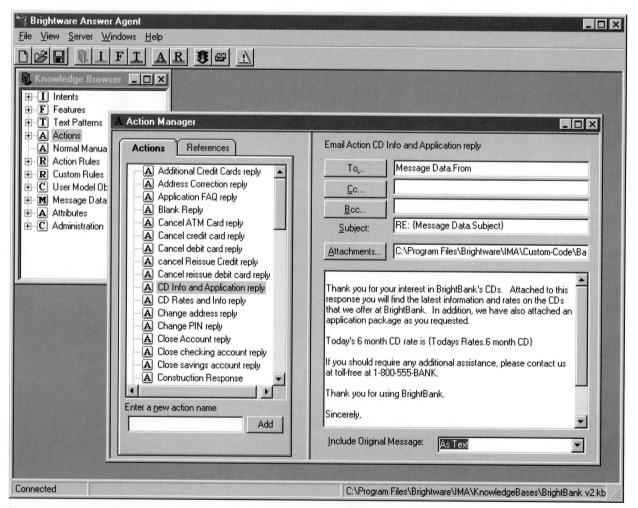

Expert systems, such as this, are used widely to capture and share the knowledge of experts.

question is asked, the explanation facility will provide the rule that is being tested and the reason why the information is needed to test this rule. Similarly, when a "how" question is asked, the explanation facility will show the line of reasoning or **logic trace** that was used to arrive at the current conclusion.

Quick Review

1. Why is groupware considered a form of knowledge management?

2. What are the parts of an expert system?

⊙ Summary

To summarize this chapter, let's answer the Learning Objectives questions posed at the beginning of the chapter.

What is organizational memory? *Organizational memory* can be defined as an organization's electronic record of data, information, and knowledge that is necessary for transacting business and making decisions. It is composed of three elements— data, information, and knowledge. Data are raw facts usually in a textual form (letters and numbers). Information is the result of processing data into a usable form. Information can be in the form of text (tables and reports), hypertext, graphics, images, audio, and video. Knowledge is the human capacity to request, structure, and use information. *Structured organizational memory* refers to forms of memory that can be easily searched, whereas semistructured organizational memory is not easily searched.

What is a database, and how does it store data in a structured form? Data are stored in structured form in databases or data warehouses. A database is a collection of different types of data organized in such a way as to make them easy to be manipulated and retrieved. A data warehouse is a subject-oriented snapshot of the organization at a particular point in time. Database management systems are used to reduce problems associated with data redundancy, data integrity, and data dependence. The data hierarchy is the way data are organized in organizational memory and is made up of bits, characters, fields, records, files, and the database.

What are the key elements of a relational database? A relational database uses a table structure where the rows correspond to records and the columns correspond to fields. Each row must have the same number of columns, and the same specific format must be followed throughout. Each table has a primary key that uniquely identifies each record. When a primary key is included in another table, it becomes a foreign key, which is used to relate the tables. The tables, fields, and relationships that are being used to provide needed data are referred to as a data model. The primary use of a database is to obtain information from it in a usable form by constructing queries to the database. These queries can be used to retrieve fields for matching records from one or more tables that can be edited or deleted. It is also possible to add new records to the database. For a relational database, these queries are written in a special language known as SQL (Structured Query Language), and they enable database users to find records from a table that meet some stated criterion or to create composite records from multiple tables that meet the criterion.

What methods are being used to improve the management of information? Information is typically stored in documents, books, reports, invoices, bills, and so on, in both paper and digital form. The newest form of information is the millions of Web pages available on the World Wide Web that store all of the information formats mentioned earlier. Much of the information on paper is being converted to digital form through imaging, whereby documents are scanned into a computer. Semistructured digital information includes Web pages and e-mail messages, that is, it is difficult to search through them to find needed information. Indexed Web sites, reports, charts, and manuals are structured information where indexing is the process of using data values or descriptors to search through documents.

What are the types of knowledge, and why is it so important to manage that knowledge? The three types of knowledge are organizational culture (how things work in the organization), social networks (who can do what), and models for handling problems (how to solve problems). Social networks and problem solving are often associated with a person or a team that can leave at any time. The people who have this type of knowledge are often referred to as human capital. Another way of classifying knowledge is as explicit knowledge or tacit knowledge. In general, organizational culture and problem solving knowledge are typically explicit knowledge, and social networks knowledge is tacit knowledge. The objective of knowledge management is often to simply find a way to share one person's or one team's knowledge with others in the organization.

What are two commonly used ways of sharing knowledge? Sharing information can be divided into two categories: group sharing and individual sharing. In group sharing, it is assumed that no one person or group has special knowledge that needs to be shared. On the other hand, almost every organization has one or more individuals (usually known as experts) who because of their knowledge (usually explicit) are essential to the successful operation of the organization. Finding ways to have these individuals share their knowledge with others in the organization is often essential to the continued success of the organization. Groupware systems are typically used for group sharing of knowledge, whereas expert systems are used for individual sharing.

⊗ Review Questions

1. How does organizational memory fit into the IS cycle? What are the components of organizational memory?

2. What is the difference between structured and semistructured organizational memory? Give some examples of each.

3. In what ways are data stored in a structured form? What do files, records, fields, and characters have to do with structured data storage?

4. What is a data warehouse? How is it used to help the organization?

5. What type of database management system is most widely used today? Why is it so named?

6. What is a data model? What is a primary key? What is a foreign key?

7. What is SQL? How is it used in database management?

8. What is imaging? What does imaging have to do with organizational memory?

9. What are the various ways in which knowledge can be classified? Which types are the most difficult to store?

10. What is the difference between groupware and expert systems? Which system is used to store the knowledge of an individual?

⊗ Discussion Questions

1. Discuss the extension of hypertext to include accessing other types of data, including images, voice, and video.

2. Discuss possible relationships between object-oriented databases and multimedia databases.

3. Discuss a topic for which you are an *expert* and the ways it could be incorporated into an expert system.

> **CASE**

WildOutfitters.com

"…three, four, five…." It was inventory day at Wild Outfitters. Alex and several friends were counting the items in the store while Claire tried to make sense of the sales transaction printouts that they had filed away for safekeeping. Twice a year, the Campagnes invited friends and neighbors to help them audit the inventory and then treated them to a barbecue as thanks for their help. It was becoming a tradition.

Claire walked from the backroom office with an armload of papers and said, "It's never seemed to take so long with these records before. All of the new orders from the Web site have really made the pile bigger."

"It doesn't look like you'll be done with those any time soon. We're almost done in here. Maybe I should get the food started on the grill," Alex offered.

"Good idea, otherwise we could have a hungry worker revolt," replied Claire, still keeping a sense of humor despite the work that would delay her fun.

The Wild Outfitter filing system had worked well enough in the past, primarily due to their low sales volume. Now that both their store and online sales have increased, they are becoming overwhelmed by the amount of data generated. Their current practice is to simply print out the transaction and file a copy of each sales transaction in chronological order. Then when it's time to do the books, one of them would compile the information and form calculations for all sales since the date of the last inventory. They have been able to determine when to restock an item through simple observation of the number on hand. Now, with the increased sales volume, they are starting to see that their current file system is becoming unmanageable. In addition, they are finding that they are running out of items unexpectedly at times, which forces them to put valuable customers on hold.

In reality, there is a lot of valuable information available in their transaction records if it were only more readily accessible. For each sales transaction, a number of data items are printed on the invoice. Part of this information identifies a customer. The customer's name and contact information appear on each invoice. This includes the street address, the city and state, the zip code, daytime phone number, and e-mail if available. The invoice also includes information about the products purchased. Product information includes the name, price, and quantity of each item purchased along with product details, such as size and color. In addition, each invoice is assigned an order number and marked with the type of sale, in-store or online.

The Campagnes realize that they need to do something to improve this situation. They would like to take advantage of their new network infrastructure to automate these recordkeeping tasks. They are ready to incorporate database technology to provide organizational memory for Wild Outfitters.

When Claire finally joined the festivities, Alex was taking the last of the ribs off the grill.

"It's a good thing that I kept a close eye on the barbecue rib inventory," Alex teased. "I would fear for my life, if I had to make you wait for a back order."

"Fear can be a good motivator. You should keep that in mind and get a database set up soon," Claire said, as she gnawed hungrily at her food.

1. What benefits would organizational memory provide for Wild Outfitters? Explain.

2. How would you categorize the sales records of Wild Outfitters? Are they composed of data, information, or knowledge? Is it structured or semi-structured?

3. What steps would you take to make these records a part of organizational memory? What other kinds of organizational memory do the owners of Wild Outfitters have?

4. *(Hands on)* You may download a database file (WildOutfit.mdb) for this case from www.harcourt-college.com/infosys/mckeown. Use MS Access or a comparable database management system to answer the following questions:

   a. What are the names of the tables in the database?

   b. For each table, what are the primary keys and foreign keys?

   c. Create a query to determine the number of sales transactions that occurred from the Web site.

   d. Create a query to find the total number of camping equipment items sold.

   e. Create a query to find the name and zip code of all customers who purchased the Litewalkers Hiking Boots.

   f. Create a standard invoice using your DBMS reporting function. The invoice should include: customer information; a listing of the transactions that make up the invoice including each product, quantity, and price; a calculation of the subtotal, tax (use a 5 percent sales tax rate); and total.

CHAPTER 6

Preparing for the Future with Decision Support Systems

> Learning Objectives

After reading this chapter, you should be able to answer the following questions:

> What is a decision support system (DSS)? What types of decision support systems are in use today?

> How are decisions made?

> How does an information-based DSS support decision making?

> How do top-level executives and the information they require differ from other managers?

> In what ways does a data-based DSS provide answers to questions?

> How does a model-based DSS answer questions from decision makers?

F o c u s   o n   M a n a g e m e n t

Web Site Analysis at Bell Atlantic

As with many companies, New York-based Bell Atlantic Corp. uses its Web site[1] to provide information to its many communications customers in the northeastern United States. But, Bell Atlantic also wants to use its Web site to market itself, create new business, improve customer relations, and save money. To find ways for its site to do these jobs better, Bell Atlantic uses data mining software that gives it data on Web site visits enabling it to form a profile of user tendencies and site usefulness. For example, the data mining software showed the site managers that many visitors to its site were using the search engine and then leaving the site. This encouraged them to add a QuickFind feature that enables users to find useful information easily on other parts of the site. This improves service for Bell Atlantic customers because they can use the Web site for "high-volume, low-value" transactions, such as looking for an area code or ordering a new phone book, instead of waiting for a telephone representative to answer a telephone call.

The reports generated by the data mining software are far more extensive than just logging "hits" to a Web page. They enable the site managers to use cost-per-user analysis to justify the amount of money spent on developing Web content areas. The software has also helped individual business managers use site data to monitor campaigns involving direct mail and online or print advertisements to determine which promotion was most effective. Finally, the actual layout of the Web pages was modified as a result of the analysis of data supplied by the software. Pages using frames were reduced, and the navigation tools were repositioned on pages.

Source: Scott Peterson, "Bell Atlantic Drills for Site Analysis," *PC Week,* February 15, 1999, pp. 33, 37.

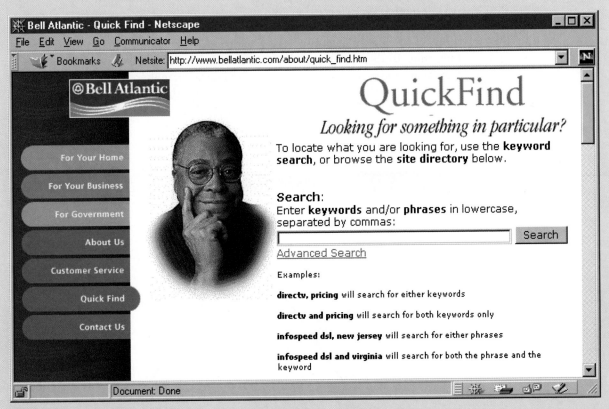

The Bell Atlantic Web site provides important data to company managers.

---

1. http://www.bellatlantic.com.

Preparing for the Future

In earlier chapters, the information system (IS) cycle model was presented (see Figure 6-1) in which organizations handle the present, remember the past, and prepare for the future in the networked economy. In this model, the organization uses transaction processing systems to handle the present. In the process, data on transactions are generated and must be stored as a part of remembering the past. These data are used to manage the transaction processing system and as a basis for helping the organization to prepare for the future using decision support systems like the one discussed in the opening Focus on Management box. In this chapter, we discuss the use of decision support systems to prepare for the future by aiding the decision-making process. The resulting decisions will, in turn, determine how the day-to-day operations (the present) are handled in the future. The decision support system uses data and information from organizational memory and external sources, as well as mathematical models, to support decision making.

Although decision making has always been the key element in the long-term survival of any organization, whether it be a business or a political unit, in the networked economy not only are good decisions necessary, but also they must be made quickly. Failure to react to the quickly changing environment of the networked economy and to handle adequately the increased level of innovation risk can result in a CEO losing their job or a company going out of business. As discussed in the opening Focus on Management box, companies are finding that having just a Web site is no longer enough—it now must be designed correctly and must be monitored constantly to ensure that it is doing the job for which it was designed.

To make good decisions quickly requires a decision support system that can quickly provide the decision maker with needed data, information, or answers to questions. In this, as in many other areas, the movement is toward Web-based systems that can be accessed by managers and decision makers from their Web browser. No longer can they wait for a paper-based report; the information or the answers to questions are needed yesterday!

Figure 6-1 Information System Cycle

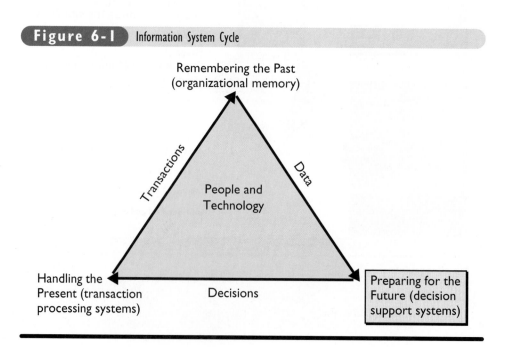

Defining Decision Support Systems

To understand the types of systems that are needed by decision makers to help them make decisions in the fast-paced networked economy, let's start by defining **decision support systems (DSS)** as information systems that provide a decision maker with information, data, or answers to questions. Included in this broad definition are three basic types of DSS: information-based DSS, data-based DSS, and model-based DSS. Traditionally, some of these types of decision support systems have gone by other names, including management information systems, executive information systems, database management systems, and, simply, *decision support systems*. However, because all are aimed at supporting decisions and differ only in the way in which they do this, we have grouped them under the broad name of decision support systems. The three types of decision support systems are shown schematically in Figure 6-2, where the segments of the pie are *not* meant to represent the proportion of use in aiding decision makers.

It is important to note that, in many cases, the person using a decision support system to find answers to questions is not the same as the person making the decision. Individuals with the title of *analyst* interact with the decision support system to find answers to questions posed by the actual decision maker. This is especially true with data-based and model-based decision support systems, where a great deal of specialized knowledge is often necessary to work with these systems.

Types of Decision Support Systems

As mentioned, we have divided decision support systems into three types: information-based, data-based, and model-based. In this section, we will discuss all three and then devote an entire section to each later in the chapter. An **information-based DSS** makes it possible for individuals at all levels of the organization to view information needed to make decisions. This is true throughout, from an employee determining the current status of a production process for which they are responsible or a salesperson checking the availability of a product or the status of an order to the company CEO comparing the performance of the company's stock to that of its competitors. Software is used to process specified internal and/or external data into information that is displayed to the user in a format that makes it possible for people to make needed decisions. In more and more cases, this information is being reported in the form of Web pages, which the employees or managers are viewing with Web browsers. Usually, analysts in the organization have spent a great deal of time determining the information needs of employees and managers to ensure that the right type of information reaches them. Once they receive it, they must spend even more time analyzing the information to understand its implications for the decisions they must make and for the organization as a whole.

It should be noted that the information-based DSS to which we are referring have traditionally been known as management information systems or executive information systems, depending on the format of the report and the audience at which it

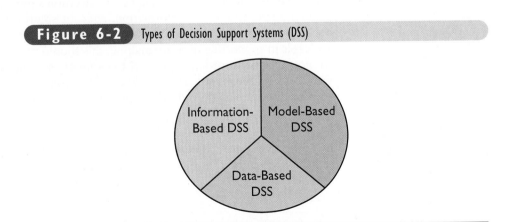

Figure 6-2 Types of Decision Support Systems (DSS)

was directed. **Management information systems (MIS)** were originally developed as paper-based text reports on internal operations. Although these reports were at one time adequate for mid-level managers, it was soon found that they were often difficult to read and did not always provide the type of information required by top-level executives. Instead of the reports provided by an MIS, top-level executives needed specialized information from a wider variety of sources in a specific format. To meet this need, **executive information systems (EIS)** were created and used graphical on-screen displays to provide information to executives. Today in the networked economy, such paper-based reports provided by an MIS are often out-of-date by the time people receive the reports. With the advent of the Web browser, it is now possible to provide up-to-date information to all managerial levels in an easy-to-use graphical format. As a result, the differences between MIS and EIS have, to a large extent, disappeared. For this reason, we refer to any system that provides information to an employee or manager as simply an information-based DSS.

A **data-based DSS** makes it possible for analysts within the organization to use data in databases and data warehouses to answer questions about the organization's operations. Quite often these questions are of an *ad hoc* nature—that is, questions created for the purpose at hand rather than planned carefully in advance. The questions are answered through a variety of approaches, including SQL, online analytic processing (OLAP), and data mining. As was discussed in chapter 5, SQL is a special language for querying databases. On the other hand, OLAP enables a user to selectively extract data from a database using different points of view. Finally, data mining is the analysis of data for relationships that have not previously been discovered. The opening Focus on Management box describes a data-based DSS that enables Bell Atlantic to understand the pattern of usage of its Web site by visitors.

When questions require mathematical or statistical analyses, a **model-based DSS** is used. As mentioned earlier, the term *decision support system* has been historically applied only to this type of system, but we are expanding its definition to include information-based and data-based systems as well. Model-based DSS combine data from the database or data warehouse with mathematical models to answer questions asked by management. This often involves generating forecasts, carrying out statistical analyses, simulating situations, or searching for the best allocation of resources.

In thinking about these three types of information systems, you should be aware that this is a somewhat artificial differentiation because it is possible to carry out activities associated with one type of DSS with software that is aimed at one of the other two types. For example, OLAP tools can also support some type of information reporting. In fact, today all three types of DSS may be accessed from the same Web site over an intranet—a so-called **enterprise information portal (EIP)**—that allows the individual seeking help with a decision to use all three types of information systems without worrying about which one is being used. An enterprise information portal acts as a *Web-based doorway* to the decision support systems through which the user enters to find the information, data, or solutions needed to make a decision.[2] Although each type is discussed separately to help you understand each system's role in supporting decision making, this should not be taken to mean that they are not integrated into a single decision support system that is available over the Web. Before discussing these three types of decision support systems, we will look at how decisions are made and the role of information in decision making.

Quick Review

1. List the three types of decision support systems.
2. Which type of decision support system is described in the opening Focus on Management box?

---

2. See http://www.sagemaker.com/company/lynch.htm for more information on EIP.

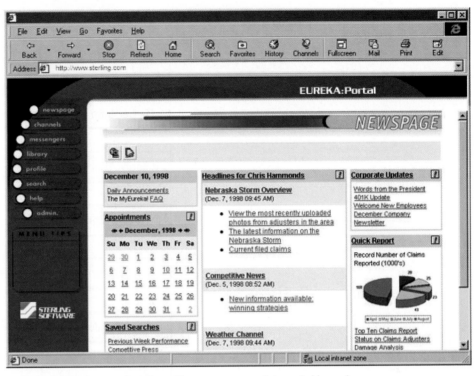

Enterprise information portals, such as this one, are a great help to decision makers.

Decision-Making Concepts

It is universally agreed that decision making is a key managerial activity—maybe *the* key activity—that often decides the fate of most organizations. That is, good decision making usually leads to the long-term survival of an organization, whereas poor decision making can quickly lead to the demise of an organization. By **decision making,** we mean recognizing problems, generating alternative solutions to the problems, choosing among alternatives, and implementing the chosen alternative. Figure 6-3 shows one model of the decision-making process.

In looking at Figure 6-3, you can see that the decision-making process begins with the definition of the problem requiring a solution or decision. One must be careful here to find the actual problem and not the symptoms of the problem. Note that problems are not inherently bad; they may actually be opportunities that must be taken advantage of in order to gain a competitive advantage. Defining a problem requires an effective intelligence component of the information system to monitor internal activities and the business environment to determine the existence and nature of the problem or opportunity. Note also that the decision-making process does not occur in a vacuum—there are environmental constraints on the process as well as strategic resource and organizational constraints. These constraints ensure that the final decision is one that actually can be used to solve the problem.

Once the problem is defined, information is gathered on the problem or competitive opportunity; this is also an important intelligence effort, and information is important in this endeavor. The information systems discussed in this chapter were developed to provide information to decision makers. In the next step, alternatives must be identified to resolve a problem or to exercise a competitive initiative. Again, an effective information system must be in place to help generate an array of feasible alternatives. These alternatives must be evaluated in light of criteria established by

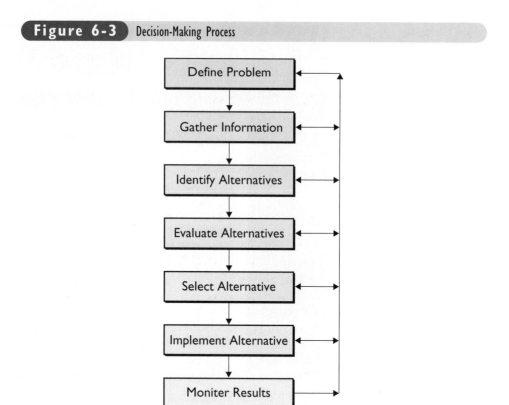

Figure 6-3 Decision-Making Process

the organization. Sometimes this is not so simple, given various organizational and political constraints as well as conflicting objectives within the organization. Nevertheless, the most appropriate alternative is selected. Next, the alternative course of action selected is implemented. This is often the most difficult part of decision making because it often requires convincing others in the organization to "buy into" the decision and enthusiastically work to make it a success. Many good decisions have failed to solve the original problem because they were not successfully implemented.

Finally, as shown in Figure 6-3, the results of the implementation are monitored to provide feedback to management for review of the selection criteria, the alternatives, and the decision. An effective information system is also necessary to carry on these monitoring activities.

Throughout this entire process, the decision maker needs to access the necessary information to size up the problem or the competitive opportunity, to assess the alternatives under consideration, to decide on selection criteria, to evaluate the alternatives, to implement a course of action, and to monitor compliance with the decision. This is a difficult task, and organizations will attempt to control the complexity of this task in several ways.

Types of Decisions

Decisions can be structured or unstructured. **Structured decisions** (also called **programmed decisions**) are those that can be made by following a set of rules and are usually made on a repetitive basis. The type of problem in this scenario is especially amenable to solution by computerized mathematical models. Examples of structured decisions include ordering raw materials or parts based on the current level of inventory, assigning checkers in a grocery store based on the time of day and day of the week, or deciding what action to take when a machine varies from acceptable tolerances.

Table 6-1	Comparison of Types of Decisions		
Type of Decision	**Information Required**	**Identification of Alternatives**	**Selection of Alternative**
Structured	Well defined	Limited	Use rules
Unstructured	Not well defined	Ambiguous	Use intuition and judgment

On the other hand, **unstructured decisions** (also known as **unprogrammed** or **ad hoc decisions**) involve complex situations and often must be made on a "once only" or ad hoc basis using whatever information is available. These are the tough decisions for which no clear-cut solution methodologies exists and require a high-degree of human intuition and judgment. Examples of these types of decisions include deciding whether to move into a new product line, deciding on which applicant to hire for a critical job, or choosing which merger or buyout offer to accept. Table 6-1 compares structured and unstructured decisions in terms of the information required, identification of alternatives, and selection of alternatives.

At one time, it was thought that various types of decisions could be associated with managerial levels of the organization. That is, structured decisions were associated with those employees who managed the day-to-day operations of the organization, whereas unstructured decisions were made solely by managers who dealt with the tactical and strategic issues facing the organization. However, with the movement toward empowering employees at all levels to make decisions about their jobs without waiting for approval from their supervisors, this is no longer necessarily the case.

Decisions Facing fareastfoods.com

All organizations face three types of risks: demand risk, innovation risk, and inefficiency risk. In chapter 4, we discussed the decisions facing fareastfoods.com in terms of carrying out transaction processing more efficiently (i.e., dealing with inefficiency risk). In that case, the company was trying to find faster and less costly ways to handle the present by taking orders, accumulating food items into an order, and shipping those orders to its customers. In the previous chapter, we discussed ways that fareastfoods.com was remembering the past through organizational memory. In this chapter, we look at ways in which fareastfoods.com is preparing for the future by making decisions. These decisions involve the company avoiding demand risk by making decisions to increase its demand in one of several ways, including:

- Making market penetration
- Developing new markets
- Developing new products or services
- Diversifying

In the first case, making market penetration involves finding ways to increase the amount of an existing product or service sold into an existing market. For example, management at fareastfoods.com might decide to use an e-mail marketing campaign similar to that used by AirTran Airlines as described in chapter 1. Developing new markets involves finding ways to sell existing products or services in new markets (e.g., fareastfoods.com might decide to try to sell its Oriental food products in Brazil because of the very large population of Japanese who have immigrated to

Focus on the Internet

Dealing with IT Acronyms

A common complaint from many people regarding information technology (IT) is the numerous acronyms that abound in the field. From terms like RAM in the computer itself to DVD for storage, LAN for networks, and Y2K for the Year 2000, there are hundreds of acronyms in the field. Keeping up with the existing IT acronyms is hard enough, but dealing with the new ones is almost impossible. Acryonyms like SAN, NUMA, VRML, and so on are difficult to figure out. However, there are many Web sites devoted to providing you with the necessary information. Two very useful sites are WhatIs.com and Computerworld's QuickStudy series. WhatIs.com (www.whatis.com) is a type of encyclopedia that provides a one or two paragraph description of the word. Words are combined alphabetically so, when you access the site, you can click on the first letter of the word and then find the word among all of those beginning with that letter. For example, to find out what VRML is, go to WhatIs.com, click on the letter V, and find and click

on VRML, where you will discover that it is an acronym for Virtual Reality Modeling Language, which is a language for describing three-dimensional (3-D) image sequences and possible user interactions with them. WhatIs.com goes on to provide more information on VRML and to provide links to other Web sites on this topic.

To find out more about a topic, you can use the Computerworld QuickStudy Series at www.computerworld.com/QuickStudy. While not nearly as many terms are included in the QuickStudy series as in WhatIs.com, each term is explained in much greater detail, with diagrams where necessary. For example, the QuickStudies discussion of a VRML begins with a succinct definition and then provides a very complete discussion of virtual reality modeling language including pictures of how it works. By combining WhatIs.com and the Computerworld QuickStudy series, you can keep up with the rapidly changing world of information techonology.

that country). Developing new products involves selling new products or services in existing markets (e.g., fareastfoods.com might want to add Caribbean food products and spices to its existing catalog of Oriental foods for sale in the U.S. markets that it currently serves). Finally, diversifying involves selling new products and services in new markets (e.g, fareastfoods.com might decide to sell the new Caribbean foods and spices in the Bahamas and Jamaica markets). Table 6-2 shows the new products and services and new markets and how they relate to these four decision areas. Management at fareastfoods.com must have data and information to make decisions about the courses of action to follow.

Quick Review

1. List the steps in the decision-making process.
2. List the differences between structured and unstructured decisions.

Table 6-2 Ways of Avoiding Demand Risk

Products	Markets	
	Existing Markets	**New Markets**
Existing products	Market penetration	Develop markets
New products	Product development	Diversify

Information-Based Decision Support Systems

An important role of information systems is to provide information to the organization in a form that can help it prepare for the future by aiding in decision making. As shown in Table 6-3, data, information, and answers to questions are needed in all seven steps of the decision-making model. For example, the first step of the decision-making process is to define a problem requiring a decision. Typical data or information required to do this includes data and information on problems in current operations, new opportunities available to the organization, or threats to the continued existence of the organization.

To obtain the data, information, or answers to questions for the various steps of the decision-making process shown in Table 6-3, a DSS is needed. In this section, we will concentrate on providing information to decision makers; later sections will also look at providing data and answers to questions.

An important method of providing information to decision makers in a form that is appropriate to them is using an information-based DSS. This is a generic name for many types of information systems that have the same goal. The primary method for providing this information is using a Web browser over an intranet. Recall that an intranet is a network that uses Internet protocols but restricts the access to employees of the organization. For example, an intranet Web server at fareastfoods.com might allow only full-time employees to have access to the information stored on it while not allowing temporary employees access. An intranet is essentially a fenced-off mini-Internet within an organization.

Web browsers have become the application of choice for information-based DSS because they are familiar to virtually everyone today and are easy to use. They also enable the same software to be used by all employees regardless of their position in the organization, with the difference being in the contents of the Web pages. If the employee is responsible for only a single machine, operational information on the current status of the machine can be sent to a Web server that formats it as a Web page that the employee can retrieve on a regular basis, or the page can be *pushed* to the employee's Web browser whenever the status of the machine changes. Based on this information, the employee can make a decision to correct any problems that may arise. Such **operational decisions** are usually considered to be structured because rules can be used in making those decisions.

| **Table 6-3** | Uses of Information in Decision Making |

Decision-Making Step	Information Required
Define problem	Problems with operations; new opportunities; threats from competition
Gather information	Information about the problem defined in first step
Identify alternatives	Alternative solutions to problem; ways to take advantage of opportunities or to deflect threats
Evaluate alternatives	Information on consequences of selecting each alternative identified in previous step
Select alternative	Rules or shared knowledge from organizational memory
Implement alternative	Individuals or organizational units that must be involved in implementation; problems with implementation process
Monitor results	Was decision implemented? Information on result of implementing decision

Similarly, a salesperson who needs information on product availability, price, or specifications can dial into the company intranet to find this information. This can help the salesperson make a decision on the terms to quote a potential customer and help avoid demand risk due to poor customer service.

On the other hand, a manager who is responsible for one or more units of the organization will want to see summary information regarding those units in order to make **tactical decisions** to implement the policy or **strategic decisions** made by policy makers in the organization. For example, assume that the policy at fareastfoods.com is for shipments to be sent out within twenty-four hours of receiving an order. However, the manager in charge of the shipping department determines that orders are taking up to thirty hours to be shipped. In this case, the manager must find out why there is a problem and make one or more decisions on ways to reduce the time to ship an order. Note that just finding out about the problem requires an information-based DSS that gathers data on shipments and summarizes them into a Web page that the manager can access. Determining the cause of the delay will require the manager to investigate the shipping process, possibly by looking at the Web pages created for the individual workers on their jobs. In a sense, the manager must *drill down* to the more-detailed information to find causes of the problem.

Similarly, executives responsible for policymaking will want to see internal information on the entire organization. They will also want to see external information on the organization's suppliers, customers, and competitors so they can stay aware of the environment. These decisions tend to be even more unstructured than those of tactical managers, often requiring a different type of knowledge and judgment on the part of the managers. If an executive sees a problem in the summary information, they may want to drill down to the tactical level or even to the operational level to determine the source of the problem. For example, if the CEO at fareastfoods.com determines that the company is losing market share, he or she will seek information both internally and externally to shed light on the cause of this problem. The process is shown in Figure 6-4, where the flow of summary information moves from the operational level out to the tactical level and from there out to the strategic level. On the other hand, the drill down for more-detailed information goes in the opposite direction. We have also shown the flow of external information into the strategic level.

Figure 6-4 Decision-Making Levels in the Organization

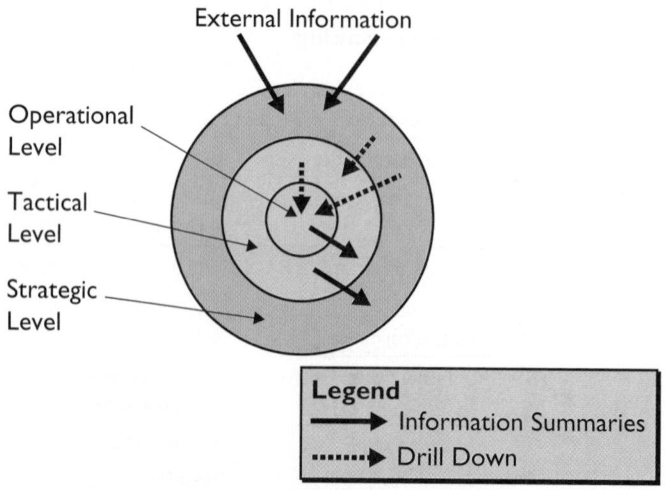

Types of Reports

Even though information-based DSS are primarily Web-based, with the information being displayed as a Web page on a computer screen, it is usually formatted as a *report*, which is a series of pages that impart information about a specific topic. These reports are tailored to meet the decision-making needs of the people who use them. For example, the shipping manager at fareastfoods.com will look at a Web page report with information on the on-time delivery of shipments.

Regardless of the managerial level—operational, tactical, or strategic—three types of reports are generated by virtually every type of information-based DSS: scheduled reports, exception reports, and demand reports. Each serves a different purpose to the managers and employees of the organization, but all are important.

Scheduled reports reflect the periodic and historic information on the organization's operations and are automatically generated by the information system on a schedule (e.g., daily, weekly, monthly, etc.). They are often the result of categorizing and summarizing the information produced by the transaction processing system. These reports provide managers with periodic information on which to make decisions or to decide to request more information. For example, the fareastfoods.com shipping manager might receive a daily report on the time to ship items for her department. This report might include average shipping time, worst case, best case, and other statistics. Based on this report, if there are problems with products being shipped late (i.e., more than twenty-four hours after an order is received) the shipping manager might decide to drill down to the operations level to seek information that will help her determine if it is a particular product or group of products that is causing problems or if it is an employee problem instead. Figure 6-5 shows a typical scheduled report for the shipping manager at fareastfoods.com.

Exception reports are generated only if some condition—usually an exceptional event—activates the generation of a report. The definition of what will cause the generation of an exception report must be defined in advance by management and must be programmed into the information system software that generates the

---

Figure 6-5   Scheduled Report at fareastfoods.com

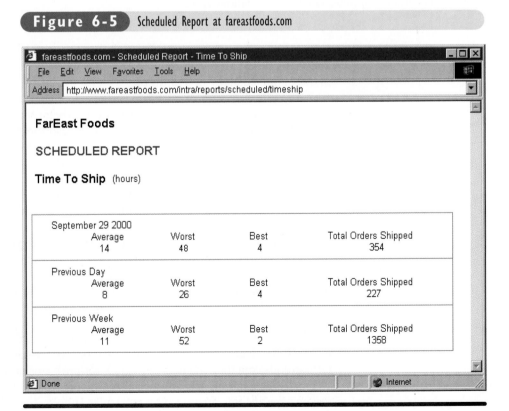

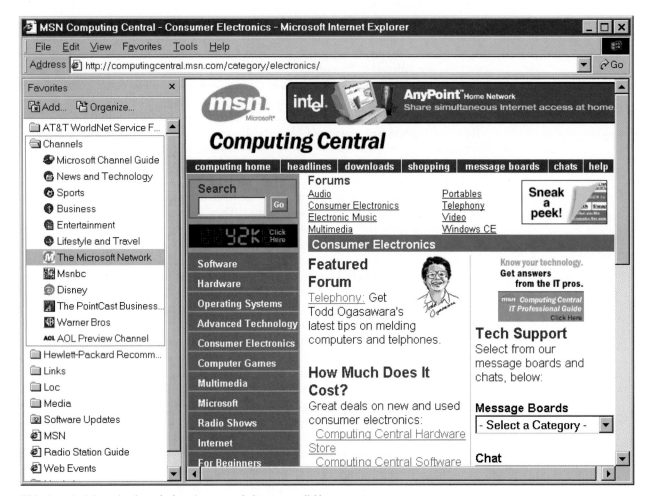

With channels, information is *pushed* to the user as it becomes available.

reports. In many cases, a manager will detect a problem using a scheduled report and then request an exception report so that whenever this problem arises again, he or she is immediately alerted. In this way, an exception report is useful to the manager for early detection of problems, an essential part of good management. At the same time, an exception report does not overwhelm the manager with unnecessary information. Today, a manager can receive exception reports in **real time** (i.e., as they are occurring) rather than waiting for a paper-based report to be written, printed, copied, and delivered. Delivery can be over the Web using **push technology,** in which Web pages are *pushed* to specific users by the server rather than being *pulled* by users going to a specific URL to retrieve a page. Given the speed at which decisions must be made in the networked economy, real-time exception reports are essential for avoiding or solving problems.

For example, an exception report for the fareastfoods.com shipping manager might be generated whenever some fraction of the shipments go out late. The shipping manager will have to decide on the threshold value at which the exception report will be generated. This report might prompt the manager to investigate the possible reasons for the excessive late shipments. In this case, the exception report provides immediate information on a known problem area so the manager does not have to wait for a scheduled report or to search through the report for the needed information. Figure 6-6 shows an exception report for the shipping manager at fareastfoods.com that will help her watch for problems in on-time delivery of orders.

Finally, **demand reports** are specialized reports that a manager may request when needing specific information on a particular subject. Often this request results from an unexpected outcome in one of the other reports or from outside information. In

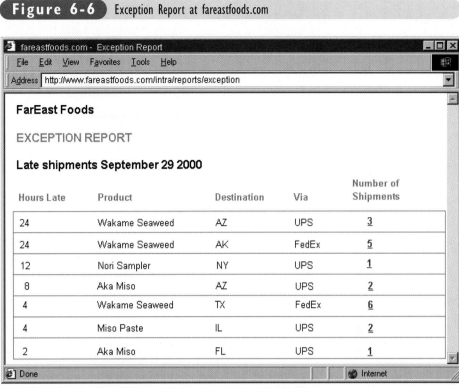

Figure 6-6 Exception Report at fareastfoods.com

the example of the shipping manager, she might request a demand report on the effects of adding a second shift in order to improve the on-time performance of the shipping department. Once again, Web or e-mail technology can be of great use to the manager by allowing her to click a link on the Web site or reply to the e-mail requesting more information on something she saw in a scheduled or exception report.

As you have seen with the example of the shipping department at fareastfoods.com, the reports mentioned are typically customized to fit the various departments (i.e., the scheduled, exception, and demand reports will be different in the finance department or the personnel department from those in the shipping department or other departments or areas in any company). Although the Web browser will be the same for all employees, and although overall design of the Web pages used to deliver the information may be the same, the information being delivered will be different. One of the strengths of a Web-based information-based DSS is the capability to deliver the right information to the right person in the organization.

Information for Top Executives

Earlier, we discussed the three levels of decision making—operational, tactical, and strategic. Although people at all three levels use a Web browser to view information that is pertinent to their operation—whether it be a department, division, or entire company—as we mentioned, there are differences in the types of information required at each level. These differences are most notable between the strategic level, where company policy is set, and the other two levels, where policy is implemented.

To understand the need for different types of information by those at the strategic level, we need to look at what these executives do. The top policymaking executives of any organization often carry titles of CEO (chief executive officer), COO (chief operating officer), CFO (chief financial officer), CIO (chief information officer), and so on. These and other members of the "executive suite" are responsible for the long-term well-being of the organization. Figure 6-7 shows a typical organization chart with those positions that would normally be classified as executives enclosed in dotted lines.

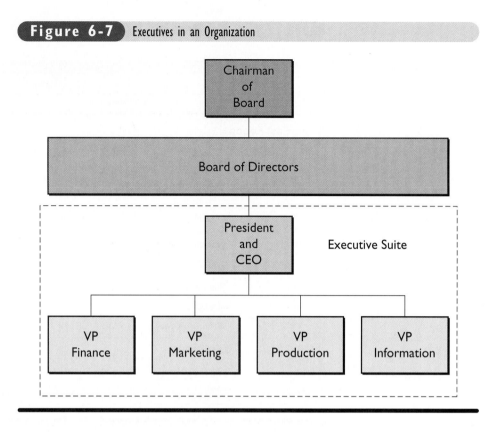

Figure 6-7 Executives in an Organization

Such executives are not just middle-level managers who make more money and have more "perks"; they must have a vision of the organization beyond just their department or the budgeting period. In terms of handling innovation risk, this group constantly must scan the environment for indications of new technology or for new approaches to doing business that will affect the organization. Although lower-level managers can generate incremental innovations in their department or division, the top-level executives can really make innovative changes that will effect a dramatic change in the direction of the company.

Executives also have a wider range of responsibilities and interests and tend to do different types of work from lower-level managers. Various researchers have tried to determine the various roles that executives carry out. Classical management theory said there are five managerial functions: plan, organize, staff, direct, and control. However, this says little about what managers actually do. In 1968, Mintzberg[3] observed five executives for a sufficient period to develop three types of roles: interpersonal, informational, and decisional. These three types, and the actual roles that are included in each type, are shown in Figure 6-8.

In looking at Mintzberg's roles, we see that an executive must do many different things each day but has only a finite amount of time to do all this. For this reason, time is an executive's most precious commodity. Also, one role in particular requires information of all types: the monitoring role. In this role, the executive is vigilant for problems that will need to be solved. Although much of this information comes from the many meetings an executive attends each day, information also comes from other sources, including that available from databases and data warehouses and from internal (intranet) and external (Internet) Web sites. However, unless that information is current and easy to obtain, it will be of no use to the executive.

Other studies have shown that executives want information in a specific form and that the form often varies from person to person. Some executives may want to

---

3. Henry Mintzberg, *The Nature of Managerial Work* (New York: Harper & Row, 1973).

Figure 6-8 Mintzberg's Roles

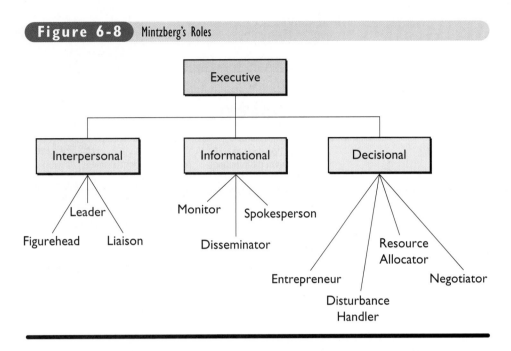

be able to see the price of their firm's stock or that of competitors, customers, or suppliers on a real-time basis, whereas others may want to see a daily report on production schedules. Each executive has a different indicator that they follow as a part of their monitoring role, and any information-based DSS must match this information requirement. For this reason, the information-based DSS for an executive is often called a "personalized presentation system" that shows the information the executive wants in the form they desire. This requires work on the part of an analyst to ensure that the right type of information in the right form is available to the executive.

Finding Information on the Web

The World Wide Web quickly has become the source of a vast amount of information, all of which is available on your desktop—if only you can find it! There are a number of ways to search for information on the Web, including directories like Yahoo![4] and search engines like AltaVista and Excite.[5] There are even *meta-search engines* like Dogpile[6] that search all of the other search engines available on the Web to help you find information. The problem with many of these searches is that you receive many references *(hits)* to Web sites that have nothing to do with your query. This is because almost all search engines work the same; they search over the entire Web indexing the pages found there using a wide variety of information on the page. Indexing is typically done on words in the title, the first words on a page, and to frequent recurrences of a word on a page. Indexing is also done on words listed in a special type of invisible HTML tag called a **meta tag** that is *supposed* to describe the page. The reason you receive so many spurious hits is that the search engine is finding one word somewhere in the page that matches your query or the page developer has used popular but incorrect words in the meta tags.

Another way to search the Web is to use a type of software known as an intelligent agent. An **intelligent agent** is a program that gathers information or performs some other service without your immediate presence and on some regular schedule.[7]

---

4. http://www.yahoo.com.

5. http://www.altavista.digital.com and http://www.excite.com.

6. http://www.dogpile.com.

7. http://www.whatis.com.

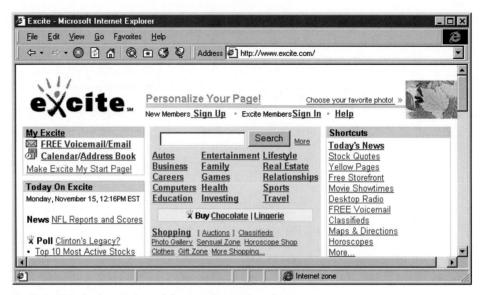

The Excite Web site (www.excite.com) is a popular search engine.

Typically, the agent searches all or some part of the Internet, gathers information you're interested in based on parameters you have set, and presents it to you on a periodic basis. An intelligent agent is a type of **artificial intelligence** because it tries to replicate actions normally associated with human behavior. Also known as **bots,** intelligent agents come in a wide variety, including those used to shop the Web for the best price on a particular item. For a complete listing of available bots, go to http://botspot.com.

Another form of artificial intelligence that can be used for searching the Web is **natural language processing (NLP),** which enables you to seek information by asking a question in a natural language. For example, if you ask: "What are the best companies for working women?" of the Ask Jeeves Web page,[8] you will be sent to the www.womenswire.com Web site. The Ask Jeeves technology also is utilized by both Dell and Microsoft to answer questions on their support Web sites. Also known as **chatbots,** NLP programs can be very useful if you have a specific question to ask.

You should be aware that search engines, intelligent agents, and NLP programs are all the result of programs written by humans and not artificial in any way. Most researchers agree that true artificially intelligent computers, like HAL in the movie *2001: A Space Odyssey* (and its sequel) are a long way from becoming a reality.

Quick Review

1. Why did we include management information systems and executive information systems under the same type of decision support system?
2. In what ways will a decision support system for a top-level executive differ from that for a mid-level executive?

Data-Based Decision Support Systems

In making decisions, employees and managers depend a great deal on Web-based information that has been developed by others. However, there are also many situations in which the decision maker has questions for which there is no available information. In these cases, the decision maker may turn to an analyst for help in finding answers to his or her questions in a database or data warehouse. This

---

8. http://www.askjeeves.com.

Ⓕocus on Technology

Improving Customer Service with Bots

As the networked economy grows, and more people take advantage of electronic commerce, customer service will have to change to match the new ways of doing business. Already, customers are finding e-mail to be better than being placed on hold waiting to talk to a customer service representative or paying per-minute charges to talk to a technical support person. As a consequence, companies are being bombarded with hundreds of e-mails from valued customers expecting a quick response that some firms are not prepared to give. However, just as technology created the problem, it can provide a solution through the use of software call *bots,* which reads the mail, guesses what the writer is requesting, and sends an appropriate (hopefully) response. Other systems attempt to detect the subject of the e-mail and route it to the appropriate person in the organization. In either case, providing efficient yet inexpensive customer service via e-mail is one very important use of bots.

There are a number of Web sites that provide demos of bots answering questions, including Red at www.neuromedia.com, Dudley at support.dell.com/askdudley/, and Andrette at www.bigscience.com. In each case, the bot is a virtual customer service representative attempting to answer your question. In the case of Red and Dudley, they are cartoon characters but Andrette is a picture of a women (called a Klone) that tells you all about the company but won't accept any dates.

Unfortunately, natural language understanding—the ability of computers to understand and respond appropriately to written sentences—has not advanced nearly as far as speech recognition. Even the best systems will respond with an inappropriate answer to a question. For example, if you ask Dell Computer's Dudley (which uses the Ask Jeeves technology discussed in the text) how much RAM you need, it gives an appropriate answer, but if you ask about ROM, it fails to recognize your question. Asking it "How fast is my machine?" yields information on cleaning the computer! However, these systems are only expected to improve, yielding better customer service through e-mail.

Source: Richard A. Schaffer, "The Robots Are Here." *Fortune.com,* March 1, 1999. http://www.pathfinder.com/fortune/technology/shaffer/1999/03/01/index.html

requires some type of data-based DSS. Such analysis is also referred to as **ad hoc analysis** because the questions are generated on an *ad hoc* basis by the decision maker.

One type of data-based DSS was discussed previously in chapter 5: the use of SQL queries to request information from a relational database. In fact, the development of relational databases and SQL by Codd was initiated by the need to create ad hoc queries to a database—something that was not possible with then-existing databases. In addition to using SQL to query relational databases, there are two other widely used methodologies: online analytical processing (OLAP) and data mining. Both of these methodologies have become popular over the last few years for answering questions about data or finding relationships in the data that were not previously known. The opening Focus on Management box concerning Web site analysis by Bell Atlantic is an example of data mining to learn more about customer visits to its Web site.

Both OLAP and data mining are based on the data warehouse concept. To review, a data warehouse (or its smaller cousin, the data mart) is a subject-oriented snapshot of the organization at a particular point in time. It is typically used for analyzing past data rather than for handling current transactions and is designed to help decision makers understand more about their organization and its environment.

Online Analytical Processing

Online analytical processing (OLAP) is a software tool that enables an analyst to extract and view data from a variety of points of view. It is used for planning and decision making using an analysis of existing data in a data warehouse. Typical applications include market analysis and financial forecasting. For example, in analyzing a market, an analyst at fareastfoods.com might ask questions about units sold by market, time

Figure 6-9   Flat Table in a Relational Database

Product	Market	Time	Units
Fish Sauce	Seattle	Q1	1,185
Fish Sauce	Seattle	Q2	1,303
Fish Sauce	Seattle	Q3	1,521
Fish Sauce	Seattle	Q4	1,779

period, and product, such as "What were unit sales in the Seattle market for Fish Sauce during the third quarter?" Trying to do this with a table in a relational database like that shown in Figure 6-9 would be difficult, especially when the analyst wants to consider many combinations of time, product, and market. Note that in the figure only one of the three dimensions (time) is being varied to see the difference in units sold.

Instead of using a flat table representation of the data, OLAP uses **multidimensional databases** in which each dimension represents one of the parameters that can be varied to determine the effect on the variable. This results in a n-dimensional cube in which each edge of the cube represents one of the dimensions. For the current example, the variable is the number of units sold, and the dimensions are product, market, and time, so we can represent it as a three-dimensional cube, as seen in Figure 6-10. The use of a multidimensional cube to represent data is, in many ways, closer to the way that employees and managers actually think about their data. For example, it is more natural to view data by product and market over time than by a series of flat tables.

Multidimensional databases for use with OLAP are typically stored in data warehouses because they are used for analyzing historical data rather than for updating databases as the result of **online transaction processing** (OLTP). Because the names are quite similar, the two are often confused. However, they are very different, as shown in Table 6-4.

In looking at this table, we can see that the purposes of the two systems are quite different, with OLAP analyzing data, whereas OLTP updates a database as each transaction is processed. The screen format of OLAP is customized to the user's needs, whereas that of OLTP is standardized. OLAP carries out numerous calculations with the data to provide information to the user, whereas OLTP makes few, if

Figure 6-10   Multidimensional Database

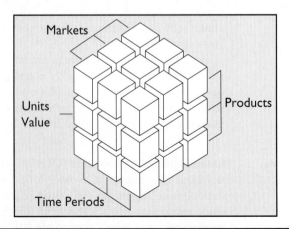

Table 6-4	Comparing OLAP and OLTP	
Characteristics	**OLAP**	**OLTP**
Operation	Analyze	Update
Screen format	User-defined	Unchanging
Calculations with data	Considerable	Little
Level of detail	Aggregate	Detail
Time	Historical, current, projected	Current
Orientation	Fields	Records

Source: Paul Gray and Hugh J. Watson, *Decision Support in the Data Warehouse* (Upper Saddle River, NJ: Prentice-Hall, 1998), p. 125.

any, calculations with the data. OLAP works with aggregate (summarized) data that have been pulled from the detail database maintained by OLTP. The time frame for OLAP is typically historical, with projections being made based on this data. On the other hand, OLTP works in a current time frame as it handles the present. Finally, like most database management systems, OLTP is record-oriented, whereas OLAP is interested in the contents of a multidimensional cell of the database.

Data in a multidimensional database can be analyzed in many ways. An analyst can choose to *view* data from different perspectives (e.g., that of the product manager or of a financial analyst) by slicing through the cube from different directions. Commonly known as **slicing and dicing,** this technique enables the user to extract portions of the aggregated data and study them in detail. For example, product managers at fareastfoods.com can study one product across many time periods and markets by slicing along the product dimension. Similarly, a financial analyst can study unit sales for all products and markets over one or more time periods by slicing across the time dimension. An analyst at fareastfoods.com could use OLAP to determine the unit sales of Lemongrass for Boston for a single quarter, for the entire year, or for as many quarters as data exist. Market and time views of data in a multidimensional database are shown in Figure 6-11.

In addition to "slicing and dicing" data in a multidimensional database, to answer "who?" and "what?" questions about the data, OLAP gives the analyst the capability to drill down into the database to answer "what if?" and "why?" questions about the data. These calculations are usually more complex than just summing

Figure 6-11 Views of a Multidimensional Database

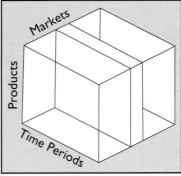
Market Slice

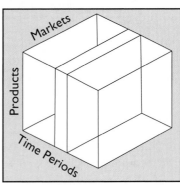
Time Slice

data; they often involve projections of future results or predicted values that would result if a decision were made. For example, at fareastfoods.com, OLAP might be used with the multidimensional database to predict future unit sales of a particular product or in a specific market. Or, OLAP might be used to predict the effect on unit sales for next year if a product (e.g., Plum Sauce) were no longer available.

Data Mining

In the previous section, we discussed the use of OLAP to analyze data stored in a multidimensional database in a data warehouse. Another way to analyze data in a data warehouse where a specific database form is not required is to use data mining. **Data mining** is a search for relationships within the data. In many cases, the relationships that are found are unexpected or are not the direct result of questions from decision makers. For example, an analysis of unit sales data for fareastfoods.com might result in the discovery that there is a seasonal variation in the sales of Tom Yam soup. This discovery might lead the marketing manager to create e-mail marketing campaigns with special prices on this product to bolster its sales in months when they are typically down.

Data mining typically includes a search for patterns or tendencies in the data using one of four approaches: associations, sequences, classification, and clustering. These four approaches, the objective of each approach, and an example of each approach are shown in Table 6-5.

Once one or more of these approaches to data mining have been used to find relationships, they can be used to improve the relationship with the customer, which, in turn, often results in a higher volume of sales. For example, a key use of data mining is for database marketing. In **database marketing,** advertisers use data mining and data warehouses to select a group of individuals who are most likely to buy their products, allowing them to spend their time and money on fewer prospects. For example, credit agencies can use their data warehouses to find individuals who tend to make only the minimum payment on a credit card and to sell their names to credit card companies. They then send "preapproved" credit card applications to this group of consumers, knowing in advance that, if the individuals use their card, the individuals will end up paying a large amount in interest and finance fees. Similarly, database marketing allows the jeweler at your local mall to advertise more efficiently by mailing advertisements only to individuals who live within ten miles of the mall and have an income of at least $100,000. And, if a company has access to multiple data warehouses, either by purchasing access or by reciprocal agreements with other companies, it is possible to combine data from them to produce the needed picture of the consumer.

Table 6-5 Data Mining Approaches

Approach	Objective	Example
Associations	Finding an event that is correlated to another event	Finding that a purchase of beer is often associated with a purchase of diapers
Sequences	Finding that the occurrence of one event leads to a second event	Finding that some percent of all persons becoming certified in scuba diving take a trip to an ocean resort within the following six months
Classification	Recognizing patterns that lead to rules about the data	Analyzing credit card utilization that results in recognition of patterns of normal usage
Clustering	Finding new ways to organize data into groups	Grouping customers by the amount and frequency of purchases from Web sites

In the credit card area, data mining has also been very helpful to both customers and credit card companies by stopping the use of stolen credit cards. It does this by first finding patterns of typical credit use for the customer. Then, if a credit card is detected as being used in an atypical manner (e.g., for a very large purchase) the company can call the card holder and ask them if they are the one using the card. If they are not, the sale is stopped and the card is canceled on the spot.

The process of data mining can be thought of as a seven-step process, as shown in Figure 6-12. Note that the process starts out with the analyst understanding the application and selecting the target data for discovery using data mining. These two steps involve the analyst knowing what relevant knowledge about the application exists, the goals of the data mining project, and what data exist in the data warehouse. In the third step, the analyst uses their knowledge to simplify the problem by reducing the number of variables being considered. The analyst then applies one of the data mining approaches shown earlier (i.e., association, sequences, classification, clustering, and time-based relationships) based on their knowledge of the application.

Once the data mining approach has been selected, the actual data mining can begin using a variety of software products developed specifically for this purpose. Such software is called **siftware** because it *sifts* through the data. Many of these products use statistical methods or clustering analysis, whereas others use a variety of other methods. One of the more useful approaches is neural networks. Popularized as the brains behind the cyborg in *Terminator 2,* **neural networks** are being used for many situations where it is difficult to write a computer program to cover all contingencies. Neural networks differ from other software approaches to data mining in that it is not necessary to decide in advance the approach or data to be used in the analysis. Instead, the neural network is *trained* to look for patterns in the data. As with training animals or educating humans, the neural network "learning" process depends on repetition to train the software component of the neural network.

Neural networks are most useful for detecting patterns in data. They have been used in various areas, including finance, speech and image processing, and data mining. In

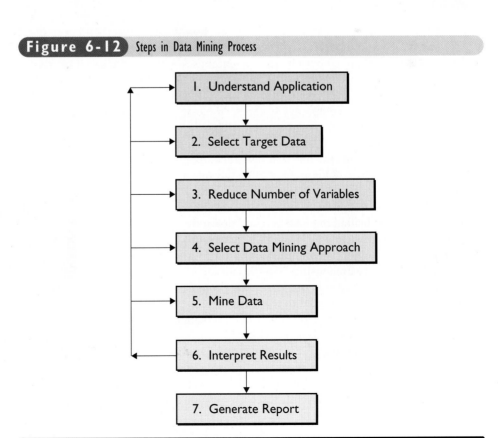

Figure 6-12 Steps in Data Mining Process

1. Understand Application
2. Select Target Data
3. Reduce Number of Variables
4. Select Data Mining Approach
5. Mine Data
6. Interpret Results
7. Generate Report

the financial area, neural networks are being used for risk analysis, fraud detection, and predictive modeling. In the database exploration area, neural networks are being used to help companies search through their databases for useful information. For example, a neural network could be used to search through fareastfoods.com's data warehouse for inactive customers who are most likely to purchase again if contacted by e-mail with a special "getting reacquainted offer."

Once results have been obtained from the data mining, the analyst must again use their knowledge to determine if the results are meaningful. This is done by checking the results for possibility, internal consistency, and plausibility. *Possibility* means that the results are physically possible, whereas *internal consistency* means that the results are not contradictory. Finally, *plausibility* means that the association or relationships found are believable. If any of these tests are failed (e.g., the results are impossible, inconsistent, or implausible) then the analysis can be rerun with a new target data set, a different set of simplified variables, or a different data mining approach (e.g., looking for sequences rather than associations). This capability to *iterate* through the data mining process was denoted in Figure 6-12 by the return arrows to the various steps.

Finally, if the results are found to be possible, consistent, and plausible, the analyst will need to interpret the results and generate a report to the decision maker(s) who was asking the original question about the data. The decision maker can then take actions based on the results, ask more questions or do nothing, depending on the situation.

Quick Review

1. How does the database used by OLAP differ from that used in an SQL query?
2. How do OLAP and data mining differ?

ⓕ o c u s   o n   P e o p l e

William Inmon

Accurate and consistent databases are key to both data-based DSS and model-based DSS. However, in the late 1980s it became obvious that the databases used in transaction processing would not work because they constantly were being updated. To solve this problem, various companies began to look at the use of databases, which were essentially snapshots of the TPS databases, to which they gave a variety of names including the one that has stuck: data warehouse. In 1992, William H. "Bill" Inmon, a veteran of many years of database technology, wrote the book, *Building the Data Warehouse,* that codified the ideas behind the field and laid down the four basic rules for defining one. As a result of this early work, Bill Inmon is commonly referred to as the "father of data warehousing." Since both OLAP and data mining depend on data warehouses, Inmon's work also contributed to their use.

Inmon has written thirty-nine books on data management, data warehouse, design review, and management of data processing that have been translated into nine languages. He is a regular contributor to trade journals with over five hundred articles to his credit. He founded and is currently the chief technol-

ogy officer and founder of Pine Cone Systems, a Colorado-based company whose mission is to create innovative software tools that address the complex and critical issues of managing and controlling data warehouse/data mart environments. Inmon conducts seminars and conferences in the United States, Europe, Canada, Asia, and Australia and holds two software patents for metadata management.

Sources: www.pine-cone.com
Private communication with William Inmon.

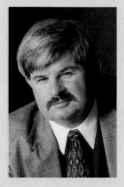

William Inmon is commonly referred to as the "father of data warehousing."

Model-Based Decision Support Systems

Information-based DSS are aimed at providing decision makers with information from internal and external sources. Data-based DSS are aimed at exploring data warehouses to analyze data found there to answer questions from decision makers. In neither case do the systems provide alternative solutions to the problems they might reveal. This is usually handled by a third type of analysis system known as model-based DSS. This type of analysis tool was developed to address the need for an information system that would help managers find solutions to problems. A model-based DSS does this through the use of quantitative and graphical models.

Model-based DSS have been used for such diverse activities as ski resort development, financial planning, and school bus routing. The system can be as simple as a spreadsheet on a PC or as complex as a full-scale financial planning and forecasting package on an application server or workstation.

Parts of a Model-Based Decision Support System

A model-based DSS has three major parts: the **database,** the **model base,** and the **user.** The database for the model-based DSS contains the data necessary to carry out the needed analyses. The model base contains a variety of types of models that can be used to analyze the data from the database. Finally, the user is the decision maker or analyst who is seeking the solution to a problem.

To make a model-based DSS work, the user must select a model and data to use in analyzing the problem. To make this possible, three software systems are necessary: a **data management system,** which manages the retrieval of data from a database as needed; a **model management system,** which is used to select a model that can be used to help arrive at a solution; and a **user interface system,** which handles the interactions between analyst and computer.

The data management function must be available to the analyst so that needed information from the company's database may be retrieved on demand. The analyst also selects a model using the model manager and combines the data and the model to develop alternative solutions. The models are a group of computer programs that will perform specific operations on the data from a database. The various alternative solutions can then be portrayed in a tabular or graphical form. To make a model-based DSS easy to use, the user interface allows the decision maker to change data and models as needed. For example, the user may request a graph of data on the screen. The user interface allows the user to select the data to be graphed and the model to be used to create the graph. Once a model has been chosen, the user interface combines the model with the data to arrive at the desired graphical display. To a large extent, the user interface should make the data management and model management functions invisible to the user by handling all of the interactions. The user interface makes the model-based DSS a truly useful tool by allowing the analyst to move about freely within it. Figure 6-13 shows the interaction between the user and the parts of the model-based DSS using the various software systems.

Using Models

In addition to being able to obtain needed information from an information-based analysis system or data from a database or data warehouse using a data-based DSS, the decision maker or analyst must be able to use software to determine the effect of changes in the information or data. For these changes to be observed, a model must be developed that represents the physical, economic, or financial situation being studied. A **model** is a simplified version of reality that captures the interrelationships between important variables in the situation. Once the model has been created, the analyst may then use it to answer questions. There are four primary types of models: forecasting, statistical, optimization, and simulation. In a **forecasting model,** historical data, assumptions, and a forecasting formula are combined to predict what the

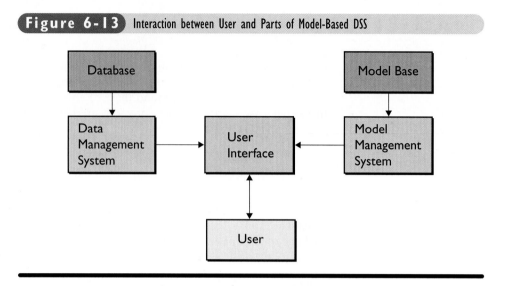

Figure 6-13   Interaction between User and Parts of Model-Based DSS

future may hold. Companies are constantly making predictions as to what sales will be in the future based on various independent variables. In a **statistical model,** the objective is to learn about tendencies within the data set or to prove that differences exist between parts of the data. In **optimization,** the user implements a mathematical equation that will determine the best possible solution to the model. For example, we may wish to find the maximum profit associated with a particular product where production is constrained by the availability of raw materials, labor hours, and so on.

Finally, with **simulation,** probability-based models are used to simulate the situation under study. Usually, simulation is done when the model that has been developed is too complex to respond well to optimization techniques or when more than just the "best" solution is needed. With a computer, several years of conditions and results can be simulated in just a few seconds. Once the results are compiled and analyzed, they can be used to determine the effect of a change in one or more of the values that control the model. The Focus on Management boxed insert about road-planning in Atlanta describes a large-scale simulation of the effect of building another expressway on the traffic patterns in Atlanta.

The Model-Based Decision Support System User

Although the ideal user of the model-based DSS is the person making the decision, this is not always the case. Decision makers, especially executives, often do not have the time to learn how to use a sophisticated decision support system. Instead, they may ask others to spend the time to become familiar with the system. These users fall into two categories: staff analysts and the executives's assistant. In the first case, the staff analysts are specialists in the decisions area (e.g., finance, marketing, production, etc.). As members of the support staff, these users can become very familiar with the system and spend as much time as necessary to develop alternative solutions to the problem being considered.

On the other hand, the executives's assistant becomes a *chauffeur* for the decision maker. In this role, the assistant actually handles the interface with the system. To do this, the assistant spends the time necessary to become familiar with using the software and interpreting the results. By so doing, the assistant can ask the right questions and provide the needed results to the decision maker.

Quick Review

1. List the three models most often used in a model-based DSS.
2. Why is an executive not always the person using a model-based DSS?

(F) o c u s   o n   M a n a g e m e n t

Simulating Commuting Problems in Atlanta

One of the biggest decisions facing the metropolitan Atlanta area is finding a way to reduce the traffic congestion during the morning and afternoon commute periods. Atlanta already has the longest commute time in the nation, with the northern leg of the perimeter highway often resembling a parking lot more than a highway! In addition, Atlanta has such serious air quality problems that the Federal government has restricted the building of any new expressways in the Atlanta area until they are solved. One solution that has been suggested is to build an "outer perimeter" thirty to forty miles outside of Atlanta to take some of the traffic off the highly congested I-285 perimeter. However, this approach is opposed by many who feel it is far too expensive at an estimated cost of $5 billion, would create more automobile-dependent urban sprawl in now rural areas, or would create the same type of air quality problems in the affected areas as now affect Atlanta.

To test the effect of the proposed highway on Atlanta traffic, the Georgia Department of Trans-

portation ran simulations for the so-called "northern arc" that would run on a generally east–west path, north of Atlanta. To most people's surprise, the simulation showed that this proposed northern leg of the outer perimeter would have limited use as a bypass with only 7 percent of the traffic being traffic going around Atlanta. While trucks would make up 17 percent of the traffic, they would be far outnumbered by automobiles, most with a single driver making local trips. The simulation also showed that the new road would have little effect in reducing traffic on the northern leg of the "inner" perimeter—I-285. There is so much demand for this route that it would quickly fill up to replace any traffic diverted to the outer perimeter. These results will be combined with others to help the state of Georgia make decisions on ways to solve Atlanta's commuting problem.

Source: David Goldberg, "A Computer-Generated Puzzle," *The Atlanta Journal-Constitution,* March 1, 1999, pp. E1–E5.

(>) S u m m a r y

To summarize this chapter, let's answer the Learning Objectives questions posed at the beginning of the chapter.

What is a decision support system (DSS)? What types of decision support systems are in use today? A decision support system is an information system that provides a decision maker with information, data, or answers to questions. A decision support system helps the organization prepare for the future using data from organizational memory as well as other types of data and information. Three types of decision support systems are in use today: information-based DSS, data-based DSS, and model-based DSS. An information-based DSS makes it possible for individuals at all levels of the organization to view information needed to make decisions. This is usually done through intranet-based Web pages. A data-based DSS makes it possible for analysts within the organization to use data in databases and data warehouses to answer questions about the organization's operations. The questions are answered through a variety of approaches, including SQL, online analytic processing (OLAP), and data mining. A model-based DSS combines data from the database or data warehouse with mathematical models to answer questions asked by management. This often involves generating forecasts, carrying out statistical analyses, searching for the best allocation of resources or simulating situations. Intranet-based enterprise information portals (EIP) allow the individual seeking help with a decision to use all three types of information systems without really having to worry about which one is being used.

How are decisions made? Decisions are made through a seven-step process:

1. Define problem
2. Gather information
3. Identify alternatives
4. Evaluate alternatives
5. Select alternative
6. Implement alternative
7. Monitor results

During this process, the decision maker needs to access the necessary information to size up the problem or the competitive opportunity, assess the alternatives under consideration, decide on selection criteria, evaluate the alternatives, implement a course of action, and monitor compliance with the decision. Decisions can be either structured (programmed) or unstructured (unprogrammed), depending on whether they can be made using predefined rules.

How does an information-based DSS support decision making? *Information-based DSS* is a generic name for many types of information systems that have the same goal: to provide decision makers with the information they need in a form that is appropriate for them. The primary method for providing this information is via a Web browser over an intranet. It supports decision making by providing the types of information required at all steps of the decision-making process. This includes information on problems in current operations, information on new opportunities available to the organization, and information on threats to the continued existence of the organization. Operational, tactical, and strategic decisions are all supported by an information-based DSS. Three types of reports are generated by virtually every type of information-based DSS: scheduled reports, exception reports, and demand reports. Each serves a different purpose to the managers and employees of the organization, but all are important. Scheduled reports reflect the periodic and historic information on the organization's operations. Exception reports are generated only if some condition—usually an exceptional event—activates the generation of a report. Demand reports are specialized reports that a manager may request when he or she needs specific information on a particular subject.

How do top-level executives and the information they require differ from other managers? The top policymaking executives of any organization are responsible for the long-term well-being of the organization. They must have a vision of the organization beyond just a single department or one budgeting period. Executives also tend to do different types of work from lower-level managers. It has been observed that executives carry out three types of roles: interpersonal, informational, and decisional. An executive must be doing many things each day, and time is his or her most precious commodity. An executive must be vigilant for problems that will need to be solved and, as such, requires information from many sources in an easy-to-use form that differs from person to person. For this reason, the information-based DSS for an executive must be a "personalized presentation system" that shows the information the executive wants in the form he or she desires.

Searching the Web has become a popular way for individuals at all managerial levels to find needed information. Search engines can help this search but often return useless Web sites. Intelligent agents (bots) are one way to improve this search process.

In what ways does a data-based DSS provide answers to questions? In many situations the decision maker has questions for which there is no available information. This requires some type of *data-based DSS* to use in finding the answers, including SQL, online analytical processing (OLAP), and data mining, where the latter two methodologies access data in a data warehouse. OLAP is a software tool that enables an analyst to extract and view data from a variety of points of view using a multidimensional database. This can involve a "slice and dice" approach to answer "who?" and "what?" questions or drill down to answer "what if?" and "why?" questions about the data. On the other hand, data mining is a way to search relationships within the data in a data warehouse. Typical data mining approaches include searching for associations, sequences, classifications, groups, or time-based relationships in the data. A seven-step approach is used to search for these patterns. Neural networks are one approach to data mining.

How does a model-based DSS answer questions from decision makers?
Finding solutions to problems facing decision makers is usually handled by a *model-based DSS,* which does this through the use of quantitative and graphical models. A model-based DSS has three major parts: the database, the model base, and the user. The database contains the data necessary to carry out the needed analyses. The model base contains a variety of types of models that can be used to analyze the data from the database. Finally, the user is the decision maker or analyst who is seeking the solution to a problem. To make this possible, it is necessary to have three software systems: a data management system, which manages the retrieval of data from a database as needed; a model management system, which is used to select a model that can be used to help arrive at a solution; and a user interface system, which handles the interactions between analyst and computer. The models are a group of computer programs that will perform specific operations on the data from a database where a model is a simplified version of reality that captures the interrelationships between important variables in the situation. There are four primary types of models: forecasting, statistics, optimization, and simulation.

⊙ Review Questions

1. How do decision support systems fit into the information systems cycle?

2. List the three types of decision support systems in use today. Which used to be the only one with this name?

3. What types of information systems have we included as part of an information-based DSS?

4. Name the three types of reports generated by an information-based DSS. Explain the purpose of each.

5. In what ways do top-level executives differ from mid-level managers? How does this affect the type of information they need and the manner in which it is delivered?

6. What two methodologies are typically included in a data-based DSS? Where do the data come from?

7. What is the difference between "slicing and dicing" and "drill down" in an OLAP?

8. What are the four commonly used approaches to data mining? How are neural networks used in a data-based DSS?

9. What are the three key components in a model-based DSS? How are they implemented?

10. What is the role of a model in a model-based DSS? Name and discuss the four types of models commonly used in DSS. Which one tries to find the best solution to a problem?

> ⊘ Discussion Questions

1. Discuss why a good information-based DSS is, to some degree, invisible. Does this indicate that it is losing its importance to the organization?

2. Discuss the concept of an enterprise information portal as it relates to decision making.

3. Discuss the concept of the analyst in the use of decision support models.

> ⊘ CASE

WildOutfitters.com

"You should set up to run trips, you could do much better than those guys. I mean it was the funniest thing that I ever saw!"

Alex was leaning over a counter of the Wild Outfitter booth at the Gauley Riverfest listening to one of their regular customers describe what he had seen that day on the river. The Gauley Riverfest is an annual festival put on by rafters and paddlers timed to correspond with the release of water into the Gauley, a Class IV–VI river in West Virginia. Water is released into the river only over a period of four weekends in the fall of each year. The festival has developed into a sort of trade show for rafting and paddling equipment, as well as a chance to party after a day on a world-class river.

The Campagnes have set up a booth with the goals of advertising their presence in the area and selling a few products.

"I bet most of the clients were asking for refunds …" the man continued. Alex nodded, only half listening. His mind had begun to wander at the time the man said that he and Claire should run trips.

For a while now, Alex and Claire have been thinking of offering adventure travel packages. Typical adventure travel packages revolve around an outdoor activity, such as whitewater rafting or mountaineering. They have been on several such trips and have also had the opportunity to observe others while going about their own adventures. Based on these observations, coupled with their own experience, they feel that they are very qualified to add these adventure travel packages to the Wild Outfitters product line.

They are eager to expand their business into this new area, and so far they have discussed a few of the decisions that they need to make. First, they have decided what types of activities to offer. The packages will also include various levels of amenities, ranging from simple guide services to more elaborate lodging and food services. Thus, they have planned a mixture of services and activities for each package. They then tried to get some

idea of what resources are required to offer these services. These resources include such items as equipment and personnel for the trips, as well as general business resources. An accurate forecast of the resource needs is an important step towards predicting the monetary resources that will be required. Their next step is to obtain financing in the form of a loan to cover their expansion.

To apply for the loan, Alex and Claire will need to provide projected financial statements and a cohesive, clear business plan. A main function of a business plan is to provide a communications tool that conveys the ideas and plans of the business to others. There are some basic elements of a business plan. These elements include: a summary of the basic business idea, the products or services that will be offered, who will comprise the market for the products, how the products or services will be provided, how many employees will be needed, any production plans, and the expected cash requirements. Besides building and equipment needs, a business should also have enough money on hand to cover operating expenses for at least a year. These expenses include the owners' salaries and money to repay the loans. The plan should also answer the typical questions asked by lenders: How will the loan be used? How much is needed to borrow? How will the loan be repaid? The financial statements, including forecasts, will be needed to support the business plan. A balance sheet, which is a record of assets, liabilities, and capital; and the income statement, which is a summary of earnings and expenses over a given period of time, are the statements most often prepared. These will demonstrate a business' past performance as well as provide forecasts of the expected future performance after the expansion. Any assumptions made when making the forecasts should also be included.

"… How they could have the rafts, the guides, and the clients at the river and ready to go without the rest of the equipment I'll never know," the man went on. Laughing, he gave Alex a good-natured smack on the back, breaking him out of his reverie. "I've heard of being up the creek without a paddle, but never thought I'd see it with my own eyes."

Alex decided to leave the business thoughts behind and began to pick up the conversation again. After all, Gauley Riverfest only happens once a year.

1. Make a list of several decisions that need to be made by a small business such as Wild Outfitters. For each decision, describe how a decision support system could help the Campagnes to make more effective and efficient decisions.

2. How would you classify the decisions that need to be made by Claire and Alex in this case? Are they structured or unstructured? Are they tactical, operational, or strategic? Identify any data and model requirements.

3. *(Hands on)* Using a spreadsheet software package (such as MS Excel) develop a quantitative model to forecast Wild Outfitters' expected earnings from the current business and expected earnings with the addition of an adventure travel service. A text file containing a Wild Outfitters balance sheet, income statement, and forecasting assumptions is available on the text's web page at www.harcourtcollege.com/infosys/mckeown. The model should be designed for "WHAT–IF" scenarios so that the forecast values change automatically with changes in input values. It should also use the graphics capability of spreadsheet software to create appropriate charts for your results.

4. *(Hands on)* Using a business presentation software package (such as MS PowerPoint) prepare a presentation in the format of a business plan to show to potential investors. Be sure to incorporate the major elements of a business plan discussed in the case as well as the forecasts and charts from your spreadsheet model of question 3.

Preparing for the Future with Electronic Commerce

⊙ Learning Objectives

After reading this chapter, you should be able to answer the following questions:

⊙ What is electronic commerce, and how does it relate to the networked economy?

⊙ How is electronic commerce changing the way business is carried out?

⊙ How are technologies used to facilitate electronic commerce?

⊙ Which electronic commerce strategies should companies consider using?

⊙ How are electronic commerce transactions protected from criminal activity?

⊙ What are the various electronic commerce payment methods in use today and predicted for the future?

Ⓕocus on Management

Electronic Commerce at Dell Computers

If there were to be a poster child for electronic commerce, it would have to be Dell Computers. Started by college student Michael Dell in 1984, at age nineteen, in his Texas dorm room, Dell has been highly successful in the personal computer market by selling directly to its customers with no middleman. Dell initially did this by using telephone sales but more recently has aggressively moved into electronic commerce as a way of connecting with its customers. Online sales in 1999 were over $14 million *per day*, with 20 percent of all sales conducted via the Web. This number is expected to reach 50 percent of sales by the year 2000. Although Dell has only 10 percent of the PC market, it earns between 70 and 80 percent of the industry's net profit. At the same time that IBM was posting a $1 billion loss in PC sales for 1998, and Compaq was firing its CEO, Dell was showing a 55 percent increase in earnings with $1.46 billion in profits.

The Dell Web site (www.dell.com) has made the direct sales model the heart of its approach to electronic commerce. By providing greater convenience and efficiency to its customers, the Web site has further simplified the process of selecting and purchasing a computer. Dell custom builds every computer so that customers get exactly what they want and, by having no middlemen with old inventory to push, the customer always gets the latest in technology. Although Dell serves all markets, it has been extremely successful in the corporate market by cre-

ating "Premier" Web pages for each of its large customers to make their purchasing process even easier. Dell also improved its support services by making the Web work as a front end to its internal databases so that its customers and suppliers can see the same support information it uses internally.

Michael Dell started Dell Computers as a teenager. The company has enjoyed great success selling directly to its customers.

Electronic Commerce and the Networked Economy

In the previous three chapters, we have considered the use of information systems to help organizations handle the present, remember the past, and prepare for the future. In this chapter, we will complete that discussion by considering the ways in which electronic commerce also will help organizations prepare for the future. This topic should not be altogether new to you because it has been mentioned in all of the first six chapters. You might have noticed that the opening boxes for the first seven chapters have involved the use of electronic commerce or the Web to provide customer service. In addition, our example company, fareastfoods.com, uses electronic commerce to market, sell, and distribute a variety of Oriental food items.

Whether it is called e-commerce, e-business, e-tailing, or some other name, electronic commerce is changing the business world. Where at one time the debate in most businesses was whether or not to engage in electronic commerce, today the debate is over exactly how to go about engaging in electronic commerce. Companies like Dell Computers, which do the best job of using the Internet and the World Wide Web, are the most likely to be successful, whereas some other companies may find themselves out of business. Even companies that do not engage actively in marketing their services over the Web will be affected by electronic commerce through the wide variety of comparison Web sites that enable a user to make an informed decision between companies offering similar products. Although the subject of electronic commerce could take up an entire book (and does),[1] this chapter will try to summarize most elements of this important topic as they relate to your understanding of information technology and the networked economy.

To begin our discussion, we need a concise definition of this topic. **Electronic commerce** is the use of computer networks to improve organizational performance. Increasing profitability, gaining market share, improving customer service, and delivering products faster are some of the organizational performance gains possible with electronic commerce. Electronic commerce is more than ordering goods from an on-line catalog. It involves all aspects of an organization's electronic interactions with its **stakeholders**—the people who determine the future of the organization. Thus, electronic commerce includes many activities, such as establishing a Web site to support investor relations or communicating electronically with college students who are potential employees. In the case of Dell Computers in the opening Focus on Management box, it has links on its Web pages for all stakeholder groups and has found ways to link customers and suppliers directly into its customer support databases.

The Effects of Electronic Commerce

The growth of Web-based electronic commerce has affected companies around the world in one way or another. To help you understand the ways in which companies have been affected, they can be categorized into five groups. Notice that we do not say "types of companies that are affected" because all companies will be affected, for better or worse. Obviously, you would like to work for a company that will be positively affected, so you might want to keep this discussion in mind when choosing an employer. The five categories of companies are shown in Table 7-1.[2]

In looking at Table 7-1, Internet companies are those that provide services for accessing the Web or facilitate using the Web. They did not exist prior to the introduction of the Web and would go out of business if the Web ceased to exist. Companies like Yahoo! (a directory of Web sites—www.yahoo.com), Alta Vista (a popular Web

Table 7-1 Categories of Companies Affected by Electronic Commerce

Category	Description	Examples
Internet companies	Companies that exist because of the Internet and Web	Yahoo!, Mindspring
New approaches	Companies that use the Web to carry out already-existing business activities in a new way	Amazon.com, Net.B@nk
Transformed	Companies that have used the Web to creatively destroy their existing business, transforming themselves into a different type of company or a company that has different business activities	UPS, Edmund's, Dell Computers
Adapting	Companies that are trying to adapt by using electronic commerce for an existing business activity	Delta Airlines, Lands' End
Hurt by electronic commerce	Companies that will be endangered by the introduction of electronic commerce or are ignoring it	Malls, construction companies

1. Richard Watson et al., *Electronic Commerce: The Strategic Prospective* (Fort Worth, TX: The Dryden Press, 1999).

2. This discussion is based on *e-Commerce: Virtually Here* by Jeanne G. Terrile, first vice president of Merrill Lynch & Co. http://e-commerce.research.ml.com/41209903.PDF.

search engine—www.altavista.com), and Mindspring (a large Internet service provider—www.mindspring.com) are examples of this category. Because of their close association with the Web and Internet, companies in this category are often referred to as *Internet companies* and have been the subject of great interest as their stock went up dramatically in 1998 and 1999. Another Internet company is America Online (AOL). Although AOL existed before the introduction of the Web, it has used the Web to greatly expand its business of providing information to users at www.aol.com. As long as there is a need for the Web, companies in this category will continue to exist, and new ones will be added to meet new needs.

On the other hand, companies in the second category (new approaches) did not exist before the introduction of the Web but have taken an existing business model and used the Web to implement it differently. These include companies like Amazon.com (books and CDs), eBay (auctions), PriceLine.com (reverse auction), and Net.B@nk (banking). By going electronic, these businesses have been able to reduce their overhead and fixed costs, allowing them to offer goods and services at a lower cost (hopefully) with no loss in customer service. Because the incremental cost of handling an additional transaction is so low, some of these firms have placed their emphasis on gaining market share rather than on increasing profitability. Their strategy is to exclude competitors by controlling a large portion of the market.

In the third category (transformed), companies are using electronic commerce to creatively destroy their previous business model and transform themselves into a new type of business. Most of these companies existed before the introduction of the Web but are now doing things differently. For example, prior to the introduction of the Web, Edmund's was a respected publisher of automotive information in magazines and books. When the Web was introduced, the company decided that its existing business model was no longer appropriate and began publishing the same information on the Web *for free* at www.edmunds.com with revenue being generated by advertising and links to other companies.

The fourth category (adapting) includes the vast majority of businesses in existence today. They are aware of the potential that electronic commerce offers and realize that they must take advantage of it. However, they are still trying to find ways to adapt it

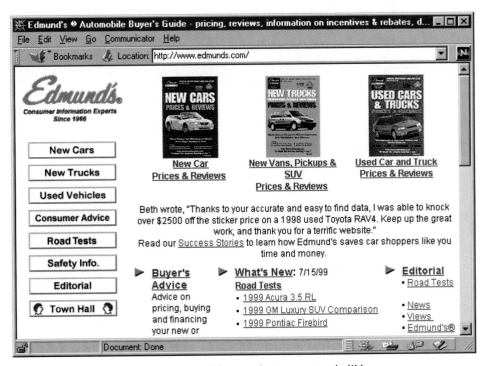

Edmund's has creatively transformed itself by giving away its contents over the Web.

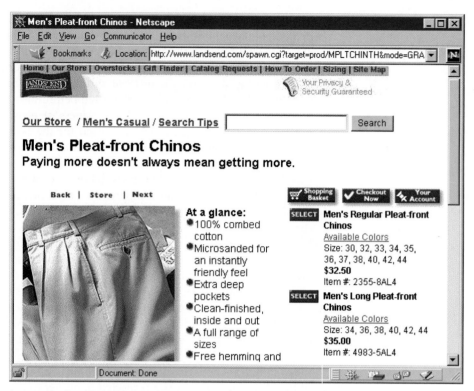

Some companies adapt existing businesses to take advantage of electronic commerce.

to their business model or vice versa. For example, while airlines like Delta (www.delta-air.com) are using the Web to enable their customers to make reservations and purchase tickets, they are still exploring other ways to use the Web to serve their customers better as are catalog companies like Lands' End (www.landsend.com).

Finally, the last category shows that there are companies that will be hurt by the Web, primarily because they are unwilling to practice creative destruction and find new ways of carrying on business that take advantage of the new electronic infrastructure. For example, companies that own, manage, or build large amounts of retail space will need to find new ways of using their existing infrastructure or skills. Ignoring electronic commerce is one sure way for companies to be hurt by it as they begin to lose customers to firms that do employ electronic commerce.

Quick Review

1. List two other so-called Internet companies with which you are familiar.
2. Why is the concept of creative destruction of great importance to companies today?

A Different Way of Doing Business

Just as the networked economy is changing the way we look at many elements of our lives, so, too, are Internet technology and the World Wide Web creating a revolution in business. The Web does this in a number of ways, including leveling the playing field, reversing the direction of communication between buyers and sellers, and changing the nature of intermediaries. As a result of these changes, companies are being affected in one way or another. In this section, we will consider the changes that Web-based electronic commerce is bringing about and how these changes are affecting companies.

Leveling the Playing Field

Typically, large businesses have advantages over small businesses because of their size and resources. A large business has greater access to the customer because of its many outlets and its capability to advertise more. It also tends to have a greater voice—that is, it can drown out its competitors by the volume of its advertising. A large business can also exclude potential competitors by raising barriers to entry into the market, say, by dominating the distribution channels. For example, a company like fareastfoods.com would have great difficulty trying to compete with the large national grocery chains due to their size and number of outlets. However, the Web levels the playing field in business in a variety of ways, including:

- Making access opportunities essentially equal for all companies, regardless of size
- Making the share of voice essentially uniform—no company can drown out others
- Making initial setup costs so low as to present minimal or nonexistent barriers to entry

In the first case, small companies with a well-designed Web site can look every bit as professional and credible as a large, multinational company. Visitors can't tell if the business operates from a Manhattan skyscraper or a garage. A small business can establish a Web presence for less than $20 per month and be just as accessible as the corporation spending $50,000 a month on its Web site. In addition, building a Web site for a business no longer requires a knowledge of hypertext markup language, graphic design, and handling credit cards. Companies such as IBM are making electronic commerce Web site creation services available over the Web for a modest cost.[3]

The IBM HomePage Creator software allows small businesses to create e-commerce Web sites.

3. See www.ibm.com/hpc.

Similarly, in traditional advertising media, the big corporation can dominate because it has more to spend. On the Web, no one can dominate because all Web sites are equally accessible. Finally, a company can use the Web combined with package delivery companies to avoid the traditional barriers to entry put up by existing firms. Firms like fareastfoods.com with its well-designed Web site, e-mail marketing, and fast delivery of a variety of types of Oriental foods can compete with any of the large chains.

Reversing the Flow of Communications

Electronic commerce has reversed the flow of communication: Instead of sending messages to customers, a firm now wants customers to converge on its Web site. **Customer convergence** is the key to Web marketing. Unless customers find a firm's Web site, the entire effort is wasted. This means a firm must ensure that its Web site is found by any of the search engines a customer may elect to use. Even more, a firm with many products must ensure that potential customers converge on the page that describes the product or service of greatest potential interest. Thus, a camera manufacturer must first make certain that photography enthusiasts find its Web site and then help the potential customer, possibly with the aid of an expert system, navigate to the pages describing the cameras or lenses of interest.

The shift from traditional broadcast advertising to customer convergence fundamentally changes the relationship between the advertiser and the customer, as summarized in Table 7-2. The initiative moves to the customer, who now decides which Web pages to view, when to view them, what part of the message to read, and how the message is presented. For example, a customer may decide to ignore an advertiser's message by never visiting its Web site or to disregard an important element of a message by not playing audio clips.

This **communication flip-flop** is a fundamental change in the nature of the relationship between buyers and sellers. With electronic commerce, the customer is royalty, and customer service is the primary element that will keep customers coming back to the Web site. As buyers increasingly use the Web to learn about new products and services, sellers will have to find ways of attracting visitors to their Web site, enticing them to read their messages, buy their products, and, most importantly, come back again. In many cases, sellers do this by gathering information about the customer that they can use to better serve the customer on future visits. For example, if you visit an online bookstore or CD mart, it will often alert you to new books or CDs that match what the Web site has learned from your previous visits. Referred to as **mass customization,** this personal touch for every buyer is a way of building customer loyalty because going to a competing Web site will require that we "teach" it our interests and buying patterns—a time-consuming task.

Changing Role of Intermediaries

In traditional commerce, we are used to the role of **intermediaries**—individuals and companies that act as *middlemen* or brokers between the consumer and the company providing the good or service. In many industries, there is a real need for intermediaries (e.g., the fresh fruit business). None of us really wants to try to deal

Table 7-2 Communications Flip-Flop	
Traditional Advertiser	**Web Customer**
Decides audience	Decides advertiser
Decides schedule	Decides schedule
Decides message content	Selects and customizes content
Decides media for distribution	Decides how message is presented

ⓕ o c u s   o n   P e o p l e

Tim Berners-Lee

When one thinks of electronic commerce, the immediate response is the World Wide Web because it is the primary operation that has facilitated so much of the commercial activity on the Internet. It is interesting to note that, where the creation of the Internet was the work of a group of people, the Web was invented by a sole individual—Tim Berners-Lee. While working at CERN (the European Particle Physics Library in Geneva) for six months in 1980, Berners-Lee began thinking about ways to store random associations of disparate things on computers. As a result of this thought, he wrote a program that actually saved information with random links. This program, named "Enquire", though never published, was the predecessor of the Web.

In 1984, Berners-Lee went back to work for CERN and, in 1989, proposed a project that would use hypertext to link random "pages" of information. This project was to be known as the World Wide Web, and the idea was to enable users to work together by sharing information in a *web* of hypertext documents. He began work on the first Web-server software and the first browser in 1990, and made both available within CERN in December of that year and on the Internet at large in the summer of 1991. Between 1991 and 1993, Berners-Lee worked on the design of the Web based on feedback from Internet users. The first Windows-based browser, Mosaic, was released in 1994 and the rest is history. In that same year, Berners-Lee joined the Laboratory for Computer Science (LCS) at the Massachusetts Institute of Technology (MIT) and, in 1999, he became the first holder of the 3Com Founders chair. He is also a director of the World Wide Web Consortium, which coordinates Web development worldwide.

Source: www.w3.org/People/Bemers-Lee/Longer.html.

Tim Berners-Lee invented the World Wide Web and, as a result, changed the face of business.

directly with the banana grower, so we are happy to buy just the bananas we want from a market. However, as discussed in the Focus on Management box on Dell Computers, electronic commerce can remove the need for intermediaries through such programs as Dell Direct. Similarly, although travelers customarily have used a travel agent, who acts as an intermediary between us and the airline or tour company, this is also changing. Today, because it is so easy to find the cheapest airfare from Chicago to Lisbon, Portugal, and to buy the ticket directly from the airline, the need for travel agents is shrinking. The same thing is true about insurance brokers; why go to an insurance broker when the prices and terms are all on the Web? You can probably think of many more cases where intermediaries could be eliminated by the Web.

The process of eliminating intermediaries is termed **disintermediation** and this process is casting a large shadow over many segments of business whose primary function was gathering information from suppliers and passing it along to consumers. Although many intermediaries will cease to exist, others like Manheim Auctions will find ways to recast themselves to meet new needs in electronic commerce. As discussed in chapter 4, Manheim Auctions has moved from being strictly an intermediary at physical auctions to being an electronic intermediary with the Manheim Online service. This is a process known as **reintermediation.**

Quick Review

1. In what ways is electronic commerce changing the way business is carried out?
2. Give two examples of communications flip-flop.

Electronic Commerce Infrastructure

Electronic commerce is built on top of a number of different technologies. These technologies created a layered, integrated infrastructure that permits the development and deployment of electronic commerce applications, as shown in Figure 7-1. Each layer is founded on the layer below it and cannot function without it.[4]

National Information Infrastructure

The **national information infrastructure layer** is the bedrock of electronic commerce because all traffic must be transmitted by one or more of the communication networks comprising the **national information infrastructure (NII)**. The components of an NII include the TV and radio broadcast industries, cable TV, telephone networks, cellular communication systems, computer networks, and the Internet. The trend in many countries is to increase competition among the various elements of

Figure 7-1   Electronic Commerce Infrastructure

| Electronic Commerce Applications |
| Business Services Infrastructure |
| Electronic Publishing Infrastructure |
| Message Distribution Infrastructure |
| National Information Infrastructure |

---

4. This section is based on P. G. McKeown and R. T. Watson, *Metamorphosis: A Guide to the World Wide Web and Electronic Commerce,* V 2.0 (New York: John Wiley, 1997), pp. 127–128.

the NII to increase its overall efficiency because it is believed that an NII is critical to the creation of national wealth.

Message Distribution Infrastructure

The **message distribution infrastructure layer** consists of software for sending and receiving messages. Its purpose is to deliver a message from a server to a client. For example, it could move a hypertext markup language (HTML) file from a Web server to a client running a Web browser like Netscape Navigator or Internet Explorer. Messages can be unformatted (e.g., e-mail) or formatted (e.g., a purchase order). Electronic data interchange (EDI), e-mail, and hypertext transfer protocol (HTTP) are examples of messaging software.

Electronic Publishing Infrastructure

The Web is a good example of the **electronic publishing infrastructure layer.** It permits organizations to publish a full range of text and multimedia. There are three key elements of the Web:

- A uniform resource locator (URL), which is used to uniquely identify any server
- A network protocol (TCP/IP)
- A structured markup language (HTML)

Notice that the electronic publishing layer is still concerned with some of the issues solved by TCP/IP for the Internet part of the NII layer. There is still a need to consider addressability (i.e., a URL) and to have a common language across the network (i.e., HTTP and HTML). However, these are built upon the previous layer, in the case of a URL, or at a higher level, in the case of HTML.

Business Services Infrastructure

The principal purpose of the **business services infrastructure layer** is to support common business processes. Nearly every business, for example, is concerned with collecting payment for the goods and services it sells. Thus, the business services layer supports the secure transmission of credit card numbers between a customer and an online merchant. In general, the business services layer should include facilities for encryption and authentication (see the section on electronic commerce security, later in this chapter).

An Electronic Commerce Application

Finally, on top of all the other layers sits an application with which the customer interacts. This is the part of the electronic commerce infrastructure where the transaction takes place, and any Web site where you have purchased a product or compared products has just such an electronic commerce application. We have discussed this layer in detail in chapter 4, which considered transaction processing from both a consumer and a business point of view. Examples of well-known business applications are the extensive catalogs of books and CDs available at a number of Web sites, the listing of automobiles available at the Manheim Online Web site discussed in chapter 4, and the database of machine parts available from the Kompass International site in chapter 5.

Although all of the other layers of this model are located on the server, the application layer is a classic example of the four-tiered client/server model discussed in earlier chapters—that is, a browser on the customer's computer communicating with a Web server, which in turn communicates with application and database servers. For very simple applications, the database, applications, and Web servers are one and the same, but for high-volume or complex applications, the database and application servers are located on separate machines. In any case, the Web browser on the client machine interacts with the Web server software to complete the transaction, as shown in Figure 7-2.

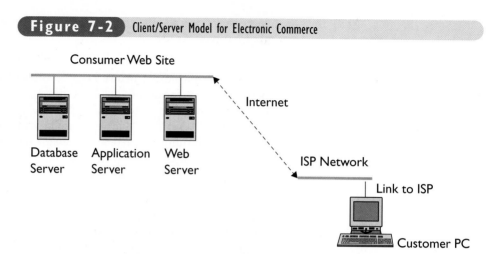

Figure 7-2 Client/Server Model for Electronic Commerce

Figure 7-3 Electronic Commerce Infrastructure for fareastfoods.com

Electronic Commerce Applications	Food Item Catalog
Business Services Infrastructure	Encryption
Electronic Publishing Infrastructure	HTML
Message Distribution Infrastructure	HTTP
National Information Infrastructure	Internet

Application to fareastfoods.com

For an example of the electronic commerce infrastructure, consider again fareastfoods.com with its online catalog of food items. The electronic commerce infrastructure for this example is shown in Figure 7-3. In this case, the application is fareastfoods.com's food item catalog with its capability to transact purchases from customers and have orders created and sent to them. The business services infrastructure uses encryption to protect a customer's credit card number. Because this is a Web site, the electronic publishing infrastructure involves the use of HTML, and the message distribution infrastructure uses HTTP to deliver the Web page to the customer and to deliver the order form back to the company. Finally, the NII uses the Internet to send the messages between the customer and fareastfoods.com.

Quick Review

1. List the five layers of the electronic commerce infrastructure.
2. What is the purpose of the message distribution infrastructure?

Electronic Commerce Strategies

Each organization needs to consider its electronic commerce strategy as a way to reduce the risks it faces (i.e., demand risk, innovation risk, and inefficiency risk). Because the organization's strategy will be developed around its Web site, understanding types of Web sites is essential to developing the strategy. Finally, not only must the Web site be of the correct type, but also it must attract customers who will purchase goods and services. In this section, we will discuss the issues involved in creating a Web-based electronic commerce strategy.

Handling Risks

The first question that any organization should ask itself is: Why should we be engaged in electronic commerce? To answer this question, the organization should consider the three types of risks faced by every organization, as discussed in chapter 4—demand risks, innovation risks, and inefficiency risks—and then look for ways by which electronic commerce can reduce one or more of those risks. We have already discussed reducing inefficiency risks in earlier chapters. Demand and innovation risks can also be reduced through the use of electronic commerce. In terms of demand risks, because the Web is global, millions of people have Web access, and this number is growing rapidly, there is unlimited potential to create demand through electronic commerce. Furthermore, many Web users are well-educated, affluent consumers—an ideal target for consumer marketing. Any firm establishing a Web presence, no matter how small or localized, instantly enters global marketing. The firm's message can be read by anyone with Web access. Thus, the Web offers an excellent opportunity for reducing demand risk by diversifying into new markets.

A new medium for advertising, the Web enables firms to develop a Web site where their products and services are described and promoted in considerable detail. A particular advantage of Web advertising is that it can be changed very quickly. Advertisements for traditional media (print, radio, and TV) are not as fortunate. For example, a glossy brochure may take weeks to prepare and distribute, and there is still the danger that many customers are referring to an older version. A Web site can be updated easily and quickly, and customers always see the latest version. Web advertising means that firms can react quickly to changing demand and adjust customer communication with great speed.

In terms of innovation risk, Internet communication (e-mail, lists, and news) can be used to create open communication links with a wide range of customers. E-mail can facilitate frequent communication with the most innovative customers. A list can be created to enable any customer to request product changes or new features. The advantage of a list is that another customer reading an idea may contribute to its development and elaboration. Also, a firm can monitor relevant newsgroups to discern what customers are saying about its products or services as well as those of competitors.

A firm can use the Web to pilot new ways of interacting with customers and other stakeholders. For example, it might experiment with different ways of marketing and delivering products and services; or, it can develop new communication channels with employees. Above all, firms need to be innovative in using the Web and in finding ways to access creative innovations.

Types of Web Sites

In order to develop a Web-based electronic commerce strategy, it is useful to understand the types of Web sites. There are a number of ways to classify Web sites, ranging from business versus personal Web sites to the topology of the Web sites to the types of applications that they are being used for. In our case, we will consider only business-related Web sites. For these sites, we can use the same Internet technology classification system introduced in chapters 3 and 4—Internet, intranets, and extranets. Recall that the **Internet** is global in extent, whereas an **intranet** is limited to the organization, and an **extranet** is based on business partnerships. In terms of electronic commerce Web sites, these can be thought of as the three **Web topologies** that are used, with each having a different audience, as shown in Table 7-3. Intranets are included in this classification because electronic commerce was defined as using networks to improve organizational performance, and the use of an intranet to facilitate organizational communication does just that. The use of extranets for handling business-to-business transaction processing, which is an essential part of electronic commerce was also discussed previously. We will use this classification system in the discussion of other aspects of electronic commerce.

Although a company will usually be quite aware of the audience to which it markets—consumers or other businesses—it may not be very sure about the appropriate business model to use in developing its Web presence. There are basically eight business models, with each having the same goal—to find a customer need, build

Table 7-3	Electronic Commerce Classifications		
Topology	**Internet**	**Intranet**	**Extranet**
Extent	Global	Organizational	Business partnerships
Type of electronic commerce	Business to consumer	Business to employees	Business to business

demand, fulfill the demand, and then repeat the process. The eight models are shown in Table 7-4, along with a description, the Web site topology used, and an example. The models are arranged from those that you are probably most familiar to those that you may not have thought of.

In looking at Table 7-4, we can see that the first four classifications are business-to-consumer models that attempt to generate revenue by selling goods and services over the Internet (e-tailers/e-malls and communities of interest), by advertising (portals), or by charging a fee for a service (auctions). The fifth business model, informediaries, generates revenue by charging members for information that they need. The last three business models are aimed at the business-to-business value chain using Internet technology.

The company that we have been following, fareastfoods.com, would be classified as an "e-tailer" company that uses the Internet to sell food items directly to consumers. It uses a value chain service provider like UPS to handle the distribution of the food items to its customers and may use a process/services improvement company to handle its supply chain management to move food items from the suppliers to the company. From this, it should be obvious that business-to-consumer companies will be using the business-to-business Web sites to help them better manage their value chain.

Table 7-4	Business Models on the Web		
Business Model	**Description**	**Topology**	**Example**
E-tailers/ E-malls	Retail sites aimed at the Web consumer	Internet	Lands' End (www.landsend.com)
Portals	Sites that are major starting points for users when they connect to the Web	Internet	Yahoo! (www.yahoo.com)
Auctions	Sites that enable an online shopping population to bid on items as well as to offer items for sale	Internet	eBay.com (www.ebay.com)
Communities of interest (COI)	Sites that create niche content and context for their members	Internet	wine.com (www.wine.com)
Informediaries	Sites that gather, organize, and link to new information and services on the Web	Internets Extranets	Chemdex (www.chemdex.com)
Process/Services improvements	Business sites aimed at improving supply chain management processes internally and externally	Intranets Extranets	Manheim Online (www.manheim.com)
Value chain service providers	Sites for companies that focus on dominating a specific function of the value chain	Extranets	UPS (www.ups.com)
Value chain integrations	Sites for companies that integrate all steps in a market's value chain	Extranets	WebMD (www.webmd.com)

Source: Adapted from Z. B. Singh, "Super Markets," *Business 2.0,* March 1999, pp. 80–85.

Ⓕocus on the Internet

The PGA Tour

Information technology has been used in sports for a number of years; however, its use to help professional golfers plan their tour schedules is new. Each of the 204 eligible golfers on the Professional Golfers Association (PGA) tour is a small business person who must manage and make decisions about their schedule, travel, accommodations, and so on. In this sense, they, like tennis professionals, are different from members of team sports like basketball and baseball, where the athlete is not involved in these decisions. For example, a typical PGA member will travel thirty weeks of the year, selecting tournaments to enter from those scheduled each week. Once a tournament is selected, the golfer must then make arrangements to enter the tournament. During the season, PGA headquarters will often need to communicate with golfers and tournament liaisons will want to send them information. If all of this communication were handled via faxes or postal mail, it would be too bulky for a golfer to carry as they traveled around the country.

To solve this problem, IBM, a tour sponsor, created an intranet specifically for tour players into which they can dial using customized laptops. Once into the intranet, players can select from over sixty areas, including ones with tournament schedules for the year, information on each tournament, and their ranking on the tour compared to other golfers. Golfers can use the schedule area to enter tournaments and they can use the information area to find information about Pro-Am events. In the first three months of operation of the intranet, all but seventeen of the tour players were participating with 20 percent of all tournament commitments being made online. The intranet also has links that help golfers manage their career, including an expense-reporting function that eases the process of tracking travel expenses; golfers can add these expenses as they occur rather than having to deal with three weeks of receipts on a weekend off. The intranet is being connected into extranet connections with tour sponsors like Delta, and hotels at tournament sites, which will further ease the golfer's job of managing their careers.

Source: Linda M. Castellitto, "Web's Now Par on the Course." *Internet World*, March 29, 1999, p. 17.

Professional golfers can use their laptops to connect to the PGA intranet to carry out a variety of scheduling activities.

Strategic Planning

Once a company has decided on the business model that it wishes to use in developing its Web presence, it must then find ways to attract customers to its site, not just on a one-time basis, but on a repeat basis. A Web site that attracts very few visitors or the wrong type of visitors is a very poor investment. Thus, organizations need to consider whom they want to attract to their Web site and how they might attract them. Because a Web site is essentially located on a one-way street with no other stores on the street, it must be an **attractor** to bring customers in on a repeat basis. As a rule, an organization should concentrate on attracting the most influential stakeholders. Remember that these are the groups that can determine an enterprise's future. Usually, an organization will want to attract prospective customers, but other groups can impact the future of the organization and can be the target of a Web site. For example, a firm can use its intranet Web site to communicate with employees, or it may want to attract and inform investors and potential suppliers. Once the targeted stakeholder group has been selected, the organization needs to decide on the degree of personalization of its interaction with this group.

There are many ways to attract people to your Web site for an initial visit, including advertising on other popular Web sites with links to yours or in other media (television, newspapers, etc.), having your site prominently displayed on a portal site like Yahoo!, or offering games or giveaways. However, to attract people on a repeat basis, your site must provide customers with something they want—a line of products, a service, or

Product giveaways and advertising in other media help attract potential customers.

information. Once you have attracted them for the first time, the real trick is to turn them into repeat customers. One feature that is common to all Web sites that are good attractors, especially for repeat visits, is **interactivity,** which is the capability of the Web site to interact with the user in some way. And, in most cases, the greater the interactivity, the greater the attractiveness of the site. The only caveat to this statement is that a high degree of interactivity should not make the site slow and unresponsive.

Although most Web sites are interactive to some degree in that they allow the user to click through to Web pages on the same site, or to Web pages on other sites, this level of interactivity often does little to make the site attractive. To achieve attractiveness, one or both of two features are usually required: use of a programming language to make the page respond to a user's requests and linkage to a database. In the first case, the computer code is either embedded in the HTML script for the page like Javascript or VBScript or is a small Java or ActiveX computer program that accompanies the Web site and is launched by the user.

In terms of accessing a database, this is absolutely essential for electronic commerce Web sites that are accepting orders for products. To provide adequate service, a Web-based retailer must be able to query a product database to determine if the product is in stock and then query a credit card database to verify that the credit card number is acceptable. Only after both databases have been queried and returned acceptable answers can the product be considered as "sold." Writing programs that are a part of the Web site and querying a database from a Web site require a good understanding of Web page mechanics, as well as programming and database skills. However, this is an exciting field with many rewards for those who choose to study this field.

A Two-Stage Model to Attractiveness

Beyond interactivity, it is often necessary to identify the strategic properties of a Web site that will make it attractive to selected stakeholders. To do this, a two-stage model has been suggested. Shown in Figure 7-4, the first stage involves using some sort of **influence filter** that makes the site more attractive to the stakeholder group selected earlier and less attractive to others. Once this group has been attracted, the degree of customization for the Web site—the **target refractor**—should be created.

Influence filters are features about the site that determine the group that will be attracted to the site. For example, the Kellogg's Company Web site[5] attracts children by having a number of features that make it fun for them to visit. One such feature lets young visitors pick a drawing and color it by selecting from a palette and clicking

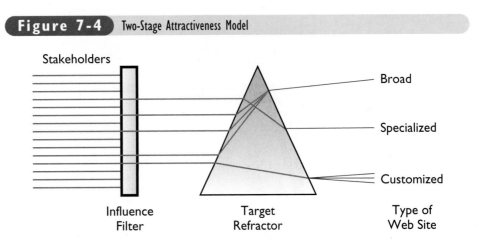

Figure 7-4 Two-Stage Attractiveness Model

Source: Richard T. Watson, Sigmund Akelsen, and Leyland F. Pitt, "Building Mountains in the Flat Landscape of the World Wide Web," *California Management Review,* Winter 1998, pp. 36–56.

5. http://www.kelloggs.com/.

on segments of the drawing. Although adults may visit this site because of the brand name, they probably would not be attracted back to the site. Similarly, the FarEast-Foods Web site attracts repeat visits through a number of features that change often enough to make it slightly different on each visit.

Both of these Web sites, designed to appeal to specific groups (young children or those interested in Oriental food), filter visitors but do not attempt to customize themselves to the visitors. For example, all children get the same portfolio of drawings to color on the Kellogg's site. To make a site worthy of repeat visits, it is often necessary to tailor it in some way to each visitor. That is, different visitors need to see a different page layout or a different set of pages or have access to different databases. For instance, although Kellogg's makes it possible for a child to select from among Web pages for the United States, the United Kingdom, Germany, and Korea, to actually customize the site, Kellogg's would need to go one step further and automate this selection based on the home country of the visitor.[6]

The second stage of strategic planning is then to decide the degree of customization of a Web site: broad, specialized, or personalized. With **broad customization,** a Web site attempts to communicate with a number of types of stakeholders or many of the people in one stakeholder category. For example, Goodyear Tire & Rubber Company's Web site,[7] with its information on tires, is directed at the general tire customer. A broad Web site provides content with minimal adjustment to the needs of the visitor. Thus, many visitors may not linger too long at the site because there is little that particularly catches their attention.

With specialized customization, a Web site appeals to a narrower audience. Federal Express, for instance, with its parcel tracking system, has decided to focus on

FarEastFoods is an example of a specialized Web site.

---

6. This can be determined from the rightmost portion of an address.
7. http://www.goodyear.com/Home/HTML/Educational/TireSchool/TireSchool.html.

current customers. A customer can enter a receipt number to determine the current location of a package and download software for preparing transportation documentation. A specialized Web site may attract fewer visitors, but nearly all those who make the link find the visit worthwhile. The Premier Web sites that Dell creates for each of its large customers are an example of very specialized customization.

The marketer's dream is to develop an interactive relationship with individual customers, and a **personalized Web site** does just that. Database technology and back-end application software enables a Web site to be personalized to meet the needs of the individual. Computer magazine publisher Ziff-Davis[8] offers visitors the opportunity to specify a personal profile. After completing a registration form, the visitor can then select what to see on future visits. For instance, a marketing manager tracking the CAD/CAM software market in Germany can set a profile that displays links to new stories on these topics. On future visits to the Ziff-Davis site, the manager can click on the personal view button to access the latest news matching the profile. Another example of a personalized Web site is www.when.com (also available on the Netscape home page). This Web site has calendaring software that can be used to save appointments and events based on a user ID and password. These appointments and events cannot be changed or viewed by anyone else. This enables the user to schedule appointments from anywhere and have them appear whenever they visit this Web site.

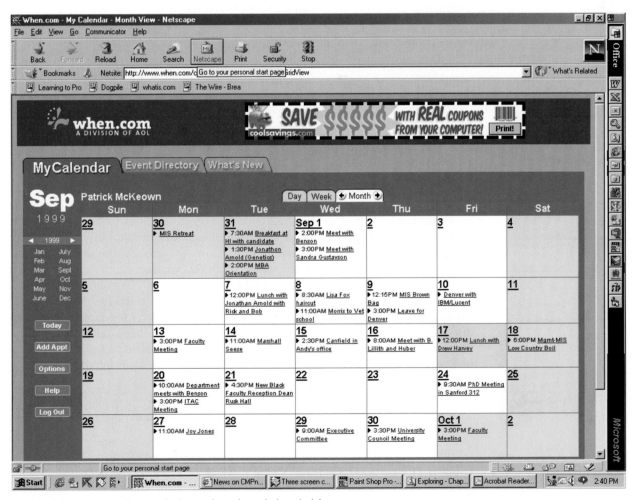

The calendar at when.com is customized to each user's particular schedule.

8. http://www.zdnet.com.

Ⓕocus on Technology

Search Engines

If the World Wide Web is the heart of electronic commerce, then search engines are its eyes and ears because they help the customer find items to purchase. With the Web containing 1.2 *billion* pages at last count, without search engines we would never find the exciting new stuff in the thirty-eight pages that are being added to the Internet *every* second. Unfortunately, the majority of Web users are unhappy with the performance of search engines, as evidenced by a study in which over 70 percent of users expressed their dissatisfaction. The problems are multiple—the Web is huge with a great deal of junk to be avoided, people are not very adept at using search engines, and the software behind the engines is not very good at determining what the user actually wants. Furthermore, some engines have admitted biasing the search results in favor of products for which a payment was made.

However, companies have been working hard to improve the search engines and the work is starting to pay off with better search results. To understand why, it is useful to understand how search engines work. In general, they take one of two approaches: computer or human. With a computer-driven search engine, technology is used to increase the breadth of the search with the largest engine including over 200 million pages in its scope. Engines like Alta Vista, Excite, and Northern Light take this approach. On the other hand, the amazing human brain is used to categorize Web pages into "directories" that provide better results than a general search. Yahoo! is the best-known user of this approach, with over 150 editors and Web surfers doing the categorizing. New computerized approaches include Google and DirectHit. Both of these use the popularity of the page to determine the pages returned. DirectHit bases its measure of popularity on how long Web surfers spend at a page while Google uses the number of pages that link to a page as its measure of popularity. In terms of electronic commerce, one of the most useful search engines may be RealNames, which allows the user to enter a product name and find the related Web site, therefore bypassing the need to enter a URL.

Source: Jennifer Tanaka, "The Perfect Search." *Newsweek,* September 27, 1999, pp. 71–72.

There are two types of personalized attractors. **Adaptable sites** can be customized by the visitor, as in the case of Ziff-Davis. The visitor establishes what is of interest by answering questions or selecting options. On the other hand, an **adaptive site** learns from the visitor's behavior and determines what should be presented. This adapting of a site to the customer's needs is usually done with a small data file, called a **cookie**, that is kept on the user's computer. Amazon.com is among the best known of the adaptive sites. It tries to discover what type of reading material and music the visitor likes so that it can recommend books and CDs. Web sites like Amazon.com have been very successful in the area of mass customization, which we discussed earlier, because every visitor feels like the site has been customized just for them through a personal welcome and a suggested list of books to consider. This is true even though thousands of people are visiting the same site each day.

Quick Review

1. What are the two stages of an attractor Web site?
2. What is the difference between an adaptable Web site and an adaptive Web site?

Securing Electronic Commerce Transactions

If any one thing has retarded the growth of electronic commerce, it is perceived security problems. Many would-be customers are afraid to use electronic commerce because they think their credit card number will be stolen. There are a variety of reasons for this concern: First, because the intent of the Internet is to give people remote access to information, it is inherently open, and traditional approaches to restricting access by the use of physical barriers are less viable, though organizations still need to restrict physical access to their servers. Second, because electronic commerce is based on computers and networks, these same technologies can be used to attack security systems. There is a perception that hackers can easily use computers to intercept network traffic and scan it for confidential information or find useful information on a server by running repeated attacks to breach its security (e.g., trying all words in the dictionary for an account password). Although this is not generally the case, and most people stand a far greater chance of having their credit card information stolen at a local restaurant or other business, the mere perception has caused many would-be buyers to avoid the Web.

To help you understand the ways in which electronic commerce transactions are secured, a brief discussion of security is provided; chapter 10 will provide a more-detailed discussion. We will discuss one issue here: using encryption to protect the contents of an Internet message and to verify the sender of a message.

Security Issues

Internet messages can pass through many computers on their way from sender to receiver, and there is always the danger that a type of computer program called a **sniffer** on an intermediate computer will briefly intercept and read a message. In most cases, this will not cause great concern, but what happens if your message contains your name, credit card number, and expiration date in an unprotected form? The sniffer program, looking for a typical credit card number format of four blocks of four digits (e.g., 1234 5678 9012 3456), copies your message before letting it continue its normal progress. Now, the owner of the rogue program can use your credit card details to purchase products in your name and charge them to your account.

Without a secure means of transmitting payment information, customers and merchants will be very reluctant to place and receive orders, respectively. When the customer places an order, the Web browser should automatically encrypt the order prior to transmission—this is not the customer's task.

Credit card numbers are not the only sensitive information transmitted on the Internet. Because it is a general transport system for electronic information, the Internet can carry a wide range of confidential information (financial reports, sales figures, marketing strategies, technology reports, etc.). If senders and receivers cannot be sure that their communication is strictly private, they will not use the Internet. Secure transmission of information is necessary for electronic commerce to thrive.

Encryption

The most widely used method of protecting Internet messages from being read by a computer along their path between sender and receiver is encryption. **Encryption** is the process of transforming messages or data to protect their meaning. Encryption scrambles a message so that it is meaningful only to the person knowing the method of encryption and holding the key to deciphering it. To everyone else, it is gobbledygook. The reverse process, **decryption,** converts a seemingly senseless character string into the original message. There are two primary forms of encryption systems: private key and public key encryption.

Private key encryption uses the same private key (a key is the bit-string used to encode and decode messages) to encrypt and decrypt a message. However, it has a very significant problem. How do you securely distribute the key? It can't be sent with the message because if the message is intercepted, the key can be used to decipher it. You must find another secure medium for transmitting the key. So, do you fax the key or phone it? Either method is not completely secure and is time consuming whenever the key is changed. Also, how do you know that the key's receiver will protect its secrecy?

On the other hand, a **public-key encryption** system has two keys: one private and the other public. A **public key** can be freely distributed because it is quite separate

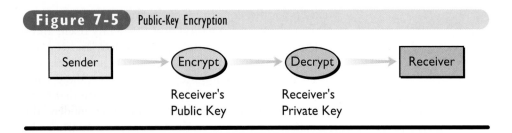

Figure 7-5 Public-Key Encryption

from its corresponding **private key.** To send and receive messages, communicators first must create separate pairs of private and public keys and then exchange their public keys. The sender encrypts a message with the intended receiver's public key, and, upon receiving the message, the receiver applies their private key, as shown in Figure 7-5. The receiver's private key, the only one that can decrypt the message, must be kept secret to permit secure message exchange.

The elegance of the public-key system is that it totally avoids the problem of secure transmission of keys. Public keys can be freely exchanged. Indeed, there can be a public database containing each person's or organization's public key. For instance, if you want to e-mail your credit card details to a catalog company, you can simply obtain its public key (probably from its Web site) and encrypt your entire message prior to transmission. Of course, you may wish to transmit far more important data than your credit card number.

Consider the message shown in Figure 7-6; the sender would hardly want this message to fall into the wrong hands. After encryption, the message is totally secure, as shown in Figure 7-7. Only the receiver, using his private key, can decode the message. A free form of public encryption is Pretty Good Privacy (PGP).

Signing

Although encryption is very useful whenever a message contains sensitive information, there are cases when the content of the message is not confidential, but the receiver may still wish to verify the sender's identity. For example, imagine that you pay $1,000 per year for an investment information service. The provider might want to verify that any e-mail requests it receives are from subscribers. Thus, as part of the subscription sign up, subscribers have to supply their public key and, when using the service, sign all electronic messages with their private key. The provider is then assured that it is servicing paying customers. Naturally, any messages between the service and the client should be encrypted to ensure that others do not gain from

Figure 7-6 Message before Encryption

```
To: Pat McKeown <pmckeown@dogs.uga.edu>
From: Rick Watson <rwatson@dogs.uga.edu>
Subject: Money
--------------------------------------------------------------------------------
G'day Pat
I hope you are enjoying your stay in Switzerland. Could you do me a favor? I need $50,000
from my secret Swiss bank account. The name of the bank is Aussie-Suisse International in
Geneva. The account code is 451-3329 and the password is 'meekatharra'. I'll see you (and
the money) at the airport this Friday.
Cheers
Rick
```

Figure 7-7   Message after Encryption

```
To:  Pat McKeown <pmckeown@dogs.uga.edu>
From:  Rick Watson <rwatson@dogs.uga.edu>
Subject:  Money
----------------------------------------------------------------------------
-----BEGIN PGP MESSAGE-----
Version: 2.6.2
hEWDfoTG8eEvuiEBAf9rxBdHpgdq1gaI7zm10cHvWHtx+9++ip27q6vI
tjYbIUKDnGjV0sm2INWpcohrarI9S2xu6UcSPyFfumGs9pgAAAQ0euRGjzy
RgIPE5DUHG  uITXYsnIq7zFHVevjO2DAEJ8OUAIX9YJD8kwp4T3suQnw7/d
1j4ed146qisrQHpRRwqHXons7w4k04x8tH4JGfWEXc5LB+hcOSyPHEir4EP
qDcEP1b1M9bH6  w2ku2fUmdMaoptnVsinLMtzWqIKQ1HMfaJ0HM9Df4kWh+
ZbY0yFXxSuHKrgbaoDcu9wUze35dtwiCTdf1sf3ndQNaLOFiIjh5pis+bUg
9rOZjxpEFbdGgYpcfBB4rvRNwOwizvSodxJ9H+VdtAL3DIsSJdNSAEuxjQ0
hvOSA8oCBDJfHSUFqX3ROtB3+yuT1vf/C8Vod4gW4tvqj8C1QNte+ehxg==
=fD44
-----END PGP MESSAGE-----
```

the information. As another example, one of your friends may find it amusing to have some fun at your expense, as shown in Figure 7-8.

If the president indeed was in the habit of communicating electronically, it is likely that he would sign his messages so that the receiver could verify it. A sender's private key is used to created a signed message. The receiver then applies the sender's public key to verify the signature, as shown in Figure 7-9.

A signed message has additional encrypted text containing the sender's signature, as shown in Figure 7-10. When the purported sender's public key is applied to this message, the identity of the sender can be verified (it was not the president).

Figure 7-8   Message before Signing

```
To:  Pat McKeown <pmckeown@dogs.uga.edu>
From:  President@whitehouse.gov
Subject:  Invitation to visit the White House
--------------------------------------------------------------------------------
Dear Dr. McKeown
It is my pleasure to invite you to a special meeting of
Internet users at the White House on April 1st at 2pm.  Please
call 212-123-7890 and ask for Mr. A. Phool for complete
details of your visit.
The President
```

Figure 7-9   Signing with Public-Key System

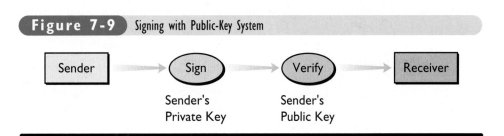

Figure 7-10 Message after Signing

```
To: Pat McKeown <pmckeown@dogs.uga.edu>
From: President@whitehouse.gov
Subject: Invitation to visit the White House
------------------------------------------------------------------------------
Dear Dr. McKeown
It is my pleasure to invite you to a special meeting of
Internet users at the White House on April 1st at 2pm. Please
call 212-123-7890 and ask for Mr. A. Phool for complete
details of your visit.
The President
-----BEGIN PGP SIGNATURE-----
Version: 2.6.2
iQCVAwUBMeRVVUb1ZxMqZR69AQFJNQQAwHMSRZhWyiGTieGukbhPGUNF3aB
+qm7E8g5ySsY6QqUcg2zwUr40w8Q0Lfcc4nmr0NUujiXkqzTNb+3RL41w5x
fTCfMp1Fi5Hawo829UZAlmN8L5hz17XfeON5WxfycxLGXZcbUWkGio6/d4r
9Ez6s79DDf9EuD1z4zfZcy1iA==G6jB
-----END PGP SIGNATURE-----
```

Quick Review

1. What is a *sniffer,* and what does it have to do with electronic commerce?
2. What is *public* about public-key encryption?

Focus on Management

United Parcel Service

While we have focused on the problems associated with attracting customers to an electronic commerce Web site and carrying out the transaction, efficiently delivering the item to the customer is a critical part of the process. No matter how attractive the Web site, or how well it handles transactions, if the purchased item does not arrive at the customer's office or home within a few days, the customer will become unhappy. Today, the vast majority of all packages are delivered by United Parcel Service (UPS), the U.S. Postal Service, or Federal Express (FedEx). Of the three, UPS has handled the largest volume of packages by far at 55 percent, with the Postal Service second at 32 percent, and FedEx third at 10 percent. There is no reason to assume that e-commerce deliveries don't follow the same pattern. In 1998, UPS delivered 3 billion packages in 200 countries, earning $1.7 billion on sales of $24.8 billion. With e-commerce expected to grow at least 30 percent a year for the foreseeable future, UPS will be a major player in the networked economy.

While everyone is aware of the big, brown trucks and brown-uniformed individuals that deliver packages to their door, many are not aware of the information technology that makes all of this possible. This includes a wide variety of network technology that enables UPS to provide a wealth of services to its business partners and customers including real-time package tracking, just-in-time shipment coordination, customs clearing, financial transactions, and Internet access. In addition, it has a telecommunications arm that connects 900,000 users in 100 countries, and its Web site (http://www.ups.com) averages 13 million hits a day as it tracks the movement of 12 million packages. To improve its tracking system that feeds into this Web site, UPS has recently moved to a new type of handheld tracking systems that transmits package information in three-tenths of a second instead of the current ten seconds. This is further evidence that UPS believes that the information about a package is almost as important as the package itself.

Sources: Stephanie Wilkinson, "UPS: Delivering Network Innovation." *PC Week Online,* September 13, 1999 (http://www.zdnet.com/pcweek).
Daniel Kadlec, "Special Delivery." *Time,* August 2, 1999.

Electronic Commerce Payment Systems

When commerce goes electronic, the means of paying for goods and services must also go electronic. Paper-based payment systems cannot support the speed, security, privacy, and internationalization necessary for electronic commerce. This section discusses three methods of electronic payment:

- Credit cards
- Electronic funds transfer
- Digital cash

Although you are already familiar with the use of credit cards, you may not be familiar with the other two types of electronic payments. We will discuss each briefly here and then in more detail in separate sections. **Electronic funds transfer (EFT)**, in its widest definition, refers to any transfer of funds electronically between two parties. However, in this context, we will use the term to mean the transfer of payments between consumers or between organizations engaged in business-to-business electronic commerce and businesses. **Digital cash** refers to the storage of value in a digital format and can be in two broad forms: card-based or computer-based. Card-based digital cash is the storage of value on a plastic card such as a prepaid telephone card or a "smart" card that can have value added or removed from it. Computer-based digital cash is the storage of value on a computer, usually one that is linked to the Internet. This allows payment directly between the customer and merchant computers.

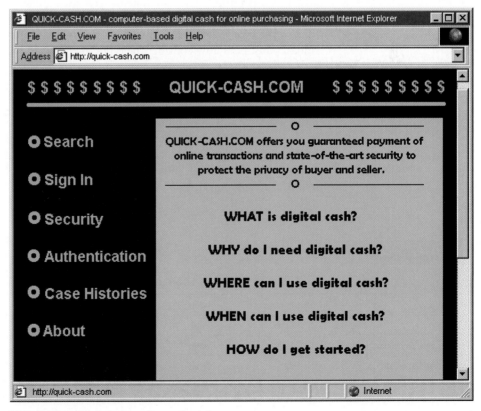

With digital cash, you don't need a credit card.

Concerns with Electronic Money

There are four fundamental concerns regarding electronic money: security, authentication, anonymity, and scale of purchase. (1) *Security* of electronic money means that consumers and organizations can be assured that their online orders are protected and that large sums of money can be safely transferred. (2) For any type of electronic money to be useful, it must be possible to *authenticate* it (i.e., verify that it is real). Otherwise, consumers will not have faith in electronic currency and will avoid using it. (3) Transactions using electronic money should retain *anonymity* (i.e., not available to persons who have no reason to see them). (4) The *scale of purchase* issue is new and is very closely associated with the rise of electronic commerce. Whereas we have traditionally thought of making purchases no smaller than the smallest denomination of a national currency (e.g., one cent in the United States), with electronic commerce this is no longer the case. Now there is a real need to make *micro* purchases (e.g., less than $1), or even *nano* purchases of less than one cent. These capabilities will enable high-volume, small-value Internet transactions such as purchasing individual newspaper, magazine, or encyclopedia articles, renting software for an hour, or accessing a technical support area.

Any money system, real or electronic, must have a reasonable level of security and a high level of authentication, otherwise people will not use it. All electronic money systems are potentially divisible. There is a need, however, to adapt some systems so that transactions can be automated. For example, there are overhead considerations that would make you not want to use your credit card to make a purchase of $0.01 On the other hand, some form of digital cash or e-cash system might work very well. The various approaches to electronic money vary in their capability to solve these concerns, as shown in Table 7-5.

Although not all of the technical problems of electronic money have been solved, many people are working on their solution because electronic money promises efficiencies that will reduce the costs of transactions between buyers and sellers. Given that counting, moving, storing, and safeguarding cash are estimated to be 4 percent of the value of all transactions, there are ample reasons to pursue the use of such systems. In addition, if electronic payment systems were used at banks, banks would have less need to have cash on hand, making more money available for investment. It is quite possible that, in the next few years, electronic currency will displace notes and coins for many transactions. Let's now consider the types of electronic money in more detail.

Credit Cards

Credit cards are a safe, secure, and widely used remote payment system. Millions of people use them every day to order goods by phone and over the Internet. Furthermore, people think nothing of handing over their card to a restaurant server, who could easily find time to write down the card's details. In the case of fraud, banks already protect consumers to some degree, depending on the national jurisdiction. For example, in the United States, credit card holders are typically liable for only the first $50 of any purchases made with a stolen credit card.

Table 7-5 Characteristics of Electronic Money

Type	Security	Authentication	Anonymity	Scale of Purchase[9]
Credit card	High	High	Low	Small to medium
EFT	High	High	Low	Small to large
Card-based digital cash	Medium	High	High	Nano to medium
Computer-based digital cash	High	High	High	Nano to medium

9. Large: > $10,000, medium: >$1,000, small: < $1,000, micro: <$1, and nano: < $0.01.

Web-based credit card systems now universally include real-time authorization and the use of secure servers and clients that make transmitting credit card numbers extremely safe. These systems include Netscape's Secure Sockets Layer (SSL) system and the Secure Electronic Transaction (SET) system supported initially by Master-Card, Visa, Microsoft, and Netscape. These systems make online purchases using encrypted credit card numbers.

Credit card systems have been expanded through the use of **electronic wallets** that enable the user to store multiple credit cards in an electronic form as a combination of software and data. When the customer purchases an item from a merchant who supports the electronic wallet system, a message is returned to the customer's computer, and the user is directed to select a credit card from the wallet.

The major shortcomings of credit cards are that they do not support person-to-person transfers, do not have the privacy of cash, and cannot now be used for micro and nano purchases.

Electronic Funds Transfer

Electronic funds transfer (EFT), introduced in the late 1960s, uses the existing banking structure to support a wide variety of payments. For example, consumers can establish monthly checking account deductions for utility bills, and banks can transfer millions of dollars. EFT is essentially electronic checking. Instead of writing a check and mailing it, the buyer initiates an electronic checking transaction (e.g., using a debit card at a point-of-sale terminal). The transaction is then electronically transmitted to an intermediary (usually the banking system), which transfers the funds from the buyer's account to the seller's account. A banking system has one or more common clearinghouses that facilitate the flow of funds between accounts in different banks. This process for a consumer purchase is shown in Figure 7-11.

Electronic checking is fast; transactions are instantaneous. Paper-handling costs are substantially reduced, and bad checks are no longer a problem because the buyer's account balance is verified at the moment of the transaction. EFT is flexible; it can handle high volumes of small consumer payments and large commercial transactions, both locally and internationally. The international payment clearing system, consisting of more than one hundred financial institutions, handles an average of $1.5 *trillion* per day.

Figure 7-11 Use of EFT for Consumer Purchase

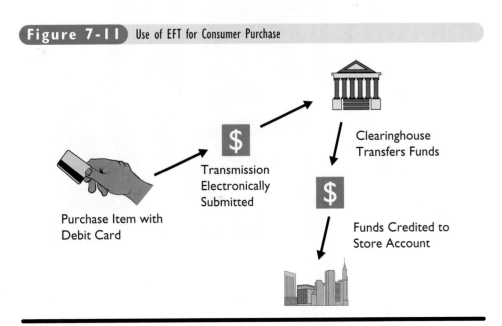

Purchase Item with Debit Card

Transmission Electronically Submitted

Clearinghouse Transfers Funds

Funds Credited to Store Account

The major shortcomings of EFT are that all transactions must pass through the banking system, which is legally required to record every transaction, and that it is inappropriate for micro and nano transactions. The lack of privacy can have serious consequences for those interested in keeping their transactions private, and the scale factor keeps it from being used for very small consumer purchases.

Card-Based Digital Cash

As we mentioned, digital cash is an electronic parallel of notes and coins. In this section, we consider card-based digital cash. Two forms are presently available: prepaid cards and smart cards. The phonecard, the most common form of prepaid card, was first issued in 1976 by the forerunner of Telecom Italia.[10] You may have also used a prepaid card for making copies at the library or for other special purposes.

The problem with prepaid special-purpose cards, such as phone and photocopy cards, is that people end up with a purse or wallet full of cards. On the other hand, a **smart card** with a computer chip with built-in memory and microprocessor can serve as personal identification, credit card, ATM card, telephone credit card, critical medical information record, and cash for micro- to medium-sized transactions. It can store as much as one thousand times more data than a magnetic-stripe card, and the microprocessor can be programmed to carry out a variety of activities.

The stored-value card, the most common application of smart card technology, can be used to purchase a wide variety of items (e.g., fast food, parking, public transport tickets). Consumers buy cards of standard denominations (e.g., $20, $50, or $100) from a card dispenser or bank. When the card is used to pay for an item, it must be inserted into a reader, where the amount of the transaction is transferred to the reader, and the value of the card is reduced by the transaction amount.

The problem with card-based digital cash, like real cash, is that you can lose it or it can be stolen. It is not as secure as the other alternatives, but most people are

Smart cards can be used for a wide variety of purposes.

10. See this card at http://www.agora.stm.it/L.Costa/firstph.htm.

likely to carry only small amounts of digital cash on their card, and thus security is not so critical. Because smart cards are likely to have a unique serial number, consumers can limit their loss by reporting a stolen or misplaced smart card to invalidate its use. Adding a PIN (personal identification number) to a smart card can raise its security level.

France, where smart cards were introduced over a decade ago, and the rest of Europe make heavy use of smart cards. For example, over twenty-five million Visa smart cards have been issued in France, and over forty million are used in Germany. Worldwide, over one billion cards were issued in 1998 alone. In addition, all eighty million citizens of Germany and Austria have been issued a smart card with health-related information on it. The United States is the one area of the world where smart cards have not become widely popular, but banks and credit card companies are continuing to work to change this attitude.

Computer-Based Digital Cash

For making purchases over the Internet, most people currently use credit cards. However, a variety of methods are now available to store value in the form of digital cash in the computer itself, either on the client software on the user's machine or on a server to pay for everyday Internet transactions, such as buying software, receiving money from parents, or paying for a pizza to be delivered without using a credit card. Digital cash provides the privacy of cash because the payer can remain anonymous.

Digital cash allows confidential online purchases.

Figure 7-12 Purchasing an Item with Digital Cash

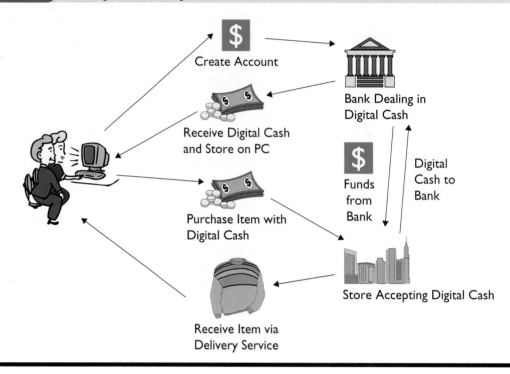

To use digital cash you need a digital bank account from one of many Internet-based banks (e.g., the Mark Twain Bank of Missouri) and client software. The client is used to withdraw digital cash from your bank account and store it on your personal computer. You can then spend the money at any location accepting digital cash or send money to someone who has a digital cash account. Transactions of virtually any size can be handled in this manner. With most digital cash schemes, you need a password to access your account, and electronic transactions are encrypted. Figure 7-12 shows the general idea behind using digital cash for electronic commerce transactions where a piece of clothing is being purchased.

Quick Review

1. What are the three electronic payment methods in current use?
2. Why is a credit card a safe way to purchase goods and services over the Web?

⊙ Summary

To summarize this chapter, let's answer the Learning Objectives questions posed at the beginning of the chapter.

What is electronic commerce, and how does it relate to the networked economy? Electronic commerce is the use of computer networks to improve organizational performance. Increasing profitability, gaining market share, improving customer service, and delivering products faster are some of the organizational performance gains possible with electronic commerce. All organizations in the world will be affected in one way or another. Companies can be classified by the effect that electronic commerce will have on them as Internet companies (companies that exist because of the Internet and Web, like Mindspring and Yahoo!), companies that use the Web to carry out already-existing business activities in a new way (e.g., Amazon.com and Net.B@nk), companies that have used the Web to creatively destroy their existing business, transforming themselves into a different type of company or a company that has different business activities (e.g., Edmunds.com and Dell Computers), companies that are trying to adapt by using electronic commerce for an existing business activity (e.g., Delta Airlines and Lands' End), and companies that will be hurt by the introduction of electronic commerce or that are ignoring it, such as malls or construction companies.

How is electronic commerce changing the way business is carried out? Internet technology and the World Wide Web are creating a revolution in business. The Web does this in a number of ways, including leveling the playing field by making customer convergence on Web sites critical to a company's success, reversing the direction of communication between buyers and sellers (communications flip-flop), and changing the nature of intermediaries through disintermediaton. In the first case, all companies on the Web have the same accessibility and large companies cannot dominate small ones. In the second case, the fundamental relationship between advertiser and customer is changed with the customer taking the initiative by demanding customization of the Web site. Finally, traditional middlemen are being eliminated in electronic commerce.

How are technologies used to facilitate electronic commerce? A variety of technologies provide the infrastructure for electronic commerce. These technologies are layered one upon the other. The lowest layer is the national information infrastructure (NII), which includes TV and radio broadcast industries, cable TV, telephone networks, cellular communication systems, computer networks, and the Internet. The next layer up is the message distribution infrastructure, which consists of software for sending and receiving messages between a server and a client. Electronic data interchange (EDI), e-mail, and hypertext transfer protocol (HTTP) are examples of messaging software. The next layer above the messaging layer is the electronic publishing infrastructure, of which the Web is a very good example. This layer addresses problems of having addressability (i.e., a URL) and having a common language across the network (i.e., HTTP and HTML). The next-to-the-top layer is the business services infrastructure, which supports common business processes, for example, supporting secure transmission of credit card numbers by providing encryption and electronic funds transfer. Finally, the top infrastructure layer is an electronic commerce application where the transaction takes place.

Which electronic commerce strategies should companies consider using? Each organization needs to consider its electronic commerce strategy as a way to reduce the risks it faces, that is, demand risk, innovation risk, and inefficiency risk. Because the organization's strategy will be developed around its Web site, understanding types of Web sites is essential to developing the strategy. Not only must the Web site be of the correct type, but also it must attract customers who will purchase goods and services. Companies are using the three Web topologies—Internet, extranet, and intranet—to facilitate electronic commerce through eight different types of Web sites. Once a company has selected the type of Web topology and type of site, it must find ways to attract customers to its Web site. This can be done through an influence filter and a target refractor. There are three degrees of mass customization: broad, specialized, and personalized. There are also two types of personalized attractors: adaptable and adaptive.

How are electronic commerce transactions protected from criminal activity? The most widely used method of protecting Internet messages from being read by a computer along their path between sender and receiver is encryption. Encryption is the process of transforming messages or data to protect their meaning. Encryption scrambles a message so that it is meaningful only to the person knowing the method of encryption and the key to deciphering it. The reverse process, decryption, converts a seemingly senseless character string into the original message. A popular form of encryption is public key encryption, which uses a public key and a private key. A variety of public key encryption that is readily available to Internet users goes by the name of Pretty Good Privacy (PGP).

What are the various electronic commerce payment methods in use today and predicted for the future? Paper-based payment systems cannot support the speed, security, privacy, and internationalization necessary for electronic commerce. Three commonly used methods of electronic payment are credit cards, electronic funds transfer (EFT), and digital cash. Credit cards are used for all types of transactions except for those involving very large or very small amounts of money. EFT refers to the transfer of payments between organizations engaged in business-to-business electronic commerce. Digital cash is the storage of value in a digital format and comes in two broad forms: card-based or computer-based. Card-based digital cash is the storage of value on a plastic card such as a prepaid telephone card or a "smart" card that can have value added or removed from it. Computer-based digital cash is the storage of value on a computer, usually one that is linked to the Internet. This allows payment directly between the customer and merchant computers.

⊙ Review Questions

1. List the five categories of companies affected by electronic commerce. Provide additional examples of Internet companies and companies using new approaches through electronic commerce.

2. In what ways is electronic commerce changing the ways in which business is transacted?

3. What is customer convergence? What is the communications flip-flop?

4. List the five layers of the electronic commerce infrastructure model. In which layer does encryption occur?

5. What are the three Web topologies? Which is used for business-to-business electronic commerce?

6. List the eight types of Web sites commonly used in electronic commerce. Provide additional examples of the first three types.

7. What are attractors? Why are they important in choosing an electronic commerce strategy?

8. What is an influence filter? A target refractor? What do they have to do with electronic commerce?

9. What is the difference between a private key and a public key in encryption?

10. What are the available payment systems for electronic commerce?

⊙ Discussion Questions

1. Choose three businesses with which you are familiar and discuss the most threatening risk to each. How might these businesses use the Web to reduce these risks?

2. Discuss the concept of disintermediation as it applies to two businesses and professions other than those discussed in the text.

3. Select three electronic commerce Web sites and analyze them in terms of topology, type of site, and success as an attractor.

> **CASE**

WildOutfitters.com

Claire had just returned from leading Wild Outfitters' first "Corporate Bonding Adventure," an adventure weekend designed specifically for business teams. The three-day package is designed to improve team dynamics by providing a unique setting and challenging outdoor activities. So far, the orders for this new service had been encouraging. Alex and Claire were discussing the events of the weekend in order to assess the lessons learned, with the hopes of applying these lessons to future outings.

"I was pleasantly surprised," Claire began. "Them thar city folk larn't good in them woods," she added in her *Jethro* twang.

Smiling, Alex responded, "I'm glad that it went well. What do you suggest for the next time? Any changes?"

"I have a couple of pages of notes about that," she replied. "But first, they gave me a few ideas that we can use with the Web site."

The ideas for the Web site that Claire mentioned came from several encounters on her trip. First, she continuously sought feedback through observation and direct inquiries about how the trip was going and what the customers were feeling. This feedback enabled her to respond more effectively to their individual needs on the trip. In addition, she took some time on the last night around the campfire to ask them as a group what they thought about the trip and their suggestions for improvement. Claire also inquired about what had attracted them to the trip in the first place and what would make them come back. These encounters gave her the content for several pages of notes specific to the "Corporate Bonding Adventure" trips.

On the way home from the trip, a light bulb went off in her head. Why couldn't similar techniques to the ones she had used to seek feedback from the trip participants be used with Web customers? If they could get good information about their online customer preferences, then they could respond more effectively to each customer on an individual basis. They could also use this information to set up special services for attracting new customers and retaining old customers.

Alex and Claire concluded that a sure way to attract customers was to offer special deals and price cuts on their products. It would be nice if they could somehow combine this with collecting customer information. One solution that they decided upon was to send targeted e-mail about specials to selected customers. For example, if a customer had a special interest in water sports, they would send the customer information about deals on water sport equipment or river trips. The e-mail would serve as both a reminder to the customer about the Wild Outfitters site, as well as serve as an attractor to the site to make a purchase. To sign up for the service, the customer would be required to fill out an online survey about their outdoor hobbies and activities. The survey information would be valuable to the Campagnes in several ways. First, it would provide them with the data needed in order to send e-mail to the appropriate targets. Second, the data could be used to gather aggregate statistics on the types of customers who are interested in and shop at their site. Finally, they could use the information for more individual customization of the site in the future.

"Wow! You really learned a lot on this trip," Alex exclaimed proudly. "Maybe we have this whole thing backwards. Those 'city folk' should have a trip to guide us around the big city."

Of course, this got Claire going again. "Reckon so, Pa," Claire cried, as she slapped her knee. "We kin do some corprit bondin' by the cement pond."

1. In which category of companies affected by electronic commerce does Wild Outfitters fit best? Which business model are they following?

2. What components of electronic commerce would be used by Wild Outfitters at each level of the electronic commerce infrastructure and how?

3. *(Hands on)* Search the Web for other examples of commercial sites for the business model used by WildOutfitters.com. List and describe the features on these sites designed to be attractors for customers. Evaluate the items on your list and rate them according to those that would most likely attract you back to the site. Which of these would you suggest for WildOutfitters.com?

4. *(Hands on)* As described in the case, the Campagnes wish to send targeted e-mail to alert their good customers about special deals and tours. Sketch out the plans for a new form on the WildOutfitters.com Web site for customers to sign up for this service. Include boxes on the form for soliciting the customers contact information, as well as questions about their product and travel interests. Add a new table to your Wild Outfitters database to store the information from your form.

Design and Development of Information Systems

In order for information systems to be of any help to organizations, they must first be created. This can be done in a number of ways including developing them internally, having someone else develop them specifically for the organization's needs, or acquiring them from a commercial software developer. If the decision is made to develop an information system internally, there are a number of approaches to doing this including ad hoc programming, structured development, end-user development, and rapid application development. Structured development, also known as systems analysis and design, is a popular approach that has been in use for over twenty years. Rapid application development (RAD) is a newer approach that attempts to speed up the often lengthy structured methodology. When internal development is not feasible, the project can be outsourced to an outside developer or it can be acquired.

In this part, we cover approaches to systems development and then provide a detailed coverage of the popular structured approach including the planning, analysis, design, and implementation stages. We also cover the use of RAD as a way to speed up the process, as is often a requirement in the networked economy. We also discuss outsourcing and acquisition as ways to speed up the development process.

CHAPTER 8

Developing Information Systems I

❯ Learning Objectives

After reading this chapter, you should be able to answer the following questions:

❯ Why is information systems development or acquisition important to all types of organizations?

❯ What are the most commonly used approaches to systems development?

❯ What are the stages in the structured approach to development?

❯ What are the steps in the planning stage of development?

❯ What are the steps in the analysis stage of development?

❯ How do data modeling and process modeling fit into the analysis of a replacement or new system?

Ⓕocus on Management

Developing the Manheim Online Web Site

In the opening Focus on Management box in chapter 4, we discussed Manheim Online and its Web site, where it sells used cars directly to automobile dealers. The development of this Web site resulted from a perceived threat to Manheim from AUCNET, a company that had been successful in Japan in auctioning cars using a television network. Wishing to blunt the threat from AUCNET, Manheim experimented with its own television-based system but decided to pursue an Internet-based system instead. To test this idea, Manheim approached Intellimedia Commerce, an Atlanta-based Internet development company, about developing such a system. Based on preliminary discussions, Intellimedia Commerce quickly developed a prototype Web site that demonstrated how dealers would be able to purchase automobiles directly from Manheim Auctions.

This initial prototype was so successful that Manheim asked Intellimedia Commerce to create a working version of the sales system. A decision was made early to make this a purchase system that would allow dealers to buy program (off-lease or company executive) cars at a set wholesale price rather than create an online bidding system. This was done to avoid problems with differences in Internet connection speeds between dealers. Although Intellimedia Commerce felt that it could solve this problem eventually, Manheim wanted a system up and running quickly.

An interesting feature of the development of Manheim Online was the *lack* of involvement by its information technology (IT) department in the development of the new sales system. Instead of having IT develop the new system, the vice president in charge chose to use an outside developer to create both the demonstration prototype and the final working version of the system. Although the developer had to interact with the IT people at Manheim to create a system that would access the data on Manheim's AS400 midrange computer, the IT department had little to do with the development of the final system.

Source: Interview with Ralph Liniado, vice president of development of Manheim Auctions, Atlanta, January 15, 1998.

Ralph Liniado was instrumental in the development of the Manheim Auctions program car sales Web site.

Systems Development

As we have discussed throughout this textbook, information systems that are used to handle the present, remember the past, and prepare for the future are an integral part of all organizations. They are used to process transactions quickly, store data, information, and knowledge, and help managers and employees to make decisions. Without information systems, most modern organizations would cease to operate in just a few days, if not hours. A problem facing all of these organizations is deciding how to obtain the information systems they need. Whereas some systems can be acquired, others must be designed and built to meet the specific needs of the organization. Properly building information systems is critical to the long-term well-being of an organization. James Martin, one of the best-known authors in the field of information technology, has said: "The building of systems for unique [competitive] capability is often the single most important activity for an

IT organization."[1] Given the importance of acquiring or building information systems, we will spend the next two chapters introducing you to it.

In acquiring or building an information system, the requirements of the organization must carefully be analyzed so that the resulting information system accomplishes the purposes for which it is being developed. The process of analyzing information requirements, designing systems to meet these requirements, and acquiring or building these systems is called **systems development.**

When Is Systems Development Needed?

The process of systems development can take place under a variety of circumstances, including a new opportunity to use information technology, a request for an enhancement to an existing system, or a problem with an existing system not meeting organizational needs. The Manheim Auctions case discussed in the opening Focus on Management box is an example of the first circumstance, where potential competition and new technology (the Internet) resulted in the development of a new information system to carry out an existing operation—selling program cars to dealers—in a different way.

In the second circumstance, existing information systems are frequently modified through enhancements that enable them to carry out additional operations. These enhancements are often requested by individuals or departments to help them to do their job better.

Finally, in the third circumstance, all systems go through an **information system life cycle,** which has three phases, as shown in Figure 8-1.

Phase 1: Development

Phase 2: Effective operational use

Phase 3: Decline in usefulness

At some point in the life cycle, the information system will need to be modified to meet changing business conditions and technology. After several modifications, a system may begin to resemble a "patchwork" of subsystems that do not work well together. This process results in **system degradations** in which the performance of the system drops off markedly, and the quality of information provided by the system suffers. Finally, the old system will have to be discarded and a new one acquired or built. The rate at which this process of development, use, and decline progresses depends on the nature of the business environment, changing business conditions,

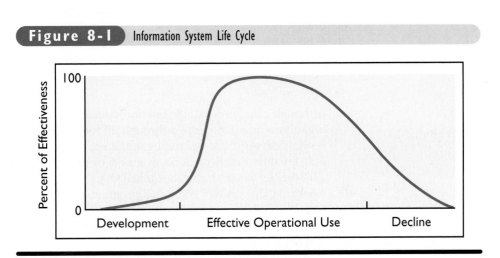

Figure 8-1 Information System Life Cycle

---

1. James Martin, *Cybercorp: The New Business Revolution* (New York: AMACOM Books), p. 104.

and technological advances. Rapid changes like those we have seen in the networked economy are dramatically shortening the length of the typical information system life cycle to the point where the life of a system is measured in months instead of years (Web years instead of calendar years!). For this reason, all information systems must continually be monitored to ensure that they satisfy current business needs and to determine when they must be upgraded, maintained, or scrapped in favor of a new system. In this chapter and the next, we will look at various approaches to the first phase of the IS life cycle—development.

Systems Development at fareastfoods.com

After scanning the environment and noting what other Internet e-tailers are doing, the management at fareastfoods.com is considering enhancing its customer ordering system to give customers rewards based on their level of spending with the company—something like a frequent purchaser plan. It is hoped that this enhancement would give fareastfoods.com a competitive advantage in the sale and delivery of Oriental foods using the Internet. Note that this is an example of the second circumstance in which information systems are acquired or built. We will use this example throughout this chapter and the next.

Quick Review

1. Why is information systems development so important to organizations?
2. What are the three stages of the information system life cycle?

Approaches to Systems Development

A variety of approaches to systems development are used today by individuals and organizations—ad hoc programming, structured approach, rapid application development, outsourcing, and acquisition. These approaches share some similarities but also have many important differences. All approaches to systems development have four basic stages: planning, analysis, design, and implementation. Note that these four development stages are quite different from the three phases of the information system life cycle shown in Figure 8-1 because they are all a part of the *development* phase of the IS life cycle.

The planning stage determines the problem to be solved, whereas the analysis stage determines what must be done to solve the problem. The design stage determines how the problem will be solved, and the implementation stage actually solves the problem. However, different approaches emphasize one or two stages over the others. It should be noted that many development projects use a combination of these approaches. Table 8-1 shows the six approaches to systems development, along with brief descriptions and comments on each. Each will be described in more detail in later sections.

Ad Hoc Programming

Although computerized information systems have been used for many years, some organizations still do not go through all four of the phases typically associated with systems development—planning, analysis, design, and implementation. Instead, an individual or a group that needs a new or revised system meets with a programmer and decides what should be done. Once this decision is made, the programmer works on the various computer programs that make up the information system, meeting with the person(s) requesting the work when questions arise. In essence, this approach has only the planning and implementation stages, with no analysis and design.

Ad hoc programming can result in a usable information system for the initial user or group, but it also results in an information system that is often poorly documented, poorly planned, not integrated into the overall organization information plan, and difficult to maintain and modify. Because these systems just evolve,

Table 8-1	Approaches to Systems	
Approach to Systems Development	**Description**	**Comments**
Ad hoc programming	Go directly from planning stage to implementation stage	Fast but very risky; may not be usable when programmer leaves
Structured approach	Systematic development using all four stages	Slow but ensures that all details are accounted for
Rapid application development (RAD)	First three stages are abbreviated	Faster than structured approach but also more risky
End-user development	User develops own system often skipping first three stages	Can be much like ad hoc programming, but done to user's own requirements
Outsourcing	Outside vendor develops system	Does not require internal expertise, but control of system can be lost
Acquisition	Purchase system from outside vendor	Fastest approach of all but may not provide competitive advantage

organizations that use the ad hoc programming approach usually have an uncoordinated "hodgepodge" information system that cannot deliver the information needed for the organization to operate in today's competitive economy.

Structured Approach

Because of the problems with ad hoc programming, structured systems development techniques were developed in the 1970s and 1980s. This is called the **structured approach** because each stage must be completed in a specific order after certain objectives are achieved in the previous stage. A specified set of deliverables must be prepared at the end of each stage, and management approval must be obtained before the next stage is initiated. This approach is useful when information requirements and the necessary data for these requirements can be specified by users, particularly for large transaction processing systems (TPS) and information-based decision support systems. This approach is also appropriate when the major components of the system must be integrated into a comprehensive system.

Because it is the most successful way of ensuring that nothing is left out of the system, over the last thirty years the structured approach has become the standard for information systems development. Major disadvantages of the structured approach are the time required to develop a new system, the requirement that all information requirements be known at the beginning of the project, and the fact that users are not always sure what they are getting. The slowness of the structured approach is becoming more of a problem given the speed at which events occur in the networked economy. Even with this problem with the speed of development, structured systems development is the standard with which anyone studying information technology should be familiar. Because it is the standard for development methodologies, structured systems development will be discussed in detail in this chapter and the next.

Rapid Application Development

Often a new system is needed quickly to meet a competitive threat. This is especially true in the networked economy when everything is moving at rapid pace. In these cases, the development process can be expedited through **rapid application development (RAD)**. There are a variety of approaches to RAD that attempt to shorten the planning, analysis, and design stages, but many involve prototyping, the approach used in the opening Focus on Management box. With this approach, a **prototype** system that contains the bare essentials can be developed and used on a trial basis. After some experience with the prototype, users can further define their requirements or try a completely different approach to solving the problem. A revised or new prototype is then designed for use. In this manner, prototyping is an iterative process. An information system is briefly analyzed, designed, used, reanalyzed, redesigned, used some more, reanalyzed, and so on, until management has a system that meets its needs. Usually, the system becomes more comprehensive with each iteration. When the user is satisfied, the prototype is implemented.

Prototyping is also useful when needs change rapidly, requirements are difficult for users to articulate without seeing the system first, the risk of developing the wrong system is high, or several alternative systems must be viewed prior to actual acceptance of a project design. The Manheim Online example discussed in the opening Focus on Management box is a good example of the first situation in that Manheim management did not have a clear idea of what it wanted. In this case, an initial prototype was created by the Web development firm to show what could be done. This prototype was then used as a starting point to create the final product. RAD will be discussed in more detail in the next chapter.

End-User Development

With the increased availability of computing power in the hands of users has come a type of "home grown" development commonly referred to as **end-user development. End users** are non-IT professionals who use the computer to solve problems associated with their job. End users are usually interested only in doing their own job better and are not interested in creating applications software for other users. When you complete computer projects as a part of this course or of other courses, you are acting as an end-user developer. The end-user developer short-circuits the often-lengthy structured development process by going directly from the planning stage to the implementation stage. As such, this process has many of the same advantages and disadvantages of the ad hoc programming approach to development, the difference being in who is doing the work and the tools used in development.

Focus on Technology

Desktop Development

Do you want to be an e-entrepreneur? More and more people are asking themselves that question with a large percentage answering with a resounding "Yes!" At one time in the distant past of Web development (four years ago), this would have required investing a large amount of time and money either to learn all the skills required to create an e-commerce Web site or to outsource the project to a Web development firm. However, with the new world of *desktop retailing,* anyone with a Web connection, ambition, and some time to spare can become the owner/operator of their own Web-based company. Just as desktop publishing allowed anyone to create slick-looking newsletters and pamphlets, as with desktop retailing, virtually anyone can become an e-merchant with desktop development. In most cases, this involves assembling a set of prefabricated objects or components in what has become known as *component-oriented programming.*

As an example of desktop development, consider James Caldwell. Jim, a high school student and a huge pro-wrestling fan, felt there was a need for a Web site devoted to this form of entertainment. With the help of a company called Nextchange, he was able to turn his avocation into a profitable Web business in about *two* hours time. On his Web site (http://www.theringsider.com/), Jim sells baseball caps and subscriptions to the WWF (Worldwide Wrestling Federation) magazine. In his case, all he had to decide was what he wanted to sell, and Nextchange helped him set up his site by taking care of the tough areas such as accepting credit cards and shipping items to customers. Jim is focused on delivering the latest news about professional wrestling and figures the few hundred dollars he earns each month makes him "pretty good at e-commerce."

Source: Thomas E. Weber, "Instant Web Stores Herald a Dizzying Era of Desktop Retailing." The *Wall Street Journal,* October 4, 1999, p. B1.

Typical end-user development tools have been spreadsheets and database management systems. With spreadsheets, the end user can use **macros** to create very sophisticated applications. For example, it is possible to create macros in spreadsheet projects that allow them to be graded electronically. Similarly, database software can be used to write applications either by using a programming language built into the software or by using database tools to create screens. The newest form of end-user tool is the **graphical applications developer** such as Microsoft's Visual BASIC, which allows end users to create menus, boxes, and so on in Microsoft Windows and then to write just the instructions needed for the specific menu or box.

Outsourcing

A popular alternative to internal development of an information system is **outsourcing** the development process to an outside organization. Outsourcing can range from having an outside company like IBM handle the entire information technology operation of an organization to hiring contractors and temporary office workers on an individual basis, with every combination between these two extremes being included. In terms of systems development, a company may choose to outsource a project because its internal information technology group does not have the skills needed to create the new system or management does not want to distract the group from other projects on which it is already working. In the Manheim case, the new project was outsourced for a combination of these reasons; the internal IT group had no experience with Web development, and members were involved in the mission critical work of processing data on the existing auction sales. The actual systems development process followed by the outsourcer will probably be either the structured approach or some form of RAD. Outsourcing will also be discussed in the next chapter.

Acquisition

Acquisition involves purchasing the information system from an outside vendor rather than developing it internally. In addition to the personal productivity packages with which you are undoubtedly familiar, such as word processors, spreadsheets, presentation software, and so on, organizations use a variety of other packaged software. Typical packages include accounting, payroll, order entry, and Internet shopping cart software. An "all-in-one" type of software called **enterprise resource planning (ERP) systems** is being offered by companies like SAP, PeopleSoft, and J. D. Edwards. ERP refers to multimodule application software that helps an organization manage the important parts of its business, including managing the supply chain, maintaining inventories, providing customer service, and tracking orders. Like RAD and outsourcing, acquisition will be discussed in the next chapter.

Internal Development, Outsourcing, or Acquisition

Determining which approach—internal development, outsourcing, or acquisition—is an important decision. Each approach has its advantages and disadvantages. For example, internal development often provides a competitive advantage for the organization but can cost more, take longer, and require more skills on the part of the internal information technology staff than either outsourcing or acquisition. Outsourcing is a good option when the skills of the internal IT professionals are not adequate for building the desired systems. In terms of acquisition, many products like word processing or spreadsheets, for which there exist standard products, are almost always acquired. Other cases are not so clear, and an analysis of the options must be carried out. The decision of whether to develop internally, outsource, or acquire an information system will be covered in chapter 9.

A Look Ahead

The remainder of this chapter will be devoted to discussing the first two stages of the structured systems development process to create customized information systems, with the fareastfoods.com customer reward project being used as an example.

The next chapter will discuss the last two stages of the structured systems development process, outsourcing, acquisition, and the use of RAD.

Quick Review

1. List the types of information systems development.
2. In which type of development are the analysis and design stages usually skipped?

Structured Systems Development

As mentioned earlier, the structured approach to systems development arose as a way to solve the problems associated with the ad hoc programming approach. Recall that this led to problems with poor planning, lack of integration into the overall organization information plan, and difficulty in maintaining and modifying the system. These problems occurred because the programmer often moved directly from a fairly simple planning stage, consisting of a conversation with the group initiating the new system, to the implementation stage, in which the computer program was written with little analysis or design considerations in between.

The ad hoc programming approach to systems development is like a builder talking with you about your visions for a house and then starting the building process the next day! Though this approach to building would work reasonably well for a dog house, a residence built this way most likely would *not* fit your requirements. On the other hand, the structured approach, which is also known as **systems analysis and design,** involves using a carefully thought-out process of planning, analyzing, designing, and implementing. In terms of our construction analogy, systems analysis and design goes from an idea to a set of preliminary sketches to preliminary plans to blueprints to the actual construction process. In both the construction of a building and the process of systems analysis, there is a step-by-step transition from a logical concept to a physical system.

This systems analysis and design process has spawned an entirely new occupation whose practitioners are known as **systems analysts.** These professionals work as a part of a development team to carry out the problem-solving process to determine the cause of the current system's problem, suggest solutions to this problem, and then see that one of these solutions is implemented. Every team includes a **project manager** whose job is to ensure that the project is completed on time and within budget and who is responsible for bringing other people onto the team. Project managers often have extensive experience working as systems analysts and are the primary point of contact for outside people. Depending on the size of the project, in addition to the project manager and one or more systems analysts, the team may include other specialists, including programmers, database designers, and technical writers.

The Systems Development Life Cycle

As mentioned earlier, the structured approach involves all four of the development stages, with each stage depending upon the successful completion of the previous stages. As we have mentioned, these four stages are:

1. Planning
2. Analysis
3. Design
4. Implementation

These four stages are commonly referred to as the **systems development life cycle (SDLC)** because they describe the conception, birth, and growth of the system. Figure 8-2 shows the four stages as they appear in the systems development life cycle.

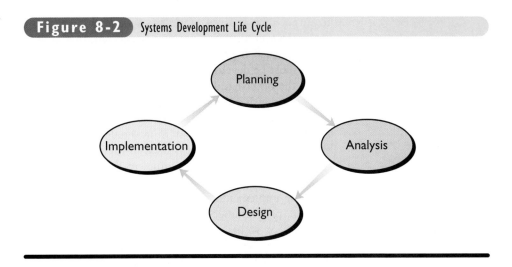

Figure 8-2 Systems Development Life Cycle

Note that we show the process as a closed loop because systems that degrade over time present problems that must be solved by repeated applications of the SDLC approach.

As we move from the planning stage through the analysis stage of the SDLC to the final implementation stage, we are moving from a broad, logical understanding of the problem to a detailed solution to the problem. Each stage of the process is composed of steps to generate deliverables in the form of written documentation or computer files that provide information about what has been accomplished and what is planned for the next stage. In each stage, different techniques are used to generate the deliverables. We will discuss these four stages briefly here and then in more detail using the fareastfoods.com example later in the chapter.

Overview of SDLC

The four stages of the SDLC begin with the planning stage, in which somebody in the organization becomes aware that either an existing system is not working correctly or a new system is needed to meet an opportunity. This process depends on many environmental and behavioral situations. For the time being, we will just assume that a problem or need has been identified and that a project has been initiated to solve it in the project initiation step. The next step is to determine if it is feasible to solve the problem or to create the new system. If it is judged to be infeasible, perhaps because of technical, economic, or organizational reasons, then the project can be terminated without going any further. If it is judged to be feasible, then a development team is formed, and a **steering committee** composed of management, users, and developers is created to oversee the project. The key deliverable of the planning stage is a document called the **project plan,** which provides a description of the desired information system. This includes a clear statement of the scope of the desired project.

In the analysis stage, the goal is to gather data that will answer the question of *what* the system will do. Only when this question has been answered does the project proceed to the next stage—design. The key deliverable from the analysis stage is the **system proposal** that describes what the new system should look like.

Note that, in the process of answering the question of what the system will do in the analysis stage, it may become clear that this system should not be developed or acquired, because either the questions cannot be clearly answered or the answers cause management to rethink the need for a modified or new system. As with the previous stage, stopping here will save a great deal of money and time compared to continuing with the wrong system or one that is unneeded.

In the next stage—design—the *how* questions are answered. The first *how* question is: *How* will the system be developed—internally, through outsourcing, or acquired? The analysis stage has provided enough information that this question can be answered. If outsourcing is selected, then a vendor must be selected and the project turned over to the vendor. If acquisition is selected, then systems requirements must be developed that will be used in selecting a system to be acquired.

On the other hand, if the decision is made to develop internally, then the design stage must also answer this question: *How* will the system operate? Whereas the *what* question was answered in the analysis stage the physical design is created to specify the details of the system in the design stage. The result of the design stage is a **system specification** that is used in the implementation stage to program the new system, outsource it, or to acquire it, depending on the decision made at the beginning of the design stage.

In the implementation stage, if the system is being developed internally or outsourced, programmers turn the system specification into working programs. If the new system is being acquired, the system specifications are used to determine the system to be purchased. Whether developed internally, outsourced, or acquired, the new system is installed and tested extensively at this stage, and the users are trained. The deliverable from this stage is an installed working system. It is important to be aware that, even when planning, analysis, and design stages are accomplished on schedule, the development process can be dramatically delayed or even aborted during the implementation stage. There can be a number of reasons for delay or termination of the project, including poorly completed early stages or programming problems, but all too often the problems are due to people in the organization subverting the implementation process when they are threatened by the changes that are associated with the new information system.

Once the project has been installed, it must be maintained by solving any day-to-day problems. During the implementation stage, if so much maintenance work is necessary to keep the system running that it becomes obvious that the system is not working as required because of changing information requirements, different business conditions, or technological innovations, we move back to the planning stage and start the systems development life cycle over again. Table 8-2 shows the four stages of the SDLC and the key deliverable for each stage.

The SDLC is often referred to as the **waterfall approach** to development because the process is much like a series of waterfalls, with the deliverable from each stage *falling down* to the next stage, as shown in Figure 8-3. And, as with a waterfall, it is often difficult (but not impossible) to go backward in the SDLC. Ideally, each step of the SDLC or waterfall method should be completed before going on to the next stage. However, in practice, there are often situations where it is necessary to go back to a previous stage to add a missing element or to fix a problem. Although this should be avoided, it is a reality in systems development. We have denoted this in the figure by showing the backward arrow as being dashed.

SDLC in the Networked Economy

Like every other facet of global business, structured systems development has been changed by the networked economy. No longer can the process be slow and tedious—it must be faster to keep up with the speed of the networked economy. This

Table 8-2   Systems Development Life Cycle

Stage	Deliverable
Planning	Project plan
Analysis	System proposal
Design	System specification
Implementation	Working system

Figure 8-3 Waterfall Development

Figure 8-3 Waterfall Development

Planning

Analysis

Design

Implementation

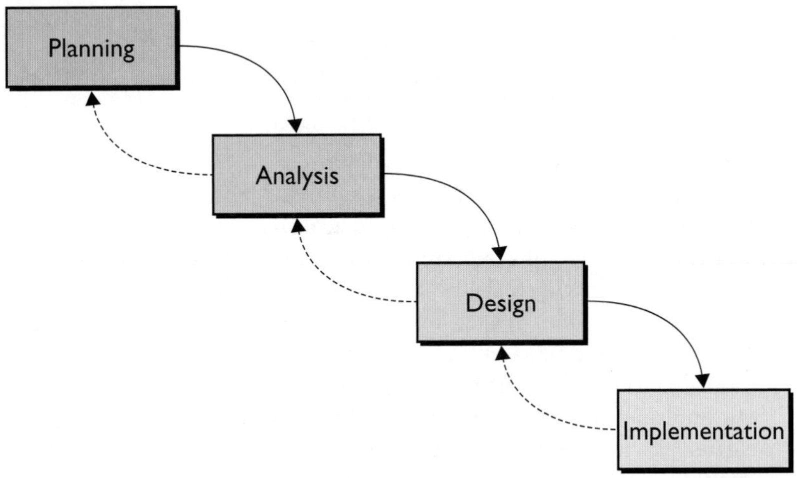

has resulted in a combining of the good features of structured systems development with those of RAD prototyping in the analysis and design stages and the use of computer languages that lend themselves to faster development. In addition, more emphasis has been placed on thinking about the implementation stage at the beginning of the process rather than waiting to the end. This often involves including implementation problems as a part of the planning process.

We will now consider the first two stages in more detail, using the enhancement to the fareastfoods.com customer ordering system as an example. The last two stages will be covered in the next chapter.

Quick Review

1. What are the four stages of the SDLC?
2. Why is the SDLC also referred to as the *waterfall approach* to systems development?

Planning Stage

In the planning stage of the SDLC process, a problem or opportunity is identified, it is determined if it would be possible to create or acquire an information system to solve the problem or meet the need, and a development team is formed. The planning stage involves five steps:

- Identifying the project
- Initiating the project
- Performing a feasibility analysis
- Creating a workplan
- Staffing the project

As a result of these five steps, a project plan containing the best estimate of a project's scope, benefits, risks, and resource requirements is created. This project plan will be reviewed by the steering committee, which will decide whether to go forward or not.

Ⓕocus on the Internet

Developing the AutoNation Web Site

Automobile dealers at all distribution levels are quickly reacting to the networked economy by creating Web sites to stay in contact with potential buyers. Manheim Auctions is doing it at the wholesale level and many new and used dealers have jumped into the market at the retail level. One such retail dealer that has done this in a big way is AutoNation, Inc., the largest seller of automobiles in the United States with more than four hundred new- and used-vehicle franchises. AutoNation's site, AutoNationDirect.com (http://www.autonationdirect.com), offers the company's entire vehicle inventory online, so customers may browse its virtual lot, model by model, to select the color, features, and price they're looking for. Customer requests are sent to an AutoNation dealership via an e-mail response to in-store salespeople known as Internet Sales Guides. Customers can also use AutoNationDirect.com to acquire financing and insurance.

AutoNation's system for processing Internet sales leads was developed from scratch in eighteen months by a four-person IT team working with several vendors. The first step was to outsource the building of a prospect-management system to Fusive.com when no off-the-shelf software met AutoNation's needs. This took six weeks and was followed by AutoNation contracting with the Cobalt Group to quickly build sites for 270 of its dealerships. The two systems ensured that leads were quickly responded to, regardless of whether they came into a dealership Web site or to the central site. This system was integrated with SkyTel Corporation's paging service to cut response times to customers' online queries from forty-eight hours to two.

Source: Bob Wallace, "Car Retailer Builds Site the Fast Way," *Computerworld,* July 12, 1999, http://www.computerworld.com.

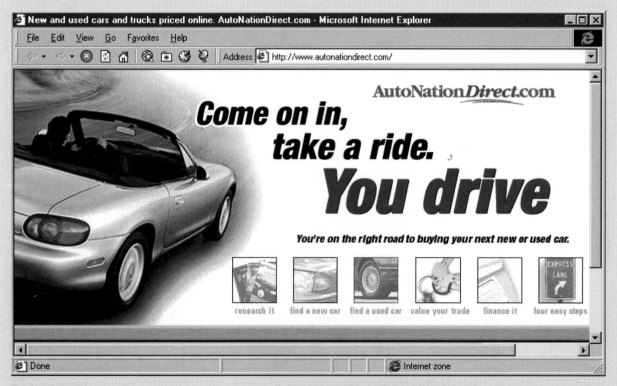

The AutoNation Web site allows prospective car buyers to search their entire vehicle inventory online.

Identifying the Project

The project identification step begins with the determination that a problem exists in the current system or that a need exists for a new system to meet an opportunity. In terms of an existing system, complaints from users of the system may signal that a problem exists, an audit may show the current system to be too expensive even though it is working, or the output from the system may not match the organizational needs. The recognition that a new system may be needed could result from the organization's strategic plans, from a need to meet competitive demands, from an idea by an employee for a new way to carry out an existing process, or from an idea to use information technology to move into a completely new area of business. Many of the so-called Internet companies and companies discussed in chapter 7 resulted from ideas that led to a new type of information system. In many cases, the company creatively destroyed itself and rebuilt around the new information system.

Like the idea for Manheim Online discussed in the opening Focus on Management box, ideas for new systems often come from individuals outside of the IT area. People in marketing, sales, production, or almost anywhere in the company can see a need for a new system that will help the organization compete. Whereas some of these ideas turn out to be impossible to implement, the ones that are possible can result in huge benefits to the company. The best case is when a person outside of IT works with the IT group to develop an idea into a workable project.

Regardless of where the recognition of a problem or the idea for a new system originates, it must have a **project sponsor** (also known as a *champion)* who has an interest in seeing the system succeed and who will provide the business expertise to the project. If a project does not have a sponsor sufficiently high up in the organization to push it, no matter how good an idea it is, the project will probably never be completed.

Initiating the Project

Once the project has been identified, the project initiation step begins. This usually involves the project's sponsor creating a **system request** that lists the business need for the project, its expected functionality, and the benefits that would like result from its completion. The system request goes to the IT department, where it is considered for development by a senior executive or an information systems approval committee. If it is approved for further study, a systems analyst is assigned to investigate the project and work with the sponsor on the next step of the process: the feasibility study.

Performing a Feasibility Study

The feasibility study that is carried out by the project sponsor and the systems analyst is aimed at answering the following questions:

1. Is the problem worth solving?
2. Is a solution to the problem possible?

If the answer to either question is "no," then the SDLC process is terminated.

In a feasibility study, the analyst does not actually attempt to find a solution to the problem or opportunity. Instead, the objective is to come to an initial understanding of the problem or opportunity and to decide whether or not it is feasible to proceed with a full-scale study of it. The feasibility study looks at the technical, economic, and organizational aspects of the problem.

- **Technical feasibility** means that technology exists to solve the problem or to meet the need.
- **Economic feasibility** means that solving the problem is an economically wise decision.
- **Organizational feasibility** means that the problem can be solved or need met within the limits of the current organization.

If a project is judged to be technically infeasible, this means that it cannot be developed with current technology or that the development group does not have the necessary skills to develop the project. To make this judgment the systems analyst must have knowledge of available technology and the skills set of the development group. Developers should also avoid using experimental technology because this can result in working on the *bleeding edge* of technology. For example, in the Manheim Online example at the beginning of the chapter, the developers decided that it was technically infeasible at that time to run a live auction on the Web where the timing of the bids was important.

Determining economic feasibility involves running a cost/benefit analysis of the project. This analysis should take into account both monetary and nonmonetary costs and benefits of solving the problem or taking advantage of the opportunity by creating a new system. At this stage in development, costs and benefits have to be approximate because the actual solution is not yet known. If this cost/benefit analysis shows that the costs will likely outweigh the potential benefits, then the systems analyst will recommend that the project be scrapped. On the other hand, if the cost/benefit analysis is positive, then the project may be considered further. In the case of Manheim Online, economic feasibility was not an issue because the company was responding to a competitive threat to its dominant position in the market. However, if the costs of setting up and running a Web site to sell cars to dealers turned out to be higher than any benefit that might result, the project would be considered economically infeasible.

Determining organizational feasibility involves assessing how well the organization will accept the new system. No matter how good the system is, if the members of the organization are unwilling to accept it, it will *not* work! As mentioned earlier, if not addressed at this stage, organizational feasibility can become a problem at the implementation stage, after a large amount of money has already been spent on the project. One way to address organizational feasibility is to use a **stakeholder analysis** to determine the effect of the change on any person or group that will affect or will be affected by the new or revised system. Typical stakeholders include the project sponsor, the IS development group, users, employees in other departments, customers, and suppliers. Failure to analyze the potential reaction of a stakeholder to the new system can result in severe problems when it is implemented. For example, in the Manheim Online example, stakeholders included the vice president (the sponsor), the IS group that was left out of the development, the dealers who would use it, and even the people who worked at the traditional auction sites who may have been threatened by the new system.

If the new system is found to be feasible on technical, economic, and organization grounds, then the analyst will recommend that the project be continued.

Creating a Workplan

If the project is approved for continuation, a project manager is typically assigned to the project, and the project is formally launched. The first responsibility of the project manager is to create a document called a **workplan,** which lists the tasks that must be accomplished to complete the project, along with information about each task, the number of persons required, and an estimated time to complete each task. This latter piece of information requires a great deal of experience on the part of the project manager, and even then it is quite possible that the actual time required to complete the project will be much different from the estimates in the workplan. Late projects are so common in systems development that they are almost an accepted part of the process. This is why redoing systems to handle the year 2000 problem was so different from the typical project—the new or revised systems could not be late or else the results could have been catastrophic.

Staffing the Project

Once the workplan has been created and approved, the next step is to bring the team members on board. As mentioned earlier, depending on the size and complexity of the project, the team will be composed of a variety of types of skilled professionals. The degree of experience will vary also as employees who are new to the systems development field are mixed with veterans in order to provide the new people with much-needed experience. The project manager will be responsible for staffing the project and assigning responsibilities to each person or subteam based on the tasks listed in the workplan.

It should be noted that the SDLC project is an organizational project and that to develop the best system possible, all functional area users must be involved in the development effort. Failure to do so could cause serious morale problems as well as design and implementation problems later in the process.

The final deliverable of the planning stage is the project plan, which is a compilation of all of the work that has gone into this stage. This includes the systems request, the feasibility studies with the cost/benefit analyses, the workplan, and the staffing assignments. It represents the team's best estimate of the project's scope, benefits, costs, time requirements, and expected results. This is the *highway map* for the project, which will be revised as the team learns more about the project during the analysis stage, which occurs next. The five steps of the planning stage are shown in Table 8-3, along with the actions taken at each step and the deliverables.

Magnitude of Effort

Although the project we will be considering as an example in this chapter is fairly small, with only a few people involved, that is often not the case. Projects like creating Windows 95 involved hundreds if not thousands of people working for several years to complete the many elements of the new system. Rewriting the code to fix the Year 2000 problem required a great deal of systems development effort. It is estimated that a typical large company spent four hundred programmer-years to fix this problem (where a programmer-year is equivalent to one programmer working full-time for one year).

Quick Review

1. What are the five steps in the planning stage of systems development?
2. What are the types of feasibility that must be considered in the planning stage?

Planning Stage for fareastfoods.com Project

It has been proposed that fareastfood.com's existing customer order system be enhanced in such a way as to provide incentives to customers to spend more at fareastfoods.com. In this case, one of the marketing employees came up with the

Table 8-3	Steps in Planning Stage	
Step	**Actions**	**Deliverables**
Identifying the problem	Problem with existing system or need for new system is identified	Problem statement
Initiating the project	System sponsor creates system request	System request
Performing a feasibility study	Systems analyst is assigned to project; works with sponsor on feasibility study	Feasibility analysis; cost/benefit analysis
Creating a workplan	Project manager is assigned to project	Workplan listing tasks, estimate times and staffing needs
Staffing the project	Other team members assigned to project	Staffing responsibilities; project plan

Focus on People

Bill Gates

Very few companies are developing more software systems than Microsoft. Products from Microsoft include its Windows operating system that runs on over 85 percent of all personal computers and is used on a wide range of servers, Micrsoft Office Suite that dominates the personal productivity market, popular programming languages like Visual Basic, Visual C++, and Visual J++, Internet Explorer and other Internet tools, and a wide variety of games and other products. Revenue from these products in 1999 was $19.5 billion, and the total value of the company was the highest in the world. As you probably are aware, the chairman of Microsoft is Bill Gates.

Gates got his start with computers as a high school student in Seattle and after a year at Harvard, he joined with Paul Allen in 1975 to form Microsoft to develop software using the BASIC computer language. Gates and Allen were successful in this market, but their real break came in 1979, when they purchased the DOS operating system from another Seattle company and licensed it to IBM for its new PC that was released in 1981. By licensing rather than selling DOS to IBM, Microsoft was able to keep control of it and sell other versions to IBM's competitors. DOS remained the primary operating system for PCs, providing much needed revenue for Microsoft until it released the first of

the Windows operating systems (Windows 3.1) in the early 1990s. Microsoft's Office Suite, Internet Explorer, programming languages, and games have become popular application software since that time. All through Microsoft's twenty-five years of growth, Gates has remained very involved in the development of new software, meeting with programmers to test and critique their work on new products, as well as providing new ideas for the company to pursue.

Bill Gates's company, Microsoft, develops a great deal of software for use in the home and in business.

---

idea after taking a vacation using frequent flier miles. She talked with her manager about this idea. The marketing manager realized that this was a great idea and put together a system request for the project. A shortened version of the system request is shown in Figure 8-4.

Feasibility Study

The system request for the customer discount program was approved by the IS approval committee, and an analyst was assigned to work with the sponsor on a feasibility study. In looking at the project, they decided that it was technically feasible to allocate FarEastBucks to customers based on the amount of each transaction, track the number of bucks in their account, and allow customers to use the bucks to make purchases. It appeared that this would require additional columns in existing database tables as well as adding functionality to handle the cases in which FarEastBucks are being used to reduce the amount due from the customer or are being created by a credit card transaction.

Because this is an *enhancement* to an existing system, we are adding new functionality to it. Most information systems are built in such a way that sections of programming instructions called **modules** can be added to enhance the existing systems. The modules communicate with the existing system by passing messages and data but operate independently to do the task for which they are designed.

Figure 8-4 System Request

> **System Request--FarEastBucks Project**
> **System Sponsor:** Chris Patrick, Marketing Manager
> CPatrick@fareastfoods.com
> **Business Need:** To increase sales and customer loyalty by providing frequent customers with FarEastBucks that they can use to purchase items from our catalog
> **Functionality:** The customer order system would be enhanced to give customers one FarEastBuck for every $20 they spend with us. When they have at least ten FarEastBucks, they could use them to purchase items from our catalog. The FarEastBucks would be stored electronically on our database, and the customers' total would appear each time they visit our Web site.
> **Benefits:** This enhancement to our customer order system could increase sales by as much as 25 percent with a very low cost to us. It would also increase customer loyalty because customers would want to increase their FarEastBucks and use them to purchase items from us.
> **Comments:** The Marketing Department is very much in favor of this project and views it as a way to build a loyal customer base.

The development process to add modules to an existing system is much the same as for an entirely new system. Although this will require some modifications to the existing customer order system, we will consider only the development of the new modules.

To check for economic feasibility, the analyst and sponsor did a cost/benefit analysis. Such analyses can be done in a variety of ways, including net present value (NPV), return on investment (ROI), and break-even analyses (BEA). With the speed at which things are changing in the current environment, one way of carrying out a break-even analysis is to look at how *long* it will take for a project to pay for itself. That is, if a project won't pay for itself in six or twelve months, a smaller, Internet-based company like fareastfoods.com may not want to invest in it because this implies a low return on investment. To see how this would work for the customer discount system at fareastfoods.com, consider the values shown in Table 8-4.

In this case, we are using a worst-case scenario for the customer discount, that is, that *all sales* will be subject to a 5 percent discount when, in actuality, customers will receive the discount only after spending at least $200 to obtain ten FarEastBucks. However, if the project pays for itself in a few months under this assumption, then it will do even better under actual conditions. The marketing manager has researched the effect that such customer discounts have had in the past and has found that monthly unit sales typically increase by *at least* 25 percent. Finally, the systems analyst has estimated that the customer discount system will cost *no more* than $100,000 to develop and can be completed in three months. The question now is: Will the increased unit sales combined with decreased unit profits result in

Table 8-4 Data and Assumptions for Customer Awards Project

Item	Value	Assumption
Current average price	$7.50	Historical data
Current average cost	$4.50	Historical data
New average price	$7.13	All sales discounted 5 percent
Old monthly unit sales	70,000	Historical data
New monthly unit sales	87,500	Unit sales will increase 25 percent based on marketing manager's research
Development cost	$100,000	Analyst's estimate

an increased monthly profit and, if so, how long will it take to recoup the cost of development? Because fareastfoods.com has a policy that a new project must pay for itself in six months or else it will not be started, this question is important.

If these data and assumptions are entered into a spreadsheet as shown in Figure 8-5, we can see that the combination of 5 percent smaller unit profits with 25 percent higher units sales results in an increased monthly profit of almost $20,000. Dividing this value into the $100,000 development cost results in a payoff period of a little more than 5 months—good enough to continue the development process.

Next the analyst considered organizational feasibility. Because this new system does not appear to affect any stakeholders other than customers (and them in a positive way), it would appear to be organizationally feasible.

Developing a Workplan and Staffing the Project

Based on the feasibility study, the steering committee gives its go-ahead to the project and assigns a project manager. She begins work immediately to develop a workplan for the project and to pull together a team that can build the new system. Some of the tasks to be performed, along with the project manager's best estimate of the time to complete each task, are shown in Figure 8-6. The staff members are shown in Table 8-5, along with the percent of their time they are expected to allocate to the project. Note in Figure 8-6 that the total of fourteen weeks required is only one week longer than was estimated by the systems analyst. Note also that two of the operations can be performed in parallel but that the last two must be performed in sequence. Finally note that in the staffing plan, in addition to the project manager and systems analyst already on the project, a lead programmer and programmer/analyst were added. The latter person is an inexperienced new hire and is expected to work on all stages of the project as a part of his training experience.

Once the workplan and staffing are completed, the project manager can combine all of the documentation into the project plan, which will be submitted to the steering committee for consideration.

Figure 8-5 Cost/Benefit Analysis

	A	B	C	D	E	F	G
1	Current Values		Projected Values		Comment		
2	Average Price		Average Price				
3	$7.50		$7.13		5 percent discount on all sales		
4	Average Cost		Average Cost				
5	4.5		4.5		Same average cost		
6	Average Profit		Average Profit				
7	$3.00		$2.63		Price - Cost		
8	Monthly sales		Monthly sales				
9	70,000		87,500		Monthly sales increase 25 percent		
10							
11	Monthly Profit		Monthly Revenue		Increased profit		
12	$210,000		$229,688		$19,688		
13							
14			Development Cost		Months to pay off		
15			$ 100,000		5.08		

Figure 8-6   Portion of Workplan for Customer Awards Project

Workplan for Customer Awards Project	
Task	Time Estimate
Determine requirements	2 weeks
Create data flow diagram	1 week*
Build data model	1 week*
Design system	4 weeks
Program system	7 weeks
*(Can be done together)	

Table 8-5   Staffing for Customer Awards Project

Name	Title	Responsibility	Time Allocation
Heather	Project manager	Oversee entire project	100
Rick	Systems analyst	Work with Heather to analyze, design, and implement project	75
Eleanor	Lead programmer	Take leadership role in implementing design	50
David*	Analyst/programmer	Support work throughout the project	100

*A new hire with very little experience

Quick Review

1. Create the spreadsheet shown in Figure 8-5 and change the increase in sales from 25 percent to 20 percent. Will the plan still meet the company's requirement of a six-month payoff?
2. Why is this considered a *worst-case analysis?*

Analysis

If the project plan is approved by the steering committee, the analysis stage of the process begins. In this stage, the development team works closely with the sponsor to understand the existing system (if one exists) and the new system that is needed. Once the team members feel that they understand what the existing system does and what the new system must do, they can develop a design for the new system in the design stage. Included in this is determining the *who, where,* and *when* of the system. This is:

- *Who* will use the system?
- *Where* will the system be used?
- *When* will it be used?

There are two main steps in the analysis stage: determining requirements and building logical models. In the first step, the development team members need to learn as much as they can about the problem or opportunity on which they are working. That is, they must learn about the *requirements* for the system they are building or acquiring. In the process of carrying out the requirements analysis, the development team will usually find both good and bad features of the existing system. The good features can be carried forward into the new system with a reduction in the design effort at the same time as the team avoids repeating the bad features in the new system.

In the second step, team members must create models of both the old and new systems, where a **model** is a simplified version of reality and as such does not attempt to capture every detail of the system. Instead, the model is useful for conceptualizing the way the system works and for determining what must be done to solve the problem or what data must be stored. These models are *logical* models in that nothing physical is involved. At this stage we are attempting to understand what the current system does and what the replacement or new system must do—not how it will be done. That must wait until the design stage.

Note that this stage is not just analysis—it is actually analysis of the existing system or need and logical design of the new system, but that is too much to say, so it is called just the *analysis stage*. Figure 8-7 shows the process through which the team will move in this stage.

Requirements Determination

To determine the requirements of the system that they are building, the team members must gather facts and information to answer a variety of questions, including:

- How does the current system function, or what need will the new system meet?
- What data are needed for the revised or new system?
- What reports does the current system generate (if there is a current system)?
- How should the replacement or new system operate?
- What reports or results should the replacement or new system generate?
- How would the new system affect jobs of employees?

Answering these questions requires that the team use a number of tools and techniques, including interviews, surveys, observations, joint application development (JAD) meetings, and reviews of output generated by the existing system. Interviews with the project sponsor and other persons closely associated with the project provide firsthand ideas on the problem or opportunity. Surveys of staff can provide less-detailed information from a wider audience regarding the problem with an existing system. JAD meetings involve the development team meeting with the project sponsor and the users to discuss the project at all stages of development. At the analysis stage, such meetings provide useful information on what is required to fix an existing system or develop a new system. Reviews of output from an existing system can be very useful in learning why it is not meeting the organization's needs. For a new system, another useful requirements tool is a throw-away prototype of the system. This tool was used very successfully in the Manheim Online project. A **throw-away prototype** is used in this step because it helps develop the system requirements but is *not* meant to be used as an actual system.

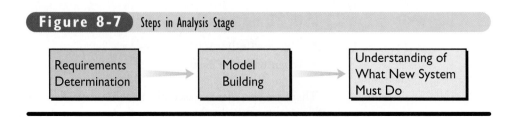

Figure 8-7 Steps in Analysis Stage

Requirements analysis is a critical step in the process of systems development because it is the source of all the information that will be used by the development team. It is important that the development team not be in a hurry in this step and miss an important piece of information that will cause the team to create the wrong system in later stages of the process.

Model Building

Once the development team members believe that they have a clear understanding of the problems with an existing system or the system that is needed to meet an opportunity, they can move ahead to the model building step. Two types of models are used in this step: data models and process models. We have already discussed data models in chapter 5 on organizational memory. Recall that a **data model** is a graphical description of the columns, tables, and identifiers in a database (usually relational). Because data are the basis for all processing in any information system, it is absolutely necessary that a correct data model be constructed before attempting to go forward.

On the other hand, process modeling involves describing the data flows within the system. This is done in the form of a **data flow diagram (DFD),** which is a graphical representation of the flow of data into and through the system and information out of the system. Only the four DFD symbols shown in Figure 8-8 are used in process modeling.

In a data flow diagram, the rectangular external source or destination symbol is used to represent parties external to the system who interact with it, such as customers, vendors, other systems, and so on. The oval internal process symbol is used to represent processing that takes place, such as calculating how many FarEastBucks should be added to a customer's account based on the amount of the sale. The storage of data is represented by the data store open rectangle, and the flow of data into and within the system and information out of the system are represented by the data flow arrow. An example of a data flow diagram will be shown later when we discuss the analysis stage for the enhanced fareastfoods.com customer order system.

A question that always arises at this stage is: Which system is being modeled—the existing system or the proposed system? The answer is both: If an existing system is being replaced, then it is necessary to understand what this system is doing in order to build a replacement system that accomplishes the same (and, usually, additional) purposes. Without understanding the existing system, there is no way to build a replacement! Then, the replacement system should also be modeled to ensure that it is accomplishing the desired purposes. On the other hand, if a completely new system is being created for which there is no existing system, then the new system must be modeled to understand what it must do.

Quick Review

1. What are the steps in the analysis stage?

2. What is the purpose of a process model?

Figure 8-8 Data Flow Diagram Symbols

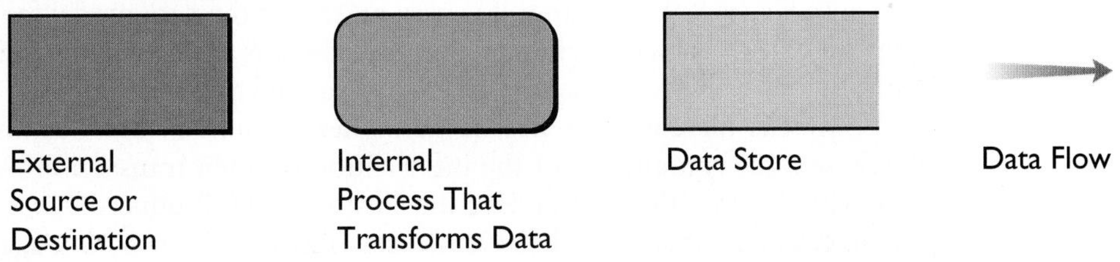

External Source or Destination

Internal Process That Transforms Data

Data Store

Data Flow

Focus on Management

Software MacKiev

If one were to guess where the largest collection of computer programmers is located, the most probable answer would be in Silicon Valley outside of San Francisco. However, this would be wrong! In fact, in the Ukrainian city of Kiev it is estimated that 15 percent of the population has a computer science degree due to the concentration of computers there during the Soviet era. For example, in the early days of computers, one of only three supercomputers in the world was located at the Cybernautics Institute in Kiev. With the fall of the Soviet Union, Ukraine became an independent country and Kiev has become a leader in capitalistic uses of its programming talent. Interestingly enough, the favorite computer in Kiev is the Apple Macintosh, due in part to the creation of a training center in cooperation with Apple's development group. This center was aimed at retraining many of the nuclear scientists and engineers for peaceful purposes. So far, over 2,000 people have been through the introductory Macintosh programming course.

As a result of this store of Macintosh programmers, Software MacKiev was founded to convert Windows software programs to run on Macintosh computers. With 107 programmers working, many of whom went through the Apple training program, it is the largest development company in the world devoted exclusively to converting Windows titles to the Macintosh and has converted over 150 such titles. The company has forty-five customers in Europe and the United States including IBM, Mattel, and Electronic Arts. The Ukrainians work fast, too: The Software MacKiev programming team completed the IBM WorldBook Multimedia Encyclopedia for Macintosh (which ships with the iMac) in just eight months. Whenever possible, they try to add features to the Mac titles not found in the Windows version. Jack Minsky, founder of Software MacKiev, is happy to note that former Soviet nuclear scientists are now writing Sesame Street programs and other peaceful projects.

Source: David Graham, "The Ukrainian Connection." *Hot News,* http://www.apple.com/hotnews/features/mackiev/

Analysis of fareastfoods.com Project

To carry out the analysis of enhancement to the customer order system, we need to begin with the systems requirement step. Recall that this involves using a variety of tools and techniques, including interviews, surveys, analyses of competitors, and so on, to answer a series of questions. We will pose those questions again along with the answers that the project development team found in Table 8-6.

Note that the answer to the question of how the new or enhanced system should operate is a list of steps that the system must follow. This is the *logic* of the system and must be carefully considered to ensure it matches the system proposed by the sponsor. This logic will become even more important in the design and implementation stages because it stipulates the manner in which the system will operate.

Model Building: The Data Model

Once the development team has been able to answer the questions listed in Table 8-6, the next step is to model the system. As mentioned earlier, this involves creating a data model and a process model for the system. The data model for the system is shown in Figure 8-9. Note that it is very much like the data model for the special request system discussed in chapter 5 in that there is the same Customer table along with Products and Purchase tables. We have added a new column for the number of FarEastBucks the customer has in his or her account to the Customer table. The Purchase table contains all of the information on each transaction—a number that uniquely identifies the transaction, the Customer ID, Product ID, the price paid for the item, the number of FarEastBucks used, the quantity purchased, and the date of the purchase. The columns for price paid and number of FarEastBucks used are

Table 8-6   Questions and Answers from Analysis

Question	Answer
How does the current system function? Or: What need will the new system meet?	The current customer order system does not provide for any type of customer award. To make this possible, new modules are required to award FarEastBucks to customers to spend on food items. The new modules will communicate with existing order entry system to update the number of FarEastBucks as they are spent or new purchases made.
What data are needed for the revised or new system?	*From Customer Order system:* Customer ID, Sales Amount, and whether FarEastBucks are being used on purchase or being created by a credit card purchase *From database:* FarEastBucks available for customer to spend
What reports does the current system generate (if there is a current system)?	Current customer order system handles orders but does not enable customer to receive awards for previous purchase amounts
How should the replacement or new system operate?	**1.** If customer is making a purchase, the amount of purchase is converted to FarEastBucks and added to existing number for the customer. **2.** If customer wants to use FarEastBucks to reduce purchase amount, a new module determines available FarEastBucks. If there are at least ten, they are subtracted from amount of purchase (up to amount of purchase). Number of bucks used is subtracted from existing number of bucks. **3.** If existing FarEastBucks are less than ten, message is sent to order system that they cannot be used for purchase.
What reports or results should the replacement or new system generate?	Total sales and FarEastBucks spent by a customer
How would the new system affect jobs of employees?	None that can be ascertained

included in the Purchase table in case there is a need for a refund. The Price Paid column contains the original purchase price, which may be different from the current product price. Similarly, the column for number of FarEastBucks used is necessary to ensure that purchasers are refunded FarEastBucks (and not a credit to the charge card) if bucks were used in the purchase. Finally, the Products table contains the Product ID as a primary key, the product name, the product price, and the quantity on hand (QOH). Although this table is not needed to work with FarEastBucks, it is a key part of the existing customer order system and is shown for completeness.

Note that the data model provides the data required in the answer to the question about data required for a new system (i.e., FarEastBucks available for customers to spend). If this were not true, the data model would need to be revised to match the data requirements. Note also the thought that goes into the data model to ensure that it handles the various operations that might occur after the purchase.

Figure 8-9   Data Model for Customer Discount System

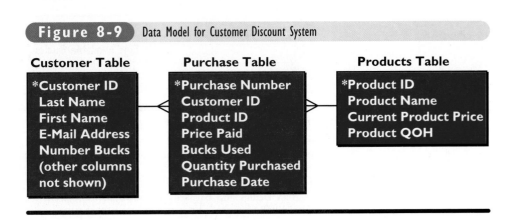

Customer Table

*Customer ID
Last Name
First Name
E-Mail Address
Number Bucks
(other columns
not shown)

Purchase Table

*Purchase Number
Customer ID
Product ID
Price Paid
Bucks Used
Quantity Purchased
Purchase Date

Products Table

*Product ID
Product Name
Current Product Price
Product QOH

Model Building: The Process Model

As mentioned earlier, the process model for any system is a data flow diagram that shows the flow of data into and through the system and information out of the system using the symbols shown in Figure 8-8. Because this is not a textbook on systems development, we do not have the space to discuss this very important technique here. Numerous articles on process modeling[2] as well as textbooks on systems development cover this topic in detail.[3] Instead, we will present the appropriate data flow diagram for a purchase involving FarEastBucks in Figure 8-10 and discuss process modeling using it. To keep this simple, we have not considered the case of a refund of a purchase using FarEastBucks—something that the development team would need to consider for a complete system.

In looking at Figure 8-10, we can see that there is only one external object—the customer order system two processes, and one data store for customer data. We treat the existing customer order system as an external entity because it already exists and operates separately from the new processes. Process 1 occurs when customers want to use their FarEastBucks to reduce the cost of a purchase and Process 2 occurs when they make a purchase creating new FarEastBucks that are added to their account. Let's consider Process 1 in more detail. For Process 1, the flow of data, in the form of Customer ID and the amount of purchase to the module, is denoted by the flow arrow from the Customer Order System. Process 1 uses this data to check the Customer Data store to determine if the customer has at least ten FarEastBucks. If there are at least ten, then the FarEastBucks can be subtracted from the Original Amount to compute a Net Amount (which cannot be negative), and the number of FarEastBucks is reduced by the number spent. The Net Amount and new number of Available Bucks are returned to the Customer Order System, which communicates with the customer. The data store is updated with the new number of FarEastBucks.

Note that the models being built in this case are of the *new* system because there is no existing system to replace. These models will be crucial in helping us design the new system in the next stage.

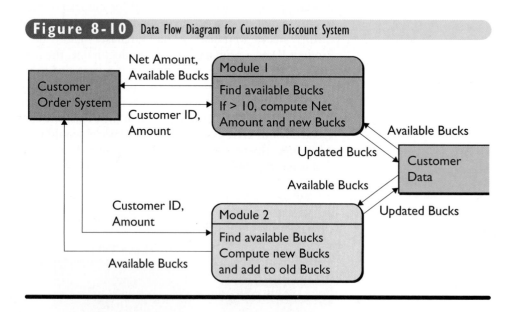

Figure 8-10 Data Flow Diagram for Customer Discount System

2. For example, a good one is J. Satzinger, "Essential Systems Analysis: Its Use and Implications," *Proceedings of the Seventh Annual Conference of the International Academy for Information Management*, Dallas, 1992, pp. 287–301.

3. See Alan Dennis and Barbara Wixom, *Systems Analysis and Design in Action* (New York: Wiley, 2000).

System Proposal

After modeling the customer discount system, the development team needs to decide if a system could be acquired or developed to meet the requirements. If, in the team's opinion, no system can be acquired or developed to meet the requirements, then this opinion should be reported to the steering committee, which will make a decision on whether to terminate the project or look for other ways of meeting the requirements, for example, by simply modifying the customer order system to give everybody a straight 5 percent discount.

The answers to analysis questions, the data model, and the processing model make up the system proposal, which is submitted to the steering committee for a decision on whether to continue or not. In this case, it was decided that the system proposed by the development team was worth continuing, and the development team was directed to begin the design process immediately. The design process will be discussed in the next chapter.

Quick Review

1. Why is it necessary to have both data models and process models?
2. Explain the logic associated with Process 2 in Figure 8-10.

⊘ Summary

To summarize this chapter, let's answer the Learning Objectives questions posed at the beginning of the chapter.

Why is information systems development or acquisition important to all types of organizations? As we have discussed throughout this textbook, information systems used to handle the present, remember the past, and prepare for the future are an integral part of all organizations. They are used to process transactions quickly, store data, information, and knowledge, and help managers and employees to make decisions. A problem facing all organizations is deciding how to obtain the information systems they need. Whereas some systems can be acquired, others must be designed and built to meet the specific needs of the organization. Properly building information systems is critical to the long-term well-being of an organization. In designing and building or acquiring an information system, the requirements of the organization must be carefully analyzed so that the resulting information system accomplishes the purposes for which it is being developed. The process of analyzing information requirements, designing systems to meet these requirements, and building these systems is called systems development.

What are the most commonly used approaches to systems development? Several approaches to systems development are used today by individuals and organizations—ad hoc programming, structured approach, rapid application development, end-user programming, outsourcing, and acquisition. All approaches to systems development have four basic stages: planning, analysis, design, and implementation. The planning stage determines the problem to be solved, whereas the analysis stage determines what must be done to solve the problem. The design stage determines how the problem will be solved, and the implementation stage actually solves the problem. However, different approaches emphasize one or two stages over the others. It should be noted that many development projects use a combination of these approaches.

What are the stages in the structured approach to development? The four stages of the structured approach to development are planning, analysis, design, and implementation. The planning stage determines that there is a problem or an opportunity and determines if it is possible to solve the problem or meet the opportunity. The key deliverable of the planning stage is the project plan. In the analysis stage, the aim is to gather data that will answer the *what* question of the system: *What* will the system do? The key deliverable is the system proposal. In the design stage, the *how* questions are answered: *How* will the system be developed, and *how* will it operate? In the design stage, the physical design is created to specify the details of the system in a systems specification. In the implementation stage, whether developed or acquired, the new system is installed and tested extensively, and the users are trained.

What are the steps in the planning stage of development? The planning stage of development has five steps: identifying the project, initiating the project, performing a feasibility analysis, creating a workplan, and staffing the project. The project identification step begins with the determination that a problem exists in the current system or that a need exists for a new system to meet an opportunity. The project initiation step involves the project's sponsor creating a system request that lists the business need for the project, its expected functionality, and the benefits that would likely result from its completion. The feasibility study is aimed at answering the following questions: Is the problem worth solving, and is a solution to the problem possible? There are three types of feasibility to be considered: technical, economic, and organizational. If the new system is found to be feasible, the project is formally launched, and a workplan that lists information on the tasks that must be accomplished to complete the project is created. Once the workplan has been created and approved, the next step is to staff the project by adding information technology professionals to it.

What are the steps in the analysis stage of development? There are two steps in the analysis stage: determining requirements and building logical models. In the first step, the development team members must learn about the requirements for the system they are building by answering a series of questions about the system. They do this through a variety of tools, including interviews, surveys, and so on. This is a very important step because all successive work will depend on the results of this step. In the second step, team members must create models for conceptualizing the way the system works and for determining what must be done to solve the problem. Data models and process models are commonly used. The models can be of either the existing system that is being replaced or of a new system.

How do data modeling and process modeling fit into the analysis of a replacement or new system? Data models are used to understand the relationship between the columns and tables in a relational database. Because data are the basis for all processing in any information system, it is absolutely necessary that a correct data model be constructed before attempting to go forward. Process modeling describes the data flows within the system in the form of a data flow diagram (DFD), which is a graphical representation of the flow of data into and through the system and information out of the system.

⊙ Review Questions

1. Under what conditions is information systems development necessary?

2. At which phase of the IS life cycle does system development occur? How has it changed in the networked economy?

3. Which approach to systems development was used in the Manheim Online case?

4. What does a systems analyst do? A project manager?

5. Why is a team needed to develop an information system? Why would a new employee be included on the team?

6. What deliverables are expected from each stage of the SDLC?

7. Why is a feasibility study necessary? What types of feasibility need to be considered?

8. What tools are used for the systems requirement stage? What is a model?

9. What symbols are used to create a process model?

10. What is the role of the steering committee in the systems development process?

⊙ Discussion Questions

1. Discuss why the structured approach was developed to respond to the problems associated with the ad hoc programming approach.

2. Which approach to systems development appears to best fit the networked economy? Why?

3. Take an information systems development situation with which you are familiar and discuss the application of the SDLC to it.

⊙ CASE

WildOutfitters.com

Alex awoke from his nap when he heard the keys in the door and began to rub his eyes.

"Wake up sleepy head," said Claire. "There are groceries to be brought in from the car."

Even though he was still woozy, Alex noticed the words CLARK'S GROCERY written in bold letters on the bags in Claire's hand.

"Why did you go there to shop?" he asked. "There are at least two grocery stores that are closer."

"Well, I've always liked the selection," she responded. "Besides, when they run my check cashing card through, I can collect points."

"Points? What can you use them for? Are you in a shopping league or something?"

"No, silly! You get points for every dollar that you spend and then when you get a certain amount you can get store coupons."

"It's kind of like that credit card we have that gives a little cash back every time we use it. They have really made loyal customers out of us. . . ." With that, Alex stopped and the two looked at each other and smiled.

What the Campagnes realized is that incentive programs like those used at the grocery store and with the credit card are designed to bring customers back for repeat business. With this realization came the sudden insight that a similar program might work for them on their Web site. They have been struggling with the question of how to attract more customers and encourage current customers. Over the next week, they begin to plan a frequent-buyer program for their site. Their strategy will be to give away special items when buyers make six purchases worth $100 or more. Before spending too much time on the project, they will need to assess the projects feasibility.

Initially, they feel that they will need to add functionality to both the Web page and their database. Additions to the Web page will, at the least, include links to the incentive program information such as rules and prizes, the ability for a customer to register for the program, and possibly secure access to their current totals. They will also need to adjust the structure of their database to include the amount of sales for each customer.

Because they are already set up with a focus on customer service, Wild Outfitters should be able to administer the program with its current staff. The major hurdle is whether Wild Outfitters has the technical ability to carry out and maintain the incentive program. The Campagnes will need to decide if they will build the system in-house or if they will need to turn to outsourcing.

After several conversations with an IS consultant and a little research on their own, Alex and Claire were able to conservatively estimate a few of the costs and benefits that would result from the project. They have estimated that an incentive program will increase their sales by 5 percent. With current monthly sales at about $76,000, this would be an extra $3,800 monthly. A rough estimate of the costs includes an initial cost of $8,500. The Campagnes would have to bear the extra costs of the prizes and the operational expenses of the program. Since they want the prizes to be meaningful, they estimate that together these costs would amount to about $1,650 per month. A banker friend of theirs suggested that it would be a reasonable to use a 12 percent annual discount rate.

With this in mind, Alex and Claire have begun the initial stages of developing the project. Once their initial analysis is complete, they then will be able to decide whether or not to continue.

After four trips to the car to lug in the groceries, Alex flopped down in the kitchen to watch Claire put them away.

"It's too bad that there isn't a shopping league," he teased. "You would be a shoe-in for the MVS—Most Valuable Shopper."

Claire smiled at his little joke as she discretely placed the steaks she had begun to thaw back in the freezer and took out the liver.

1. In which of the four stages of the SDLC is the customer incentive project at WildOutfitters.com? What deliverables should be developed?

2. Does this project sound feasible for WildOutfitters.com? Describe the criteria that you would use to make this determination in terms of technical, economical, and organizational feasibility.

What information is needed in order to make this determination?

3. *(Hands on)* Using the information in the case, along with what you have learned so far about electronic commerce, write a system request for this project.

4. *(Hands on)* Using spreadsheet software (such as MS Excel), create a model for performing a cost/benefit analysis of the project. Develop your model to determine the time to payout as the primary measure of the projects' worth. The calculations should estimate monthly values and be carried out for the first year of the projects operation. Be sure that your model includes formulas and functions in the appropriate places so that it may be used for "What–If" analysis. If the Campagnes only are willing to take on the project if it has a payout period of less than one year, what should they decide based on your analysis?

CHAPTER 9

Developing Information Systems 2

⊙ Learning Objectives

After reading this chapter, you should be able to answer the following questions:

⊙ What is the purpose of the design stage of the structured systems development process?

⊙ What operations must occur during the implementation stage, and how is computer programming involved?

⊙ What is outsourcing, and what issues should be considered in deciding to outsource a project?

⊙ If an organization chooses to acquire an information system, what are the key elements of this process?

⊙ What is RAD, and how does it differ from the waterfall approach to systems development?

ⓕocus on Management

Installing TGA at Merrill Lynch

Merrill Lynch & Company has long been a leader in the financial services field, with over $1.5 *trillion* in assets in 1999—more than the GDP of countries like England and France. However, in 1997, Merrill Lynch realized that the growth of low-cost trading over the Internet was a threat to its business. To combat this perceived threat, the management at Merrill Lynch decided to compete on the Internet by concentrating on improving its customer service. Specifically, Merrill Lynch wanted to improve information access for its financial consultants who spent their time helping clients accrue wealth. To do this, a completely new information system was required, one that was centered on providing financial consultants with the analytic tools and information they needed to develop, implement, and monitor financial plans for clients.

The resulting Trusted Global Advisor (TGA) system was completed by October 1998 for a total cost of $850 million. To implement this system quickly, Merrill Lynch set a goal of upgrading ten offices a week. Two weeks before the conversion from the existing system to TGA at each office, all employees in each office underwent mandatory training on the new system. This included training on basic functionality as well as the use of the extensive online help system containing online cue cards and multimedia demonstrations. On the Friday before the conversion, an installation team arrived at the office to remove the old technology and install the new system. On the Sunday before the new system went live, the trainers provided a three-hour review session, and on Monday morning the new system went live. The trainers stayed for a week after the conversion to provide solutions to any problems that came up. Merrill Lynch found the problems to be fewer than expected, primarily due to the intuitiveness of the new system and the thoroughness of the training.

Source: Bill Gates, *Business @ the Speed of Thought* (New York: Warner Books), pp. 80–86.

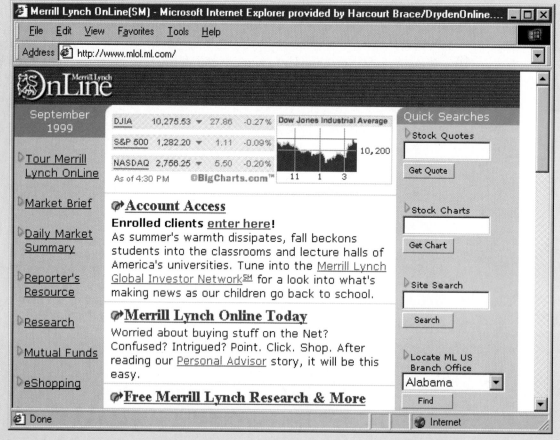

To remain competitive in the fast-paced brokerage business, Merrill Lynch installed new information systems.

Continuing the Development Process

The importance of the information systems development process to an organization and the most commonly used types of systems development, including ad hoc programming, structured systems development, RAD, acquisition, and outsourcing was discussed previously. We went into some detail regarding the use of structured systems development because it is so widely used. Also known as the waterfall approach to systems development, it is divided into four stages: planning, analysis, design, and implementation, as shown in Figure 9-1.

The first two stages of this approach—the planning and analysis stages—were discussed earlier and these stages were applied to the development of an enhancement to the customer ordering system for fareastfoods.com. If you recall, the planning stage involved determining that there exists a need or an opportunity. The result of the planning stage is the development of a project plan containing the best estimate of a project's scope, benefits, risks, and resource requirements. The second stage in the waterfall approach is analysis, which concentrates on determining *what* must be done to solve the problem or meet the opportunity determined in the planning stage. This involves the development team's learning what the existing system does and what the new system must do. There are two steps in the analysis stage: determining requirements and building logical models.

When the planning and analysis stages are complete, the development team knows the problem to be solved or opportunity to be met and what must be done to do this. The team is now ready to begin the design and implementation stages of systems development. As with the planning and analysis stages, we will use the customer awards system for fareastfoods.com as an example throughout this discussion.

Design Stage

The **design stage** is dedicated to the *how* questions, that is, how will the new system be developed, and how will the new system work? The first question of *how* the system will be developed must be answered first. If the decision is made to develop a custom system, it can be done internally or outsourced to another firm. When a project is outsourced, an entity outside of the organization is used to develop all or part of the project. If the decision is made to acquire the information system, an appropriate system must be found and purchased. If the decision is to outsource or to acquire, then the remainder of the design stage is skipped, and the implementation stage is begun.

If the decision is made to develop internally, then the design stage must answer the question of how the system will operate. It does this by moving from the logical

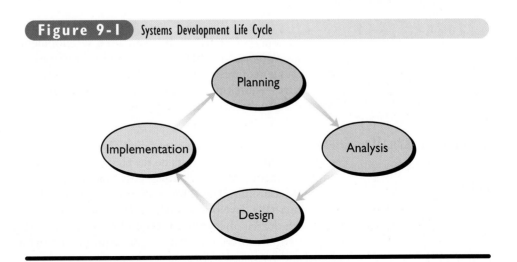

Figure 9-1 Systems Development Life Cycle

models of the analysis stage to a physical design that specifies *all* of the details of the system. For example, in the analysis stage, process modeling was used to determine what the system should do, but no effort was made to specify how the actual processes would work. In the design stage, the manner in which all of the processes in the data flow diagrams will work must be specified. The result of the design stage is a **system specification,** which is used in the implementation stage to build the new system.

Implementation Stage

Once the design stage has been completed, the design must be implemented. This involves building the system, installing it, training the staff that will use the system, and, finally, performing maintenance. If it has been decided to develop the system internally, the design must be programmed by organizational employees. In this case, the design must be sufficiently detailed so that there is no ambiguity about what the programmers are supposed to do. On the other hand, if it has been decided to outsource the development, then the vendor must deliver a working information system. Finally, if the system is to be acquired, an appropriate commercial software package must be found and purchased. Because programming is essential to all information systems development, we will provide a brief discussion of the programming process. Although this discussion is not meant to teach you to program, it should help you understand more about this very important process.

Regardless of how the information system is developed—internally, outsourced, or acquired—it must be installed in the organization and a conversion must be made from the existing system. Employees who will use the system must be trained and the system supported and maintained. Failure to appropriately carry out these steps can doom even the best system to failure. The success of the new TGA system at Merrill Lynch, described in the opening Focus on Management box, was ensured by a well-thought out installation process.

Because outsourcing and acquisition are important alternatives to internal development of an information system, we will also cover these two topics in more detail in this chapter. Finally, because the networked economy often requires high-speed development, we will discuss various approaches to rapid application development (RAD) that result in faster development than does structured systems development.

Quick Review

1. What is the purpose of the design stage of the structured approach?
2. When the implementation stage is completed, what should be the result?

Design Stage

After the analysis stage of the structured development process, the development team knows *what* must be done but has not yet worked out *how* it will be done. The design stage requires that the development team investigate the three development alternatives—develop internally, outsource, or acquire—and then present a recommendation to the steering committee.

Develop Internally, Outsource, or Acquire?

How does an organization choose whether to develop an information system internally, outsource it to an outside developer, or acquire a system? Making this decision is a function of five variables: cost, customization, time, competitive advantage, and in-house skills. There are trade-offs between each variable that must be considered. Internally developing a system or having one developed by an outsourcer leads to a high degree of customization and provides competitive advantage because the organization can control exactly the features that go into the system, the way it looks and feels, and so on.

However, internal development or outsourcing comes at a price because it takes much longer and costs more to create a new system than it does to acquire one. On the other hand, acquired systems may not fit organizational needs exactly and will probably not provide a competitive advantage because other companies can acquire the same system. Enterprise resource planning (ERP) systems have some features of both approaches; that is, a system can be acquired fairly quickly and then modified to fit your special needs. However, acquiring a product with this in mind can lead to many problems when the customization does not work and the maker of the product is under no obligation to solve the problems caused by the changes.

In terms of competitive advantage, internal development is typically superior to outsourcing or acquisition because the resulting system will be unique to the organization. However, internal development requires that the organization have employees with the skills necessary to carry out this process. If those skills are missing from the organization, then outsourcing can be used to bring in a company that has exactly those skills. It should be noted that companies often use outsourcing to develop an information system, but then use their own people to actually run and maintain it. The reverse can also occur. In addition, a compromise between internal development and outsourcing exists in which the existing staff is complemented with consultants to develop the system and use the internal staff to maintain the system. Table 9-1 compares advantages and disadvantages of three approaches to systems development.

Sometimes this decision can be made immediately after the planning stage because the organization realizes that the problem can easily be solved with acquired software or that the organization does not have the skills in-house to develop the system. In other cases, this decision is made after the analysis stage when it is known what must be done. For example, in looking at fareastfoods.com's project to create a system that will reward customers based on their purchases, it appears that this project will require that a system be developed, either internally or through outsourcing. The degree of customization required far outweighs the time it may take to develop it. In addition, this system is meant to give the company a competitive advantage over other companies providing the same product or service.

On the other hand, assume that the company has discovered that using employees provided by a temporary firm is not working very well. Too many orders are being

Table 9-1	Comparison of Development Methods	
Development Method	**Advantages**	**Disadvantages**
Internal development	• Competitive advantage • Complete control over final system • Builds technical skills and functional knowledge of developers	• Requires dedicated effort of in-house staff • Development can be slow • Costs may be higher than with other approaches • System may not work when completed or may not provide desired functionality
Outsourcing	• Outsourcer has more skilled and experienced programmers • Internal staff is not diverted from current work	• Loss of control of project • Internal developers may not learn skills necessary to maintain system • Costs may be higher than with acquisition • Outsourcer may not deliver on claims, or final system may not provide desired functionality
Acquisition	• Available sooner and has high probability of working • Lower costs because development spread out over many users	• Little competitive advantage • Must accept functionality of purchased system • May not integrate well with existing systems • May require modification to meet needs

incorrectly combined, and fareastfoods.com believes that permanent employees who can earn promotions and other benefits will have more pride in their work, resulting in fewer mistakes in combining orders. To handle this new group of employees, the company needs a payroll system that can deal with hourly employees in addition to the salaried employees who already work for the company. Because this project appears to require little customization or provide any competitive advantage and it is needed quickly to make the move to permanent employees, it is probably best to look at acquiring such a payroll system. Outsourcing and acquisition will be discussed in detail later in the chapter.

Internal Development

If the recommendation is to develop the system internally, then the development team must answer the second *how* question, that is: How will the system operate? To do this the team must develop plans for a new system and present them to the potential users for comments. It is at this stage that close contact between the team and users is extremely important to ensure that the replacement system will solve the problems in the existing system without introducing any new ones or else the new system will not solve the problem nor meet the opportunity identified in the planning stage.

Although there are many aspects to this process, we will concentrate on the three most important ones: converting the logical database model to a physical database specification, converting the logical process model into physical forms that can be used by programmers to write the necessary computer programs, and developing the interface screens with which the users will work.

The deliverables from the design stage will include a complete and detailed specification of the physical data model, physical models of each process in the process model created in the analysis stage, and the interface screens. Let's discuss each of these elements of design in order, using the fareastfoods.com example.

Physical Database Specification

Because the steering committee has chosen internal development, the next step in the design process is to create a physical database specification. In the analysis stage, we discussed creating a data model for the system under analysis. This data model includes the tables, the columns in each table, the data type for each column (for example, currency), and the relationships between the tables. Although this is essential information for understanding the system, we need to go further to design the new system by providing data about the database elements, so-called **metadata**. For the database, this includes the type of database being used (Oracle, Access, etc.), the names of the tables and the fields in the tables, the primary key for each table, and the foreign keys in each table. Although these names may be the same as those shown in the data model, they may have to be changed to meet naming requirements of the database system being used or standard naming conventions being used by the organization. Figure 9-2 shows the data model

Figure 9-2 Data Model for Purchasing System

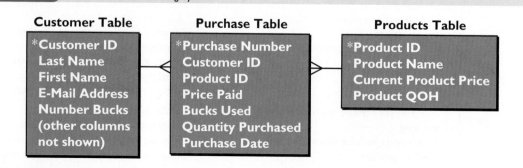

Customer Table

*Customer ID
Last Name
First Name
E-Mail Address
Number Bucks
(other columns not shown)

Purchase Table

*Purchase Number
Customer ID
Product ID
Price Paid
Bucks Used
Quantity Purchased
Purchase Date

Products Table

*Product ID
Product Name
Current Product Price
Product QOH

Figure 9-3 Access Design Screen

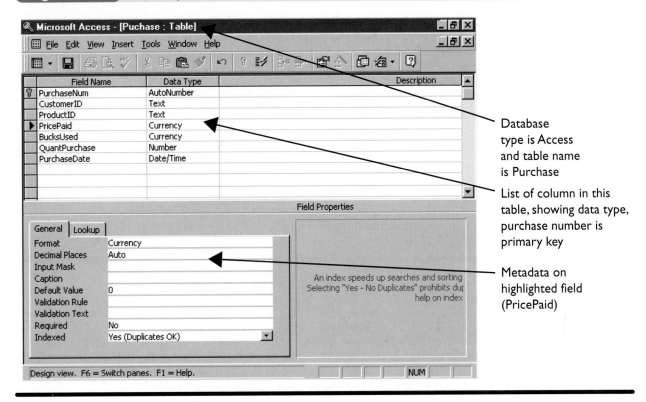

Database
type is Access
and table name
is Purchase

List of column in this
table, showing data type,
purchase number is
primary key

Metadata on
highlighted field
(PricePaid)

for the fareastfoods.com purchasing system, and Figure 9-3 shows the corresponding Access design screen for the Purchase table with key metadata labels pointed out.

Converting Process Models to Physical Forms

To design the processes that make up the information system, it is necessary to convert the logical process models into a form that programmers can use in developing the software portion of the system. This means that all of the processing ovals in the data flow diagrams (DFDs) must be converted into two physical forms: input/processing/output (IPO) tables and pseudocode procedures. In addition, the data stores in the DFDs must be related to the database tables shown in the physical data model.

As their name implies, **input/processing/output (IPO) tables** show the inputs to a process, the required outputs for that process, and the logic that is necessary to convert the inputs into the desired outputs. **Pseudocode** is a way of expressing the logic of the processing in *structured English* rather than in a computer language. Once you have developed an IPO table and the pseudocode for each process, it is often straightforward for programmers to write a computer program in the next stage that will carry out the necessary processing.

To understand how IPO tables work, let's use Process 1 from the data flow diagram created for the fareastfoods.com discount system in the last chapter. This DFD is shown again in Figure 9-4.

We have chosen to explain Process 1 because the logic for Process 2 is very simple—input the Customer ID and Sale Amount and use the Customer ID to find the number of Available FarEastBucks in the database. Divide the Sale Amount by twenty and add the result to the number of FarEastBucks. On the other hand, the logic for Process 1 is a little more interesting.

The IPO table for Process 1 should include the inputs, logic, and outputs for the process, with the logic converting the inputs into the desired outputs. The inputs are

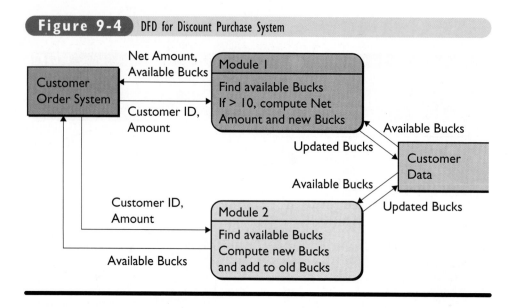

Figure 9-4 DFD for Discount Purchase System

the Customer ID and Sale Amount from the Customer Order System and Available Bucks from the Customer Data store. Outputs are the Net Sale Amount to the Customer Order System and an updated number of FarEastBucks to the Customer Data store. The logic involves three steps. In Step 1, the Customer ID is used to find Available Bucks. In Step 2, if the Available Bucks are greater than ten, the customer is queried for the number of Bucks to be used, the Net Sale Amount is calculated by subtracting the number of Bucks used from the Sales Amount, and new Available Bucks are calculated by subtracting the number of Bucks used from Available Bucks. (For simplicity, it is assumed that the number of Bucks used is less than the amount of the sale and less than Available Bucks. Also, we assume more Bucks are not earned on sales using Bucks.) In Step 3, if the Available Bucks are less than ten, then a message is displayed that Bucks cannot be used in the purchase. The resulting IPO table is shown in Figure 9-5.

Once IPO tables have been created for all of the processes in the DFD, corresponding pseudocode procedures should be created. Pseudocode is useful because the procedure for the DFD process can be expressed very clearly in structured English without worrying about the special syntax and grammar of a computer language. The pseudocode should be a set of clearly defined steps that enables a reader to see the next step to be taken under any possible circumstances. Also, the language and syntax should be consistent so that the programmer will be able to understand the designer's pseudocode. This makes it easy for a programmer to implement the DFD process as a computer program. Often, the conversion from pseudocode statement to computer language instruction is virtually line for line. As an example of pseudocode, the pseudocode for Process 1 of the DFD that was converted to an IPO table earlier is shown in Figure 9-6. Note that it is easy to follow logic in this pseudocode procedure. IPO tables and pseudocode are an essential part of the design stage because the programmers in the implementation stage will use them to guide their work.

The final step in creating physical versions of the process model is to link the data stores in the DFD to the database tables in the physical data model. In the case of the fareastfoods.com discount purchase system, the Customer Data store matches the Customer database table, so no change is needed. However, there is no requirement that the data stores have a one-to-one match with database tables; it may be necessary to split a data store into multiple data store *tables* to match the structure of the database.

ⓕ ocus on People

Ed Yourdan

With the increasing use of computers to handle large projects in the late 1960s and early 1970s came the need for a more organized way to handle the development of such projects. One of the leaders in developing the structured approach for developing large information systems was Edward Yourdan, developer of the popular "Yourdan Method" of structured systems development. Educated at MIT, Yourdan began his career with Digital Equipment Corporation (DEC—now a part of Compaq Computers) in 1964. After working for DEC and General Electric, where he was involved in the development of a number of pioneering computer technologies such as time-sharing operating systems and virtual memory systems, Yourdan started his own consulting firm, Yourdan, Inc., in 1974. Over the next twelve years, the company grew to a staff of over 150 people that trained over 250,000 people around the world in some of the concepts that Yourdan developed. In 1986, Yourdan sold his consulting firm (it is now a part of IBM). The publishing division, which has published over 150 titles on computer science topics, is now a part of Barnes and Noble.

Yourdan followed up this work on structured-systems development methods with pioneering work on the use of object-oriented methods for systems development in the late 1980s and 1990s. This included the development of the Yourdon/Whitehead method of object-oriented analysis/design and the Coad/Yourdon object-oriented methodology. The author of twenty-six computer books and over two hundred technical articles, Yourdan recently has been active in writing and speaking about the Year 2000 problem with a series of books on the subject, including a book with his daughter Jennifer: *Time Bomb 2000: What the Year 2000 Computer Crisis Means to You!*

Source: http://www.yourdon.com/bio.html.

Ed Yourdan has pioneered many of the approaches to systems development in use today.

Figure 9-5 IPO Table for Process 1

Input	Processing	Output
Customer ID, Sales Amount, Available Bucks	1. Use Customer ID to query database for Available Bucks 2. If Available Bucks >10 then Query user for Bucks to use Net Amount = Sales Amount − Bucks Used Available Bucks = Available Bucks − Bucks Used 3. If Available Bucks ≤ 10 then Send message that Bucks cannot be used	Net Amount, Updated Available Bucks

Figure 9-6   Pseudocode for Process 1

```
Begin Procedure
    Input Customer ID and Sales Amount
    Query database for Available Bucks for this Customer ID
    If Available Bucks > 10 then
            Query user for number of Bucks to use
        Net Amount = Sales Amount – Bucks Used
            Available Bucks = Available Bucks – Bucks Used
    Otherwise
            Send message to user that Bucks cannot be used
    End decision
    Output Net Amount to user and updated Available Bucks to database
End Procedure.
```

Creating Interface Screens

Although converting logical models to physical models is crucial for communicating the design of the information system to the programmers who will actually build it, this is often not a very good way of communicating with the project sponsor or potential users. Instead, it is usually mandatory that the design stage include examples of the **interface** with which the user will work. The project sponsor and potential user are usually better able to understand the design by viewing and working with the interface than with the various physical models. The interface screens can be of varying levels of complexity, ranging from a screen with little or no interactivity to one that allows the user to input values and click buttons to see results. The latter case is actually a form of prototyping known as **user-interface prototyping** in which an example interface is created. An example interface, like a test drive, enables prospective users to gain firsthand experience with the new system's interface.

With the move to Web-based electronic commerce systems such as that being used at fareastfoods.com with its standard browser interface, creating interface screens has become much easier. Users readily understand how to use a browser, so the designers need only make sure their design fits within this standardized system. For example, the interface screen for the fareastfoods.com enhanced customer order system might appear as shown in Figure 9-7. In this case, the designers have added some functionality to the screen that will enable the sponsor or users to enter a specific Customer ID and Sale Amount and see the result of using the system. They also have allowed the customer to use only a portion of their Bucks on a given purchase. In this case, the prototype is not actually querying the database but is using values that are *hard-coded* into the interface and work only for the specified ID values.

A variation of user-interface prototyping is **demonstration prototyping.** This type of prototyping is used when a company is bidding on an outsourcing or systems development project. Instead of creating a written proposal or a PowerPoint slide presentation, the company creates a user-interface prototype that demonstrates what the final system will accomplish. This approach was used by Intellimedia Commerce to win the contract to create the Manheim Online system discussed in the opening Focus on Management boxes in chapters 4 and 8.

Using Computer-Aided Software Engineering

A growing trend in developing large software systems is the use of **computer-aided software engineering (CASE).** CASE is the use of software to help in all phases of the systems development process to improve the productivity of systems development. A **CASE repository,** which is a database of metadata about the project, can be used to automate much of the paper flow typically associated with structured development. Development team members can store this information about the project in

Figure 9-7   Interface for Discount Purchase System

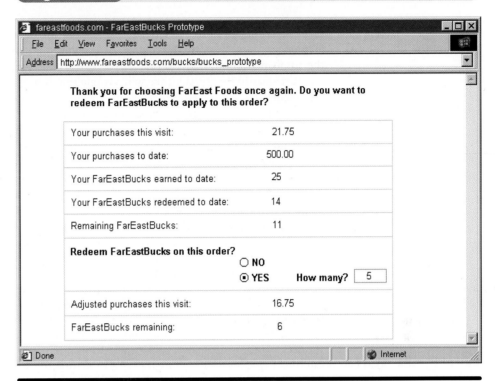

Thank you for choosing FarEast Foods once again. Do you want to redeem FarEastBucks to apply to this order?

Your purchases this visit:	21.75
Your purchases to date:	500.00
Your FarEastBucks earned to date:	25
Your FarEastBucks redeemed to date:	14
Remaining FarEastBucks:	11
Redeem FarEastBucks on this order? ○ NO ⊙ YES How many? [5]	
Adjusted purchases this visit:	16.75
FarEastBucks remaining:	6

the CASE repository on a server accessible to all team members. In addition, CASE-based diagramming software can be used to reduce the effort involved in creating process and data models, and application or code generators can automate the actual writing of the programs. CASE can also automate the documentation process so that as new versions of the program are developed, new documentation is also created. The objective of the CASE process is to have rapid production of program instructions that can be reused with other applications.

The benefits of using CASE software packages—so-called **CASE tools**—include the following:

- The duration of the overall systems development life cycle is reduced as the various stages are compressed and begin to overlap.
- Information sharing is improved as paperbound methods are automated and stored in central information repositories. This also reduces duplicated effort.
- Users are involved throughout the process, and more effort is spent in the early design stages—often the source of critical errors that are difficult to correct.
- Systems are easier to modify because system parameters and functions are stored in a central place. When one part of a system is changed, all elements of the system affected by the change automatically access the new value.

A side effect of using CASE technology is that it encourages developers to concentrate on the front end of the software design procedure: the analysis and design of new applications. The result is the production of applications that require less debugging or redesigning and go to the customer sooner.

Quick Review

1. What are the deliverables from the design stage?
2. What tools are used to convert the logical process models into physical models?

Implementation Stage

If the steering committee decides to implement the design recommended by the development team, then the final stage of the development process can begin. This is the **implementation stage,** which involves turning the information system design into a reality. In this section, we will assume that internal development has been recommended by the development team. In later sections, we will consider the outsourcing and acquisition development alternatives.

As mentioned earlier, the implementation stage for internal development of an information system involves four steps: building the system, installing the system, training staff, and performing maintenance. In the first step, the system is *built* by writing appropriate computer programs or assembling objects that implement the design created in the previous step. Once the programs have been written and debugged, the next step is to install the system on the organization's computers, test it in that location, and to convert from the old system to the new. The third step is to train the staff who will use it. Training not only prepares the employees to use the new system, but also can help avoid people problems that occur whenever there is any kind of change in an organization. Finally, once the system is installed and running in a production mode, it must be supported and maintained. All too often this last step is not given sufficient weight, even though the maintenance cost of an information system is much more than its development cost.

Building the System

Building the information system involves writing the computer programs that go together to provide the functionality specified in the first three stages of this process. Writing computer programs involves giving the computer a sequence of instructions in a computer language such as COBOL, FORTRAN, C++, Java, and Visual Basic. Regardless of the language in which the program is written, the programmer must first be able to translate correctly the logic developed in the design phase into a working program, first by learning the vocabulary and syntax (grammar) of the language and then by studying how various logical situations are handled in that particular language.

Although all five of the languages just listed can be used to write computer programs, Visual Basic, C++, and Java are quite different from the other two in that they are **object-oriented languages,** whereas COBOL and FORTRAN are not. In programming, an object is a self-contained module that combines data and instruction and that cooperates with other objects in the program by passing strictly defined messages to other objects. This methodology is easier to work with because it is more intuitive than traditional programming methods, which divide programs into hierarchies and separate data from programming code. To understand why objects are extremely valuable programming tools, it is necessary to understand that all programs consist of data that require processing and groups of instructions called **procedures** for processing that data. As long as the data and procedures remain the same, the program will work; however, if either the data or the procedures change, the program may not work. Object-oriented programming transforms programming by binding data and procedures in objects. Users can combine the objects with relative ease to create new systems and extend existing ones. Around us is a world made of objects, so the use of objects to create information systems provides a natural approach to programming.

The Programming Process

The most important concept to learn about programming is that it is a form of *problem solving* in which the design created in the design stage is converted into a computer program that implements the design. If the work has been done correctly in the design stage, programmers do not have to know very much about the original problem because their job is to follow the design. The data model, IPO tables,

```
crossword_java.txt - Notepad
File  Edit  Search  Help

void PaintQuestionArea(Graphics g) {
    Font f = new java.awt.Font("Helvetica", 0, 12);
    Font questionFont = new java.awt.Font("Courier", 0, 24);
    Font questionFont18 = new java.awt.Font("Courier", 0, 18);
    FontMetrics questionFontMetrics = g.getFontMetrics(questionFont);

    int viewWidth = kBlocksWide * kBlockWidth;
    int viewHeight = kBlocksHigh * kBlockHeight;

    int top = kPadding;
    int left = (size().width / 2) - (viewWidth / 2);
    //g.clipRect(left, top, viewWidth, kQuestionAreaHeight);

    g.setColor(Color.white);
    g.fill3DRect(left, top, viewWidth, kQuestionAreaHeight, false);

    g.setFont(f);
    String s = new String(  String.valueOf(layout[gBlockMinY][gBlockMinX]))
    s = s.concat(" - ");
    if (gDirection == kAcross)
        s = s.concat("across");
    else
        s = s.concat("down");
```

The Java language is a popular way of developing information systems on the Web.

pseudocode, and interface screens, if correctly done, are sufficient to guide the programming process.

In the networked economy, it is common today for highly competent programmers in countries such as India or Bangladesh to access the design elements over the Internet and to write the programming instructions (the *code)* and return it over the Internet. Given the time differences, this can be a very efficient way to develop an information system as the process continues around the clock with one group of programmers writing code in one time zone and another group testing it in a time zone twelve hours away. In this way, the development process runs continuously.

Assuming that the design stage has been carried out correctly, ideally five steps must be carried out before the program can be operational.

1. Programmers incorporate the step-by-step logic from the design stage into a computer program.

2. Programmers test the program extensively and correct any errors (bugs).

3. Development team tests the program.

4. Programmers and development team release program to users for additional testing in the work environment.

5. Users report errors, which programmers fix, leading to a revised release of program.

In looking at this list, in Step 1, the programmers create or build the program, and in Steps 2 and 3, the programmers and development team test the program and correct any errors that are found. Testing is an extremely important aspect of the programming process that must not be taken for granted. Once the programmers and development team believe that the program is correct, they release it to the designated users for further testing in the work environment. When (not if) users find errors, they report them back to the programming team, which corrects them and sends out a new version. This can be an ongoing process, with program versions numbered 1.0, 1.1, and so on, until an entirely new version of the software is created. Figure 9-8 shows the Visual Basic code corresponding to the IPO table and pseudocode for Process 1 shown earlier as Figure 9-5 and Figure 9-6 in which internal documentation has been added.

It is not uncommon for errors or **bugs** to be found even after extensive testing has been done in popular commercial software programs. Commercial software developers like Microsoft, Adobe, and Apple try to avoid this by engaging the services of users to test prerelease versions of software—so-called **beta testing**—and report any bugs in exchange for receiving free copies of the software. They also release revised versions of software as errors are corrected.

As an aside, it should be noted that the so-called *Y2K bug,* which has been in the news for the last several years, was not a bug at all. Instead it was the result of decisions made during the design stage when the software was being developed in the 1960s and 1970s. At that time, secondary storage was in short supply, and to conserve on the use of this scarce resource, developers decided to use only the last two years of the date in calculations. This meant that the storage required for a four-digit

Figure 9-8 Visual Basic Program

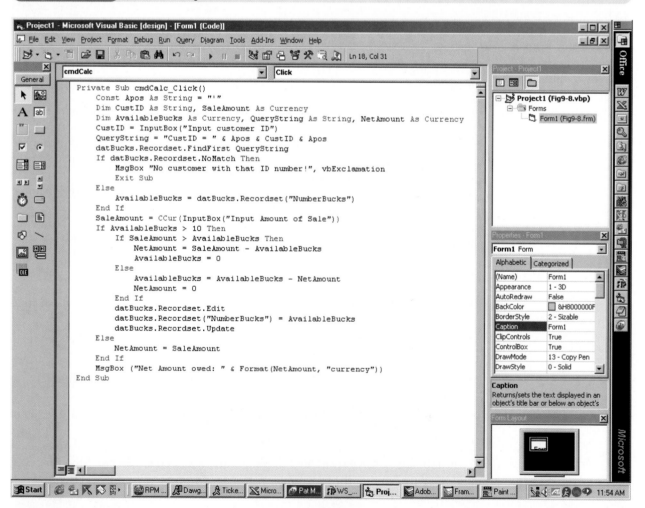

⒡ocus on Technology

Silver Linings to the Y2K Problems

By now, you know that the rollover to the year 2000 occurred with very few problems being caused by computers that did not understand dates beginning with 20 instead of 19. Reported problems included minor glitches with FAA equipment, customers of the Jacksonville (Florida) electric Authority being told to pay their bills by January 3, 1900, and the United States Naval Observatory—commonly referred to as the "nation's timekeeper"—posting the year as 19100 on its Web site during the first few hours of January 1, 2000.

All problems were due to non-Y2K compliant software and were fixed quickly once discovered. When compared to the many dire warnings (and movies) about the effect that the Y2K problem would have on society, the actual problems were minimal. In fact, there are a number of *silver linings* to the Y2K challenge that have resulted from the

massive, worldwide effort to meet the challenge. While the cost was high—an approximate $100 billion in the United States and $300 billion worldwide, the results will continue far beyond the current year. A study by the Government Services Administration (GSA) found many benefits in the networked economy for government agencies at both the state and federal level. These benefits are summarized in the following table.

Sources: Sami Lais, "Update: FAA Reports Only Minor Outages," *Computerworld,* January 1, 2000.
Linda Rosencrance, "Florida Utility Hit by Y2K Bug, Sends Erroneous Overdue Notices to 5,000," *Computerworld,* January 1, 2000.
Linda Rosencrance, "Y2K Glitch a 'Black Eye' for Naval Observatory," *Computerworld,* January 1, 2000.
"The Many Silver Linings of Y2K Challenge," http://policyworks.gov/intergov.

Item	Benefit from Preparing for Y2K Problem	Example
IT inventories	Government agencies had a much better understanding of their IT inventories	Florida now has a portfolio of key applications in thirty agencies
IT infrastructure	Many agencies were forced to renovate their IT infrastructure	The U.S. Postal Service has renovated its information infrastructure
Project management	Agencies were forced to address problems in the way they manage projects	In Michigan, new project management techniques now track the progress of projects
Partnerships	Local, state, and federal agencies have found ways to cooperate better	Howard County, Maryland, has found better ways to work with state and federal emergency agencies
Project measurements	Agencies were forced to find ways to improve quality in software	The Society for Information Management study found higher quality aspirations
Data exchanges	State and federal agencies found ways to exchange data	Florida has created a list of agency data exchanges with partners
Testing procedures	Finding all references to two-digit dates required agencies to improve their testing procedures	The Department of Housing and Urban Development (HUD) engaged in a test of all its information systems
Business continuation	Preparing for contingencies due to the rollover to the year 2000 forced agencies to consider the effects of natural and other disasters	The state of Florida now has a business continuation plan for both short and long periods without power and water
Elevation of chief information officer	Preparation for Y2K convinced many agencies of the importance of IT and the chief information officer (CIO)	In Michigan, the Y2K project has resulted in IT being viewed as an enabler to transform business processes

date could be cut in half for the two-digit version of the date. This may seem ludicrous in this day of cheap, widely available disk storage, but it saved a great deal of money at the time. The designers and programmers developing the software thirty or forty years ago never thought that the programs would still be in use today and did not consider the problems that this two-digit date convention would cause.

As a part of the program development process, it is necessary to write documentation that explains to users and other programmers how the program works. This is a very important element of the programming process that is often ignored in the rush to get a new system up and running. However, without proper documentation, both users and support personnel can quickly become frustrated when they cannot get the system to work as planned or solve problems with the system. In addition, documentation is essential to the maintenance step that keeps the system running after the development team has moved on to other projects. Once again, relative to the Year 2000 problem, inadequate documentation or documentation that was lost over time made solving the Y2K problem more difficult than it should have been.

A key concept regarding programming is that program development steps take place only *after* a great deal of planning, analysis, and design work has been done. This is an important concept because no matter how well the program is written, the objective will not be achieved if the program is being written to solve the *wrong* problem.

Installing the System

In this step, the new information system is installed in the organization. This includes installing any new computers and then loading the software onto them. In the Merrill Lynch case discussed in the opening box, an entire weekend was dedicated at each office to removing old hardware and wiring, installing new computers and Internet connections, and installing the TGA system on the new hardware.

Regardless of whether commercial software or specially developed software is used, once the system is acquired or developed, it must be installed and tested. System testing involves extensive checking of the new system's capabilities in terms of processing capability, that is, throughput, turnaround time, and access time. It must also be tested to determine its capability to handle the normal volume of transactions as well as abnormally high volumes. The system must also be tested to determine its capability to restart and recover after abnormal system termination *(crashes)*. The results of system testing must be analyzed to determine the magnitude of any problems and how they can be fixed.

Once the system has been completely tested, database files may have to be converted to the new system. This is especially true when the previous system involved several different types of files or when proprietary software was used. Careful attention must be given to integrity of new and old files; otherwise, poor decisions can be made because of bad or missing data.

After testing and data conversion are completed, the final installation steps involve system conversion. This is the process of changing over from the old system to the new one. There are four commonly used approaches to system conversion: direct, parallel, pilot, and phased. Table 9-2 summarizes the four approaches and gives the advantages, disadvantages, and risk level of each.

In looking at Table 9-2, you can see that the direct method is faster but much more risky than the conservative parallel approach in which both systems run side-by-side for a period of time. More than one job has been lost due to trying to speed up the conversion process by going with a direct conversion, only to have to revert to the old system when the new one failed to work as promised. You may note that Merrill Lynch used a phased installation of its new TGA system because the same system was being installed at hundreds of offices around the world.

Training Staff

In the Merrill Lynch case, a great deal of emphasis was given to training the potential users of the new TGA system both by giving mandatory training sessions two weeks before the system was installed and then by providing a review session the

Table 9-2 Comparison of Approaches to System Conversion

Conversion Approach	Characteristics	Advantages	Disadvantages	Risk
Direct	Simultaneously shut down old system and start up new system	Fast; lower cost	New system may not work	High
Parallel	Run old and new systems at same time	Able to fix problems with new system while old system still in operation	Slower than direct approach; expensive to run both versions; performance problems due to running two versions	Low
Pilot	Install and test system in one part of organization before installing everywhere	Find and fix problems without affecting entire organization	Problems with high volume of transactions may not be found	Moderate
Phased	System is installed sequentially at different locations	Requires less installation staff; problems at one location can be fixed before installing elsewhere	Different locations are not using the same version of the system	Moderate

day before the system went live. This indicates the importance that organizations should place on training their employees on how the new system will help them perform their job responsibilities. If employees are not given appropriate training, even the best system can quickly frustrate users and lead to eventual failure by them to accept it.

A common question is: What training should be provided to users? The answer may surprise you—the training should focus not only on how to use the system but also on how the system will help users do their jobs better. This involves helping the users understand the ways in which the new system fits into the overall mission of the organization. If the users do not understand the business aspects of the new system, they may fail to see the reasons why learning to use it are important.

Training should focus on what users need to do rather than on the features of the new system. Most users of word processing or spreadsheet packages use only a small fraction of the programs' capabilities, and the same is true of many new information systems. Unfortunately, the development team is usually so excited about its new "baby" that members want to show off all of its capabilities, often overwhelming the users with features. Training should concentrate on the 20 percent of the system's features that will be used by 80 percent of the users, thereby enabling the vast majority of the users to become confident of their ability to use the new system. Users can learn about the more advanced features when they need them by reading the documentation or by talking with members of the development team.

Types of training include classroom training, one-on-one training, and **computer-based training (CBT)**. Classroom training is commonly used when a large number of users must be trained simultaneously, but it is often not as effective as one-on-one training or CBT. On the other hand, one-on-one training and CBT are more expensive than classroom training *unless* the same training is going to be used repetitively in many situations. In this case, the startup cost of creating a CBT program can be spread over many trainees. It should be noted that the movement toward using the standard browser interface for software applications has reduced the amount of training needed because most people are already quite comfortable with this interface.

Training is critical not only to provide users with the knowledge they need to use the new system but also to avoid problems with resistance to change. It is a well-known aspect of organizational behavior that any change will bring about

Computer-based training is one type of training that companies can offer to its employees.

resistance. Unless the change process is well planned with adequate training, employees who are being asked to change the way they do their jobs can resist to the point of ensuring that the new system fails. In actuality, the change process should have started much earlier by involving potential users in the earlier planning, analysis, and design stages of the systems development process. If this is done, the users often feel that they had a big part in designing the new system and can be enthusiastic about the change rather than resistant.

Performing Maintenance

Any system, no matter how well designed, will need to be continually modified to handle changes in input, output, or logic requirements. This is done through **maintenance:** the ongoing process of keeping a system up-to-date by making necessary changes. Although it may seem like a minor part of the analysis, design, and implementation process, maintenance is an important aspect of keeping information systems running as designed. In fact, programmers spend almost 70 percent of their time maintaining information systems. This has certainly been the case over the last few years as companies have had to rewrite existing computer systems to update them to handle dates beginning with the numeral 20 rather than 19. The interesting part of this maintenance problem was that many of the systems were written in COBOL, a language for which many companies had to bring back retired programmers at a high consulting fee to find and change all of the data references.

Maintenance consists of two important steps: determining what changes need to be made and then making the changes. Determining needed changes is very similar to the planning stage in that it requires a systems analyst to study a situation and to then pinpoint the problem or to respond to a request from a user for an upgrade. Once the problem or change is identified, changing the existing system is a small-scale version of the systems life cycle shown in Figure 9-1. This is why we show the life cycle as a continuing process.

The ease with which an existing system can be maintained depends a great deal on the system documentation and the quality of the computer code. This documentation is made up of the descriptions and instructions provided with the hardware and commercial software or the documentation for software written internally. Without this documentation, changing the system may be virtually impossible, and the existing system may have to be junked in favor of an entirely new system—a potentially expensive process.

Quick Review

1. What are the four steps in the implementation stage?
2. Why can the quality of training on a new information system "make or break" the new system?

Outsourcing and Acquisition

As discussed earlier, an important outcome of the design stage is a decision on how the information system will be developed: by an internal development team, by an outside development team (outsourcing), or by a commercial software company (acquisition). We have discussed the first alternative already, and we will cover the second and third alternatives in this section. Although each has advantages relative to internal development, each also has definite problems, which we will point out. Both outsourcing and acquisition also require special consideration of the selection of the vendor for either outsourcing or software purchase. In addition, consideration needs to be given to the type of outsourcing contract that is used.

Outsourcing

Outsourcing is an arrangement in which one company provides for another company services that could also be or usually have been provided in-house.[1] Outsourcing is a growing trend with a market that is expected to exceed $120 billion in the year 2000. Although outsourcing for information technology purposes represents only around 30 percent of all outsourcing, we will restrict our attention to that segment of the market. Outsourcing can range from the use of contractors, temporary employees, or offshore programmers like those mentioned earlier to the use of the entire information technology operation of a company. The extent of the outsourcing depends on the degree to which the company believes that IT contributes to its competitive advantage.

As shown earlier in Table 9-1, there are advantages to outsourcing, including:

- Outsourcer has more skilled and experienced programmers
- Internal staff is not diverted from current work

The development of the Manheim Online used car sales system discussed at the beginning of chapter 8 is a good example of the use of outsourcing. Manheim management realized that its internal development staff had little or no experience or skills in Web development. Management also did not want to divert the attention of the internal IT group from its primary purpose of processing auction sales data into usable information. At the same time, management wanted to add value to the company. As a result, Manheim outsourced the development of the online sales system until such time as it became a part of its competitive advantage. When it became clear that Manheim Online would be an important part of the company's future, Manheim hired IT people knowledgeable in Web development and brought the system inside the company. The reverse can also occur; that is, an organization can develop a system internally and then outsource the maintenance of it. It all depends on how the company views its use of information technology.

Another well-known use of outsourcing was in dealing with the Year 2000 problem. As noted earlier, many companies no longer employ programmers with skills in

---

1. www.whatis.com.

COBOL and other older languages. This meant that they had to hire outside contractors to rewrite the programs internally or outsource the entire project to companies, such as American Software, specializing in this type of work.

Also as listed in Table 9-1, there are a number of disadvantages to outsourcing, including:

- Control of project may be lost
- Internal developers may not learn skills necessary to maintain system
- Outsourcer may not deliver on claims
- Costs may be higher

Of particular interest in systems development is the last of these: Outsourcer may not deliver on claims. This problem is often due to the so-called *90 percent syndrome* in which team leaders almost always reply to a question about the status of their project with "it is 90 percent complete," regardless of the true stage of completion. Unfortunately, in many development projects, the last 10 percent seems to take the vast majority of the development time! This problem becomes more critical when the project is being handled outside of the organization where it is not always possible for management to visit with the development team and ask questions and view outputs that will reveal the true stage of completion.

Once the decision has been made to outsource a project, a vendor must be selected and a contract negotiated. Vendor selection is very crucial because the organization is depending on the vendor to develop a needed information system in a timely manner. Important considerations include the record of the outsourcer on meeting its commitments with similar projects, the satisfaction level of current customers, and the technical competence of its employees as evidenced by prior work.

Three types of contracts are commonly used when engaging an outsourcer: time-and-materials, fixed-price, and value-added. A **time-and-materials contract** involves payment based on the time spent on the project by the outsourcer. This can result in a large bill if the time to complete the project runs past initial estimates, but it is a good way to go if neither the company nor the outsourcer is sure about the time required to complete the project. A **fixed-price contract** is exactly that—a contract with a fixed price to complete the work. In this case, the outsourcer will usually specify up front what it will do, with additions or changes requiring an upward revision to the contract price. A disadvantage to this type of contract is the potential of the outsourcer to cut corners or reduce functionality to keep costs down. In a **value-added contract,** the outsourcer is paid based on the benefits arising from the resulting information system—usually in terms of reduced costs or increased revenues. In so doing, the outsourcer shares in the risks and benefits of the project. Table 9-3 summarizes the three types of contracts and their pricing plans and comments on each type.

Table 9-3	**Types of Contracts**	
Contract Type	**Pricing**	**Comments**
Time-and-materials	Payment is based on time spent on project and any materials involved.	Can result in large bill; good when time required for project is hard to estimate
Fixed-price	Price is fixed for development of system.	Company knows costs prior to work; can result in outsourcer cutting corners to keep costs down
Value-added	Outsourcer is paid based on benefits resulting from new system.	Enables outsourcer to share in risks and benefits of project

Acquisition

Whereas outsourcing and internal development are usually used for projects requiring a high degree of customization or competitive advantage, acquiring packaged software can be very useful when speed or cost is the primary consideration. For example, as mentioned earlier, it would probably be better to acquire the new payroll system for fareastfoods.com because it did not need to be customized and did not add to the company's competitive advantage.

In addition, you have probably noticed that we have not mentioned hardware in our discussion of systems development; this is because hardware is almost always acquired instead of being developed. The various hardware companies like IBM, Compaq, and Dell now specialize in creating hardware systems to meet almost any company's needs, so there is little need to try to build your own. However, when hardware and software are being acquired together, there is a particular sequence in which this acquisition should occur, as shown in Figure 9-9. Note that the software is specified and selected *before* hardware is specified and selected. The acquisition process must follow this general order; otherwise the new hardware may not run the new software. The only time this is not true is when the hardware is already in place; in this case, the software must be purchased to match the existing hardware.

This process starts with the design stage, in which the specifications for the software are developed, that is, it has been decided what the software must accomplish. Once this has been completed, the next step is to send out a **request for proposals (RFP)** to vendors who are known to offer software of the type under consideration. The RFP should list the specifications for the software as completely as is needed for a vendor to prepare a bid.

When the software proposals are received, they must be evaluated against the software design. This can be done by using a weighted set of criteria by which to

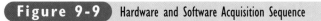

Figure 9-9 Hardware and Software Acquisition Sequence

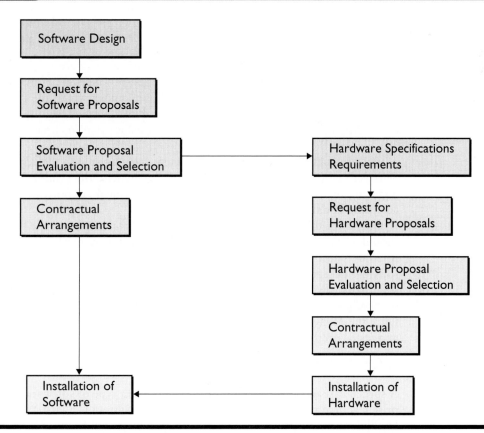

Compaq can produce a system to meet virtually all user's needs.

measure the proposals, with more weight being given to criteria that are of greater importance. Another way of comparing competing software packages is to **benchmark** them. In a benchmark test, the competing products are compared using programs and data typical of the actual conditions under which the proposed system will operate. These two methods may be combined, with the list of proposals being reduced by using the weighting method and the best two or three alternatives being benchmarked.

Once the best software option is selected, the next step in the acquisition of software is to work out the contractual arrangements with the vendor. This includes the financing of the software, arrangements for technical support, and conditions for acquiring updates to the software.

Only after the software proposals have been evaluated and the best one selected should any thought be given to selecting and acquiring hardware that matches the software selection. The selection of hardware follows the same process as acquiring software except that additional considerations are given to the contractual process. Whereas software is typically purchased or leased, hardware can be rented, leased, or purchased, so these options must be considered in the hardware acquisition. Once the hardware has been installed and tested, the software can then be installed and tested on the new hardware.

Enterprise Resource Planning Systems

A special case of the acquisition process involves a type of software known as **enterprise resource planning (ERP) systems.** An ERP system is a large, integrated system handling business processes and data storage for a significant collection of business units and business functions.[2] ERP systems are packaged software designed with a class of organizations in mind. They permit some tailoring of the business processes to be used in any given organization, but only within fixed bounds, because all of the business processes are designed to work together using a single database. ERP systems are a very popular form of software, as evidenced by the fact that by mid-1999, approximately 19 percent of U.S. companies had installed some form of ERP. A market growth of more than 30 percent is predicted by 2001, and the fastest-growing software company in the world is SAP, the maker of the popular R/3 ERP system. Other ERP companies include PeopleSoft, Oracle, and J. D. Edwards.

Business activities typically included in an ERP system are product planning, purchasing, inventory management, supply chain management, customer service management, and order tracking. In addition, ERP can include modules for managing the finance and human resources sides of a business. Figure 9-10 shows a screen shot from a popular ERP vendor.

To understand the use of ERP, we need to see that it is based on three key concepts: standardization, restrictions, and integration. In terms of standards, ERP requires

Figure 9-10 Web-Based Method for Selecting an ERP System

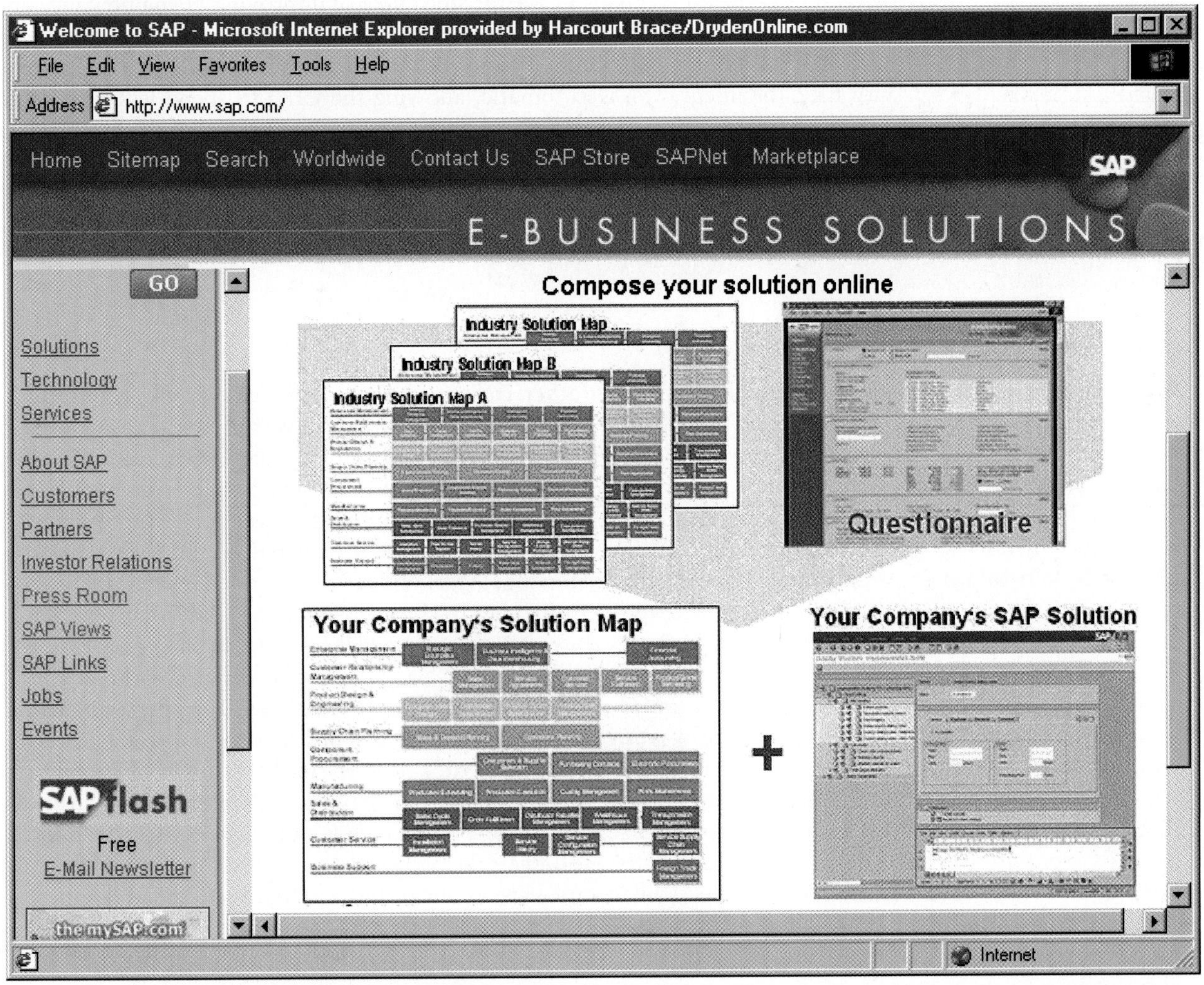

---

2. Thomas Gattiker and Dale Goodhue, "The Downside of ERP: Will the Ugly Duckling Always Turn into a Swan?," working paper, Terry College of Business, University of Georgia, 1999.

standardization of data and processes. This means that a single database with common units of data must be used throughout an organization for an ERP system to be implemented. If two plants are using different databases, then they cannot be on the same ERP system. Process standardization implies that all units within an organization using a single ERP system must carry out a process in the same way. It would not be possible for one unit to use a system of payment for raw materials that is different from that used in other units. It turns out that in many cases, data standardization forces process standardization onto the organization.

ERP also restricts the type of business processes that an organization can use to a set of options that is built into the software. These options are based on a set of *best practices* as selected by the software developer. This restriction means that many companies have to revise the way they do business to be able to use an ERP system. Finally, integration is a key feature of an ERP in that it links many (if not all) of a company's locations and functions so they have access to all relevant information. Installing ERP is not just the installation of a new software product; rather, in many cases it is a whole new way of thinking about the organization and its business processes.

ERP can be beneficial to a firm by improving communication and coordination as well as by improving organizational efficiency by forcing the firm away from inefficient processes for which there was no real rationale for continuing them. The enforced standardization can also have the side effect of improving IT maintenance and the deployment of new IT systems. Before ERP, if a CEO wanted the "big" picture on the firm, he would have to obtain it from each department head and then integrate it. With ERP, the integration is automatic, allowing the CEO to spend less time determining what is going on and more time improving the operations of the firm.

ⓕocus on the Internet

mySAP.com

Although it is widely known as a leader in enterprise resource planning (ERP) application software, until mid-1999, SAP was not known for its Internet strategy. In fact, SAP's premier ERP product, R/3, is decidedly different from what users are accustomed to seeing when working with a Web browser's colorful point-and-click interface. Many users complain about its monochrome colors and difficult to understand interface. In addition, it was created to run on terminals connected to powerful application servers and mainframes rather than on PCs connected to the Internet. However, with its May 1999 announcement of a Web portal site, SAP moved to extend its reach beyond traditional ERP users. This portal, to be known as mySAP.com (www.mysap.com), will attempt to link its SAP back office software into electronic commerce. Eventually, hundreds of SAP applications will be available through this Web site enabling users to view many applications—such as spreadsheets or maps generated by a geographic information systems (GIS)—via a Web browser rather than requiring a full-scale workstation. To actually carry out the more complex transactions, such as actually generating the GIS map, will still require a high-powered workstation; mySAP.com does this through four elements: Marketplace, Workplace, Business Scenarios, and Application Hosting. Marketplace is intended to be an open electronic business-to-business hub that enables business-to-business (B-to-B) relationships for buying, selling, and communicating. Workplace is aimed at providing users with a personalized, Web-browser-based work environment that offers everything they need to do their jobs. The Business Scenarios in mySAP.com will demonstrate a variety of business-to-business and business-to-consumer solutions available through SAP and third-party software applications. Finally, Web-based Application Hosting will also be available to provide a quick, cost-effective delivery mechanism that enables companies to adopt mySAP.com solutions.

Source: www.mysap.com.

Although ERP can improve a firm's operations, it is not without a great deal of work. This starts with deciding to go to an ERP system and selecting the correct package. There are numerous stories of companies that decided to abort the ERP installation process after installing one (or none) modules. This often occurs because the company did not completely understand its own business processes and how ERP would work with them. Selecting and installing an ERP package must begin with a thorough study of the firm's business processes.

Problems with ERP include costs, functionality, and implementation problems. ERP is expensive in terms of both time and cost. An ERP system from SAP can cost $4 million and take three years to install. In terms of functionality, an ERP system may not support a particular business process desired by the company. Finally, there can be implementation problems associated with installing the ERP system and with changing business procedures. Installation of an ERP system often requires the use of consultants who specialize in the type of system being installed. What can be worse is that if the consultants do not transfer their knowledge to the in-house staff, they may never leave. In addition, business procedures must be changed to use ERP. In this case, employees must learn both the new business process and the new ERP system at the same time.

Although ERP is a type of software package, choosing to use this approach to business integration is much more than just purchasing software. It requires a total dedication of the business to the practices built into the ERP system: something that all too many businesses fail to comprehend until they are deep into installing a system they don't understand.

Quick Review

1. How do outsourcing and acquisition differ? How are they similar?
2. Why is ERP an important type of packaged software?

Rapid Application Development

Although the structured approach to systems development has been the most widely used methodology over the last twenty years for creating information systems, the speed at which things change in the networked economy is forcing developers to look for faster ways of doing things. Even though the CASE methodology discussed earlier has speeded up the structured approach by computerizing much of the paper flow associated with the waterfall method, the process is still too slow for many applications, particularly those in electronic commerce. By the time the planning, analysis, design, and implementation processes are completed for an electronic commerce project, the project may no longer be appropriate or the company may have gone out of business while waiting for the new system. For example, the discount purchase system at fareastfoods.com is planned to take almost six months using the structured approach, but by that time there is no telling what kinds of changes will have occurred or if somebody else will have beat the company to market with the idea. After all, six months is close to three Web years! As one developer so aptly put it, "We can't wait nine months to have a baby anymore; we have to do it in two. And it has to come out perfect and it has to run when it's two weeks old."[3] The ideas expressed in this quote are far truer today than when it was said *over ten years ago*, before the commercialization of the Internet.

To respond to the need for faster development in the networked economy, a number of approaches have been suggested. We have already discussed two approaches to rapid application development—outsourcing and acquisition, and we will discuss

---

3. Quoted in Robert L. Schier, "Taking the Quick Path to Systems Design," *PC Week*, June 19, 1989, p. 65.

another approach, prototyping, in this section. Outsourcing can be quicker than internal development because the company doing the work will have a more skilled development team that does not need to be trained in, say, Web development techniques. Acquisition is possibly the fastest approach to systems development if the company is willing to accept the loss of flexibility and competitive advantage associated with using an off-the-shelf software package. On the other hand, if the company wants fast development combined with customization and competitive advantage, it may want to take a hard look at using prototyping.

In **prototyping,** the development team creates a "quick and dirty" version of the final product, using either advanced languages or software tools. Prototyping can help the developer to *short-circuit* the often-lengthy structured systems process by replacing some of the planning, analysis, and design steps with prototypes of the final system. Prototypes can be created by using languages like Visual Basic that allow quick creation of interfaces or by using HTML editors like Microsoft FrontPage or Netscape Composer. Although some of these prototypes are not meant to provide the *industrial-strength* programming necessary to actually handle the volume of transactions in the final application, they do provide important user feedback about the system.

Types of Prototypes

A variety of types of prototypes can be used to speed up the development process. We have already discussed two types of prototypes in the section on the design stage: the user interface prototype and the demonstration prototype. In addition, there are two other types of prototypes: the throw-away prototype and the evolutionary prototype. All four types of prototypes are shown in Table 9-4, along with comments about their primary use and the development tools.[4]

ⓕocus on Management

Web Development at What's Up Inc.

For the director of Internet Operations at What's Up Inc., life at work is never dull. It could mean meeting with potential clients to talk about a possible project, talking with existing clients to update them on the work on their Web site, plotting corporate strategy with the firm's owners, or even "getting her hands dirty" by writing some HTML to finish a project by the due date. Not quite what Ashley Connell envisioned for herself when she was finishing work on an art degree at the University of Georgia (UGA) in 1995. However, on the suggestion of a roommate, Ashley took a course in Web publishing in her final quarter of school. With just this one course, she received three job offers in the field. She accepted a staff position at UGA helping other students with their Web projects and a year later she joined What's Up in her current position.

Working on Web projects has enabled Ashley to use her background to tie artistic ideas and visual communications together with the technical aspects of the Web to create electronic commerce Web sites. A typical Web site takes ten to twelve weeks to finish from concept to completion and involves a development team of people from different fields. For example, on the development of the *Popeyes* Web site, Ashley oversaw the work of two designers from an outside firm, two programmers who built the site, and one copywriter/proofreader. The design of the site was based on the desire of the director of marketing at Popeyes for the site to speak to a range of people from consumers to potential franchisees. Ashley's biggest challenge is keeping up with the incredible speed of change on the Internet and being able to talk with people that have widely differing understandings of the Internet as a communication tool.

Source: Tammy Joyner, "What's Up? On the Web, It Could Be Anything." *The Atlanta Journal-Constitution,* October 6, 1999, p. D10.

---

4. Much of this discussion is based on Steve McConnell's book, *Rapid Development* (Redmond, WA: Microsoft Press, 1996).

Table 9-4   Types of Prototypes

Type of Prototype	Primary Purpose	Development Tools
User interface prototype	Used in design stage of development process to explore interfaces of final applications	Special purpose computer language or final computer language Browser/HTML
Demo prototype	To show a potential client the manner in which the application will look and act	Special purpose computer language
Throw-away prototype	Used in analysis stage to determine specifications; also used to explore factors critical to system's success	Special purpose computer language that results in much faster development than final computer language
Evolutionary prototype	Development of actual system in an iterative fashion that can be modified to meet user's feedback	Any of a number of computer languages

In looking at Table 9-4, we can see that, rather than being systems development methodologies, the first three types of prototypes are tools used by the system developer in the development process. The **throw-away prototype** tends to be more complex than the user interface or demo prototypes because it is used to do exploratory work on critical factors in the system rather than being used just for interface designing or for demonstrating an idea to a client. However, like the user interface and demo prototypes, the throw-away prototype is meant for that purpose—to be thrown away and not used as the final product. It is thrown away because its purpose is not to be used in the final product, but rather to help in determining information requirements.

Because throw-away prototypes are not meant to be used as the final application, they are often created using a special purpose computer language that enables interface creation but is inappropriate for creating a final working project. Occasionally, user interface prototypes are created in a language that could be used for the final application. This enables a user interface prototype to be evolved into the actual application.

Evolutionary Prototyping

The prototype that we will discuss in more detail is the **evolutionary prototype,** which is meant to evolve into a working application. The emphasis here is on the word *evolutionary* because the prototype is meant to evolve over time as the user has an opportunity to work with it. Features of evolutionary prototyping include:

- Development is an iterative process with short intervals between system versions and rapid feedback from the user. The emphasis is on *speed*.
- The user is closely involved in the development process.
- The initial prototype has a low cost that does not require justification.
- With the iterative nature of prototyping and the feedback it provides, users develop information requirements while seeing what a new system can do.

Note that the emphasis of prototyping is on four things—speed, low cost, user involvement, and iterative development. Although you undoubtedly understand speed, low cost, and user involvement, **iterative development** is a new idea. By this we mean a process by which the user tries out the latest version of the information system and provides feedback on it to the development team. Based on this feedback, the team makes changes in the system and gets additional feedback from the user. To keep this process moving as fast as possible, the user must be willing to try out the system and provide feedback as quickly as possible. Compare this to the waterfall method of development in which "backing up" and changing the deliverable from a previous step is difficult.

Note also that it is not assumed in evolutionary prototyping that users can specify their information requirements up front, as is assumed with the waterfall approach. Instead, because they don't always know what they want until they have used the system for some time, users develop their information requirements as they use the system and include them as a part of their feedback. This last feature of evolutionary prototyping makes it extremely useful in situations where sponsors or users do not know exactly what they want but know just that they need *something* to remain competitive in the networked economy. Evolutionary prototyping is appropriate for creating many types of electronic commerce Web sites and some types of decision support systems, especially those where the users have some idea about the information they need but may not know how it should be presented.

If these features of prototyping are compared to the waterfall approach, we see that several differences exist. First, where user involvement is mandatory with evolutionary prototyping, the user may not participate at all in the waterfall approach other than to provide information in the planning and analysis stages and to sign off on the results of the various stages. Second, with prototyping, it is not necessary for users to be able to clearly define their information needs at the beginning of the process. However, with the waterfall approach, users must be able to clearly define information needs at the beginning of the process. Finally, where the emphasis with prototyping is on speed and low cost, the emphasis with the waterfall approach is on achieving completeness and ensuring that every detail has been considered. For this reason, evolutionary prototyping may not be appropriate for creating complicated transaction processing systems where many options must be considered because the lack of complete planning, analysis, and design stages can result in important elements of the system being missed or left out.

The steps in the evolutionary prototyping process are listed below and are also diagrammed in Figure 9-11, with the step number in the upper-righthand corner of each box. Note that when the prototype is completed, it can be actually used as a production information system, or it can be used as a design model for the implementation stage of the structured approach to development. In the former case, as with any information system, the new information system must be maintained by updating its features and correcting problems.

Steps in the evolutionary prototyping process are:

Step 1: Developer identifies user's problem through discussions with user and determines if a system that solves the problem is feasible.

Step 2: Working prototyping is developed for a key element of system.

Step 3: User works with prototype, learns more about information requirements, and provides feedback to developer, who refines and enhances the prototype until it meets user's information requirements.

Step 4: The prototype is either implemented or used as a model for the implementation phase of the structured process.

Step 5: Information system is documented and maintained.

As with any approach to systems development, there are both advantages and disadvantages of using evolutionary prototyping, as shown in Table 9-5. In general, the advantages have to do with the increased speed and lower cost of development, along with greater user involvement. On the other hand, the disadvantages have to do with the lack of clear planning, analysis, and design stages or with users not understanding the purpose of evolutionary prototyping or being unwilling to do their work in testing the prototype and in providing feedback to the development team. Another disadvantage is that users keep wanting to add more features to the system as they use it. Both users and developers need to guard against this so-called **feature creep.**

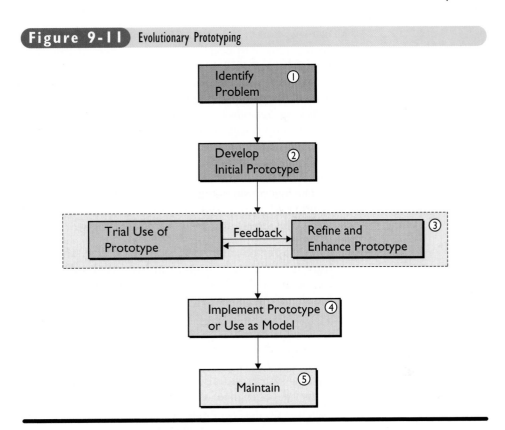

Figure 9-11 Evolutionary Prototyping

- Identify Problem ①
- Develop Initial Prototype ②
- Trial Use of Prototype ←Feedback→ Refine and Enhance Prototype ③
- Implement Prototype or Use as Model ④
- Maintain ⑤

Table 9-5 Advantages and Disadvantages of Evolutionary Prototyping

Advantages	Disadvantages
1. Users understand and react to prototypes far better than paper specifications.	1. Quick, rough design may replace well-thought out design.
2. It is usually quicker to build prototypes than to create paper specifications.	2. Evolutionary prototyping may encourage users to continually change their minds about requirements, resulting in feature creep.
3. Reality testing is introduced into project at early stage.	3. Users' expectations may be too high based on early prototypes.
4. It can help avoid systems with inadequate or wrong features.	4. Users may not want to go from prototype to production system; they may want to keep the prototype.
5. It encourages creative input from users.	5. Users may not understand why the final cost for the full system is so high.
6. It enables errors and weaknesses to be caught before expensive design and programming are done.	6. Users may not work hard enough to identify flaws in the prototype.

Quick Review

1. What are the four types of prototypes commonly used in systems development?
2. List three ways that evolutionary prototyping differs from the waterfall approach to systems development.

⊙ Summary

To summarize this chapter, let's answer the Learning Objectives questions posed at the beginning of the chapter.

What is the purpose of the design stage of the structured systems development process? The design stage is dedicated to the *how* questions, that is, how will the new system be developed, and how will the new system work? The first question of *how* the system will be developed must be answered first. If the decision is made to develop a custom system, it can be done internally or outsourced to another firm. When a project is outsourced, an entity outside of the organization is used to develop all or part of the project. If the decision is made to acquire the information system, an appropriate system must be found and purchased. If the decision is to outsource or acquire, then the remainder of the design stage is skipped, and the implementation stage is begun. If the decision is made to develop internally, the design stage must answer the question of how the system will operate. It does this by moving from the logical models of the analysis stage to a physical design that specifies *all* of the details of the system.

The logical process models must be converted to physical models using such tools as IPO tables and pseudocode. Interface screens are also used to specify the look and feel of the screens with which the users will work.

What operations must occur during the implementation stage, and how is computer programming involved?

The implementation stage involves four steps: building the system, installing the system, training staff, and, finally, performing maintenance. In the first step, the system is *built* by writing appropriate computer programs that implement the design created in the previous step. Once the system is built, the next step is to install the system on the organization's computers, test it in that location, and to convert from the old system to the new. The third step is to train the staff who will use it. Training not only prepares the employees to use the new system, but also can help avoid people problems that occur whenever there is any kind of change in an organization. Finally, once the system is installed and running in a production mode, it must be supported and maintained.

Computer programming is at the heart of the step during which the new system is built. A variety of computer languages can be used for this process, with object-oriented languages becoming more popular. Regardless of the language, a great deal of attention must be given to testing the system to find errors known as *bugs* in the programs. This programming depends heavily on the design work that goes before it.

What is outsourcing, and what issues should be considered in deciding to outsource a project?

Outsourcing is an arrangement in which one company provides for another company services that could also be or usually have been provided in-house. Advantages of outsourcing include: More-skilled and experienced programmers are available, internal staff is not diverted from current work, and costs are possibly lower. Disadvantages of outsourcing include: Control of the project may be lost, internal developers may not learn skills necessary to maintain the system, and the outsourcer may not deliver on claims. An important aspect of outsourcing is selecting a vendor and writing the best type of contract. Important considerations include the record of the outsourcer on meeting its commitments with similar projects, the satisfaction level of current customers, and the technical competence of its employees as evidenced by prior work. Three types of contracts are commonly used when engaging an outsourcer: time-and-materials, fixed-price, and value-added.

If an organization chooses to acquire an information system, what are the key elements of this process?

During the acquisition process, it is important to always specify, select, and acquire the software *before* acquiring the hardware that matches the software. Otherwise the new software may not run on the new hardware. This process starts with the design stage in which the specifications for the software are developed. Once this has been completed, the next step is to send out to vendors a request for proposals (RFP) that lists the specifications for the software. Resulting software proposals must be evaluated against the software design. This can be done by using a weighted set of criteria or by benchmarking them. Only after the software has been selected can the hardware be acquired by a similar process. Only if the hardware is already installed is this process reversed.

An important type of package software in use today is enterprise resource planning (ERP) software. ERP is a large, integrated system that handles business processes and data storage for a significant collection of business units and business functions. ERPs permit some tailoring of the business processes to be used in any given organization, but only within fixed bounds because all of the business processes are designed to work together using a single database.

What is RAD, and how does it differ from the waterfall approach to systems development? RAD is an acronym for *rapid application development,* and it applies to a variety of approaches used to speed up the traditional approaches to systems development. Both outsourcing and acquisition are RAD approaches. For internal development, the most popular approach to RAD is prototyping, which involves creating a "quick and dirty" version of the final product, using either advanced languages or software tools. Prototyping can help the developer *short-circuit* the often-lengthy structured systems process by replacing some of the planning, analysis, and design steps with prototypes of the final system. Types of prototypes include user interface, demonstration, throw-away, and evolutionary prototype. The evolutionary prototype is often used to replace or supplement the waterfall method. It is a lower-cost, faster iterative approach involving heavy user participation in the process. Dangers of using evolutionary prototyping include a quick, rough design replacing a well-thought out design, users never converging on a final set of requirements for the prototype, users having overly high expectations, or users not providing adequate feedback to the development team.

⊙ Review Questions

1. Why is it necessary to specify metadata for a data model?
2. What is CASE, and how is it used in the development process?
3. Why are user interface screens a necessary part of the design stage?
4. What are the four steps in the implementation stage?
5. How does object-oriented programming differ from traditional programming?
6. List the four types of conversion that are commonly used in installing a new information system. Which are the highest and lowest risk types?
7. In what cases would outsourcing be a better approach to systems development than internal development? In what cases would outsourcing be a worse approach?
8. Why should software be selected and acquired *before* acquiring hardware? In what case does this not apply?
9. Why is ERP becoming an important type of package software?
10. List the four types of prototypes used in RAD. Which is also used in the design stage?

⊙ Discussion Questions

1. Discuss the difference between the analysis and design stages.
2. Assume that your company needs software to start a business on the Web and that you have found several companies that offer "turn-key" shopping cart software for doing this. Under what circumstances would you choose to purchase this software as opposed to developing it in-house?
3. Assume in Question 2 that your company has decided to develop the software in-house; discuss the conditions under which your company would choose to use evolutionary prototyping rather than the waterfall approach to development.

> ◆ **C A S E**

WildOutfitters.com

Swooosh.... Alex glided to a stop just short of the spot where Claire had settled for a rest on a felled tree. The two were breaking trail with their cross-country skis in the wooded hills behind the shop.

"Hey, slow poke. What took you so long?" The chilly air imparted a visible quality to Claire's greeting.

Alex took off one of his gloves and grabbed the thermos that she offered. After a couple of deep breaths and a swig of the warm liquid, he replied, "Too many nights in front of the computer I'm afraid. I'm a little out of shape and my herringbone technique is rusty. I nearly lost it on that hill back there."

"Speaking of computers," Claire said. "Since you weren't around to talk to, I've been giving some thought to the customer incentive project for the Web site."

As he settled down beside her, Alex said, "Please tell me your thoughts, oh Nordic Queen of the Web."

Based on their initial feasibility studies and cost/benefit analysis, the Campagnes have decided to go forward with adding a customer incentive program to their Web site. Their lives had become very busy with the success of their business and they took the time to discuss important issues like this whenever they could find it.

First, Claire explained the objectives of the project. The primary goal is to improve their market share and customer loyalty by providing an incentive system. The incentive system will keep track of the dollars spent on the Web site and will then offer "freebies" to customers whose total purchases are over a specified amount. The new system should be an enhancement to, and a fully functional part of, the current Web site. Finally, they want to have the new system up and running in three months from the current date.

Whether they develop the system themselves or decide to outsource, the project team will need to fulfill several requirements. They will need to plan the Web pages for content, functionality, and compatibility. This plan should be accompanied by a written specification. The team will be responsible for the look and feel of the pages as well as the front-end and the back-end functionality. The new pages will be hosted on the current facility; therefore, the capacity of the current facility will need to be analyzed. If changes to the current hosting facility are needed, the team will need to provide a solution for these changes.

The Campagnes envision that customers who wish to take part in the incentive program will first register with the site. Upon registration, entries are made into the database designed to keep up with the spending of the customer. When the customers spending level crosses the target level, the customer will be notified via e-mail and will be allowed to choose from the current items available. The registration process should capture as much demographic data as possible. The team's proposal should include how this will be done along with the specific modifications to the database. Claire would also like for the team to explore the possibility of using a cookie system. A cookie could be used in a couple of ways. First, it could help registered users with automatic log on to the site and tracking of their spending level values. Second, it could allow WildOutfitters to analyze where site visitors go and how they interact with the site. The team's proposal should explain their solution for cookies and the features the system will offer.

The team will need to develop a detailed project report that describes the hosting requirements, maintenance, training considerations, and all technical considerations. The report should include specifications for all resources needed for the system including software, hardware, and personnel requirements. Software specifications should discuss the programming languages used as well as any third party software that will be used. Hardware specifications will describe the additional hardware needed, if any, to incorporate the new system into the Web site. Personal specifications should define the number of human resources needed for developing and maintaining the system and the appropriate skills that these people should have.

With these thoughts in mind, the Campagnes now need to incorporate them into a formal document describing the projects mission. Then they will decide how to complete the project.

"Well, enough mixing business with pleasure," Claire said vigorously. "Race you back to the house." With that she arose and with a quick, kicking motion started gliding down to the base of the next hill.

Alex groaned and forced himself up over his skis. He was thinking about the four miles of mostly uphill "pleasure" back to the shop as he began to follow after his wife.

1. In which of the four stages of the SDLC is the customer incentive project at WildOutfitters.com in now? What deliverables should be developed?

2. Would outsourcing be a good choice for the development of the customer incentive system? Explain. What advantages and disadvantages will the Campagnes experience if they decide to develop the project through outsourcing?

3. *(Hands on)* Assume that the Campagnes would like to pursue outsourcing for the project. Use word

processing software to prepare a request for proposal (RFP). Remember that the RFP should list the specifications for the system as completely as possible. Feel free to add your own ideas to supplement the information that is provided in the case. A template with instructions for the RFP may be downloaded from www.harcourtcollege.com/infosys/mckeown.

4. *(Hands on)* Take the role of a company that provides outsourcing services. Prepare a presentation using a variety of software tools (word processor, spreadsheet, presentation software, etc.) that your company may use to convince the Campagnes to hire you for the job. Be sure to address the major points that you provided in your RFP.

P A R T ④

Issues in the Networked Economy

The growth of the networked economy means that information technology is a part of everyone's life in one way or another. Crime, security, privacy, ethics, economics, health, and lifestyle issues are just as much a concern in the networked economy as they were in the industrial economy, if not more so. Criminals are finding methods to use information technology to carry out their illegal activities in new and different ways; therefore, security becomes an even bigger concern to organizations and individuals who buy or sell goods and services over the Internet or who use information technology to carry out some element of their daily life. Because we are becoming an online society, privacy quickly is becoming one of the hottest issues that concerns many of us. Similarly, because we are becoming dependent on information technology, ethical issues in its use are important to all of us. Finally, because of our widespread use of information technology—economic, health, and lifestyle issues associated with its use are issues with which we, as a society, must deal.

In part 4, crime and security, privacy and ethics, and societal issues involving our health, our lifestyles, and the economy are covered.

Crime and Security in the Networked Economy

❯ Learning Objectives

After reading this chapter, you should be able to answer the following questions:

❯ How has the face of crime changed in the networked economy?

❯ What types of crime are having the greatest impact on individuals and organizations in the networked economy?

❯ What kinds of attacks are being made on information technology and users?

❯ How can organizations protect themselves from crime in the networked economy?

❯ In what ways can an organization protect its enterprise network from intrusions over the Internet?

Focus on Society

The Woodside Case

When Jayne Hitchcock and other aspiring writers received an e-mail from the Woodside Literary Agency of Queens, New York, or saw its advertisement posted in the misc.writers newsgroup, many of them took advantage of the offer to have their work reviewed for possible publication. However, as they soon discovered, the agency was not all that it claimed to be. Writers who submitted a manuscript to the agency were asked to pay $150 for a "reviewer's fee," a practice that is not common in the publishing industry. Those who were told that their manuscripts were "publishable" were then asked in a telephone call for an additional amount of several hundred dollars for further reviewing and for the cost of "processing manuscripts," also an unusual request in this industry.

Writers who were initially irritated by the aggressive e-mail ad campaign run by Woodside began to e-mail one another about the company's practices. Several of them felt that Woodside was running a fraudulent operation. To test this theory, the writers submitted what they considered to be a "bad" piece of writing to Woodside for consideration. All but one of these authors were told that they were among the special one-in-twenty applicants who were accepted by the agency and were asked for more money. As a result of this experiment, the authors notified the New York State Attorney General's office, which, in turn, investigated their complaints and prosecuted the agency for fraudulent practices. In February of 1999, a New York judge ordered the Woodside agency to stop its Internet-publishing scheme, provide restitution to authors, and post a $100,000 bond to protect future writers.

Source: Heidi Kriz, "Stranger than Fiction," http://www.wired.com/news/, February 18, 1999.

The Changing Face of Crime

In most cases, information technology is used for completely legal purposes. Unfortunately, as illustrated in the opening Focus on Society box, individuals and organizations have found ways to use information technology for illegal purposes. And unfortunately, the volume of crime associated with information technology can be expected to grow right along with the growth of the Internet and electronic commerce. The movement into the networked economy means that criminals will not go away, but rather will just change their objectives and the way they achieve these objectives. For example, instead of using the telephone to peddle worthless stocks, real estate, or cancer remedies, they will use the Web to do it. The fraud discussed in the opening Focus on Society box is a good example of criminals switching from using magazine and matchbook advertisements to using e-mail and newsgroups to find victims.

In this chapter, we will cover crime and security as they relate to information technology (IT). An **IT crime** is an illegal act that requires the use of information technology, and **IT security** comprises the methods used to protect the hardware, software, data, and user from both natural and criminal forces.

Introduction to IT Crime

The extent of IT crime in the United States is unknown because many companies are reluctant to prosecute the people involved for fear that the general public will lose confidence in the companies. Companies also worry that discussing details of the crime in open court may encourage someone else to try to replicate the crime elsewhere. Although we may not know exactly what the cost of IT crime really is, there is little doubt that it involves a large and growing number of companies. For example, a joint 1998 Computer Security Institute/FBI survey revealed that 81 percent of the respondents said they had suffered a computer security breach in the last twelve months or *did not know* if they had. The same survey found that organizations that

Table 10-1 Types of Computer Crime

Type of Crime	Purpose
Theft	Steal hardware, data, or information from individuals or organizations either directly or through networks
Fraud	Use computers and the Internet to steal money by deceiving victims
Copyright infringement	Illegally use software, music, or trademarks that in many cases are obtained over the Internet
Attacks on organizations and individuals	Attack organizations and individuals over the Internet or other networks with a goal of damaging software, data, information, or reputation

had experienced computer fraud reported losses averaging almost $3 million.[1] Compare this to the average armed robbery that nets only $6,600 and the average embezzlement that nets $19,000. With potential losses so great, IT crime has become a very important topic for networked economy organizations.

An IT crime can be committed in a variety of ways, but in general, it involves theft, fraud, copyright infringement, and attacks on information technology or users. The first category includes stealing computers, peripherals, company data, or private corporate information either directly or through networks. In the second category, information technology is used to carry out fraudulent activities like those discussed in the Focus on Society box. In the third category, the illegal reproduction of software and music is a very large problem for companies that develop and sell software or produce music. Finally, information technology or users are attacked through the use of damaging software or through e-mail, chat rooms, or newsgroups. It should be noted that all of these acts involve computer networks and the Internet—not surprising in the networked economy. Table 10-1 provides a summary of the four types of computer crime and the purpose of each.

IT Criminals

IT criminals may be grouped in three major categories: employees, outside people, and organized criminals. These three categories are shown in Table 10-2, along with their objectives.

Although outside parties are often given the most publicity, most surveys have shown that employees or ex-employees form the largest group of computer criminals, usually because they have the easiest access to the computer. The criminal may be a disgruntled employee wishing to get back at the company either by attacking the company's information technology or by using it to steal from the company. At other times, the employee finds a way to perform an illegal act with the organization's computers or other IT infrastructure.

People outside the organization have used the Internet and other networks to break into computers for various reasons. The best known are the teenaged "whiz kids" who

Table 10-2 Types of IT Criminals

IT Criminal Type	Objective
Employees	To steal money from the company or to harm it in some way
Outside people	To steal from the company or to damage its infrastructure in some way
Organized criminals	To use the company's information technology for monetary gain

---

1. http://www.gocsi.com/losses.htm.

Kevin Mitnick, one of the most widely publicized hackers, is now in prison for his computer crimes.

Table 10-3 Changing Nature of Crime

Aspect of Crime	Industrial Economy (1950)	Networked Economy (2000)
Location	Local	Remote
Impact	Low	High
Format	Physical	Electronic
Risk	High	Low

seek unauthorized access "for the fun of it." These individuals are often referred to as **hackers** because they "hack away," trying to gain illegal entry to computers. Numerous movies have glamorized this group, but in an increasing number of recent cases, hackers have been involved in criminal activities. In addition, the process of "hacking" into a computer has the potential to damage computer programs and files.

Organized criminals have discovered that IT can be extremely useful in furthering its objectives. For example, Asian gangs in California are heavily involved in counterfeiting Microsoft products—not just the floppy disks or CD-ROMs but also the boxes, warranty cards, end-user licenses, and even the hologram that Microsoft uses to authenticate its products. Police raids on these operations have netted as much as $6 million in fake Microsoft products in one case and four million pieces of fake products, as well as replicating machines, in another case.

The Changing Nature of Crime

To understand the changing nature of crime, consider Table 10-3, where the industrial economy, represented by the year 1950, is compared with the networked economy, represented by the year 2000. This comparison uses four aspects of crime: location, impact, format, and risk. *Location* refers to whether the crime is local or at some remote distance. *Impact* refers to the amount of money (low or high) that can be involved in the crime. *Format* refers to the manner (physical or electronic) in which the crime is carried out, and *risk* refers to the risk (high or low) facing the criminal.

In looking at Table 10-3, we can see that because crime in the 1950s was usually face-to-face, it was local with low impact because it was difficult to physically steal large amounts of money. It was also physical, and the risk to the criminal was high. On the other hand, computer crime in the 2000s is remote with a potentially high impact in terms of amount stolen. The format is electronic with a low risk to the criminal.

IT Crime and fareastfoods.com

Small companies like fareastfoods.com need to be most concerned with outside people and their employees (or ex-employees). In the first place, they need to work to keep intruders out of their network. In the second case, they must closely check the background of any employee that will have access to the company servers and other IT equipment.

Quick Review

1. Why is the extent of IT crime unknown?
2. What are the three types of computer criminals?

Types of IT Crime

IT crime can be classified into four categories: theft of hardware, data, or information; fraud; copyright violations; and attacks on individuals or organizations.

Theft of Hardware, Data, or Information

When most computers were mainframes, the theft of hardware was a fairly small problem involving a few terminals or other peripherals because a high level of security surrounded a mainframe and the computer center. However, with the almost universal use of PCs as network clients has come the widespread theft of hardware items. This theft involves entire PC systems, laptops, printers, or computer elements such as keyboards and monitors. As a result of the dramatic increase in computer theft, especially laptops, the National Computer Registry[2] has been set up to help recover stolen equipment.

A two-year study carried out in 1997–1998 by the Rand Corporation found that the cost of stolen equipment and parts to companies was approximately $4 billion, which included the value of lost goods as well as indirect costs such as insurance, security, and lost sales. A favorite target of thieves is shipments of semiconductor chips used in the manufacture of information technology equipment. A single shipment of chips can be worth several million dollars but is often treated by shipping companies the same as much less valuable freight.

Although it is expensive to replace stolen hardware, the real cost is in the software, data, and information stored in the computers. For example, Ontrack Data International has found that most companies value one hundred mbytes of data at over $1 million.[3] In many cases involving laptop theft, it has been found that the equipment was actually stolen with the intent of acquiring competitive information stored on the hard disk or to gain access to corporate servers and intranets through the passwords and remote-access software stored in the computer. In one company, the loss rate of laptops among the field sales staff was an almost unbelievable one in twelve!

Criminals also can steal data and information through a network. By making a location on the Internet or other network appear to be a trusted computer, criminals can trick organizational computers into sending data and information to them.

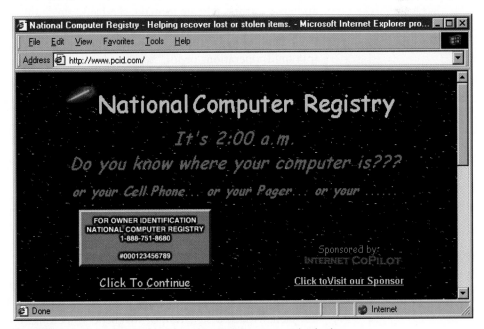

The National Computer Registry has been set up to help recover stolen hardware.

2. http://www.pcid.com.

3. http://www.ontrack.com.

Figure 10-1 Growth in Internet Fraud Reports

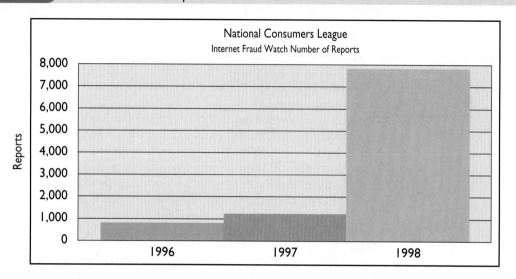

Source: http://www.natlconsumersleague.org/favorite.htm#ifraud.

Fraudulent Use of IT

The use of information technology to commit fraud over the Internet is one of the fastest-growing types of IT crimes. Over six million users in the United States reported some type of fraud in a 1999 Harris Survey.[4] In addition, the Internet Fraud Watch (run by the National Consumers League) reported that Internet fraud complaints were up over 600 percent in 1998 compared to 1997. Figure 10-1 shows the number of Internet fraud reports for 1996–1998.

One reason for this increase is that running a fraud over the Internet is very cheap compared to other methods; criminals only have to interest a small fraction of their audience in their scheme to make the fraud profitable. Information technology has been used to lure individuals into sending money to unscrupulous operators for services that are normally free, or individuals send money for multilevel marketing (pyramid) operations or for "work at home" operations. In addition to this type of fraud, there are at least four other types of IT fraud:

- Credit card fraud
- Investor fraud
- Medical and drug-related fraud
- Auction site fraud

All of these types of IT fraud are compounded by people believing that everything they read on the Internet is true, even when it is put there by people they do not know. Information on the Internet is often like that found on bathroom walls: It may be interesting but should not always be accepted as the truth! Let's take a closer look at these types of IT fraud.

Credit card fraud. With the rapid growth of electronic commerce have come problems for merchants accepting credit cards for payment. Because Internet credit card transactions lack a signature or magnetic stripe on the back of the card, merchants must agree to pay full cost plus any penalty fees for sales made using invalid credit cards. This means that criminals with either bogus cards that appear to be valid or stolen cards can purchase items over the Internet, and when the credit card company

---

4. http://www.nclnet.org/NCLSURV5.HTM.

Ⓕocus on Technology

Busting a Hacker Ring with a Data Tap

As we move further into the networked economy, all facets of society will be changing—including law enforcement agencies—as they work to find ways to keep pace with increasingly sophisticated hackers. One of the first illustrations of the changing face of police work involved an eleven-member group of hackers known to the FBI as the "Phone Masters" because of their interest in manipulating the computers that route telephone calls. This group was able to gain access to telephone networks of most of the large, long distance carriers including AT&T, British Telcom, GTE, MCI Worldcom, Sprint, and so on. At various times, they were able to eavesdrop on phone calls, poke around in secure databases, and redirect phone calls in any way they wished. For example, they were able to cause one police department's telephone number to appear on thousands of pagers, causing havoc when people returned the fake call. Unlike many of the earlier hackers, this group was in it for money; they sold the telephone access numbers, credit reports, and other records stolen from various databases.

Catching the "Phone Masters" required that the FBI invent a totally new type of telephone interception device called a "data tap." The purpose of the data tap, which was built at the FBI's engineering lab in Quantico, Virginia, was to reverse the process of the typical telephone modem; instead of converting keystrokes into analog sound signals, it converted the analog back to keystrokes that could be recorded by the FBI. Before using it, the FBI had to convince a federal court of the need to intrude on the data coming from one of the hackers. Once the data tap was approved and installed, along with a traditional tap on the voice line, the FBI was able to record both voice and data transmissions from a hacker's telephone. For example, they caught the hackers in the act of raiding a long distance database for over eight hundred access codes that they sold to a contact in Canada for $2 apiece. The evidence gathered from the data tap was used to obtain convictions of three of the group.

Source: John Simmons, "How a Cybersleuth, Using a 'Data Tap,' Busted a Hacker Ring." *The Wall Street Journal,* October 1, 1999, pp. A1, A6.

---

disallows the charges the merchant is liable. For new Internet merchants, the fraud rate can run as high as 20 to 50 percent of all transactions and can quickly put them out of business. This problem is especially bad with international transactions. For example, Web transactions account for only 2 percent of Visa's international business, yet they account for almost 50 percent of disputed charges and fraud in that market.

A high percentage of this type of credit card fraud originates from free e-mail accounts such as those offered by Yahoo! and Microsoft, which make it very hard to track down the person making the fraudulent purchase. Criminals will either use credit card-generation programs available on the Web or set up so-called *gypsy* Web sites that mimic those of legitimate merchants but with unbelievably low prices offered to those who pay with credit card. These sites do not actually have any merchandise to sell; they are there to take orders to obtain valid credit card numbers. This information can then be used to make bogus purchases of real merchandise or the credit card numbers can be sold on the Web to others with a criminal intent. It should be noted that this type of fraud is primarily a problem for merchants, whereas most other types of fraud are problems for individuals.

A system called **secure electronic transaction (SET)** has been created to eliminate this type of credit card fraud. SET has been endorsed by Visa, MasterCard, American Express, and Japan's JCB Credit Card Corp. Unfortunately, SET has not been widely adopted by businesses in the United States. The process of using SET is shown in Figure 10-2.

Another type of credit card fraud involves criminals billing credit card holders for services they did not request, such as subscriptions to adult-oriented Web sites. In some cases, computer programs are used to generate the credit card numbers to which the charges are made. An example of this type of fraud was found with the

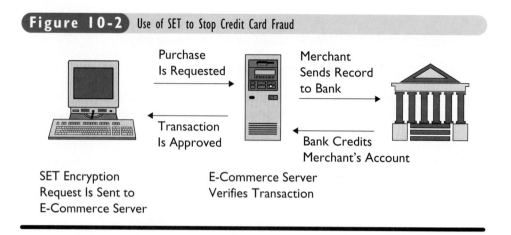

Figure 10-2 Use of SET to Stop Credit Card Fraud

1999 arrest of a California man by federal agents who charged him with $45 million in fraudulent charges in hundreds of thousands of transactions.

Investor fraud. With the widespread use of the Internet for stock market trading by investors has come a dramatic growth in stock-related fraud. This is partly because many of the Internet-based investors are new to the stock market and are more prone to fraud. Types of investor fraud include e-mail campaigns improperly touting stocks, false information spread in chat rooms and newsgroups, and forgeries of legitimate brokerage Web sites. In the first case, promoters send a large number of junk e-mail messages to target groups, often the elderly. The objective of these mailings can be to sell stock in investment opportunities that do not exist or to pump up the value of a real stock so the promoters can then sell their shares at a profit.

In the second case, promoters will use chat rooms to create a phony conversation between two or more fictitious investors to generate interest in a stock. As with the junk e-mail approach, the objective can be to sell a fake stock or to make a profit on their own shares. It also is easy to post messages to newsgroups that make fraudulent claims about a stock offering with the same intent.

Finally, sophisticated promoters can create a Web site that appears to be one for a legitimate investment company. They accept money for stock purchases but never buy the stock for the investor. By the time the investor has figured out that they do not own any stock shares, the promoters have closed the Web site and opened another. This is an important point: Promoters can close down a Web site and can move on much faster than they could move on in pre-Internet days. Before the Internet, they would need at least six months to restart their operation; today, it takes only a few days to be up and running again.

Medical and drug-related fraud. Medical fraud has been around as long as there have been remedies for sickness. In the nineteenth century, "snake oil dealers" peddled remedies from the back of a wagon, whereas in the second half of the twentieth century, radio and television were the source of many advertisements for such products. The advent of the Internet has given the people who sell these products a new way to reach their target market—those who are medically naive and those who are desperate for a cure. As with stock fraud, junk e-mail, chat groups, and professional-appearing Web sites are the major channels for medical fraud. Examples of this type of fraud include false claims for:

- A cure for arthritis made from beef tallow
- A shark cartilage remedy for cancer and HIV/AIDS
- Magnetic therapy for high blood pressure and liver disease

A study by the Federal Trade Commission (FTC) found that the Internet has become a primary source of health and medical information. The study reported that twenty-two million adults in the United States had searched online for this type of information. Many of these citizens visit the Web for information before they visit a physician. As a result of this study, the FTC, in June of 1999, announced an effort to combat the problem of health-related fraud.

Another health-related issue involving the Web is physicians who dispense drugs over the Internet. Because the patient and physician usually have never met or spoken with each other, a physician–patient relationship does not exist; the dispensing of drugs over the Web is considered "unprofessional conduct" and can lead to the physician's loss of license.

Auction site fraud. Since its beginning in 1995, the eBay auction (and others like it) has been an extremely popular Web site where individuals and organizations buy and sell items. However, unlike a physical auction, the buyer and seller are not actually at the auction, nor is the buyer's money or the item being sold. This situation can quickly lead to problems when buyers fail to send the funds for the purchase or when sellers fail to send the item that has been purchased. In fact, this type of fraud, by far, is the cause of the largest number of reports of Internet fraud to the National Consumers League.

Another problem faced by eBay is people who engage in the auction process when they have no intention of actually buying the items. This occurred at eBay in 1999 when a thirteen-year-old boy bid over $900,000 on various items—money he did not have to spend!

In response to these problems, eBay, which originally had a "hands-off" policy toward the bidding and payment process, has instituted new policies to discourage this type of fraud. In addition, electronic escrow services like i-Escrow[5] have begun to be used by eBay members. These services hold the funds in escrow until the item arrives, at which time the funds are turned over to the seller.

Fraud protection at fareastfoods.com. Because it handles a high volume of food orders over the Internet that are paid for by credit card, a relatively small company like fareastfoods.com could easily be put out of business if its credit card fraud rate is much above 1 percent. To avoid this problem, the company has subscribed to the SET protocol to protect itself and its customers. Fareastfoods.com also does not allow its employees to save passwords on their laptops, which would allow entry into the corporate network if the laptops were stolen.

Quick Review

1. What are the motives for the theft of laptop computers, besides their hardware value?
2. Why does credit card fraud affect merchants more than consumers?

Copyright Infringement

Copyright infringement (i.e., using copyrighted material without paying the copyright holders a fee or having their permission to use the material) is a crime. Copyright infringement is now widespread in two areas—software and music. Commonly referred to as **software piracy,** illegally copying or sharing software is now a very big business that costs companies like Microsoft a great deal of money each year. Illegally downloading music files from the Internet is referred to as **music piracy,** and this piracy is being fought by the major music labels and publishing groups.

---

5. http://www.iescrow.com.

Software Piracy

With the introduction of PCs in the late 1970s came a new type of crime: the illegal copying of computer software. Before PCs, when mainframes and minicomputers were the only sources of computing power, this was not a significant problem because users could use only whatever software was available at their computer center. In this environment, there was seldom the need or the facility to copy the commercial software from the computer. However, once PCs came into use, with software being distributed on floppy disks and now on CD-ROMs and over the Internet, users started illegally copying or sharing the software rather than buying the software.

This problem is now a very large one for software developers. A study by the Business Software Alliance (BSA) and the Software and Information Industry Association (SIIA), two software trade associations, found the worldwide cost in 1998 to be around $11 *billion*. The same study found that almost two out of every five new software packages installed today are illegal copies. In the United States alone, 27 percent of all new software installations involve pirated software, resulting in an estimated 130,000 lost jobs, $5.3 billion in lost wages, and $1 billion in lost tax revenue annually.[6]

In response to this problem, the software industry has acted strongly against the worst domestic offenders and against retailers around the world. The industry has filed lawsuits or sent cease-and-desist letters to many offenders and distributed a software package that companies can use to audit their own computers (SoftScan or MacScan, which can be downloaded from the BSA Web site at www.bsa.org/freeware). However, some foreign countries are still referred to as "one-disk countries" because of the widespread software piracy practiced there. For example, the BSA-SIIA study found that more than nine out of ten business software applications are pirated in Vietnam, China, Indonesia, and Russia.

Although not exactly the same as software piracy, the sale of stolen software has the same effect of denying the rightful parties of profit from sales. In a 1999 case, a father and son in Massachusetts were found guilty of conspiring to sell more than $20 million in stolen Microsoft software.

Software Piracy and the Law

To understand how copying commercial software for personal use and committing software piracy differ, it is necessary to look at the 1980 Software Copyright Act. In this act, and others before it, a distinction is made between copying a piece of software for backup purposes and copying it to sell or give away. It is perfectly legal to copy a disk for backup purposes. It does not matter how many copies are made, as long as all are retained by the user. The minute a copy is given or sold to anyone else, a federal law has been broken. The penalties include damages to the copyright holder—in this case the software developer—as well as loss of any profits made by the person who has distributed the program. In cases of willfully copying and reselling, prison terms can be imposed. Enforcement of the copyright law is reserved for the most blatant offenders because of the cost of prosecution. This means that the person who copies a program and gives it to a friend is probably not going to be prosecuted, but copying and reselling software in large quantities will bring quick action by the U.S. Attorney's office. One must remember that the software developer has put a great deal of money and effort into creating that software and expects a fair return on the investment. Every time someone gives away a copy of the program, the developer suffers a loss. If this were to happen enough times, there would be no incentive for companies to develop software.

Another part of the copyright act permits the user to modify the program to the extent necessary to make it useful. A user may change a program to meet special

---

6. http://www.bsa.org or http://www.siia.net.

needs, but no matter how much it is changed, it still cannot be resold as a new product. The U.S. Attorney's office has become involved in several cases in which people have either knowingly or unknowingly modified software and tried to resell it as a new product.

In 1997, a law aimed at software and other types of piracy was passed. The No Electronic Theft (NET) Act makes distributing illegal copies of online copyrighted material a federal crime if the value of the material is $2,500 or more.

Hundreds of pirated CDs are destroyed in India.

Music Piracy

Starting in 1997, a new type of copyright infringement began to occur—in music. In that year, the popular MP3 Rio player was made available to consumers. This device allows users to download compressed music files in the MP3 format from the Internet and play them. The MP3 format (MP3 stands for Motion Picture Entertainment Group or MPEG version 3) enables music files that would ordinarily take up to fifty mbytes of storage space to be reduced to four or five mbytes. This compression, resulting in a very slight loss in sound quality, makes it feasible for files to be downloaded over the Internet.

Although it is legal for individuals to create their own files and keep them for themselves, or to download songs with the permission of the copyright holder, it is illegal to download or trade copyrighted songs without permission. Illegally downloading compressed music files falls under the NET Act of 1997. Several industry groups have acted to restrict the availability of MP3 downloads, and other standards have been suggested to make music available over the Internet while still ensuring that the copyright holders receive income. This issue is not resolved at this writing, but with a potential market for downloadable music from the Internet approaching $1 billion in the next few years, there is a great deal of interest in this topic.

Other Issues on the Web

There is a growing battle over copyright and trademark questions that could have a much bigger impact on what appears on the Web than issues of software and music. As more and more companies are jumping into electronic commerce, they are realizing that they need to protect their assets from trademark infringement, copyright violation, and unfair competition. Whereas the NET Act spells out some of the conditions, other conditions are being worked out case by case. In many instances, Webmasters are being asked to change a Web site or remove content that is copyrighted. To see what you can and *cannot* do in terms of Web sites, visit the Web site at http://builder.cnet.com/Business/Law/ for a discussion of these complex but very important issues.

Quick Review

1. Under what conditions is it *legal* to make a copy of a software program?
2. What is a *one-disk country*?

Attacks on Information Technology

Although information technology can be attacked physically by terrorists or other criminals, attacks are much more likely to be through the Internet. In these cases, the objectives are typically IT software and data, a Web or e-mail server, or an IT user. Software and data attacks involve various types of destructive software called *viruses* and *worms*. In each case, a destructive computer program is introduced into the computer to destroy software and data. Attacks on Web and e-mail servers involve either taking control of the server or sending so many requests or messages to the servers that they collapse under the load. Attacks on IT users often involve using e-mail, chat groups or newsgroups, or fictitious Web pages to destroy the reputation of the users.

Viruses and Other Types of Destructive Software

The most common type of destructive software is the virus. A **virus** is a program that attaches itself to specific files. When an infected file is executed, the virus replicates itself with potentially harmful results. Hundreds of viruses for PCs are active at any one time. They go by such names as "Chernobyl," "Melissa," and "Michelangelo." The number of computers that have been infected by viruses is unknown, but the Computer Security Institute/FBI study mentioned earlier found that 90 percent of the respondents had a virus infection during the previous twelve months. Two examples of such viruses were the Melissa virus and the Chernobyl virus.

Focus on the Internet

Securing Electronic Documents

As we move into the networked economy, the use of electronic documents will undoubtedly grow dramatically over the coming years. Instead of searching for; ordering; and paying for raw materials, parts, and finished goods using traditional paper catalogs, invoices, and checks; this function as well as many others (taxes, permits, etc.) will all be handled by business, industry, and individuals over the Internet or private networks. Many businesses are already using Electronic Data Interchange (EDI) for these operations and many more will use EDI, Extensible Markup Language (XML), or other methods in the near future. Even transactions with government increasingly are being handled electronically. As we move into a "less paper" economy, there will be an increasing need for ways to secure copies of the electronic documents. Just as we need to store paper federal tax returns for at least three years, we will need to store copies of our electronic tax returns in a secure location for the same length of time. Doing this at home or in the office can be risky with the potential for loss of files due to hard disk failure, theft, or damage to the PC from fire, water, electricity, or storms. Unauthorized access can also be a problem.

For many years, one of the safest ways to securely store paper documents, as well as other valuables, has been a safe-deposit box at the bank. Now, you can do the same with your electronic documents at www.safedepositbox.com. This service provides users with the capability of securely storing important files in an electronic safe deposit box. The files can be saved by transferring them directly from a PC to a restricted access, high-security data center using a secure Internet connection. The service offers the capability for shared access to the documents by multiple people, document encoding to provide further protection to especially sensitive files, and document recovery in case the user loses their key to the box. Like physical safe-deposit boxes, the electronic ones on safedepositbox.com are associated with banks like NetB@nk, the largest FDIC-insured bank operating solely on the Internet.

Source: www.safedepositbox.com.

The Melissa virus was released on Friday, March 26, 1999, and by the end of that weekend, it had infected at least 100,000 machines in over eight hundred organizations. As viruses go, Melissa was quite benign because all it did was e-mail itself to the first fifty people in the computer's address book when the recipient of an e-mail opened the attached document. However, even the act of e-mailing itself to fifty people caused some e-mail systems to crash from an overload of messages. The author of Melissa was caught within a week through cyberdetective work and was charged with a variety of crimes that could put him in jail for up to forty years, plus a fine of as much as $480,000.

Far more destructive than Melissa was the Chernobyl virus. So-named because it strikes on April 26 of each year—the anniversary of the 1986 Chernobyl nuclear disaster in the former Soviet Union—in 1999 it caused over 540,000 computers to crash, mostly in South Korea and Turkey. The virus wiped computer hard drives clean and, in some cases, destroyed a key chip in the computer. Only about ten thousand systems were hit in the United States. The lesser damage in the United States was thought to be because the United States was aware of viruses from the Melissa attack and because the Chernobyl virus was carried on pirated software that is thought to be widely used in the hardest-hit countries.

The virus process is shown in Figure 10-3. Note that the virus enters the computer through pirated software, through software obtained from a friend, or over a computer network. A virus must be attached to an executable program that is installed in the computer. Once the infected program is executed in the object computer, the virus is activated, at which time it often copies itself to the files of the operating system and then into RAM. From RAM it replicates itself and makes copies on any disks inserted into the computer or sends itself back out over the network, where the process starts over.

Figure 10-3 Virus Generation Process

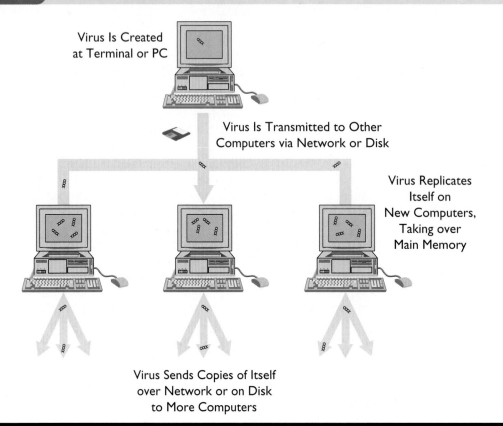

Virus Is Created at Terminal or PC

Virus Is Transmitted to Other Computers via Network or Disk

Virus Replicates Itself on New Computers, Taking over Main Memory

Virus Sends Copies of Itself over Network or on Disk to More Computers

To combat viruses, users should avoid using any software that is not "shrink-wrapped" or from a certified clean download site on the Internet. Users should also avoid opening attachments that come in e-mail from unknown people or that they are not expecting from people they do know. The latter warning is due to the fact that it is possible to make e-mail look like it is coming from a friend when it is not. You should also have up-to-date antivirus software running at all times that will check every file that is introduced into your computer and set off an alarm or automatically clean any infected files.

A **worm** is similar to, and often confused with, a virus because both can replicate themselves. The difference is that a virus must attach itself to another program, whereas a worm is a freestanding program that can continually execute without outside influence. A recent example of a worm is a program known as W32/ExplorerZip.worm, which was unleashed in June of 1999. Like the Melissa virus, this worm arrives by e-mail, but unlike Melissa, it is far from benign. It deposits itself on the hard drive and searches for a variety of file types and attempts to erase them in such a way that utility software cannot restore them. Also, unlike Melissa, this worm replies to legitimate e-mail messages with an attachment that recipients are likely to open because it is in a reply to their own message.

In addition to viruses and worms, there are a variety of other types of destructive software with which you should be familiar. A **trojan horse** program appears to do one thing but actually does another. For example, a Trojan horse program might seem to be antivirus software but actually will be a destructive program. A **time bomb** is a program timed to execute itself on a certain date, whereas a **logic bomb** executes whenever a certain command is given or an event occurs. Both types of "bombs" can be stored in a computer, waiting for a date or command to go off. For

David L. Smith created the Melissa virus and released it onto the Internet.

example, an employee may place a logic bomb in the company computer. As long as the employee's name is on the payroll file, the bomb does nothing. However, if the employee is terminated and his or her name is removed from the payroll file, the logic bomb goes off, usually erasing files from secondary storage.

Software developers may include a **trapdoor** in a computer that allows them to circumvent any security systems and access the computer whenever they desire. Developers have installed software and then, when they were not paid on time, they have used the trapdoor to enter the program and turn it off.

Attacks on Web and E-Mail Servers

The ease of access to the World Wide Web and e-mail is at the heart of the tremendous growth of these two Internet applications. However, the same ease of access makes Web and e-mail servers susceptible to outside attack. This susceptibility is also attributable to the underlying TCP/IP Internet protocol and the UNIX operating system, which many of these servers run. Both TCP/IP and UNIX were developed in the 1960s and 1970s for use in research and academic environments where security was of little or no concern. A number of well-known "holes" (i.e., ways in which an intruder can gain access to the system) in both TCP/IP and UNIX can allow hackers to break into them and cause mischief. Today we use TCP/IP and UNIX for electronic commerce and e-mail, which require a high level of security, and they do not always work as well as we would like.

The Web, on top of the TCP/IP protocol, uses a series of protocols that are also not very secure. This means that hackers can often break into a Web site and change the contents of a Web page, such as when hackers vandalized the official U.S. Senate

Web site in 1999 and changed the welcoming page. Web sites can also be attacked by being flooded with too many requests for access. This occurred on May 12, 1999, when the U.S. President's Web site was deluged with requests and had to be shut down for twenty-four hours. It is not even necessary for multiple people to be involved because widely available computer programs can generate the volume of requests needed to crash a Web site.

E-mail servers suffer from the same types of problems (i.e., they can be broken into through security holes and crashed by receiving too many requests for service). When hackers break into an e-mail service, they can wipe out e-mail files or capture passwords for future use. Occasionally, a "hacked" e-mail system will have to be shut down so that the security hole can be found and fixed.

Attacks on IT Users

With the tremendous growth of information technology has come an increase in cyberattacks on individuals and organizations. The attacks are not on the information technology being used but rather on the reputation of the person or organization. It is easy to send an e-mail to a widely distributed listserv or group of listservs that makes negative remarks about an individual or organization. Similarly, chat rooms, newsgroups, or electronic bulletin boards are wide open for postings of negative comments. In addition, it is easy to create an entire Web site dedicated to spreading negative information about an individual or organization. For example, Jayne Hitchcock, the person mentioned in the opening Focus on Society box, has brought civil action against the owner of the Woodside Literary Agency for harassing her with e-mail. According to her suit, the owner went so far as to forge posts to the misc.writer newsgroup that appeared to be from Hitchcock's e-mail address, contained her telephone number and address, and involved sexual activities. According to the New York Assistant Attorney General on the case, Woodside harassed other writers who attempted to warn writers about the Internet scam being run by the agency.

For the individual or organization that is defamed on the Internet, it is very difficult to rectify incorrect information. Bad news travels very fast on the Internet, and corrections or retractions seldom reach the same number of readers as did the original message. With Internet law still in its infancy, there are no strict rules on what is libel when posted electronically. Although there is a culture of "anything goes" on the Internet, observers feel that the courts will eventually have to rule on what constitutes libel, just as they have on similar questions after the advent of radio, television, and VCRs.

Legal Aspects of IT Crime

Prior to 1986, although computer criminals reaped large sums of money from crimes, they usually did not spend much time behind bars when convicted—for two reasons. First, not many laws actually covered IT crime, and even when they did, prosecutors had difficulty obtaining a conviction. In many cases, the only thing stolen was information or computer time, neither of which would constitute a crime under theft laws enacted prior to the age of computers. Often the only law that came close to applying to IT crime was the mail fraud law. Even when money was taken, the thief usually got off—because he or she was young, clean-cut, and had no previous record. The thief might also be excused if the jury considered the crime "victimless" because the injured party was a large corporation. In addition, the intricacies of the computer were often very difficult to explain to the judge and jury, so the prosecution may have had a hard time demonstrating how a crime was committed. Second, computer criminals went unpunished because companies were hesitant to take action against former employees. These companies did not wish to risk the negative publicity of a trial or the appearance of not having adequate security for the company computer system. As a result, many white-collar computer criminals have been allowed to resign quietly from the company, in some cases moving to a similar position in another company.

To rectify the problem, the federal government and all fifty states have passed laws covering IT crime. The most recent federal law is the NET Act. The Computer Fraud and Abuse Act of 1986 made it a crime to damage data in any government computer or in any computer used by a federally insured financial institution (this includes most banks). It also made it a crime to use a computer to view, copy, or damage data across state lines. Under this act, if a victim can show that at least $1,000 in damage was done or that medical records were in any way damaged, the alleged offender can be prosecuted. This act also made it a felony to set up or use bulletin boards that list individual or corporate computer passwords. People convicted under the Computer Fraud and Abuse Act can be sentenced to up to twenty years in prison and fined up to $100,000. The author of the Melissa virus may be prosecuted under this act. The 106th U.S. Congress is also considering a number of bills that would cover a variety of criminal activities.

IT crime is not restricted to the United States. Other countries, such as Canada and the United Kingdom, have either enacted laws similar to those discussed here or are exploring other legal avenues to combat IT crime. For example, a German court sentenced an American to four years in jail for importing illegally copied software.

Quick Review

1. List the three objects of an attack through the Internet.
2. Why is it so difficult for people defamed over the Internet to clear their names?

Information Technology Security

Information technology security is the protection of the IT assets—including hardware, software, data, information, and the user—of individuals and organizations. Given the huge potential losses involved in IT crime, IT security has become a very important topic for individuals and organizations. IT security includes the wide range of methods used to protect IT and IT users from natural and criminal forces. (We include natural forces because fire, water, wind, or earthquakes can be as devastating as the criminal who seeks personal gain.) Types of security range from a commonsense approach of locking doors to sophisticated methods of protecting intranets from outsiders.

Threats to Computer Systems

Although unauthorized access by outside parties is the most publicized threat to a computer system's security, most experts do not consider it the most important. More pressing concerns include errors in data and omission of data by employees; the actual theft of the computer and peripheral devices (printers, monitors, etc.); misuse by disgruntled or dishonest employees; and damage from terrorist acts, fire, water, or natural disasters.

Although not everyone will agree with a particular ranking of threats to computer hardware, software, and data, no one will deny that security must respond to all of these threats. Another way to look at the security problem for computers is to consider physical security, data security, and Internet security. **Physical security** is the protection of computer hardware from theft or damage, whether caused by nature or humans, in the same way that other office equipment would be protected. **Data security** is the protection of software and data from manipulation, destruction, or theft. Finally, **Internet security** is the protection of information technology from outside intrusions through the Internet.

Physical Security

Methods of protecting computer hardware from outside forces include employing procedures that exclude unauthorized people from the organizational servers, protecting hardware and software from theft, and protecting the hardware as much as possible from natural disasters and from fire and water damage. A key part of any physical security plan is to have a plan for recovery of critical data and programs in case of disaster. This plan should consider the worst-case scenarios facing the organization and set up ways to recover from them. Scenarios should include weather or terrorist disasters as well as problems caused by hackers or malicious employees. Failure to plan ahead could easily result in the organization's going out of business.

Unauthorized people can be excluded by controlling entry to the areas where servers are kept by using fingerprints, eyeprints, or voiceprints to identify individuals and, as simple as it may seem, by keeping doors locked. Protecting computers, especially laptops, from theft is a growing problem that requires constant vigilance on the part of owners. Keeping serial numbers of computers on file is another important part of physical security because they are the best hope for recovering lost machines. Portable secondary storage devices like floppy disks, zip disks, or writable CD-ROMs are even easier to steal than computers when they are left lying around or are stored in an unlocked desk drawer or cabinet. Keeping doors locked may be even more important for the security of personal computers than for the larger, less portable computers.

Damage from fire or water is somewhere on everyone's list of dangers, but these dangers are not often treated with the respect they deserve. Like any electronic machine, the computer is always in danger from an electrical fire caused by a short circuit. Nonelectrical fires can also cause great damage if water is used to extinguish them, because water can do great damage to the delicate circuits of a computer. For this reason, the danger of water damage must be considered in planning the security system for the computer. Sprinkler systems are a common protection against fire in commercial buildings, but they can cause more damage to a computer than the fire itself. A number of years ago, a government agency's sprinklers went off by accident, soaking the computers and causing many related problems. Newer fire-suppression systems use combinations of gases to deprive a fire of oxygen, instead of using water.

This eye detection system provides a fast and secure way of protecting the facility.

This UPS will provide power to an IT device in the event of a power loss.

To avoid a complete loss of data in a disaster, there should be a policy of regularly backing up files on the system and storing the backups in an area physically separate from the main computer center. In this context, a **backup** is a second (or even a third) copy of a data file on a secondary storage device separate from the primary disk secondary storage. Unfortunately, personal computer users tend to put this task off as long as possible. To avoid the expensive problems that can occur if the hard disk crashes or an errant command destroys all data on the disk, making backups on disk or tape should be a policy of every user.

In addition to securing a personal computer against theft, individuals and companies must protect the personal computer from environmental harm. The normal precautions taken to protect any piece of office equipment against fire, water, dust, and other physical damage apply. Besides these, the user must protect the computer and its data against, of all things, electricity. Too much electricity, too little, the wrong kind, or the right kind applied in the wrong manner can cause problems. If a computer is hit by a **voltage surge,** or **spike,** in which lightning or some other electrical disturbance causes a sudden increase in the electrical supply, the delicate chips and other electrical parts can be destroyed. For this reason, **surge protectors** are a necessity to protect the computer against uneven electrical power. These devices are quite inexpensive and plug into a normal wall outlet. The computer and its peripherals are then plugged into outlets in the surge protector. When a surge hits the wall outlet, a circuit breaker is thrown in the surge protector, and the computer and its peripherals are protected.

Just as too much electricity can damage a computer, too little electricity—in the form of a brownout or a blackout—can cause the loss of all data from internal memory. Because RAM is volatile and depends on a constant power source to retain the information, loss of power means loss of memory. Devices called **uninterruptible power supplies (UPS)** continue the power to a personal computer if electrical current is disrupted. Although a UPS is more expensive than a surge protector, it is commonly used by organizations that have a LAN or by people who use a computer on a daily basis. However, if you do not have a UPS, the best defense against a power outage is frequently saving information in RAM to disk. Figure 10-4 shows the spectrum of electrical power and the effects of too much or too little power.

Figure 10-4 Electrical Spectrum

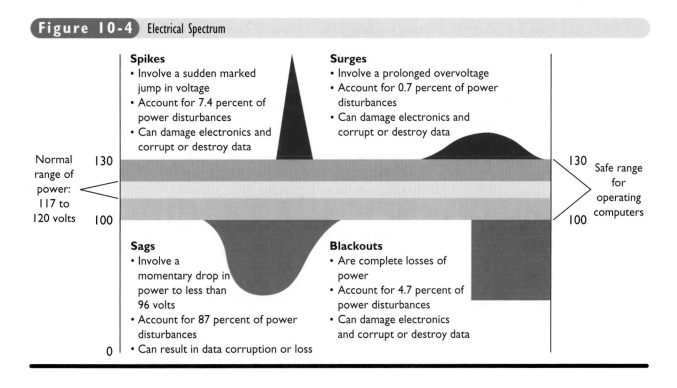

Spikes
- Involve a sudden marked jump in voltage
- Account for 7.4 percent of power disturbances
- Can damage electronics and corrupt or destroy data

Surges
- Involve a prolonged overvoltage
- Account for 0.7 percent of power disturbances
- Can damage electronics and corrupt or destroy data

Normal range of power: 117 to 120 volts

130

100

130 Safe range for operating computers

100

Sags
- Involve a momentary drop in power to less than 96 volts
- Account for 87 percent of power disturbances
- Can result in data corruption or loss

Blackouts
- Are complete losses of power
- Account for 4.7 percent of power disturbances
- Can damage electronics and corrupt or destroy data

0

Security at fareastfoods.com. The servers at fareastfoods.com are secured in a server farm that has locked doors that check the eyeprint of everyone entering the room. There are duplicate servers for each operation so that, if one goes down, the operation can continue uninterrupted. There are also duplicate communication links to the Internet so that, if one line is cut, the company can continue to operate. All servers are protected by surge protectors, and each has its own UPS that is good for two hours of continuous power. There is also a generator that can be used if necessary. The servers are backed up each night to ensure that data are never lost. All in all, there is a good deal of redundancy to protect fareastfoods.com's capability to operate.

Data Security

Protecting the software and data is an entirely different problem from providing physical security. It is generally agreed that although computer hardware can almost always be replaced, an organization's data are its most important asset and may be irreplaceable. Even if data are not destroyed, having data fall into a competitor's hands can have disastrous implications for private companies and national governments. The primary tool for protecting access to software and data on computer systems is the password. A **password** is a sequence of letters and/or digits, supposedly known only to the user, that must be entered before the computer system can be accessed. Most people have become accustomed to using a type of password called a **personal identification number (PIN)** to access a bank account from an automatic teller machine (ATM). Unfortunately, many passwords are common words such as *test, system,* or the name of the user's significant other, child, or pet.

Given the importance of passwords in protecting software and data on computer systems, **password policies** that define how a password is assigned, when it is changed, and who should have a password are an important element of any security system. These policies should include the following elements:

- Do not allow users to choose their own passwords, and require that the password be longer than four letters or digits.
- Users should have their passwords changed immediately if any evidence exists that security may have been breached.
- All passwords should be changed periodically to make guessing a password more difficult.
- If an employee with supervisory-level network access is fired or leaves under less than pleasant circumstances, *all* passwords to which he or she had access, not just the ex-employee's, should be changed. Failure to change all relevant passwords can leave the system open for intrusion.

In addition to password policies, other tools used to protect computer software and data include systems audit software, data encryption systems, and antivirus policies and software.

Systems audit software keeps track of all attempts to log on to the computer, giving particular attention to unsuccessful attempts. An audit of the system log would indicate who has been on the system at any given time and therefore should reveal if an unauthorized user has been on the system. **Data encryption systems** protect the data being transmitted over a network by converting them into an unreadable form. The process is one of transforming **plain text** (a readable form) into **ciphertext** (an indecipherable form) at the source computer and then back to plain text at the destination computer. The quality of an encryption system is measured by the number of bits in the key that is required to convert the ciphertext back to plain text. The higher the number of bits in the key, the more effort required to guess the key because if there are n bits in a key, there are $2n$ possible combinations in that key. Modern encryption systems use at least 128-bit keys. The Pretty Good Privacy (PGP) system is a popular public key encryption system (discussed in chapter 7) that is free to users at a variety of sites in the United States and around the world.

Ⓕocus on People

Phil Zimmermann

One of the best ways to provide security for data and information is to encrypt it. As discussed in chapter 7, encryption involves converting text from a readable form into an unreadable form and decryption converts it back. While the CIA and other government agencies have very sophisticated methods of encryption, almost anyone can use a type of encryption known as Pretty Good Privacy (PGP). PGP is a public key form of encryption in which users exchange digital keys that enable them to encrypt and decrypt messages. PGP was invented in 1991 by a software engineer named Phil Zimmermann. He had been interested in encryption since childhood and, after completing a bachelor's degree in computer science, he became serious about finding a *workable* encryption. By workable, we mean one that is easy to use while not being easily broken. The result of his work was PGP.

After inventing PGP, rather than trying to sell it, Zimmermann gave it away to anyone requesting it. That got him into trouble with U.S. authorities, because it was illegal at that time to export encryption technology. (In September 1999, the Clinton White House proposed ending encryption export restrictions.) In spite of this government effort to stop his work, PGP quickly became the most widely used encryption software in the world. After a three-year effort to prosecute him, the U.S. Justice Department dropped its case and Zimmermann founded PGP, Inc. This company was purchased by Network Associates, where Zimmermann is now a senior fellow. Although he has received a number of awards for his work, including the 1998 Lifetime Achievement Award from *Secure Computing* magazine, he is very proud of the fact that many human rights activists are documenting the atrocities of their governments by encrypting documents with PGP.

Sources: http://www.pgp.com/phil/phil.cgi#about
http://www.animatedsoftware.com/hightech/philspgp.htm

Phil Zimmermann is the inventor of the popular PGP public key encryption system.

Viruses and other destructive software are threats to computer data. **Antivirus policies** are organizational policies that protect the computer system from destructive software. These policies include not allowing untested software to be used on organizational computers and running a virus test every time a computer is started. In addition, if a virus is detected, **antivirus software** can be used to remove the virus from the computer.

Protecting data at fareastfoods.com. At fareastfoods.com, passwords to access the server are generated randomly for each person and are changed every month. Encryption software is used to decrypt the order information coming in from browsers over the Internet, and antivirus software is updated as soon as new data become available on the Web, but no less than once a month.

Quick Review

1. What are the three types of threats with which IT security is concerned?

2. What is the primary way to protect data on a computer from outside intrusion?

Internet Security

Because the Internet has become the primary method for accessing data and information on computers around the world, Internet security has become very important to organizations. Web and e-mail sites are often the object of outside attacks by destructive software. Protecting Web and other Internet servers from these attacks is part of Internet security. The organization must consider the trade-offs between making its Web, e-mail, and other Internet-related servers easily available to its stakeholders and protecting the servers from unwanted intrusions. This requires the organization to consider how it will secure its network environment.

Securing the Corporate Internet Connection

For an organization to secure its connection to the Internet, it must first decide how it wishes to connect to the Internet. There are two basic choices: direct and indirect. A **direct Internet connection** means the company enterprise network is connected to the Internet through its own server and communications link. On the other hand, an **indirect Internet connection** is one in which the company connects to the Internet through an ISP. Each type of connection has its advantages and disadvantages: A direct connection is faster and more flexible but subjects the company to more risks from outside intrusion. An indirect connection tends to be slower and less flexible but provides the company with more protection from outside forces and, possibly, additional technical expertise.

Once a company decides how it wants to connect to the Internet to establish a Web presence, it must consider how it will handle the security risks resulting from its Internet connection. Certainly those companies that have their enterprise network directly connected to the Internet will most likely need to install the higher levels of security. Three types of security that individual computer systems also apply to networks are:

- Installing virus protection software to protect against viruses and other destructive software
- Using passwords to control access to a network
- Using encryption to protect the contents of messages being transmitted over the Internet

In addition, companies with direct connections to the Internet need to consider two other forms of security: fixing known security holes in the UNIX operating system and Internet protocols and employing firewalls to protect themselves.

Fixing known security holes. The UNIX operating system and Internet protocols were not designed to provide a high level of security. One feature of the UNIX operating system, under which many Web servers operate, is that approved users can log on from anywhere, at any time, to administer the system. By gaining access to the main folder of the server, they can manipulate files and gain entry to a corporate network. Unfortunately, so can hackers who know how to exploit these features of UNIX. Fortunately, much of the server and operating systems software can be altered to greatly improve its level of security.

Some well-known holes in the security armor of a company's UNIX-based server can be fixed by a knowledgeable system administrator. **System administrators** are those people who manage security and user access to an intranet or LAN. Other holes are not easily fixed, and some are still unknown. One of the best ways to protect mission-critical information is to move it onto other servers or networks that are not connected to the Internet. Still, there may be some critical information that needs to be available on the portion of the corporate network that is accessible to the Internet. In this case there are several steps to improve corporate network security.

To stay on top of who is trying to break into the organization's computer, server logs should be monitored. Monitoring software keeps track of all successful and *un-successful* attempts to access the server. It is estimated that 5 percent of all intrusions are detected and that of those detected only 5 percent are reported. Intruders' latest tricks can be observed and thwarted by monitoring the server logs for any unusual activities. When intrusions or attempts at intrusion are found, the server needs to be fixed quickly to guard against similar attacks. Many copy-cat hackers will attempt to break into a system by exploiting system flaws found by other hackers.

One way to begin to find the security holes on a network or your server is to run a program that is designed to identify potential security holes. Many of these scanner programs are controversial because hackers can use them to find holes in a network that they can exploit. Knowing that hackers have these tools at their disposal, you would be better off using them yourself in order to close the windows to your server that the hacker can easily identify and crawl through. Satan (Security Administrator Tool for Analyzing Networks) is one such scanner program, as is NMap.

Finally, when the known holes are fixed, the network administrator needs to stay on top of who may be trying to break into company computers and what is happening at other sites on the network. To stay on top of security violations on the Internet the network administrator may want to join one of the mailing lists run by Computer Emergency Response Team (CERT)[7] or another mailing list that alerts the network administrator of known security problems. The network administrator can also find a wealth of information about the state of security of the Internet by browsing various Web sites.

Firewalls. Firewalls are the dominant technology used by businesses to protect their networks from hackers. A **firewall** is a set of related programs, located at a network gateway server, that protects the resources of a private network from users

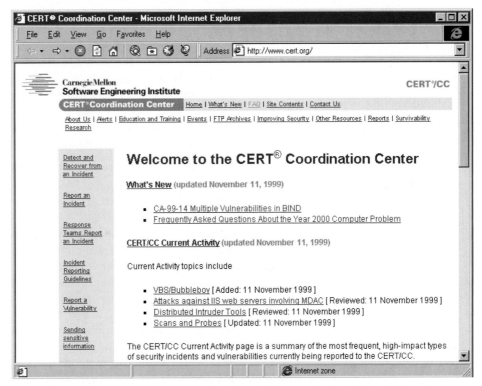

The CERT Web site can be a tremendous aid to network administrators in thwarting outside intrusion.

---

7. http://www.cert.org/.

Figure 10-5 Firewall around Enterprise Network

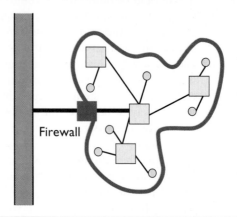

Firewall

from other networks by enforcing a security policy.[8] Firewalls must protect the enterprise network from outside intruders while also making it possible for users inside the firewall to access the Internet. There is a trade-off between user flexibility and the level of security provided for the internal network. Although no firewall is perfect in balancing these two competing demands, many come close. Figure 10-5 shows a conceptual view of a firewall around a corporate network.

Once a corporation decides to put in a firewall it needs to program the firewall to support its security needs. A firewall can be restrictive or flexible, depending on the company's goals. For instance, specific services can be limited in order to reduce the probability of break-ins. One of the most common ways for a hacker to break into a server is through the File Transfer Protocol (FTP) software on the server; as a result, many corporations have decided not to allow access to that service from outside the firewall.

The primary purpose of a firewall is to look at every piece of information that is either sent in or out of the internal network. Firewalls will act on a message on the basis of user identification, point of origin, file, or other codes or actions. A firewall can take four basic actions when it looks at a piece of information:

1. The piece of information can be dropped (not forwarded) entirely.
2. An alert can be issued to the network administrator.
3. A message can be returned to the sender after a failed attempt to send the information through.
4. The action could just be logged.

A common way to attack a network is through **IP-spoofing.** IP-spoofing takes advantage of the fact that the UNIX operating system presumes that anyone who logs in to a server using a previously approved TCP/IP address must be an authorized user, which is not always the case. By altering the source IP address someone can "spoof" the firewall into believing a message is coming from a trusted source. Then, once inside the network, the message can wreak havoc. To combat this problem, many firewalls reject all packets that come from outside the firewall but carry an internal source address.

In summary, Figure 10-6 shows the methods that can be used to protect the organization's enterprise network. Note that an employee who wishes to access the intranet server has to pass a human guard, some type of identification system, a

---

8. http://www.whatis.com.

locked door, and then log on to an intranet client that is linked via a LAN to the server, using a personal identification code or user name. The employee then has to provide an acceptable password and may have to go through an additional authentication procedure. At this point, the employee is logged on to the system and passes through an encryption process before actually accessing the intranet server. A user wishing to access the server from the Internet has to go through a firewall before following the same process as the inside user.

Internet security at fareastfoods.com. In addition to using SET (Secure Electronic Transaction) to protect all orders and credit card numbers coming into fareastfoods.com, to protect company software and data, the system administrator runs the latest scanning software periodically to find new holes in the UNIX operating system that runs the servers. Fareastfoods.com also has a firewall that is constantly updated to keep rogue messages out of the system.

Legal Issues

Many companies overlook the potential legal issues they face when they connect to the Internet. The popular media have focused attention on many of these issues, including the availability of child pornography, bootlegged software, and ease of infringement of copyright laws. Network administrators must be aware of these potential dangers and take measures to protect their company and its employees from lawsuits and loss of valuable copyrighted data.

If FTP access is allowed to a corporate server, a good policy is not allowing external users to place files on the server or purging files from it frequently. This will guard against unwanted guests using the server as a clearinghouse for pirated software.

Figure 10-6 Summary of Network Security Methods

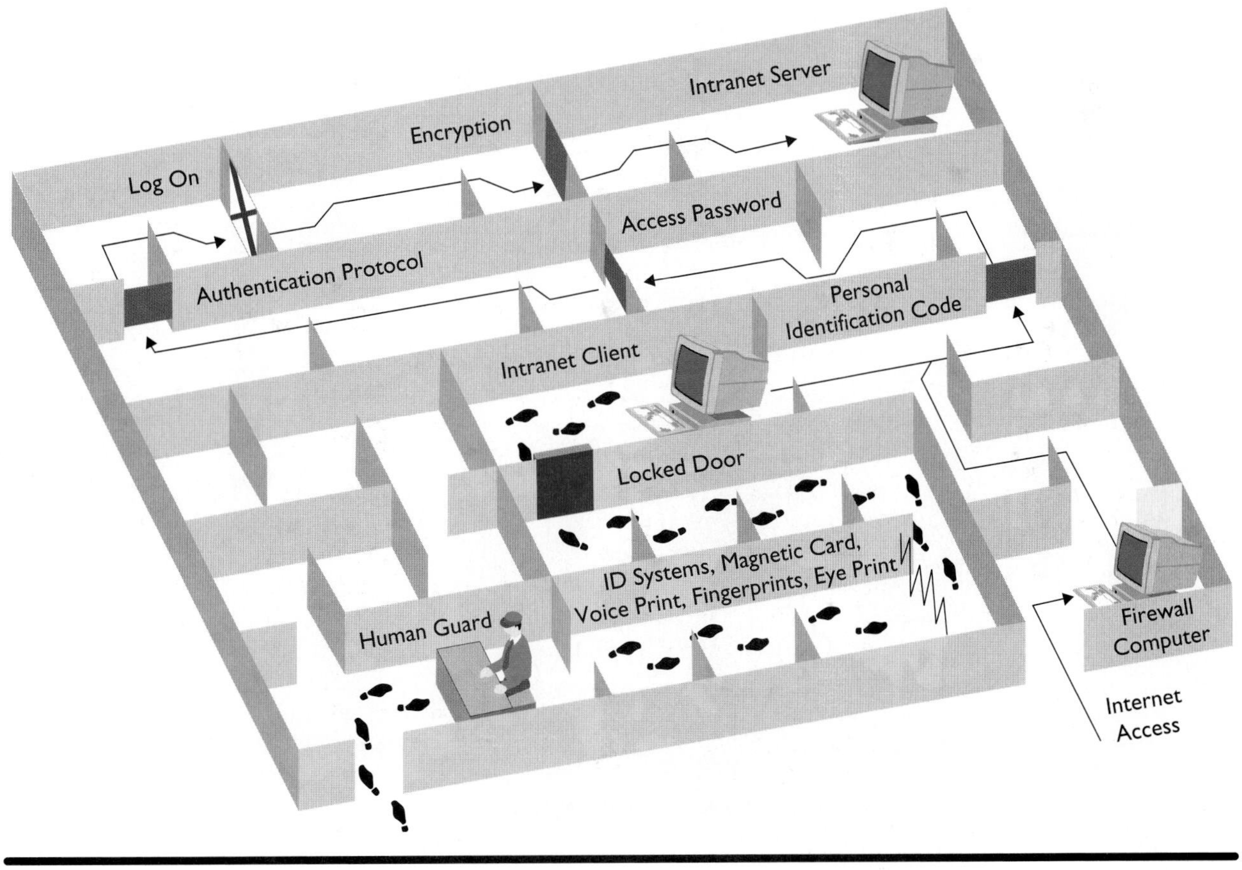

Focus on Management

From Russia with Bits

In what is being called the first post-cold war cyberwar attack, hackers from Moscow were found to have breached American computer security in the Defense and Energy Departments. The attacks were serious enough for the Department of Defense (DOD) to have all of its civilian and military employees change their passwords, a first in such large numbers. It is believed that the hackers were from the Russian Academy of Sciences, a government-supported organization that interacts with Russia's top military labs. DOD officials believe the repetitive intrusions began in January 1999 at a low-access level and were detected almost immediately. When they were followed, the trail led to Moscow. Shortly thereafter, the attackers returned with new tools that allowed them to enter undetected but left electronic traces that could be reconstructed later. Some perpetrators even gained "root level" access (the level restricted to a few network administrators) on some systems.

A key question regarding this intrusion is whether the culprits managed to jump from the un-classified but nonpublic systems that they had penetrated to classified DOD networks containing extremely sensitive data. Defense Department security experts insist that firewalls between the classified and unclassified networks would have prohibited such an intrusion, but other sources are not so sure. In any case, the unclassified databases to which the hackers gained access often contain data than can be combined to create an accurate picture of secret information. Of more pressing concern is that the last detected intrusion was on May 14, 1999, and no one knows if the attacks stopped or if they reached a level of sophistication that rendered them untraceable. Both Russia's SVR Foreign Intelligence Service and the Academy of Sciences denied any knowledge of the intrusions, noting that the hackers could be amateurs seeking thrills or agents from a third country using servers in Moscow as their jumping-off place to hack into U.S. systems.

Source: Gregory Vistica, "We're in the Middle of a Cyberwar." *Newsweek,* September 20, 1999, p. 52.

Hackers, who appeared to be from Moscow, were able to break into DOD computers.

One well-publicized case occurred at a major university where unknown individuals were using a seldom-used computer as a storage facility for pirated software. It is not unthinkable that the owners of a server might be found liable for what resides on their computer, regardless of their knowledge, and be brought to court for copyright infringement laws.

To curb the access to sexually explicit materials, many companies are restricting access to a variety of newsgroups. Although this may cut off that source, there are other ways for users to gain access to such materials. The only hope a company has in guarding against such actions is to educate employees on what type of behavior the company will not tolerate and to enforce aggressively such stances. There is no way to monitor the actions of all employees, but by creating an environment that does not condone such behavior the company may be able to reduce the likelihood of such incidents.

Employees also need to be educated on copyright laws. Although it is fairly well known that copying commercial, nonshareware computer programs is illegal, other forms of copyright infringement may not be as obvious. Downloading a copyrighted music file or distributing an article copied from a Web site without citing it can also be violations of copyright laws. Furthermore, the company needs to be concerned not only with what the employees obtain but also with what they may post outside of the company. An employee may unwittingly release private company information to others on the Internet and jeopardize company data or potential profits. Once again, the only way to guard against such situations is through employee education. When in doubt employees should contact the company legal department or the network administrator.

Insurance against IT Crime

Beginning with Lloyds of London in 1981, many insurance companies have been offering coverage for IT crime. In many cases, this coverage is part of a more general insurance policy for criminal activities, and most large corporations are covered to some degree.

Beginning with Lloyds of London in 1981, many insurance companies have been offering coverage for IT crime. In many cases, this coverage is part of a more general insurance policy for criminal activities, and most large corporations are covered to some degree. However, there tend to be many exclusions that relate to criminal activities—by either internal employees or hackers. For example, the traditional insurance policy only covers theft from the insured by people outside the firm and does not cover harm to the company from insiders or due to business interruption. It also usually refers only to money or property. In response to these exclusions, newer policies are aimed at coverage against crimes committed by insiders or hackers, loss of business due to such activities, and activities carried out by a hacker using the company computer. These new policies extend the definition of fraud from "theft when related to the use of any computer" to covering more than theft, to the extent that they protect a company from going out of business due to a "hacking" event.

Unfortunately, these new policies are expensive with the policy offered by Lloyds having a minimum premium of $10,000. This may be too much for all but the largest corporations, therefore leaving smaller companies uncovered.

Human Aspects of Computer Security

The human role in ensuring the security of a computer system is every bit as important as the technological role. First, education is the primary means of changing people's attitudes toward security. People must understand that unauthorized intrusion, no matter how innocent it may seem, is a crime punishable by a fine or imprisonment or both. Second, management must be willing to run a complete background check on each prospective employee to determine if any security problems occurred in that person's previous position. It is not uncommon for individuals convicted of some type of IT crime to apply for a similar position once released from incarceration.

Another way to tighten computer security is to involve users in the design of the security system. Although failure to involve users may still allow a system to be secure, users may end up spending more time devising ways to circumvent the security measures than doing their work. Finally, users of the system need to recognize that people, not machines, have the real responsibility for computer security. This aspect of computer ethics is growing in importance as the use of computers grows.

Quick Review

1. In which ways can an organization's enterprise computer network be connected to the Internet?
2. Which two methods are often used to provide security for an enterprise network connected directly to the Internet?

⊙ Summary

To summarize this chapter, let's answer the Learning Objectives questions posed at the beginning of the chapter.

How has the face of crime changed in the networked economy? In the networked economy, individuals and organizations have found ways to use information technology for illegal purposes. Unfortunately, the volume of information technology crime can only be expected to grow right along with the growth of the Internet and electronic commerce. The movement into the networked economy means that criminals will not go away but rather will just change their objectives and the way they achieve these objectives. An IT crime is an illegal act that requires use of information technology and can be committed in a variety of ways, but in general it involves theft, fraud, attacks on information technology or users, or copyright violations. IT criminals may be grouped in three categories: employees, outside people, and organized criminals.

What types of crime are having the greatest impact on individuals and organizations in the networked economy? IT crime can be classified into four categories: theft, fraud, attacks on information technology or users, or copyright violations. Theft involves stealing hardware, data, or information from individuals or organizations, and fraud involves using the Internet to steal money by deceiving victims. Attacks involve attacking organizations and individuals over the Internet with a goal of damaging software, data, information, or reputation.

Types of fraud include convincing users to send money for unneeded services, work-at-home schemes or multilevel marketing schemes, and committing credit card fraud, investor fraud, medical fraud, and auction site fraud.

Copyright infringement involves the illegal use of software or music by using copyrighted material without paying the copyright holder a fee or not obtaining permission to use copyrighted material. Two types of copyright infringement are illegally copying or sharing software (software piracy) and illegally downloading music files (music piracy). Software piracy cost software companies $11 billion in 1998, and music piracy cost approximately $1 billion.

What kinds of attacks are being made on information technology and users? Kinds of attacks include using destructive software to destroy data, attacking Web or e-mail servers, and attacking an individual. The most widely used destructive software are viruses and worms. Attacking Web or e-mail servers can either change or delete contents or cause the servers to crash by receiving too many requests. People are attacked when somebody uses the Internet to hurt their reputation. The primary laws used against IT crime are the Computer Fraud and Abuse Act of 1986 and the NET Act of 1997.

How can organizations protect themselves from crime in the networked economy? Information technology security is the protection of IT assets—including hardware, software, data, information, and the user—of individuals and organizations. IT security includes a wide range of methods used to protect IT and IT users from natural and criminal forces. Types of security range from a commonsense approach of locking doors to sophisticated methods of protecting intranets from outsiders. Security can be divided into physical security, data security, and Internet security. Physical security is the protection of computer hardware from theft or damage, whether caused by nature or people, in the same way that other office equipment would be protected. Data security is the protection of software and data from unauthorized manipulation, destruction, or theft.

In what ways can an organization protect its enterprise network from intrusions over the Internet? Internet security involves protecting Web and other Internet servers from attacks. The organization must consider the trade-offs between making its Web, e-mail, and other Internet-related servers easily available to its stakeholders and protecting the servers from unwanted intrusions. This requires that the company think about how to secure its network environment by fixing holes in the UNIX operating system and using a firewall to keep out intruders.

⊘ Review Questions

1. Why is it difficult to determine the actual value of IT crime?
2. List the types of crimes involving information technology.
3. List and discuss the three types of IT criminals. Which type of criminals is considered to be the largest?
4. Why are computer chips often a prime target of criminals?
5. List the various types of IT fraud. Which affects the merchant but not the individual?
6. Why is it legal to make a backup of software but not to copy it for a friend?
7. List the various types of destructive software. Which is the most widespread?
8. What three types of security does a computer need?
9. List three password policies that organizations should follow to protect their data.
10. What is the purpose of a firewall, and how does it work?

⊘ Discussion Questions

1. Discuss one of the types of IT crime in detail.
2. Research and discuss the No Electronic Theft (NET) Act of 1997. What penalties are given for computer criminals in this act?
3. Investigate whether any of the IT crime-related bills before the 106th Congress were passed. If any were, discuss one.

⊘ CASE

WildOutfitters.com

Claire was in the kitchen preparing dinner when she heard what she thought sounded like "gribble nix . . . jabber twillig hacked" grumbled from the upstairs office.

"What's the matter dear?" she inquired. "Did your exertions on the trail give you a bad cough?"

"No!" the exasperated voice said a little closer now, as Alex descended down the stairs to the kitchen. "The

Web site has been hacked! Come up and take a look!"

The two rushed upstairs to the computer. Alex reloaded the browser and pulled up the WildOutfitters.com home page. At first, all appeared normal. Claire looked at her husband inquisitively and was about to speak when suddenly the page seemed to burst into flames before her eyes. The flames seemed to incinerate the home page, leaving a background that appeared to be scorched paper. In big flaming letters, a message appeared in the center of the screen saying: "Congratulations, you're a victim of the Spoiled Hackers and Miscreants Club."

Alex and Claire are learning the hard way that the Internet is a difficult environment for maintaining the security and integrity of their information. Almost anyone from any country can connect to the Internet and possibly gain unauthorized access to connected systems. In addition, the uncontrolled growth of the Internet has made it difficult to develop technical and legislative remedies for security violations. The Campagnes have given little thought to security so far, thinking that their site would be an unlikely target for IT crime. As they are finding out, in the networked economy, everyone who is connected is a potential victim.

Fortunately, all of the pages for the site were stored on backup tape. Alex immediately shut down the site by replacing the home page with a message about technical difficulties. He then began to remove and replace the site's pages with the 'clean' pages from the backup tape. Later that evening, he began to look at the HTML code for the site to see if he could determine how the 'hack' was accomplished. It seemed that the only changes he could find were in the home page. Somebody had inserted a simple JavaScript program to redirect the browser to the S.H.A.M. page after fifteen seconds. Finding that the hackers had made only this small change brought Alex just slight relief. He still did not know how the hackers had been able to put the JavaScript code on the page in the first place.

This attack on their site turned out to be just a minor nuisance and disruption. It did, however, bring to light a problem with the Wild Outfitters' systems. Alex began to worry about what could happen in the future if something wasn't done to protect their systems. Someone had already gained unauthorized access to their network and made alterations to the Web

pages. What if they could also gain access to the database? There was a lot of valuable information in the database for the company as well as for the customers. What if the information was destroyed or used to violate the privacy of a customer? Could Wild Outfitters be held liable? Could a hacker enter the system and place bogus orders? What kind of financial problems would that cause? Are they insured for this? All of these questions ran through his mind and frightened him. Alex resolved to call in someone familiar with IT security to evaluate their system and help them make it more secure. The sooner the better, he thought.

After a few minutes of discussion about what they should do Alex said, "Scary, isn't it, and so realistic. It's almost as if I can smell the home page burning."

Looking puzzled, Claire sniffed the air and then cried, "Supper!"

She ran downstairs to see what she could salvage while Alex picked up the phone and pressed the speed dial button for the local Chinese takeout.

1. How would you classify the type of IT crime perpetrated against WildOutfitters.com? Which type of IT criminal performed the crime?

2. Do you think that the Campagnes should report this crime? Explain your choice by discussing the pros and cons.

3. *(Hands on)* Search the news and the Web for recent examples of IT crime. Describe several of these incidents. What categories of IT crime did you find? Who were the victims? Do you notice any trends in the crimes that you found?

4. *(Hands on)* Pretend that you are an IT security specialist. Prepare a presentation for the Campagnes describing the IT security problems that they might be vulnerable to and what they can do to protect themselves against these problems.

CHAPTER ⓲

Privacy and Ethical Issues in the Networked Economy

⊙ Learning Objectives

After reading this chapter, you should be able to answer the following questions:

> Why has privacy become an important issue in the networked economy?

> What is the trade-off between privacy and customer service?

> How is information technology used to collect privacy data and information?

> What types of threats to personal privacy exist in the networked economy?

> What approaches are being used to protect personal data?

> What ethical issues must be dealt with in the networked economy?

Focus on Society

Are Your Records on the Internet?

You probably automatically answered a resounding "no" to this question, but think for a minute—is your name in one of the phone books on the Web? For example, try either Bigfoot (http://www.bigfoot.com) or Switchboard (http://www.switchboard.com) and see if you are listed. If you find it on Switchboard (and you probably will), it will show a map of your neighborhood. If you need a more detailed map of your location, go to MapQuest (http://www.mapquest.com) and have it show you a map with your location pointed out!

Although having your name, phone number, and even a map to your home listed on the Internet may not be so bad, what happens when confidential or embarrassing information is out there? Recent cases have shown just how insecure the Web can be. For example, in early 1999, Hallmark Cards discovered that it had inadvertently made a file available on the Internet. This file contained names, e-mail addresses, and intimate messages of some electronic greeting card customers and was wide open for viewing by those with a little technical knowledge and an interest in such things. In another case, in December of 1998, entrants in a CBS Sportsline Web site contest found that their names, addresses, phone numbers, and e-mail addresses were available to anyone who could use a Web search engine. Finally, consider the case of the University of Michigan Health Center. Its patients learned, in 1999, that their medical records had been available for months to anyone on the university network with a Web browser. In each case, the problem was fixed as soon as it was found, but it is unknown what kind of problems were caused before it was fixed.

Source: Michael J. Himowitz, "Net Privacy Affects Everyone," *The Atlanta Journal-Constitution*, February 28, 1999, p. P6.

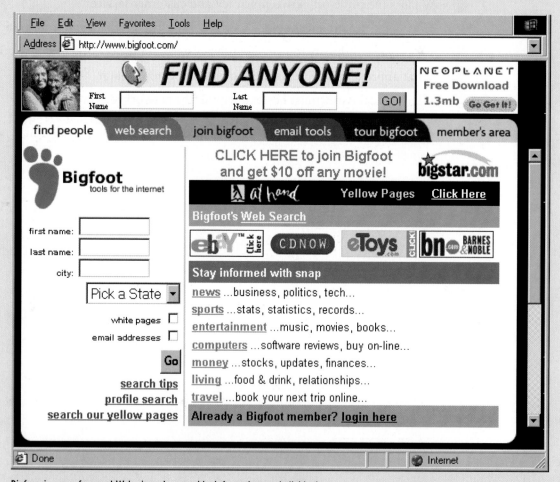

Bigfoot is one of several Web sites that provide information on individuals.

Information Technology and Privacy

In this chapter, we consider the impact of the networked economy on the individual consumer's personal privacy. This is an important area for you to consider, both as a consumer in the networked economy and as an employee in a networked economy organization. As a consumer, you should know the threats to your privacy and how you can deal with them. As an employee, you should know the privacy concerns of your customers and how your organization balances them against its need for information about its customers in order to serve them better. This latter consideration requires a look at ethics in the networked economy because although it is often not illegal, invasion of privacy can be unethical.

Privacy can be defined as the freedom from unauthorized intrusion.[1] In the case of the Internet, this definition can be expanded to mean that users have the right to control personal information about themselves and the capability to determine if and how that information should be obtained and used. Privacy is often confused with confidentiality, but privacy is much broader because confidentiality is involved only with protecting already acquired information from outside intrusion. It is interesting to note that we all think we have a right to privacy in the United States. However, the word *privacy* appears *nowhere* in the U.S. Constitution. In fact, the only country with an explicit constitutional guarantee to privacy is Germany.[2]

Privacy usually falls under the broader aegis of *common law,* meaning that it is considered to be a given right that does not need to be guaranteed by a constitution. However, advances in technology associated with the Internet have pushed this concept to the limit and beyond. There are virtually no laws that restrict the sharing of personal information between companies, often resulting in the concerns that are discussed in this chapter.

How big is the consumer concern with privacy? A survey of experienced Web users in the United States showed that 87 percent of them were somewhat or very concerned with threats to their online privacy. Respondents were particularly concerned with the personal information they provided online being shared with third parties without their consent.[3] The fact that many prospective customers are concerned with threats to their privacy is felt to be one of the major impediments to continued growth of electronic commerce.

Privacy versus Customization

Although electronic commerce is currently only a small fraction of the overall global economy, it is predicted to grow at a rapid rate over the next few years. Business and industry are constantly striving to create Web sites that attract customers and other stakeholders. One way that they do this is through **mass customization**—making the Web site customized to each visitor by learning about the visitor's preferences. They can do this by asking for information about the visitor or by tracking the visitor's purchases and learning about their buying habits. In either case, to customize itself to a customer's preferences, the Web site has to create a profile of the customer. This information makes the Web site more useful to customers but requires that customers give up some of their privacy in order for the site to achieve increased usefulness.

This trade-off between customization and personal privacy is not new to the networked economy; improved service of almost any type has always required additional knowledge about the customer and a resulting loss of privacy. The major

---

1. *WWWebster Dictionary*, http://www.m-w.com/cgi-bin/dictionary.
2. Ann Cavoukian, "Go beyond Security—Build in Privacy: One Does Not Equal the Other," Cardtech/Securtech 96 Conference, Atlanta, May 14–16, 1996.
3. Lorrie Cranor et al., "Beyond Concern: Understanding Net User's Attitudes about Online Privacy" p. 5 (1999), http://www.research.att.com/projects/privacystudy.

difference is that previously, customized service was available only to the few who could afford to have servants and tailor-made suits. In the networked economy, customization is available to all if they are willing to accept an associated loss of control over personal information.

Privacy Concerns

Although you may think that our concerns for privacy are a function of our heavy dependence upon information technology, previous technology advances brought their own new concerns for privacy. For example, the introduction of both the telegraph and telephone in the latter half of the nineteenth century raised questions. Would telegrams be protected by mail privacy laws, or would they be open to reading by the authorities? Could authorities listen in on telephone conversations if protecting the public good seemed to warrant it?

Information technology (IT) brings a number of new privacy concerns. First, the growth in the use of the World Wide Web and Internet for research, commerce, and recreation has opened new avenues for organizations to gather personal data on users. Second, tremendous amounts of this personal data can be stored on modern database servers and then matched with data on other databases in a matter of *seconds* to create a very complete picture of groups of consumers or even of individual consumers. Without information technology, such a search would require *days,* if possible at all. Finally, as in the opening Focus on Society box, personal data collected and stored for legitimate reasons can become public through software or employee errors, causing problems for the people about which the data were collected.

The current privacy concerns have their roots in the mid-1960s when, after hearings before the U.S. House of Representatives, a Bureau of the Budget proposal to set up a national database on citizens was turned down. It was feared that such a database of information on individuals, often called a **data bank,** would give the government too much power. Although the United States does not *currently* have a national data bank, numerous public and private data banks have evolved, and their number increases almost daily. The personal computer has allowed small organizations to set up data banks of clients, customers, and so on and, at the same time, to communicate with larger database servers storing data banks. Many of these public data banks exist for federal and state government use, but numerous private data banks also exist. Table 11-1 provides examples of various public and private data banks, divided into broad categories.

Today, people have become concerned about the threat of organizations and individuals using the Internet to access public and private databases to invade their privacy. This is because almost anyone with a personal computer and modem can access the Internet, through which they can search a database and retrieve information about prospective employees, tenants, or other individuals. In general, we can define five threats to personal privacy:

- Exposure of information
- Data surveillance
- Information brokers
- Identity theft
- Junk e-mail

An example of exposure of information is discussed in the opening Focus on Society box, but it also can be the result of hacker attacks. Data surveillance involves combining data from multiple databases to create a statistical "picture" of individuals or groups. Information brokers are people or organizations that find information on individuals or groups. Identity theft occurs when a person takes over the identity of another. Finally, the widespread sending of junk e-mail is an increasing problem for heavy users of e-mail.

Table 11-1 Examples of Data Banks

Category	Data Bank
Law enforcement	FBI—National Crime Information Center (NCIC) Security clearances Defense Department surveillance of citizens
Taxes and regulatory agencies	Internal Revenue Service State revenue departments Car and boat registration Professional and driver's licenses Hunting and fishing licenses
Human services	Social Security registration Aid to Dependent Children Food stamps Veteran benefits Employment and unemployment Armed forces discharge records
Financial	Credit bureaus Credit card companies Financial institutions Landlord listing of renters Insurance company policy holders Magazine subscription lists Affluent consumer lists Potential debt problem lists Names of individuals more than sixty days past due on credit cards
Organizations	Personnel files, including intelligence, aptitude, and personality tests, and supervisor appraisals Political party and club membership lists
Medicine	Hospital and doctor records Psychiatric and mental-health records Insurance records Workers' compensation records
Travel	Airline reservations Lodging reservations Car rentals
Communications	Telephone call records Cellular phone records E-mail messages

The Changing Nature of Privacy

To understand the changing nature of privacy, consider Table 11-2, in which we have compared the industrial economy, represented by the year 1950, with the networked economy, represented by the year 2000. This comparison uses three aspects of privacy: searchability, protection, and integration. *Searchability* refers to the ease with which information can be found about someone, whereas *protection* refers to the level of security provided for truly critical information. Finally, *integration* refers to the degree that data from disparate sources can be integrated.

Table 11-2 shows that searchability was difficult in 1950, but is easy today. This is because so much information is available today over the Internet using search engines, whereas to find a fraction of this information in 1950 you would have had to visit many offices, go through many books, and ask many questions of people in the offices. However, because searching was such a difficult task in 1950, there was not as much need for protection. We all have seen movies where private detectives talk

Table 11-2 Changing Nature of Privacy

Aspect of Privacy	Industrial Economy (1950)	Networked Economy (2000)
Searchability	Difficult	Easy
Protection	Little	Much
Integration	Very little	Moderate

their way into an office to look for information in a filing cabinet. Although much information is freely available over the Internet, truly critical information is protected. Finally, there was almost no integration of personal information in 1950 because it was kept in a variety of locations with little or no communication. Today, because software can link widely separated databases to create a fairly complete picture of an individual, we say there is moderate integration because a Social Security number can be used to link records in different files. A high level of integration would assume that these databases are automatically linked with no need of additional software.

This means that privacy in the networked economy is at greater risk than it was in the industrial economy because of increased searchability and integration, but privacy can also be better protected if the organizations retaining personal information follow good security practices. Consumers are most at risk of having their privacy threatened when organizations choose to cooperate in sharing information, use the information inappropriately, or do not follow proper security procedures.

Quick Review

1. What is a data bank, and what does it have to do with privacy?
2. Why do we say that it is easier to search for information in the networked economy but that protection is better?

Data and Information Collection Using IT

A variety of threats to privacy involve the use of data or information that has been collected using information technology. Data and information collection using IT can be divided into three types: data on transactions, data collected from Web visits, and data collected from communications using the Internet. We separate Internet communications data from Web-visit data because they are generated by different Internet protocols. The three types of data that can be collected using information technology are summarized in Table 11-3.

Table 11-3 Types of Data

Data Type	Source	Contents
Transactional data	All noncash transactions and some cash transactions	Data on transactions using credit or debit cards, car rentals, airline tickets, lodging reservations, ATM transactions, and so on, either face-to-face, by telephone, or over the Web
Web-visit data	Visits to Web site	Data and information provided to Web sites by user or collected by the Web server during the visit by user
Internet communications data	Newsgroups, chat groups, bulletin boards, e-mail	Postings to a newsgroup or bulletin board, conversations in chat rooms, contents of e-mail

Transactional Data

The first type of data and information is a special type of data called **transactional data.** This type includes all data generated by noncash transactions involving face-to-face, electronic, telephone, mail, or Web transactions. Note that the noncash nature of these transactions requires that customers identify themselves in some way. Included are Web-based and point-of-sale purchase systems, as well as travel, credit, and communication services. For example, every time you make a purchase with a credit card, make a long distance or cellular telephone call, rent a car, purchase an airline ticket, or carry out an automatic teller machine transaction, you are creating transactional data that are stored in at least one database. The only way to *not* create transactional data about yourself as you go through life would be to use cash or money orders for all transactions and to not have any Internet, telephone, power, water, or cable accounts. This would require one to live like a hermit.

Consumers also create data about themselves and their buying habits whenever they provide "product registration" or contest information, either on paper or on the Web. This information is combined with transactional data to create private data banks or is sold to data banks by organizations who collect these data as a sidelight of their main business. For example, when you complete a change of address form at the post office, probably the last thing on your mind is that you are

ⒻocusonPeople

Roger Clarke

Although the commercialization of the Internet has brought a great deal of attention to privacy issues, for some writers and researchers, these issues existed before the Internet's popularity. One of these writers is Roger Clarke, an Australian lecturer, author, and consultant in the field of privacy. Clarke's interests in privacy go back over twenty-five years when he prepared a series of papers for the New South Wales Privacy Committee. Since 1982, he has written over one hundred papers on the subject, many of which are available at http://www.anu.edu.au/people/Roger.Clarke/. He divides these into theory, practice, policy, and papers specific to Australia. Clarke is also a regular participant at the Computers, Freedom, and Privacy Conferences that are held annually. His notes on these conferences are linked to his Web page.

Clarke's Web page is a treasure-trove of information for anyone interested in privacy. An area of privacy in which Clarke specializes is *dataveillance,* which is the systematic use of personal data systems in the investigation or monitoring of the actions or communications of one or more people. He introduced this topic in a paper that appeared in the *Communications of the Association for Computing Machinery* and was twice reprinted. Other privacy topics in which he is interested include identification and anonymity, privacy im-

plications of digital signatures, and person-location and person-tracking technologies.

Source: www.anu.edu.au/people/Roger.Clarke/.

Roger Clarke has lectured, written, and consulted on privacy issues for over twenty-five years.

Table 11-4 Data Collection Methods

Collection Method	Description
Web browser	Date, time, and amount of all transactions are recorded
ATM	Machine records time, data, amount, and location of transaction; may also capture your image
Prescription drugs	Druggist keeps a record of all drugs purchased, including date and payment method
Employee ID scanner	Scanner records date and time of every entry into the building, including employee name
Cellular telephone	Date, time, and length of every call are recorded; calls can be intercepted
Credit/debit cards	Date and amount of every transaction are recorded
Toll booths	Electronic payment of tolls enables date and time of passage through toll booth to be recorded
Long-distance telephone calls	Date, time, and duration of all calls are recorded
Bar code scanners	Registering for coupons can allow store to track every item purchased
Surveillance cameras	Many banks, liquor stores, convenience stores, and public buildings now videotape on a 24/7 basis
Product registration	Registration provides personal information as well as information on buying habits

Source: Joseph Quittner, "Invasion of Privacy," http://cgi.pathfinder.com/time/reports/privacy/cover1.html.

creating data for a data bank. However, the U.S. Postal Service sells these names and addresses to direct marketers!

Transactional data indicate such facts as the type of clothes you buy, where you eat, where you stay when out of town, to where and to whom you make long distance calls, where and when you take trips, and when you withdraw money from the bank. Together, such data can paint a complete picture of an individual's lifestyle—something that can be of great value to companies wishing to market goods or services. Table 11-4 lists a number of the ways in which we create transactional data.

There are no U.S. federal laws against companies sharing transactional data on their customers. For example, if you have subscribed to one magazine, it will often sell your name, along with those of all other subscribers, to other magazines and catalogs, leading to a substantial increase in the amount of postal mail you receive. Banks routinely share information on their customers with credit card companies, leading to "preapproved" credit card offers. Other countries, especially those in the European Union, have laws against this practice, and many organizations in the United States are calling for similar restrictions.

In addition to transactional data generated by consumer purchases, data are often also collected on the employees handling the telephone transaction and, frequently, other types of transactions. Commonly referred to as **electronic supervision** or **computer monitoring**, this practice involves organization managers monitoring the amount of work performed by employees on networked computers for entering data, making reservations, and so on. This is accomplished by installing software in the network server to measure work rate. Typical values measured include the amount of time a telephone operator takes to answer a request, the number of keystrokes a data entry operator makes each second, and the number of errors made by users. The types of employees who are monitored include customer service representatives, catalog sales representatives, and reservation agents. It is also possible to monitor

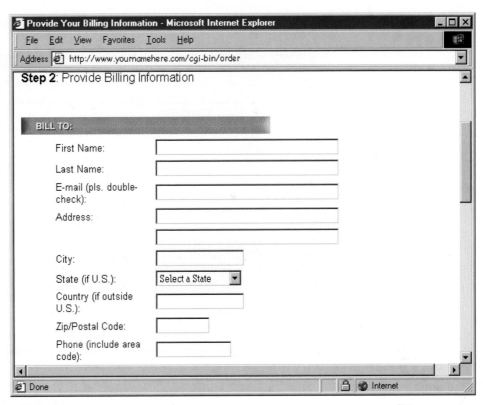

Web sites, such as this one, collect data on consumers.

what is on an employee's screen and how long a computer has been idle. Although many employee organizations believe that this sort of computer monitoring is an invasion of employee privacy, it is virtually unregulated in the United States at either the state or federal levels.

Web-Visit Data

Web-visit data include data that are unique to the Web in that a "transaction" in the traditional sense of the word does not have to occur—any visit to a Web site generates a great deal of data about the user's computer. To see what a Web site knows about you, go to http://www.anonymizer.com and click on the underlined word *you*. Figure 11-1 shows *some* of the information gathered by this site on the author's computer. Note that this Web site shows the monitor resolution, the time and date, and the type of files accepted by the browser. Although not shown here, the Web site also knows the computer's IP address and "name" as well as other information about the system.

This information may or may not be specific to you, depending on how you access the Internet. If you access the Internet through a dial-up connection to an ISP like Mindspring or AT&T Worldnet, you are typically assigned an IP address and computer name *dynamically* (i.e., it is yours *only* during that dial-up session). On the other hand, if you access the Web from a LAN or from a cable modem, then your computer has a specific IP address and name assigned to it that do not change unless the network is reconfigured in some way. In the case of a dial-up connection, this means that Web sites know only the name of the ISP through which you are accessing the Internet, making it difficult to track down who is actually visiting the Web site. On the other hand, Web sites know the specific machine you are using if you access the Internet over a LAN or cable modem connection, making you more easily traceable. In either case, those who wish to "surf" the Web anonymously can use the Anonymizer Web site to do this either for free or for a fee depending on the speed at which the Web sites are accessed.

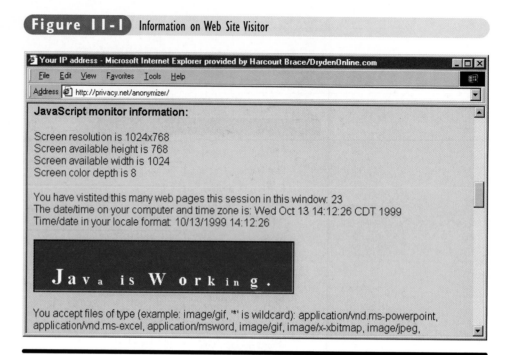

Figure 11-1 Information on Web Site Visitor

If law enforcement agencies suspect you of engaging in criminal activities, they can obtain a search warrant that will allow them to view the ISP's logs, which will show which dynamic IP address you were using during a dial-up session. The author of the Melissa virus was tracked through a search of IP addressees. Hosting companies like AOL that allow users to assign themselves screen names are also subject to search warrants or subpoenas to turn over that information to the courts.

In addition to the data that can be collected by a Web site whenever it is visited, many Web sites request information from the visitor such as name and e-mail address, which is saved in a database. In most cases, if visitors return to that Web site and enter the same information, the Web site will remember their preferences. In electronic commerce terms, this is an **adaptable Web site** because it adapts itself to the information you choose to give it. On the other hand, many Web sites are **adaptive Web sites** because they adapt themselves to patterns they find in your interests and purchases. For example, as shown in Figure 11-2, the adaptive Web site recognizes the author and knows from his previous purchases that he is a Jimmy Buffett fan. Based on this information, it suggests other CDs by this artist and suggests CDs by artists that other Jimmy Buffett fans have purchased. Most electronic commerce sites are becoming more adaptive because this is less intrusive on the customer.

When you go to adaptive sites like the one shown in Figure 11-2, they may welcome you by name without requesting that you sign in. This is accomplished via the use of a computer file that is known as a **cookie,** which the Web server stores on your hard disk, stored in a subfolder of the browser folder. Cookie files are necessary because the Web's http protocol makes each visit to a Web page independent of all others. This means that a Web server has no memory of what pages it has previously sent to a user (e.g., instead of having to log on to a calendar Web site, the cookie does this for you). Although it is easy to set up your browser to reject the storage of cookie files or to provide the option of whether or not to store the files, remember that by so doing, you lose the customized features of the Web sites. Figure 11-3 shows a cookie file for one of the author's computers, with each Web site visited adding more lines to the file, which Web sites read when a page is requested by a computer.

Figure 11-2   Example of Adaptive Web Site

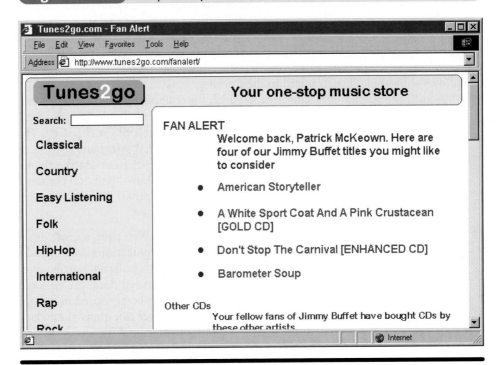

Figure 11-3   Cookie Text File

```
# Netscape HTTP Cookie File
# http://www.netscape.com/newsref/std/cookie_spec.html
# This is a generated file!  Do not edit.

        FALSE   /C|/Program Files/Netscape/Users/pmckeown/mail  FALSE    941432400
www.webpromote.com      FALSE   /cgi-bin/       FALSE   942189278       webpcode
www.goto.com    FALSE   /d/search       FALSE   1221232885      UserID  7A25108B3EA97AEC
keyword.netscape.com    FALSE   /keyword        FALSE   1606953551      sbkwtime
keyword.netscape.com    FALSE   /keyword        FALSE   1606953551      kwtipcount
e12.zdnet.com:8080      FALSE   /clear  946684724       cgversion       2
www.msd.ucns.uga.edu    FALSE   /msd    FALSE   944035381       SHOPPERMANAGER%2FMSDCAT
wwwp.goto.com   FALSE   /d      FALSE   1220182172      UserID  9E9DDDEC2B2B07FF
www.e2consult.com       FALSE   /       FALSE   1293753902      EGSOFT_ID       128.192.
videofitness.com        FALSE   /       FALSE   942189282       NGUserID        cfd5334b
www.usatoday.com        FALSE   /       FALSE   946684946       USATUID 128.192.28.186-7
www.babson.edu  FALSE   /       FALSE   1293753746      EGSOFT_ID       128.192.28.186-9
.inquiry.com    TRUE    /       FALSE   942189328       INTERSE 128120896815715
.doubleclick.net        TRUE    /       FALSE   1920499140      id      2fa26c87
.amazon.com     TRUE    /       FALSE   2082787345      ubid-main       002-3298294-8782
www.cdnow.com   FALSE   /       FALSE   942189305       cookTrack       369584103-896818
home.netscape.com       FALSE   /       FALSE   942190337       NGUserID        cc98a716
.looksmart.com  TRUE    /       FALSE   1212673478      LookSmartPIN    1849ca7636d3111f
www.ihs.ac.at   FALSE   /       FALSE   946511999       RoxenUserID     0x18bf4
.imgis.com      TRUE    /       FALSE   1055003543      JEB2    0EDD9DC4D5F0101E80C01CBA
.excite.com     TRUE    /       FALSE   946641734       registered      no
.excite.com     TRUE    /       FALSE   946641734       UID     5D59D141357C0453
.preferences.com        TRUE    /       FALSE   1182140555      PreferencesID   nC0rqorm
.pathfinder.com TRUE    /       FALSE   2051222532      PFUID   cc47f21e357c07454ea61000
gm.preferences.com      TRUE    /       FALSE   1182140553      CPreferencesID  WWZNF+uU
redback.news.com.au     FALSE   /       FALSE   942189371       NGUserID        a545013c
.focalink.com   TRUE    /       FALSE   946641718       SB_ID   08979170610000214351104G
.snci.com       TRUE    /       FALSE   946684905       INTERSE s28h1868968899524182
.travelocity.com        TRUE    /       FALSE   1609459200      auto    PHDDAWG|KELLY
.adobe.com      TRUE    /       FALSE   946684868       INTERSE 128.192.28.1861336190008
www.adval.org   FALSE   /       FALSE   1293753855      EGSOFT_ID       128.192.28.186-1
www.webtravels.com      FALSE   /       FALSE   1293753698      EGSOFT_ID       128.192.
www.vbxtras.com FALSE   /       FALSE   1293753952      EGSOFT_ID       128.192.28.186-2
```

Many privacy advocates are concerned about the collection of data by Web sites, either on the server or on cookies. However, customers must make that trade-off between privacy and customization of the Web site to their needs. If you rejected all cookies, then you would always have to sign in to all Web pages, like Amazon.com, rather than having them recognize you. If no information on Web visitors was retained on the server, then electronic commerce applications would never be customized to their needs.

One area in which the collection of data has been restricted is Web sites aimed at children. As the result of a Federal Trade Commission (FTC) report, the **Children's Online Privacy Protection Act of 1998** was passed. This law requires that commercial Web sites that collect personal information from children under the age of thirteen must obtain prior parental consent. At the time of this writing, the FTC had not formulated rules on exactly how "parental consent" could be sent; would e-mail be sufficient, or would a signed postal letter be necessary?

Internet Communications Data

In addition to data collected by Web sites, a great deal of data exists on other Internet applications. **Internet communications data** include e-mail messages, "conversations" in chat rooms, postings to bulletin boards, and messages to newsgroups. In terms of structured and unstructured data, the data collected by Web sites are typically structured because they are being stored in a database. This means that the organization running the Web server can query these data to learn more about specific customers or groups of customers. With structured data, it is possible to combine information from multiple databases to create an accurate picture of a customer.

On the other hand, Internet communications data tend to be unstructured because they are not organized into database form. This does not mean that the data cannot be used; it just means that querying the data involves searches for words or phrases and that any integration across data sets must be done manually. Even with these problems, Internet communications data are closely watched by organizations because chat rooms, newsgroups, and bulletin boards are often the place where complaints, rumors, and the like are voiced. For example, a woman voiced

This search engine has returned the names of newsgroups that discuss the Java language.

unhappiness with her HMO in a health care newsgroup and was surprised to receive a call from a representative of the HMO to discuss her complaints. The HMO monitored such newsgroups and followed up on any complaints posted there.

At the same time that there are complaints about public and private data banks, the capturing of transactional data, and Web sites using cookies, many people are telling the world about themselves on newsgroups or chatting with people they don't know as if they were old friends. In reality, each piece of correspondence is available for viewing by millions worldwide for years to come and is a fertile source for cyberdetectives seeking information. Newsgroup postings are even searchable just like Web sites.

In the networked economy, e-mail has become the method of choice for sending messages. Most people believe that e-mail has the same constitutional guarantees of privacy that postal mail has, and it does have similar protections with one big caveat: E-mail sent or received on an employer's computer is the property of the employer. This means that employers have the right to read employees' e-mail at any time to protect themselves from potential liability and to ensure that computers are being used for legitimate business purposes. In fact, an employer's rights concerning computers go further than this; the employer can remove the computer or just the hard disk at any time and search it. Although most employers do not snoop into employees' e-mail, if damaging or threatening e-mail messages are being sent from a company computer, they have the right to take action to stop it.

Along the same lines, as Microsoft and many other companies have found, any e-mail saved on a company computer is subject to subpoena in a criminal or civil court action. This is also true in freedom of information (FOI) cases for government agencies; anything on an agency computer is subject to search and release in an FOI case.

ⓕocus on Management

E-Mail Monitoring a Growing Trend

As e-mail has become an indispensable part of most organizations communications systems, it has brought problems with it. Several high-profile court cases, including the Microsoft case, have involved e-mail as evidence. In addition, companies are concerned about protecting their intellectual property, guarding themselves against litigation resulting from e-mail messages, and protecting their employees from receiving hate mail and unwanted messages. To do this, many organizations are installing e-mail monitoring systems. In fact, in one survey, 31 percent of seventy-five corporate e-mail managers used e-mail monitoring systems either regularly or for spot checks and, of those that did not monitor e-mail, 21 percent were planning to install an e-mail monitoring system. The three primary reasons given by managers for monitoring e-mail were:

- Legal liability from information contained in e-mail

- Leaks in corporate secrets
- Use of e-mail for racial or sexual harassment

The software used for monitoring e-mail usually works by looking for keywords in messages. Messages containing these keywords can be blocked or sent to a reviewer. Most companies use this software only after an irregularity has occurred or use this software on a random basis. They have found this approach to be an effective way to stop employees from using the company e-mail system for personal or inappropriate messages. Experts in this field suggest that putting a company's e-mail policy in writing is critical to its acceptance by employees.

Source: Dominique Deckmyn, "More Managers Monitor E-Mail." *Computerworld*, October 18, 1999, pp. 1, 97.

Data Collection at fareastfoods.com

Because fareastfoods.com is a Web-based company, it collects a great deal of data on its customers to help it customize its Web site to their needs. Fareastfoods.com uses an adaptive Web site that customizes itself based on the customer's previous purchases. For example, if the customer had previously purchased only Thai food items, this is the portion of the site that the customer would automatically see. Much of this data, plus the customer's log in ID and password, are stored on the customer's computer as a cookie.

Quick Review

1. List the three types of data that are collected by information technology.
2. What are the ways that Web-visit data are collected?

Threats to Privacy

The four types of threats to privacy in the networked economy—information exposure, data surveillance, information brokers, and identity theft—are summarized in Table 11-5.

Information Exposure

As discussed in the opening Focus on Society box, exposure of confidential information can be embarrassing and a potential threat to a person's financial and personal well-being. Such exposure can be accidental or intentional. Accidental exposures are usually caused by the person running the server failing to close security holes or to fix known bugs in server software. In the case of an intentional attack from an outside person, the hacker is either searching for information on someone or wanting to expose the entire database to the outside world. In the first case, the hacker may wish to embarrass someone or find information that could be used in criminal activities, whereas in the second case the hacker may wish to create mischief or embarrass an entire organization.

In both the accidental and the intentional cases, the solution is for the technical group running the servers to fix all security holes and software bugs immediately upon their being discovered. This is the same problem that organizations face in providing security for their networks.

Data Surveillance

A common objective of organizations is to find individuals who fall into segments or groups of interest to them. For example, universities seek to find students who will be successful in their academic programs, and retailers look for people who can afford their products and may have an interest in them. Although not all uses of information technology to find groups of people who fall into certain categories are problematic,

Table 11-5 Threats to Privacy

Type of Threat	Source	Information at Risk
Information exposure	Accidental exposure Hackers	Almost any type of information that is stored in a database connected to a network
Data surveillance	Public or private organizations wishing to identify individuals who fall into a group	Information about a person's lifestyle, spending habits, travel history, and so on
Information brokers	People or organizations paid to find information about individuals	Information about a person's lifestyle, spending number, workplace, and so on
Identity theft	Criminals	Name, Social Security number, credit rating, anything that identifies a person

governments or private groups using information technology for surveillance purposes can present a threat to privacy. **Data surveillance** is the systematic use of information technology in the investigation or monitoring of the actions or communications of one or more people.[4] Data surveillance includes methods such as computer matching and profiling to push from marketing to segments to one-to-one marketing.

Computer matching is the merger of data from two or more databases to create a list of individuals who match certain criteria. Computer matching takes advantage of the fact that an individual's record in one data bank will usually have one or more attributes in common with that same individual's record in other data banks. In many cases, this attribute is the Social Security number, which has become virtually a universal identifier for residents of the United States. For example, a credit bureau like Experian can combine its data on people's income, jobs, bank accounts, purchasing behavior, and credit limits with public data it draws from motor vehicle and public property records, such as those shown in Table 11-1, to create sophisticated lists of consumers. For example, it might generate the names of all people in Gwinett County, Georgia, who purchased (and registered) a Mercedes automobile within the last six months, make more than $125,000 per year, and have no more than two children. The process of computer matching is shown in Figure 11-4. Note that after a list of "raw" hits is created, it must be filtered and edited to remove erroneous items to create a list of "solid" hits that goes into the matching organization's database.

Figure 11-4 Computer Matching Process

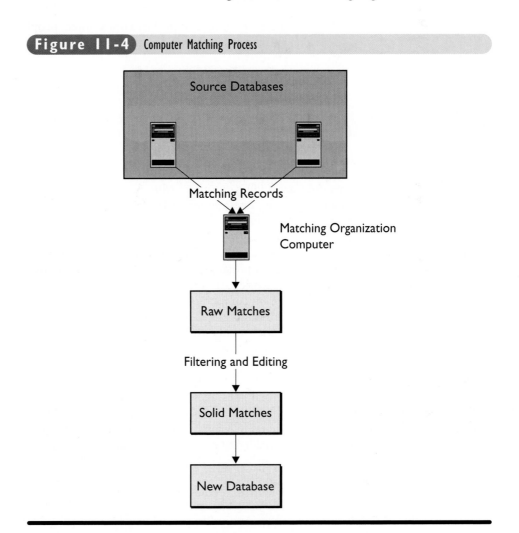

4. Roger Clarke, "Introduction to Dataveillance and Information Privacy, and Definitions of Terms," http://www.anu.edu.au/people/Roger.Clarke/DV/Intro.html.

A danger exists if some of these data are wrong and an individual is refused credit because of the error.

The U.S. government made heavy use of computer matching in the 1970s and 1980s to try to increase its "efficiency." For example, it was reported that individuals who had not repaid their government student loans were matched with individuals eligible for tax refunds. This enabled the IRS to collect some of the money (an average of $544.91 per case for a cost of only $3.70)owed the government. However, in response to many complaints about federal computer matching generating many erroneous "hits," the **Computer Matching and Privacy Protection Act 1988 (CMPPA)** took effect in January 1990. It established a number of fair information practice provisions to apply to matching programs in the federal government but excludes many programs and agencies.

Profiling is similar to computer matching in that databases are used to generate lists, but the criteria tend to be broader and the search may cover only a single database. Specifically, profiling is the use of past experience to infer characteristics about groups of individuals and then searching databases for individuals with a close fit to those characteristics.[5] Although you might automatically think of the television program *Profiler* or the use of profiling to single out air travelers for searches by customs agents, it has many other uses.

The profiling process consists of five steps:

1. Select a class of people to profile. For example, people who might be interested in having an irrigation system installed in their yards.

(F)ocus on Technology

Self-Destructing E-Mail

As more and more Internet users are finding out, the various forms of communication on the Internet (e-mail, chat rooms, bulletin boards, instant messaging systems, etc.) are not completely private. In terms of e-mail, even if the wrong people don't have access to your messages, it is almost impossible to completely erase them. Even if both sender and receiver delete an e-mail, copies remain on computers beyond their reach. And, since network administrators regularly back up their computers, e-mails live on for a long time on backup tapes, long after they have been removed from the computers. For example, much of the evidence in the 1998–1999 Microsoft antitrust trial was based on e-mail messages. Individuals involved in these and other judicial proceedings have probably wished that there was an electronic equivalent to the paper shredder to completely wipe out e-mails.

Such an electronic e-mail shredder is now available from Disappearing Inc., a San Francisco company. To understand how this system works, assume that you send a message to a friend using Disappearing Inc.'s system. When you select "Send," a software add-in to the e-mail client encrypts the message with a key that is available to only the sender (you) and any receivers you choose. The unique element to this form of encryption is that you can control how long the key is good for, from a few minutes to a few months. In any case, at the end of the defined life span of the key, it is permanently deleted from the computers at Disappearing Inc., leaving the message as binary garbage. For companies, this will mean they can use e-mail for sensitive messages that will not hang around forever. For individuals, this will mean that they can send messages secure in the knowledge that only the addressee can read it and that the message will eventually become unreadable.

Source: Jack Smith, "Virtual Shredder." ABCNews.com, October 7, 1999.

---

5. Roger Clarke, "Introduction to Dataveillance and Information Privacy, and Definitions of Terms," http://www.anu.edu.au/people/Roger.Clarke/DV/Intro.html.

2. Define a profile for that class of people. For our example, such a profile might include people who own homes appraised at more than $150,000.

3. Acquire data from pertinent databases about a relevant population. In the example, this would be the tax assessor's list of citizens who pay property tax in the county and the local telephone directory.

4. Search the list for individuals who match the profile. In the example, the list of property taxpayers would be searched for those who own homes with assessed value higher than $150,000 and who have applied for an exemption based on the fact that they live in the home, that is, it is not commercial or rental property or an empty lot. Match this with telephone numbers from the directory.

5. Take action on the resulting list of people. In this case, place a telephone call to people matching the profile.

This process is illustrated in Figure 11-5.

Target marketing is profiling applied to the private sector. Recall that **target marketing** is the use of databases by companies to select a group of individuals who are most likely to buy their products. The selected group is then the subject of specific advertising or special offers. The databases used in target marketing often contain transactional or Web data because these data can be used to create a very clear picture about a consumer's spending habits. Profiling in the form of target marketing can be an efficient method for alerting consumers to products in which they may have an interest while not bothering them with products of little interest to them. However, companies also can prejudge the economic behavior of consumers, thereby limiting some group's access to information about goods and services. Profiling can also lead to annoying telephone calls from telemarketers or unexpected and sometimes disconcerting offers from businesses that you have never visited. For example, several days prior to your birthday you might receive a birthday card and a coupon from an electronics store that you have never visited, or you might receive an offer of a discount on a smoking cessation drug shortly after you fill a prescription for a nicotine replacement patch. In the first case, a public database has been combined with transactional data on your shopping habits to indicate you might be willing to purchase electronic items. In the second case, transactional data in the form of a prescription have indicated you are trying to stop smoking, and the pharmaceutical company is taking advantage of this information.

Figure 11-5 Profiling Process

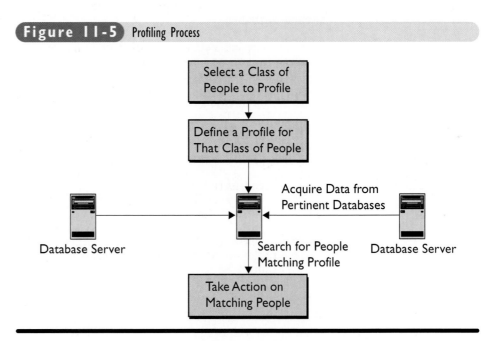

Both computer matching and profiling have the potential to pinpoint victims of fraudulent marketing schemes. For example, it would be very easy to match several data banks to create a list of elderly widows with high equity in their homes. Unscrupulous individuals could use the list to market fraudulent home equity loans. There have been numerous calls for regulation to protect the public from the abuses of data surveillance, but legitimate companies using the technology point out that the same technology has been used to do background checks on potential employees and to find fathers who are delinquent in child-support payments. And, in at least one case, the technology helped track down a relative of a child who required an organ transplant.

Information Brokers

With the proliferation of both private and public databases containing information on people, a new breed of people and organizations called **information brokers** has found ways to profit from these databases. Information brokers will use almost any means—usually legal, but sometimes not so legal—to provide information on an individual of interest to their customers. Typical information provided by information brokers includes credit reports, criminal histories, unlisted phone numbers, and so on. Information brokers find this information in a variety of ways, some the electronic way and some the "old-fashioned" way—through personal contact. In the first case, information brokers use a growing number of online proprietary databases that store public information. As recently as ten years ago, information such as death records, marriage licenses, and property deeds was stored in courthouse basements, requiring a personal visit to review it. Now companies like Choicepoint make much of this information available online for a fee. Finding information on a person still requires a great deal of research, but now it can accomplished from the researcher's computer. Figure 11-6 shows the type of report (for a fictitious person) that is possible from an information broker.

Figure 11-6 Information Broker's Report

```
SAINT LOUIS,MO 63121
DOB: 5/5/55
SSN:444-44-4444

RECORD RETURNED.

RESULTS: RECORD FOUND ON NAME AND DATE OF BIRTH MATCH
ADDRESS LISTED AS: MILES ROAD, ST. LOUIS, MO.
HEIGHT: 5'2"    WEIGHT:110 lbs.    EYES: BLUE    HAIR: BLONDE

CASE#: 2-6229-2378-M

FILE DATE: 5/3/97 ST. LOUIS COUNTY, MISSOURI

TYPE OF OFFENSE: FELONY        CHARGE:GRAND THEFT MOTOR VEHICLE

 DISPOSITION DATE: 5/24/97
 DISPOSITION: PLEA GUILTY , 1 YEAR PRISON SUSPENDED,
       2 YEARS PROBATION

 DISPOSITION DATE: 7-17-97
 DISPOSITION: VIOLATED PROBATION, PROBATION REVOKED
    SENTENCED TO 1 YEAR WITH CREDIT FOR 13 DAYS SERVED.

END OF Criminal Report
---------------------
```

In the second case, some unscrupulous information brokers acquire information through an industrial economy-type process known as *pretexting*. The information broker calls a business or agency under the *pretext* of being the person on whom they are seeking information and asks about their account. If the information broker has the person's Social Security number, he or she can find almost any type of information on the target individual; if not, the information broker has to work a little harder, but eventually, the broker usually finds the needed information. Often this is done by having a person at the business or agency use a computer to look up the information. Many companies engaged in information brokering have spoken out strongly against this use of deception to find information.

Identity Theft

When even a small amount of information about a person falls into the hands of criminals, the worst type of privacy invasion can occur—**identity theft**. Credit card numbers, ATM PINs, and Social Security numbers all offer ways for thieves to steal your identity. This information can be stolen in a number of ways, including:

- Theft of pocketbook, purse, wallet, or mail
- So-called "dumpster diving"—going into a trash bin to retrieve credit card receipt carbons, medical records, and so on
- Insiders using their connections to credit agencies to access information about employees or others
- Fraudulent schemes in which the criminal fills out a change of address form and has the victim's mail sent to a new address
- Pretexting to fool people into providing information on the victim

Once they have this information, criminals can use it to apply for driver's licenses, telephone service, credit cards, or to steal benefits such as pensions and Social Security payments. Sometimes identity thieves are individuals who have credit problems, but organized crime is often the culprit. By one estimate, about one thousand people a day in the United States fall victim to identity theft.

Victims often don't find out that their identity has been stolen until they are denied a loan because of unpaid bills or until bill collectors try to collect on credit card bills the criminal has run up. Then victims start finding out that someone has used their name, Social Security number, and other personal data for criminal purposes. Finding out about the identity theft is only the tip of the iceberg—convincing the creditors and police that your identity has been stolen and restoring your credit rating can be a very long and difficult task. Until recently, making matters worse was that the person whose identity had been stolen was *not* even considered a victim; only the credit grantors who had a monetary loss were legally victims of this crime! This was rectified by the **Identity Theft and Assumption Deterrence Act of 1998**, which made stealing someone's identity a crime punishable by up to fifteen years in jail.

It should be noted that in the United States, Social Security numbers are often used as personal identifiers although they were never meant for that purpose. However, because Social Security numbers are used as personal identifiers, once stolen, they can be easily used for identity theft. In general, a consumer should closely guard their Social Security number. Unfortunately, stealing a Social Security number is all too easy. Some states use them as driver's license numbers, and many universities use them as student ID numbers.

Junk E-Mail

Just as junk mail and telemarketing calls have been used in the industrial economy as ways of advertising or attempting to sell products and services, e-mail is now being heavily used in the networked economy for similar purposes. Commonly referred to as **spam,**[6] junk e-mail is extremely inexpensive to send and also inexpensive (at least in monetary terms) to receive. Because of the low cost, the sender needs to be responded to by only a small proportion of those receiving the e-mail. One of the first uses of spam was by a pair of Arizona lawyers who sent repeated e-mail messages to as many newsgroups as they could find. The message was always the same: They could help noncitizens apply for the resident alien lottery for $100 (the process is easy and free, so no lawyer is needed). They received a great deal of publicity (mostly negative but still useful to them) about their spamming of newsgroups and have since gone into Internet marketing full time.

As with the Arizona case, spam is often sent to individuals who post messages to particular newsgroups. Others unknowingly sign up for it when they register at a Web site. Because many people replied to spam by *flaming* the sender (i.e., sending a nasty reply) or by overloading the spammer's server by sending many messages or very large messages, spammers now use *nonrepliable* messages in which they leave off the reply-to address. Instead of replying by e-mail, you have to use fax or the postal service to reply to the "wonderful" offer in the e-mail.

In most cases, the best way to respond to spam is to simply delete it before reading. Replying at all usually adds your e-mail address to several other spam lists. Figure 11-7 shows an example of spam received by the author in which the "From" and "To" addresses (which have been deleted) were the same and not that of the author!

It should be noted that although there have been attempts to prosecute spammers under state and federal laws, this has been successful in only a few cases. Some foreign governments, notably Austria and Australia, have passed laws against sending spam, but these may be difficult to enforce given the global nature of the Internet. There appears to be no movement in the United States to pass similar federal legislation.

Using Information at fareastfoods.com

Fareastfoods.com has been offered a number of opportunities to purchase e-mail lists from target marketers for use in spam campaigns. It also has been solicited to sell information about its customers. In both cases, the company has resisted

Figure 11-7 Example of E-Mail Spam

Subject: Watch Your Business Take Off With E-Marketing
 Date: Tue, 20 Jul 1999 03:18:09 +0100 (WET DST)
 From:
  To:

```
E - M A I L   M A R K E T I N G   W O R K S ! !

It's a fact!  If you're not using your computer to generate
income, you're leaving money on the table.

Or, if you're financially independent, then just hit delete
and we won't bother you again.

But, "the proof is in the pudding", and if $50,000 to $151,200
per year makes you tingle with excitement, then this message is
for you. Don't worry, this has nothing to do with Chain Letters
or any of the many offers you receive, this is pure and simple
E-MAIL MARKETING...
```

---

6. The product Spam is a type of lunch meat produced by Hormel. The origin of the term in relationship to unwanted e-mail is shrouded in the myths of the Internet but is thought to have some relationship to the Monty Python skit of the same name.

because employees know that their future success is based on the goodwill of their customers and that using spam could backfire on them.

Quick Review

1. List the four major threats to personal privacy in the networked economy.
2. What is spam, and what does it have to do with privacy?

Protecting Privacy

Now let's take a look at five widely accepted principles of privacy protection and see how they are being applied. These principles, known as the **Fair Information Practice (FIP) Principles,** have been developed by government agencies in the United States, Canada, and Europe. They were prompted to a large extent by a 1973 report by the U.S. Department of Health, Education, and Welfare (HEW) on privacy protections in the age of data collection *(Records, Computers, and the Rights of Citizens)*. These five principles are notice/awareness, choice/consent, access/participation, integrity/security, and enforcement/redress and they are listed in Table 11-6, along with a short description of each and an example.

The first two principles are key because without notice or awareness, the others have no meaning. Also, without choice or consent, consumers cannot "opt out" of having their data collected. Legislation and self-regulation are the two primary approaches to ensuring that these principles are being applied to personal privacy. In the first case, government takes the responsibility for ensuring privacy, whereas in the second case, business and industry do so for themselves.

Table 11-6 Fair Information Practice (FIP) Principles

Principle	Description	Example
Notice/awareness	Consumer is notified that information is being gathered and with whom it is being shared	Web site informs consumer that information is being gathered and with whom it will be shared
Choice/consent	Consumer is given option to not have information gathered	Web site allows consumer to opt out of having information gathered
Access/participation	Consumer is given access to data and has right to contest data's accuracy and completeness	Web site shows consumer the information that has been gathered and gives the opportunity to correct errors
Integrity/security	Data collected are accurate and secure	Data collected by Web server are verified before being used; they are also kept secure against intrusion
Enforcement/redress	There is some mechanism for enforcing these principles and redress for consumer when not enforced	Consumer can report Web site to an industry watchdog group or to a government agency if it fails to follow these principles

Legislative Approach   The proposal for a national data bank in the United States in the 1960s, and its subsequent rejection, was the beginning of a period of legislative action on the privacy issue. This resulted in the following legislation between 1970 and 1987 (in addition to the more recent laws already discussed):

- Fair Credit Reporting Act of 1970
- Freedom of Information Act of 1970
- Privacy Act of 1974
- Electronic Communications Privacy Act of 1986
- Computer Security Act of 1987

The **Fair Credit Reporting Act of 1970** regulates some actions of credit bureaus that collect credit information on individuals. When a person wishes to borrow money (or engage in other activities, including applying for a job), the potential lender runs a **credit check** on the person by requesting information from a credit bureau. Unfortunately, the tremendous increase in computing power since 1970 has caused widespread abuse of this law.

The **Freedom of Information Act of 1970** gave individuals the right to inspect information concerning them held in U.S. government data banks. The **Privacy Act of 1974** attempted to correct most of the recordkeeping practices of the federal government. The **Electronic Communications Privacy Act of 1986** extended wiretap laws protecting aural conversations to include communications between computers. The **Computer Security Act of 1987** was aimed at ensuring the security of U.S. government computers. Public electronic mail is protected by this act, but court decisions have made corporate electronic mail messages the property of the organization.

In addition to these laws and the more recent legislation already discussed, at the time of this writing numerous pieces of legislation were awaiting action in either the U.S. House or Senate.

It should be noted that Canada and Europe have passed stronger laws regarding the protection of personal privacy and data. This difference of opinion has led to problems regarding the transmission of data between the European Union countries and the United States. These problems are still being negotiated at the time of this writing. It is interesting to note that some representatives of business and industry in the United States point to the lack of such laws in the United States as being the reason why electronic commerce is more advanced in the United States than in Europe. On the other hand, European governments believe that their citizens are better protected than those in the United States.

Self-Regulation

The other approach to protection of personal privacy in the networked economy is that of self-regulation. In this approach, the electronic commerce industry is allowed to develop ways to implement the Fair Information Practice Principles without government intervention. However, as seen in a variety of recent surveys, the Fair Information Practice Principles have not been as widely applied to electronic commerce Web sites as one might hope. The results of one such survey of 361 of the most popular Web sites by the FTC in 1999 are shown in Table 11-7. Note that whereas 93 percent of the sites collect information, only 10 percent post a disclosure for all of the Fair Information Practice Principles.

In its report, the FTC recommended that the online industry be allowed to continue to provide self-regulation rather than legislation being used to control it for adults. Whereas privacy advocacy groups were not happy with this recommendation, business and industry applauded it. Efforts at self-regulation have included industry group guidelines, the use of privacy seals of approval, advertiser pressure, technology, and user education.

In the first case, in 1998, the Online Privacy Alliance (OPA), a coalition of industry groups, announced its Online Privacy Guidelines, which implement the FIP principles. OPA members agree to adopt and implement a posted privacy policy, but there is no monitoring of members.

In the second case, a **privacy seal of approval** is an icon that the Web site can display if it has agreed to follow the FIP principles as defined by the seal-granting organization. Such seals of approval enable consumers to identify online businesses that follow specified privacy principles and enable businesses to demonstrate compliance with such principles. By mid-1999, there were two such privacy seal organizations: TRUSTe (http://www.truste.org) and BBBOnline, which is sponsored by the Council of Better Business Bureaus (http://www.bbbonline.com). For example, TRUSTe claims that its seal assures that the Web site will disclose what information is being gathered, how it will be used, and who it will be shared with. Such Web sites are also supposed to provide choices to users as to how information will be collected, safeguards to protect the information, and ways for users to update or correct information. The privacy seal organizations monitor the compliance of the online businesses that display the seals.

In terms of pressure from advertisers, two of the largest Web-based advertisers, Microsoft and IBM, have policies that require the Web sites on which they advertise to have clearly defined privacy policies. Obviously, one way for Web sites to meet this requirement is to obtain the privacy seals of approval from either TRUSTe or BBBOnline.

A group directed by the inventor of the Web, Tim Berners-Lee, the **World Wide Web Consortium (W3C)**, has proposed a technology-based solution to the privacy

---

Table 11-7 Federal Trade Commission (FTC) Reported Study

Item	Percent of Total
Sites collecting personal information	93
Sites posting any privacy disclosure	66
Sites posting a privacy policy online	44
Sites posting a disclosure of FIP principles	10

Source: "Self-Regulation and Privacy Online: A Report to Congress," Federal Trade Commission, July 1999.

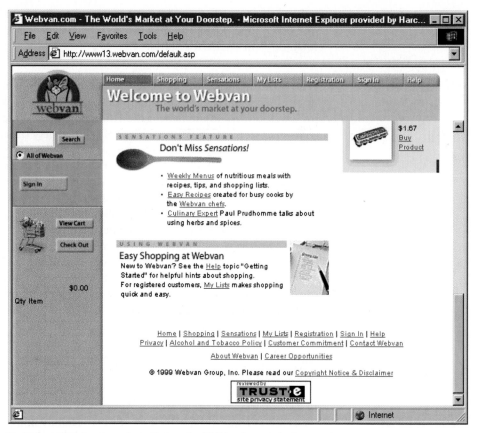

The Webvan Web site shown here displays the TRUSTe privacy seal of approval.

problem. Referred to as the **Platform for Privacy Preferences (P3P),** this technology would give consumers control over their own personal data by building the necessary mechanism into Web browsers such as Netscape and Internet Explorer. However, before any testing of the technology had taken place, a patent was issued to a company in Seattle. This may keep the technology from becoming an open standard available to all users at no cost.

User education in the area of online privacy is possibly the best way to ensure that personal data are protected. This is the aim of such groups as the OPA and the privacy seal sponsors. Many privacy advocates agree that the best way for consumers to protect their privacy is to take control of personal data themselves. Some suggestions about how you might protect your personal data are shown in Table 11-8, along with comments regarding the effects of taking this action.

Quick Review

1. What are the five Fair Information Practice Principles?
2. What two ways are being used to protect personal privacy?

Ethical Issues in the Networked Economy

All cultures and economies have had to develop rules about whether certain acts are "good" or "bad." These rules are known as **ethics** and are inherently value judgments that have resulted from a consensus in society. Such rules are often formalized as laws. The networked economy is no different from previous economies in terms of ethical issues. For example, is it ethical to write virus programs that annoy users without destroying anything? Is it ethical for employers to read their employees'

| Table 11-8 | Protecting Personal Data |

Suggestion	Comment
Supply your Social Security number only when required by law	Ask if you can obtain a different identifying number
Find your cookie file and erase it, then set your browser to give you the option to reject cookies	This will allow you to customize only those adaptive Web sites that you trust and refuse to do so for unknown Web sites
Visit Web sites anonymously by going through sites like www.anonymizer.com	This will effectively kill all customization of Web sites to your habits
Pay cash whenever you can	This will reduce generation of transactional data but will require forethought as well as effectively cut you off from electronic commerce
Be careful about your use of chat rooms, bulletin boards, and newsgroups	These can provide a wealth of information about you, even if you use a pseudonym
Think twice about filling out warranty cards or contest entries	Receipts are sufficient for most warranties. Have you won any sweepstakes recently?

e-mail with no reason (it is legal, but is it *ethical*)? Similarly, is it ethical to compile personal information on customers with or without their knowledge? We could discuss a host of ethical issues, but we will use a code of ethics developed by the Computer Ethics Institute as a framework for our discussion.

Known as the Ten Commandments of Computer Ethics, the list of rules shown in Figure 11-8 covers many of the issues facing computer users in the networked economy. (Like any list of general rules, problems can be found with it.[7]) You should note that these commandments were developed by the Computer Ethics Institute in 1992 and have *not* been modified to reflect the tremendous growth in the use of the Internet since that time. However, they are still appropriate if, when you see the word *computer,* you include any networks (including the Internet) to which it is linked. Your university almost certainly has its own code of computer ethics that provides guidance for faculty, staff, and student use of its computers.

| Figure 11-8 | Ten Commandments of Computer Ethics |

1. Thou shalt not use a computer to harm other people.
2. Thou shalt not interfere with other people's computer work.
3. Thou shalt not snoop around in other people's files.
4. Thou shalt not use a computer to steal.
5. Thou shalt not use a computer to bear false witness.
6. Thou shalt not copy or use proprietary software for which you have not paid.
7. Thou shalt not use other people's computer resources without authorization or proper compensation.
8. Thou shalt not appropriate other people's intellectual output.
9. Thou shalt think about the social consequences of the program you write or the system you design.
10. Thou shalt use a computer in ways that show consideration and respect for your fellow humans.

Source: http://www.brook.edu/its/cei/cei_hp.htm.

7. http://www.ccsr.cms.dmu.ac.uk/resources/professionalism/codes/cei_command_com.html.

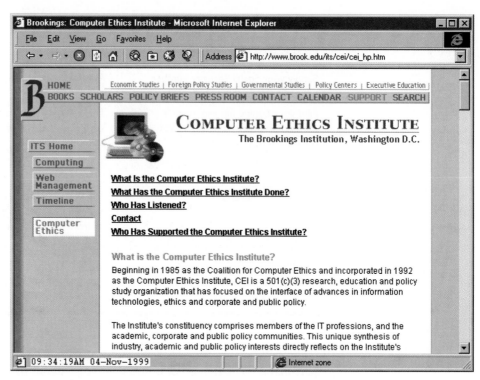

The Computer Ethics Institute developed the Ten Commandments of Computer Ethics.

Discussion and Application of the Ten Commandments of Computer Ethics

To help you understand the ethical issues facing computer and Internet users in the networked economy, we will discuss each of these ten rules and give examples.

1. *Thou shalt not use a computer to harm other people.* In this commandment, the key term is *harm* and it can be interpreted to mean any type of harm—physical, emotional, monetary, or otherwise. For example, just as it is unethical to harm people by planting a bomb in a public building, according to this rule, it is also unethical to post instructions for bombmaking on the Internet. Hacking into a credit union database and accessing personal financial data would also be considered unethical (as well as illegal) under this commandment, as would purposefully causing personal data to be exposed on the Web or collecting personal data without permission of that person.

2. *Thou shalt not interfere with other people's computer work.* *Interfere* is the key word in this commandment because it now very easy to send viruses and other programs over the Internet to interfere with or even destroy other people's computer work. Sending even nondestructive viruses to other computer users can be a form of interference if they interfere with work by taking over internal memory. Also, sending an overwhelming number of e-mails or requests for Web pages to a server with an intent of crashing it would be considered unethical, no matter what your feelings are about the purpose of the server.

3. *Thou shalt not snoop around in other people's files.* Files on computers owned by individuals (not organizations) either are the personal property of the individuals or are software that has been licensed to that person. In either case, it is unethical (and, in many cases, illegal) to access these files. This includes e-mail sent from personally owned computers. On the other hand, files on computers owned by organizations have been ruled to the property of the organizations. Some employee organizations feel that it is unethical for employers to read their employees' e-mail.

4. *Thou shalt not use a computer to steal.* Using a computer to steal from individuals or organizations is both unethical and illegal. The networked economy has brought with it many new types of fraud as well as old schemes repackaged for the Internet.

5. *Thou shalt not use a computer to bear false witness.* One of the well-known facts about the Internet is that bad or unflattering news spreads like wildfire. Using a Web page to spread an untruth or inaccurate information and sending an unfounded rumor to a newsgroup are examples of using a computer to bear false witness. The volatility of Internet-related stocks means that good or bad news can cause a large number of investors to gain or lose a great deal of money very quickly before the validity of the news can be determined.

6. *Thou shalt not copy or use proprietary software for which you have not paid.* Although we all know that software piracy is illegal, we may think that *borrowing* a copy of a software program from a friend is okay. However, it is definitely not! The software is *licensed* to a single user (unless a site license has been purchased), and that user is the only person who should use it. Allowing others to use software is both illegal and unethical in the same way as photocopying a copyrighted textbook. Although not always illegal, it is definitely unethical to download shareware and then not pay for it. (**Shareware** is software that can be freely downloaded from Web sites on the Internet. If you choose to use it, then you are "on your honor" to pay for it.)

7. *Thou shalt not use other people's computer resources without authorization or proper compensation.* You probably have a computer account that allows you to access your university's computer system, including access to e-mail. You may also have an AOL or local ISP account for which you pay a monthly user fee. In either case, you would not want someone else to break into the computer system and use your account. The same applies to other people's accounts—hacking into them is considered unethical.

8. *Thou shalt not appropriate other people's intellectual output.* Just as copying somebody else's math homework or English term paper is cheating, so, too, is copying somebody else's computer program. This includes copying text, illustrations, or photos from a Web site. Although it is generally conceded to be appropriate to learn design and programming techniques by investigating a Web site, outright copying of it is unethical, and, if the material is copyrighted, illegal as well. As has been done in this book, any quoting or paraphrasing of material from a Web site should be cited just like any other research source.

9. *Thou shalt think about the social consequences of the program you write or the system you design.* To apply this commandment, it is useful to include Web sites under the broad term *program*. If this is done, then you should ask yourself if the Web site you have created will in some way be harmful to society. Is it providing information that can be used in a harmful way—say, in the hands of somebody with psychological problems? Will the Web site incite anger or other hurtful emotions in those who read it? Will it degrade a group of the population or be harmful to children? As mentioned earlier, several attempts have been made in the United States to control Web site content to protect children, but most have been ruled unconstitutional on freedom of speech grounds.

10. *Thou shalt use a computer in ways that show consideration and respect for your fellow humans.* E-mail users as well as those using other Internet communication protocols sometimes feel that they can write things that they would not say in a person-to-person conversation. Sending angry e-mail messages to someone or an organization would be considered unethical under this commandment. As with any communications media, politeness and consideration are always the best policy, regardless of how you feel about the other person.

Although these commandments may not cover all possible situations, they should give you some ideas on which to base your actions.

⊙ Summary

To summarize this chapter, let's answer the Learning Objectives questions posed at the beginning of the chapter.

Why has privacy become an important issue in the networked economy? Personal privacy is an important area for you to consider, both as a consumer in the networked economy and as an employee in a networked economy organization. As a consumer, you should know the threats to your privacy and how you can deal with them. As an employee, you should be aware of the privacy concerns of your customers and how your organization balances them against its need for information needed to serve customers better. Privacy in the networked economy is at greater risk than in the industrial economy because of increased searchability and integration, but privacy can also be better protected if the organizations retaining personal information follow good security practices. Consumers are most at risk of having their privacy threatened when organizations choose to cooperate in sharing information or don't follow security procedures.

People have become concerned about the threat of organizations and individuals using the Internet to access public and private databases to invade their privacy. This is because almost anyone with a personal computer and modem can access the Internet to search a database and retrieve information about prospective employees, tenants, or other individuals.

What is the trade-off between privacy and customer service? Business and industry are constantly striving to create Web sites that attract customers and other stakeholders. One way by which they do this is by making Web sites customized to each customer by learning about the customer's preferences. This information makes the Web site more useful to customers but also requires that customers give up some of their privacy in order to achieve maximum customization.

How is information technology used to collect privacy data and information? Threats to privacy involve the use of data or information that has been collected using information technology. There are three broad types of data: transactional data, Web-visit data, and Internet communications data. Transactional data are generated by noncash transactions. Such transactions take place face-to-face, electronically, or by telephone, mail, or the Web and identify the customer. There are no federal laws in the United States against companies sharing transactional data on their customers. Data are often also collected on the employees handling the transactions.

Web-visit data about a user's computer are generated whenever a visit is made to a Web site. Adaptable Web sites request information from the visitor. Adaptive Web sites use patterns they find in consumer interests and purchases to adapt themselves to the customer's interests. These Web sites often use cookie files to save these data on the client computer. Internet communications data include e-mail messages, "conversations" in chat rooms, postings to bulletin boards, and messages to newsgroups. E-mail sent or received on an employer's computer is the property of the employer. This means that the employer has the right to read an employee's e-mail at any time.

What types of threats to personal privacy exist in the networked economy? There are four types of threats to privacy in the networked economy: exposure of information, data surveillance, information brokers, and identity theft.

Exposure of information can be caused by accident or intentionally by hackers. Data surveillance involves computer matching of databases or profiling of individuals who fall into specific groups. Profiling is often used for target marketing. Information brokers are people or groups that find information on an individual for a fee. Identity theft involves stealing a person's credit rating or other information specific to that person. Another intrusion into personal privacy is junk e-mail—so-called spam.

What approaches are being used to protect personal data? Approaches to protecting personal data involve attempting to follow the Fair Information Practice Principles. This can be done through government legislation and self-regulation. Government legislation in the United States has included a number of laws, with two being passed in 1998. Self-regulation includes industry group guidelines, privacy seals of approval, advertiser pressure, technology, and user education.

What ethical issues must be dealt with in the networked economy? Like any other economy, the networked economy has a variety of ethical issues. These issues were discussed in the context of the Ten Commandments of Computer Ethics and involve the ethics of using computers to harm other people, steal from them, spread untruths about them, look into their files, and so on.

⊗ Review Questions

1. What three dimensions are used to compare privacy in the networked and industrial economies?

2. Why is there a trade-off between customization and personal privacy? Give an example other than those mentioned in the text.

3. List five types of transactional data that you have created in the last week. How would these data create a picture of your likes and dislikes?

4. How do employees generate transactional data? Of what use is this to employers?

5. What is a cookie? How is it used to collect data?

6. Why do we say that Internet communications data are unstructured? Does this mean they cannot be searched or integrated with other data?

7. How can information exposure be avoided? Have you ever been the target of profiling? If so, how?

8. What is the major identifier used in identity theft? How often have you given it out in the last week?

9. What are four approaches to self-regulation of privacy protection?

10. Why is it unethical to copy material from other Web sites and use it in yours?

⊗ Discussion Questions

1. How is employee e-mail different from personal e-mail? Discuss the pros and cons of reading employee e-mail.

2. For a Web site of your choosing, discuss how it uses customization and the type of personal data it collects.

3. Check with your college computing center about whether it has a code of ethics for computer use. If it does, compare it to the Ten Commandments of Computer Ethics discussed here.

> **CASE**

WildOutfitters.com

Claire was awakened when she felt Alex stirring beside her. Groggily, she asked, "What's the matter, honey?"

"Nothing, I just had a strange dream," Alex replied. Before Claire could settle back to sleep, he continued. "I was climbing on a high mountain, when I came upon an eagle's nest. I was happy to see the eagle and began to ask questions in order to get to know her better. Each time that I asked her a question, I gave her a worm. The questions kept getting more personal and soon I knew almost everything about the eagle and her family."

"Wasn't the eagle nervous about answering your questions?"

"No, it seemed that as long as I had nice, juicy worms to give her she was willing to tell me anything."

Alex's dream probably can be attributed to the latest ideas that the pair had been discussing for the Web site. One of the reasons for the success of their brick-and-mortar store has been the ability to give personalized service to their customers. Admittedly, the number of regular customers to the store has been relatively small but this has allowed the Campagnes to know these customers well. This knowledge has served them on a number of occasions by enabling them to recommend trips or gear that were a custom fit with the customers' interests. Claire and Alex would like to extend this ability to the Web site but to do so would involve collecting and using more personal information from their Web customers.

Customization is not entirely new to their site. They already collect some personal information from users who register for their customer incentive program along with tracking their sales level. This information, and the use of a cookie, allows these registered users to log in to the site quickly and check how close they are to a prize. Also, for customers who want it, they have been sending targeted e-mail about special deals. They are also more confident in their ability to protect information due to the improved security of their systems.

Lately, they have been struggling with how to customize the site further. One alternative is to make their site adaptable. With this option, they would use information provided by each user to present more customized views on the Web pages. While still providing the main options and a fairly standardized look and feel, they could incorporate some objects on the pages that would vary according to the user. They might even go so far as to allow users to create their own WildOutfitter.com related home page on the site.

Another alternative is to make the Web site adaptive. Instead of requesting specific information from the customers, they could enhance the cookie to monitor the customers usage of the site. Then, using this information, they can make more subtle changes to the site when the customer visits.

For each alternative, they will have to answer several questions. What information will they need to collect and how will they collect it? What uses for this information are acceptable? At what point would their questions become too personal and obtrusive? Could this turn some customers away? What additional responsibilities would they be taking on in order to protect the privacy of their customers? The Campagnes are well aware of the trade-offs in regard to privacy that are being brought about in the networked economy. Because of the possible risks to privacy, they have decided to think very carefully about how they may use the personal information of their customers in a responsible manner.

"Strange dream, bird brain," Claire said. "What made you wake up?"

"I didn't realize that she'd had enough. I tried to give her unwanted worms with little ads tattooed on the sides," he replied. "She got mad and started to peck at my hand. That's when I woke up."

Claire giggled, "I've heard of snail-mail before, but worm-spam, that's a new one on me." She was barely able to dodge the pillow that flew her way.

1. How would you classify the data that would be collected with system discussed in the case?

2. Alex and Claire are trying to decide between making their Web site adaptive or adaptable. What are the advantages and disadvantages of each choice? Which would you choose for the WildOutfitters.com site?

3. If the Campagnes decide to make their site adaptive, should they notify their customers about the changes in the information that is stored in the cookie? Explain.

4. *(Hands on)* Browse the Web for various sites that collect personal information from customers. How many of these sites have a privacy statement? Read a few of these privacy statements to see what they contain. Do they make you feel secure about entrusting your personal information to the site? Using what you have learned, write a privacy statement for WildOutfitters.com.

Societal Issues in the Networked Economy

❯ L e a r n i n g O b j e c t i v e s

After reading this chapter, you should be able to answer the following questions:

❯ How has the rise of ubiquitous computing and communications changed our concepts of time, distance, and borders?

❯ What economic issues are we facing in the networked economy?

❯ How has telecommuting changed the lives of many employees in the networked economy?

❯ What health issues has the networked economy brought on?

❯ How has Web content caused problems for society?

❯ What kinds of changes in our society might we see in the future?

Living in Internet Time in Silicon Valley

Evan Thornley and Tracey Ellery describe themselves as living on the "bleeding edge" of Internet time. By this the two founders of LookSmart, a Web directory start-up company, mean that time in the Silicon Valley, where they live, moves at a rapid rate, with their workday often stretching until midnight. To meet the demands of their new company and their family, which includes five-year-old twins, they are using personal outsourcing to take care of as many tasks as possible. They have a nanny for the twins and personal assistants that do anything that needs to be done, including paying their bills. At home, groceries are ordered over the Web using Peapod and delivered weekly, and two companies deliver ready-made meals for those times when Evan and Tracey don't have time to cook. They also employ a housekeeper and gardener.

When the twins, Max and Ruby, go to school, they might be taken by one of the companies like Kids Kab that specialize in transporting children in Silicon Valley to and from school, sports, after-school classes, and other activities. Many parents keep their schedules on Palm Pilot organizers, which they synchronize each night; children use the Web to check their practice and car-pool schedules. Parents and children update each other throughout the day by cellular phone, pager, and e-mail as events are canceled, times changed, and meetings run late. Because 70 percent of the students at Fremont High School in Sunnyvale, California, have pagers and 52 percent of households have e-mail (as compared to only 11 percent for the rest of the country), keeping in touch is easy.

Source: Elizabeth Weise, "It's about Time, and Tech," *USA Today,* May 26, 1999, pp. D1–D2.

Kids Kab provides a personal outsourcing service to parents in the Silicon Valley by transporting their children to and from various activities.

Living in Internet Time

Life for IT professionals in Silicon Valley runs at high speed, to say the least. The Silicon Valley is a high-tech industrial region between Palo Alto and San Jose, California, where many information technology firms are located. The name derives from the use of high-purity silicon in manufacturing computer chips. Although the opening Focus on Society box is about Silicon Valley, the same could be said for professionals living and working in many other areas of the world, including Redmond, Washington, where Microsoft is located, and Bangalore, India, where many IT devices are made and programmed. In fact, more and more of us are beginning to live in Internet time—that is, our lives revolve around information technology and the Internet. Even those of us who do not work directly in the IT industry are being affected as we find our lives speeding up due to the transition to the networked economy.

A number of other trends are being noticed by anthropologists and sociologists who study changes in lifestyle. **Personal outsourcing,** by which individuals outsource as many of their nonprofessional responsibilities to someone else as they can; **reach creep,** by which individuals take on more and more work because technology allows it; and the blurring of work and home are all parts of living and working in Internet time. To live and work in the networked economy, you need to understand these trends as well as a variety of issues generated by our growing use of the Internet.

Elements of the Networked Economy

From a social issue point of view, the networked economy is built on three key elements: ubiquitous computing and communications (computer and communications technology everywhere), education, and freedom of ideas and trade. There is little argument about the importance of education and freedom of ideas and trade. The growth of Western economies can be said to have begun with the invention of the printing press. That invention led to educational opportunities for the majority of citizens through the widespread availability of printed books instead of for just the elite few who had access to extremely scarce hand-lettered books. When coupled with the freedom to express ideas and to trade goods freely, the resulting education led to inventions and new ways of doing things that generated economic growth. The key difference between the industrial economy of the last two hundred years and the networked economy into which we are now moving is the combination of education and freedom with ubiquitous computing and communications, as shown in Figure 12-1.

Figure 12-1   Elements of Networked Economy

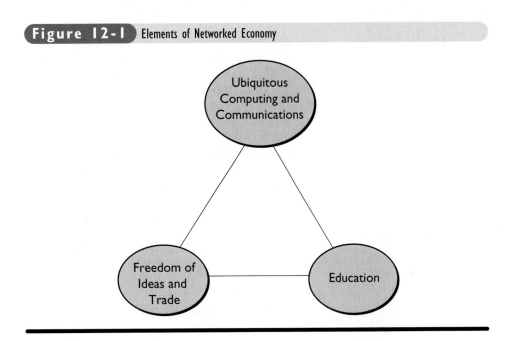

The combination of education and freedom with ubiquitous computing and communications results in a different type of economy; instead of employees with physical strength and dexterity being needed to work in manufacturing plants, power stations, and so on, employees with a knowledge of and an ability to use information technology are needed. This is going to require a higher level of education than was required in the industrial economy for an individual to be successful. This combination is also resulting in three important side effects:

- Death of distance
- Homogenization of time
- Disintegration of borders

The **death of distance** means that we are no longer restricted by geography. For example, it is now possible to use ubiquitous computing and communications to work anywhere and share your results with coworkers anywhere in the world in a matter of seconds. The death of distance has made it possible for many workers to avoid long commutes to and from work by telecommuting to work using the Internet or private networks. **Telecommuting** (also known as *telework*) is a work arrangement in which employees work at any time or place that allows them to accomplish their work in an effective and efficient manner.[1]

The **homogenization of time** means that we live in a 24/7 world where business continues somewhere all of the time. This side effect is causing the blurring of work and home as we find we can work around the clock if necessary. For example, the Internet brings the capability to work continuously on information systems development projects by having development teams in widely separated time zones working together on the same project. The homogenization of time also means that workers who telecommute must be careful to separate their professional and home lives; otherwise, they may have a tendency to work "all the time."

Finally, the **disintegration of borders** means that states and countries can no longer protect themselves from the import of ideas and electronic goods without seriously hampering their entry into the networked economy. The free flow of ideas and trade is essential to the networked economy. For example, some countries that fear the import of ideas that are felt to be dangerous to the government either don't allow Internet access or require all Web pages to be filtered before being sent to the user. In either case, the government runs the risk of being left behind in the networked economy.

An Example of Working in Internet Time

As an example of the way things are speeding up in the networked economy due to Internet use, consider the process of creating a textbook. When the author published his first textbook in 1981, he and a coauthor wrote the manuscript in longhand, and a typist used a typewriter (an electro-mechanical device that used a keyboard to print characters directly on paper) to transcribe it. The typewritten manuscript was reviewed by the authors, mistakes corrected, and then it was typed all over again (it was not stored electronically, so it could not be edited). The manuscript was then reviewed by faculty members at other colleges and universities who might eventually use the book, and changes were made to the manuscript based on their comments. This often involved retyping the manuscript all over again, but sometimes it was possible to physically cut and paste to avoid some typing. (This actually involved cutting up the manuscript with scissors and combining the pieces with newly typed material using glue.)

Once the final manuscript was complete, it was sent to a manuscript editor for editing of spelling, style, and grammar (no spell checker on a typewriter!). The edited manuscript was returned to the authors for them to check any changes made

---

1. http://www.telecommute.org.

to it. Once approved by the authors, the edited manuscript was sent to a compositor, who set the manuscript in type and printed it in long text pages called *galleys,* which also had to be approved by the authors. When finalized, the galley text was cut up and combined with any artwork by a *paste-up artist* to create *dummies.* The dummies were then converted into *page proofs* by the compositor, which were again reviewed by the authors. At this point, the approved page proofs were ready to be printed and distributed to campus bookstores. All in all, this process, the steps of which are shown in Table 12-1, took well over three years! It should be noted that, with the exception of the transcribing and correcting by the typist, all communications were via the postal service or package delivery companies and were routed through an editor at the publication company, introducing further time delays.

Today, a three-year time frame to complete a textbook is out of the question in fields such as information systems where the technology is changing so rapidly. To write a book that is up-to-date, it must be finished much faster using all the capabilities of today's software and the Internet. For example, it is now possible to research the book using the Web and then to write it using **desktop publishing software.** This software combines the capabilities of a word processor and a paste-up artist by including artwork (created by the author or others) into the text as it is being written to create a nearly final version of the text. The book chapters can be converted to a **portable document format (PDF) file** and placed on the Internet for faculty members around the world to download and review (a PDF file can be read by any type of computer). Reviewers send back their comments via e-mail, and the manuscript is corrected based on their comments.

The corrected manuscript can then be sent via e-mail or FTP to the manuscript editor who edits it electronically for style and grammar and returns it by the same route. To see what changes have been made by the manuscript editor, the author can use the desktop publishing software to compare the original and edited manuscripts. The chapters can now be converted to **postscript files,** which can be printed and bound by a print house. Instead of taking at least three years, the whole process can now be shortened to less than sixteen months (based on the author's experience with such a project). These three steps are shown in Table 12-2, and the two methods are compared in Figure 12-2 (where the circled numbers correspond to the steps in the writing process in the tables).

Table 12-1   Industrial Economy Method of Book Publication

Step Number	Activity	Communication Mode
One	Write manuscript by hand, have typist transcribe it, and make corrections	Interoffice
Two	Manuscript is reviewed by faculty experts	Postal service or package delivery
Three	Rewrite manuscript and have it transcribed	Interoffice
Four	Editor edits manuscript for spelling, style, and grammar, and result is reviewed by author	Postal service or package delivery
Five	Compositor creates galleys, which are reviewed by author	Postal service or package delivery
Six	Paste-up artist creates dummies from galleys and artwork	Postal service or package delivery
Seven	Compositor uses dummies to create page proofs which are reviewed by author	Postal service or package delivery
Eight	Page proofs are sent to printer for printing	Postal service or package delivery

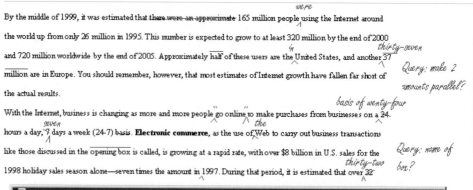

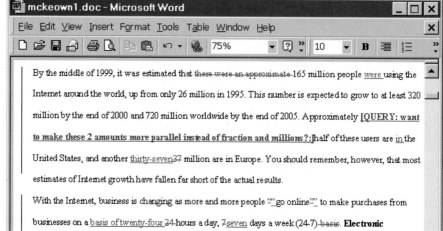

Online editing (bottom) results in much shorter publication time than traditional methods (top).

Knowing that you can use information technology and the Internet to complete a project like writing and publishing a book in much less time than before can cause all of the lifestyle changes mentioned. The author experienced personal outsourcing, reach creep, and the blurring of work and home. To write a book this quickly required that lawn care be outsourced to a landscaping company. The author also had to take on additional development responsibilities once handled by people at the publishing company because the technology made it possible to do so. Finally, knowing that writing could be done at virtually any place and any time led to a blurring of work and home life—resulting in the book being finished overseas on a laptop computer while the author was on a Fulbright Fellowship.

Table 12-2 Networked Economy Method of Book Publication

Step Number	Activity	Communication Mode
One	Author writes book in desktop publishing software and sends to reviewers	Internet
Two	Author makes revisions and sends to manuscript editor for editing of spelling, style, and grammar	Internet
Three	Author transmits Postscript files to printer for printing	Internet

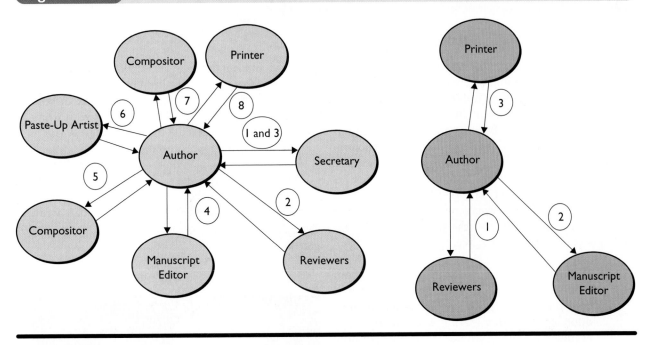

Figure 12-2 Book Production in Internet Time

The manuscript editing portion of the project was a good example of the death of distance, homogenization of time, and disintegration of borders because the author was in Europe and the manuscript editor in California. This allowed them to take advantage of the time difference by the author creating text files in Portugal eight hours ahead of the Pacific time zone and then transmitting them to California via the Internet. The editor worked on them while the author slept in Europe and transmitted back for more work the next morning. There were no borders at all.

Creation of Societal Issues

The combination of ubiquitous computing and communications, education, and freedom of ideas and trade that has created the networked economy has also created a host of societal issues. These issues include health, economy, Web site content, and the future of our society. Many times the issues are not cut-and-dry because restricting one set of actions may have undesirable effects. For example, one might say that employees should never use the Internet for nonwork activities, but if there is a blurring of work and home life, how do you define *nonwork activities*? Also, how do you know that putting a restriction on Internet use might not cause the firm to miss out on some new opportunity that is known only to Web surfers?

Quick Review

1. What are the three results of living in Internet time?
2. What are the societal elements of the networked economy?

Economic Issues in the Networked Economy

The networked economy has already brought about many changes in our lives. One dramatic change is the definition of *scarcity*. Like land, labor, and capital, consumer attention span will be a scarce commodity. Companies wishing to do business in the networked economy will have to take this change into account. The networked

ⓕocus on the Internet

Personal Outsourcing Web Sites

As mentioned in the text, *personal outsourcing* is a growing fact of life in the networked economy. This is not just for executives in Silicon Valley who need their bills paid and their children transported to after-school activites. Busy people all over are finding that paying someone else to take care of such responsibilities gives them more free time and a more relaxed lifestyle. Most are finding these services exactly where you would expect—on the Web. In fact, the push to deliver services online, straight to the customer's door, is one of the fastest growing segments of electronic commerce.

- In New York City, you can use Kozmo.com (www.kozmo.com) to find movie videos and have them delivered by bike messenger to your doorstep. No more leaving work at six in the evening and taking whatever video is left; now you can select a movie at nine in the morning from a full inventory and have it delivered whenever you want—all for $4.33. You can also have candy, popcorn, and ice cream delivered along with your movie.

- Want a gourmet meal that's ready to heat and eat? Go to CookExpress.com (www.cookexpress.com) and find the meal and have it delivered, on a same day basis if you live in the San Francisco Bay area or overnight elsewhere in the United States. *Newsweek* tried it from Manhatten and was able to have a pretty good pan-roasted halibut in a tomato vinaigrette with roasted potatoes delivered in about twenty-four hours.

- Have film that needs to be developed, shoes to be repaired, or dry cleaning to be picked up? If

you live in the Boston or Washington, D.C. areas, go to Streamline.com. For $30 per month they set up a dry storage box in your driveway and once a week, stock it with whatever you've ordered—from groceries to videos to meals from local restaurants.

While all of these services are located in large metropolitan areas, this is forecast to change as the demand grows in smaller cities and suburban areas.

Source: Jared Sandberg, "NoChores.com." *Newsweek,* August 30, 1999, p. 64.

With personal outsourcing, you can use the Internet to order a movie in the morning and have it delivered to your door in the evening.

---

economy is having other effects on society, including issues of productivity and the workplace, changing work requirements and economic dislocation, and taxation policies.

Productivity and Workplace Issues

An apparent paradox exists in the information technology industry: In 1986, the IT industry employed 469,000 production workers engaged in the manufacture of IT devices, but by 1996, this number had dropped to 363,000, with a predicted drop to 314,000 by 2006. The number of IT devices (computers, peripherals, and so on) did not drop; in fact, it has increased dramatically. Computer sales doubled between 1994 and 1998, and the percent of U.S. households with a computer increased to 45 percent in 1998, up from 38 percent three years earlier. The question is: How did

The number of workers required to run computer manufacturing facilities such as this are dropping at the same time as output is increasing.

the IT industry manage to increase production while cutting production jobs? The answer is the use of IT itself to improve the productivity of this industry. At the same time that IT production-related jobs are dropping at 1.4 percent per year, output is going up at a rate of 15 percent per year—a rate five times that of other manufacturing industries.[2]

Because the IT industry, including the Internet, is generating much of the growth in the U.S. economy, increased productivity means a low rate of inflation. In fact, the inflation rate *dropped* by 0.7 percent in 1996 and 1997. While we may not be able to expect this decrease in the rate of inflation to continue forever (and, in fact, it did rise in 1999), there are many who believe that the Internet is creating a **frictionless economy** in which goods and services are bought and sold without the need of intermediaries, thereby decreasing costs.

At the same time, the unemployment rate continues to be low by historic measures. You can be sure that most of the people who no longer work in the assembly side of IT companies are now working in the software or service side of IT or have started their own IT businesses. In fact, for those interested in the IT field, there should be plenty of jobs because computer service jobs are expected to grow at a 7 percent rate in the foreseeable future, while output will grow at a 9 percent rate.

---

2. Mark Johnson, "Computer Makers Doing More with Less," *The Atlanta Journal-Constitution,* July 28, 1999, p. D11.

One important way in which the networked economy is changing employment is in terms of gender equity. There appears to be less discrimination against women in information technology positions, possibly because this work is based on knowledge rather than strength. Women in high-level positions in this industry are quite common, and there are numerous female CEOs and presidents. When communication is by e-mail and Web page, the gender of the person at the other end of the line seems to matter less.

Changing Work Requirements and Economic Dislocation

With the number of manufacturing jobs dropping in the IT industry and the jobs shifting to software and service, most new hires will be knowledge workers. Recall that a **knowledge worker** is someone who works with information in an organization. With the onset of the networked economy, knowledge workers will be in great demand as the very nature of work changes from requiring physical strength and dexterity to requiring knowledge. A 1999 survey run by the Department of Commerce entitled "Falling through the Net II," found that 77 percent of all workers use a computer at work.[3] The same survey found that college graduates are three times more likely to use the Internet than are high school graduates and *ten times* more likely than nonhigh school graduates. Based on these rates, which are sure to increase as we move through the twenty-first century, it will be less and less possible to enter the workplace without some understanding of information technology. Even positions like that of automobile mechanics are being restructured because of the level of information technology in today's automobiles.

Not surprisingly, education is essential to adapting to the changing work requirements in the networked economy. Without education, workers will find it difficult to find a position that will enable them to share in the wealth generated by the networked economy. In fact, there is a concern that some elements of the population might miss out completely on participating in the new economy because of their lack of knowledge in this area, resulting in a widening of the division between the "haves" and "have-nots" of the world. Studies have begun to identify trends in Internet use by various traits, including education, race/national origin, geography, and family structure.

The use of the Internet and level of education are highly correlated, with more-educated people using the Internet more than do those with less education. Americans with less education, who could benefit the most from Internet use, unfortunately tend to use it less. Of particular concern is that this divide is increasing. Figure 12-3 shows the growth of a **digital divide**—that is, a difference in Internet use based on level of education. In this figure, each bar displays the difference between the Internet use of a college graduate and another educational level. For example, in 1997, the bar for high school graduates indicates that the gap between high school graduates and college graduates was about 29 percent, but by 1998, the corresponding bar indicates that this difference had grown to over 32 percent.

Global Issues

This gap between "haves" and "have-nots" is also true for countries of the world. For example, a 1999 United Nations study[4] suggested that the planet is splitting into two very different worlds: one inhabited by a minority that is using information technology to improve its standard of living and another inhabited by a majority of poverty-stricken citizens in low-tech countries. For example, for approximately one-half of the people in the world, their next telephone call will be their *first!*

One reason for this difference is that the citizens of poor countries cannot afford to purchase the technology necessary to keep up. The same study showed that the average American pays one month's wage for a computer (probably less now), whereas the average Bangladeshi would spend eight *years'* income to purchase the same machine and would then have to learn English to use it because 80 percent of

---

3. David Lieberman, "Net Hangs out of Reach of Have-Not," *USA Today,* July 9, 1999, p. 2B.
4. Marilyn Geewax, "Chasm between the 'Haves' and 'Have Nots' Is Widening," *The Atlanta Journal-Constitution,* July 25, 1999, p. F3.

Figure 12-3 Digital Divide by Educational Level

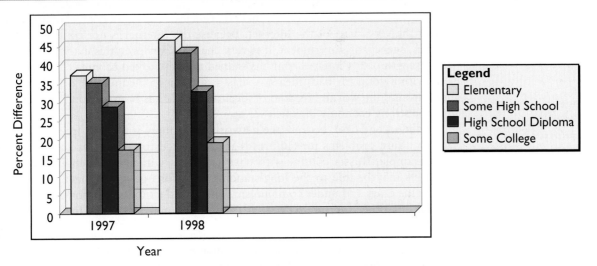

Source: U.S. Department of Commerce, "Falling through the Net: Defining the Digital Divide.

all Web sites are in English. Although there have been suggestions of taxing e-mail messages in the developed countries to support wiring underdeveloped countries, there appears to be little chance of this occurring.

Other global issues include the tension between local control and freedom of communications and the imposition of the free market system by the networked economy. In the first case, a number of countries have screened Web site content for political or religious reasons. Vietnam, Iraq, Iran, and Saudi Arabia are the best known of these countries. In some countries, all connections must go through a single computer that filters out those Web sites that are deemed objectionable. In

ⓕocus on Technology

On the Wrong Side of the Digital Divide

The so-called digital divide usually refers to socio-economic divisions in the use of the Internet, but it can also refer to a distinct division in the availability of high-speed, broadband Internet connections. Without these types of connections, which provide access at a speed at least four times that available with a 56k modem, companies can't compete. Such access is usually associated with T-1 lines, digital subscriber lines (DSL), or cable connections—connections that are not available everywhere. Rural and low-income inner-city areas appear to be most at risk of not having the necessary connections for companies to be willing to stay or relocate there.

To see the effect of high-speed connections, consider two companies: Serna Enterprises and Wayne Engineering. Serna is a small print shop in north Denver that is having trouble competing because of the lack of high-speed access. Its customers want to send art, photos, and layouts over the Internet but, using conventional phone modems, this takes twenty minutes for an eight-page brochure—too long to be competitive. On the other hand, garbage truck maker Wayne Engineering's business boomed when a cable connection enabled it to send multiple megabytes of 3-D drawings worldwide to promote sales. With the future of many small businesses riding on the availability of high-speed access, some governments are starting to see a need to ensure equal access to high-speed Internet connections. But, until this is universal over the entire United States, many companies will be at a disadvantage.

Source: David Lieberman, "On the Wrong Side of the Wires." *USA Today,* October 11, 1999, pp. B1–B2.

other countries, service providers monitor what their clients view. A schematic of the former approach is shown in Figure 12-4.

The problems facing all governmental agencies in trying to control online content are at the very heart of the Internet. Because the Internet is not controlled by any person, agency, or government, it is very chaotic. However, this extreme freedom is the strength of the Internet that has shaped the networked economy. Virtually anyone with a good (or bad) idea now has a fast, cheap medium for distributing that idea around the world. Freedom of ideas and trade has been a strong force in creating the strong economy in which we now live.

In the second case, because the networked economy is built on freedom of trade, it may cause problems for cultures that are unaccustomed to this economic form. For example, Russia continues to have problems with the free enterprise system, and this may be due to the long-standing traditions of government control, both under the czars and under communism. The introduction of electronic commerce in Russia and other countries with similar cultures could exacerbate these problems.

Taxation of Electronic Commerce

With the rapid growth of electronic commerce, there is pressure both in the United States and globally to subject it to some form of sales tax. In the United States, because sales made through electronic commerce are often across state borders, many states are losing sales tax revenue that they would otherwise collect on sales made at stores within their borders. Already, local governments estimate they are losing $5 billion each year from mail order sales, and because they rely on sales taxes for 36 percent of their revenue, states and counties worry about how much more revenue would be lost to electronic commerce. You should note that this is another example of the disintegration of borders. Because no one is sure of the long-term results of a tax on electronic commerce, the **Internet Tax Freedom Act of 1998** placed a three-year waiting period on state and local Internet taxes in the United States and created the Advisory Commission on Electronic Commerce to study this issue and make recommendations to Congress on taxing electronic commerce by April of 2000.

Figure 12-4 Governmental Control of Internet Content

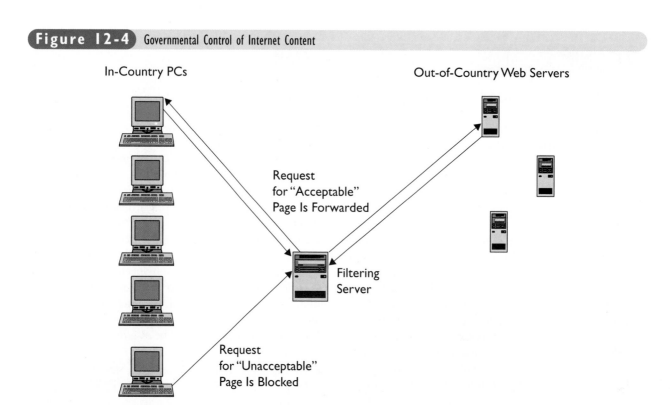

The work of this commission was immediately complicated by the failure of a task force to reach agreement in July of 1999 on how electronic commerce should be taxed. Created by the National Tax Association in 1996, the thirty-nine-member group included members from government and business. This task force had developed a proposal that would have dramatically changed the nation's sales tax system by forcing states to have only one statewide sales rate instead of the 6,600-plus sales tax rates currently in effect. The proposal was dropped when the business members failed to accept it. The failure of this task force to pass a proposal illustrates some of the problems facing the commission:

- Electronic commerce businesses hesitate to collect sales taxes in all fifty states because they fear it will open the states to imposing corporate income and franchise taxes on them. Currently, such taxes can be imposed on a business only if it has a presence in the state in the form of an office or store.
- Local governments do not want to lose their ability to set sales tax rates for fear of losing tax revenue. Many counties and cities have local option sales taxes on top of the sales taxes collected by the states that provide revenue to fund operations or new projects.

In a move to force the Internet taxation issue, Senator Fritz Hollings of South Carolina introduced legislation in August 1999 that would impose a 5 percent tax on all electronic commerce sales, with the proceeds to be used to fund teachers' salaries in elementary and secondary schools nationwide. Between the commission created by Congress, the calls for taxation from local and state governments, and the action of individual politicians like Senator Hollings, there is little doubt that this issue will continue to be in the forefront of national debate.

Quick Review

1. What are three major economic issues in the networked economy?
2. Why is education even more important in the networked economy than before?

Telecommuting

Telecommuting, the use of telecommunications to work outside the traditional office or workplace, is a growing approach to work.[5] As seen in Figure 12-5, telecommuting has grown by 15 percent per year for the last ten years, with a sharp jump between 1996 and 1998. Many companies have set up policies for telecommuting, including AT&T, IBM, and Lucent Technologies. AT&T adopted a corporate telecommuting policy in 1992. By 1997, the percentage of U.S.-based AT&T managers who were telecommuting had steadily grown to 55 percent, totaling over thirty-six thousand AT&T teleworkers.[6] Many employers provide their telecommuting employees with office furniture in addition to technology such as computers, Internet connections, and fax and copy machines.

This trend is supported by two federal laws that encourage telecommuting: amendments to the **Clear Air Act** passed in 1990 and the **Family and Medical Leave Act of 1992.** Telecommuting was widely used in Atlanta during the 1996 Olympics and is being given consideration again due to the air quality problems and long commuting times there.

A 1999 survey of one thousand workers by Rutgers University and the University of Connecticut showed that 59 percent of workers would like to have the opportunity

---

5. www.whatis.com.
6. http://www.att.com/ehs/telework/chap05.html.

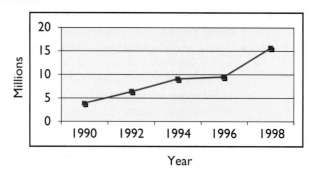

Figure 12-5 Growth of Telecommuting

Source: http://www.telecommute.org/twa_overview.htm.

to telecommute because of the increased opportunities they believe it will give them to be with their family.[7] This is despite the concern of many workers that telecommuting could affect their chance for advancement. According to the survey, almost half (46 percent) of those who do telecommute report being more productive than at the office. However, the survey appears to show a "telecommuting gap" based on education and income. Fifty-eight percent of workers earning less than $40,000 a year reported that they had an opportunity to telecommute, as compared to 76 percent of those earning more than $40,000.

Telecommuting Locations

In addition to the home, there are four other options for telecommuting: the virtual/mobile office, hoteling, the satellite office, and the telework center. With the **virtual/mobile office,** employees are equipped with the communications tools and technology needed to perform job duties from wherever they need to be—home, office, customer location, airport, and so on. With **hoteling,** temporary office space is created for drop-in use by employees. The temporary office space is equipped with standard office technology—phones, PCs, faxes, printers, copiers, e-mail, Internet access, and so on—and employees either reserve space in advance or drop in to use a cubicle on an as-needed basis. A **satellite office** is a fully equipped office where employees can reserve space and work one or more days a week closer to their homes, reducing commute times and helping ease traffic congestion. Finally, a **telework center** is like a satellite office except that the office space is utilized by employees from different organizations, with employers being charged for the space and services utilized by each employee per day. These centers are typically located closer to employees' homes than their regular office locations.

Telecommuting Advantages and Disadvantages

Telecommuting has numerous advantages for the company, the employee, and the community. For the company, various studies have shown that although the monetary benefits are difficult to measure, the company benefits from more-productive, happier workers. For the employee, telecommuting leads to a less-stressful job, a shorter (or no) commute to work, and a better family life. For the community, telecommuting leads to less traffic and air pollution.

On the other hand, telecommuters require a different type of management because they are not in the traditional workplace. In addition, telecommuting is not for every worker because it requires a large degree of self-initiative. Finally, it can

---

7. *Work Trends: America's Attitudes about Work, Employers, and Government,* study conducted February 5–22, 1999, by the John J. Heldrich Center for Workforce Development at Rutgers University and the Center for Survey Research and Analysis at University of Connecticut.

Telecommuting by working at home has many advantages but also has some disadvantages.

cause problems when the worker cannot separate their work life from home life—too much homogenization of time!

Telecommuting at fareastfoods.com

Being a Web-based company, fareastfoods.com has always encouraged its employees to telecommute. Many of its programmers work at home and FTP their programs in to the company Web server for testing. The company provides them with the latest in technology as well as giving them a $1,500 allowance for home office furniture. Telecommuters come into the office once a week to meet with other team members and their supervisor; they use the telephone for audio teleconferencing at other times.

Quick Review

1. What is the "telecommuting gap"?
2. What are the five types of telecommuting?

Health Issues in the Networked Economy

In general, computers and the Internet have been very beneficial to society and have allowed us to do many things not otherwise possible. For example, they have created virtual communities of people who otherwise would not have been able to meet. However, working at the speed of the Internet can cause health problems associated with long-term use of the keyboard and mouse. These problems are costing employers large sums of money in workers' compensation costs and lost productivity. In this section, we will discuss the various health problems and the possible solutions through a comprehensive approach that includes the use of ergonomics.

Repetitive Stress Injuries

In the early part of the twentieth century, many blue-collar occupations that required repetitive motions often resulted in a variety of aches and pains, which the workers accepted as a "part of the job." Some such injuries were "stitcher's wrist," "brick layer's shoulder," "meat cutter's wrist," and "cotton twister's hand." Today,

ⓕ ocus on Management

Telecommuting to the Salt Lake City Olympic Site

Planning for and designing the facilities for an olympics, even a Winter Olympics, is a big job that requires the cooperation of a large number of people. For the 2002 Winter Olympics, the Salt Lake City planning group needed more than one hundred architects, engineers, and contractors to create the $300 million, thirty acre complex in the downtown area. The project includes a plaza and courtyard, a multiplex cinema, retail offices, a cultural museum, and residences to be used as Olympic villages for the athletes and the media.

The traditional approach to doing the work for this project would have been to bring in everyone to the same location. However, in this case, using a system developed by the Cubus Corporation, the planners and builders from five states were brought together over the Internet. With this system, if a building needs to be changed, the architect can make the change and dozens of other users can see the change at once and provide feedback. They can talk with each other via the computer and demonstrate changes. With a project this size, faxes and phones would have bogged down the process but the software enables the process to go forward quickly to meet the deadlines associated with an olympics. The only downside is that the individuals involved in the process have to carry their computer with them everywhere they go.

Source: Karen Allen, "Salt Lake City Planners Commute On Line." *USA Today,* August 5, 1999, p. 6e.

Many of the facilities for the 2002 Salt Lake City Winter Olympics were designed by individuals telecommuting from other locations.

with the widespread use of computers, workers in computer-related occupations are having similar types of aches and pains. Often referred to as **repetitive stress injuries (RSI)**, these injuries are becoming epidemic in computer-related jobs. In fact, the use of the computer has created a dimension in occupational health and safety unique to computer users. The Occupational Safety and Health Administration (OSHA) reported that in 1996 U.S. workers experienced more than 647,000 lost workdays due to RSI (OSHA refers to RSI as "work-related musculoskeletal disorders"). RSIs now account for 34 percent of all lost workday injuries and illnesses. These injuries cost business $15–$20 billion in workers' compensation each year. Indirect costs may run as high as $45–$60 billion.[8] Although not all of these RSIs can be attributed to computer use, there is no doubt that a significant percentage can.

RSIs have increased concurrently with the increase in the number of "heavy" computer users (i.e., users who spend long, uninterrupted sessions working at the computer). That this causes problems is not surprising when you consider that a typical keyboard operator's hands travel about sixteen miles across the keyboard during an eight-hour workday while entering data. This includes striking 115,200 keys, a daily workload equivalent of lifting 1.25 tons!

At one time, RSIs were restricted to professions that made heavy use of the keyboard, but today that is no longer the case. The growth in Internet use through such activities as sending, receiving, and processing e-mail, Web surfing, participating in chat rooms, and so on has brought RSIs home to many people who would not consider themselves to be working in a profession involving heavy use of the keyboard.

RSI is also called *cumulative trauma disorder (CTD)* and *typing injury (TI)*. Regardless of the name, RSI involves numbness and tingling in the hands as well as pain and edema (swelling) of the hands, arms, shoulders, neck, and/or back. RSI occurs when muscles, tendons, and nerves are damaged by irritation resulting from prolonged use of a keyboard with the body in an unnatural, unrelaxed position. Often this is due to using an improperly designed workstation (in this context, a **workstation** is the computer and supporting furniture). RSI can totally debilitate a worker.

RSI can take several forms, including carpal tunnel syndrome and tendonitis. **Carpal tunnel syndrome** results when the median nerve becomes compressed as the result of swollen, inflamed tendons exerting pressure on a nerve. **Tendonitis** is a general inflammation and swelling of the tendons in the hands, wrists, or arms and epicondylitis is an irritation of the tendons connecting the forearm to the elbow joint (also known as tennis elbow).

Carpal Tunnel Syndrome

Carpal tunnel syndrome is the most common form of RSI. Each time a key is pressed, tendons slide back and forth in the hand and wrist. If friction occurs during this process, the tendons or their sheaths may become inflamed and painful. If the swollen tendons squeeze the arm's median nerve at the wrist, where the median nerve passes to the fingers through a narrow passage called the *carpal tunnel,* then carpal tunnel syndrome can occur. This process is shown in Figure 12-6. When the nerve is compressed, severe pain, numbness, and loss of strength result. These sensations are more common at night, often awakening the victim. Symptoms may worsen quickly if the activity is continued. As the nerve compression continues damage to the nerve can occur.

A diagnosis of carpal tunnel syndrome is made by examining a history of the computer user's activity and symptoms. Also, electrical impulse procedures assess the nerve's ability to fully handle the impulse—a delay indicates an obstruction in the carpal tunnel. Nonsurgical treatment is, of course, preferred. This includes immobilizing the hand by splinting the hand and wrist for three to six weeks and prescribing anti-inflammatory drugs. If no improvement results in two to three months, then surgical intervention becomes necessary. The surgical procedure, most often done on an outpatient basis, involves severing the transverse carpal ligament, thereby releasing the pressure on the median nerve. Complete healing takes about two months. When the syndrome is recognized and treated early, 80 percent of all cases can be reversed.

---

8. http://www.osha-slc.gov/SLTC/ergonomics/index.html.

Figure 12-6 Carpal Tunnel Syndrome

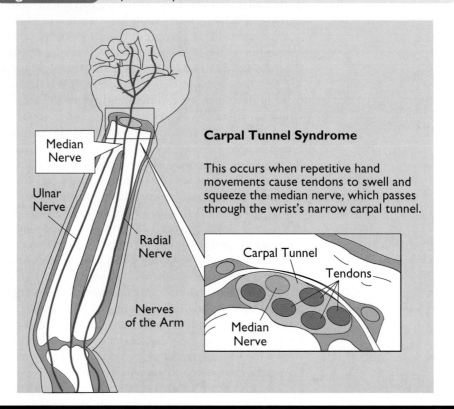

Median Nerve

Ulnar Nerve

Radial Nerve

Nerves of the Arm

Carpal Tunnel Syndrome

This occurs when repetitive hand movements cause tendons to swell and squeeze the median nerve, which passes through the wrist's narrow carpal tunnel.

Carpal Tunnel

Tendons

Median Nerve

Causes of Repetitive Stress Injuries

Research into RSI has identified a number of risk factors. Initially, heavy computer users were recognized as the most likely subjects to develop RSI. Design of the workstation is another key risk factor. Clearly, if the worker uses the keyboard for extended periods of time in a strained or unnatural position, injury is much more likely. Many surveys by labor-related organizations reveal that workers are uneducated about how the workstation should be individually designed.

Other factors include the worker's psychological state relating to production and deadline pressures, fear of losing their job, boredom with repetitive tasks, or being isolated or discouraged from socializing with coworkers. Also, certain physical factors have been identified as risks including diabetes, pregnancy, and thyroid disorders. These tendencies are not understood but are being evaluated.

Researchers have found that a comprehensive examination of the causes of repetitive stress injury and other health-related problems must consider the following issues:

1. The work "motion" required to complete the task
2. The equipment design of the workstation
3. The education provided for the worker about how to use the workstation equipment
4. The attitude of management toward the worker
5. The physical characteristics that may predispose the worker to repetitive stress injury

This comprehensive approach may provide understanding of the causes of RSI.

Mouse Problems

Although not nearly as problematic as keyboard use, improper use of a mouse can also cause shoulder, back, and arm pain. People who use a mouse positioned to the side of their computer keyboard have been found to have greater muscle tension in

One treatment for RSI is to have workers wear splints to support the wrist.

the upper shoulder, back, and arm than those who use a centrally located trackball pointer. Because the mouse is used 30 percent of the time in word processing and 80 percent of the time in graphics work, proper positioning can be critical to avoiding "mouse shoulder" or "mouse arm." It has also been found that training and short breaks can cut this tension in half.

It should be noted that keyboards are much wider now than when the mouse was introduced with the Apple Macintosh in 1984 and that the mouse has been moved farther to the side of the user. Users tend to keep their arm straight out, causing shoulder problems. By using a centrally located trackball pointer, the pointing motion is moved right in front of the user. On a personal note, the author has switched from a mouse to a trackball for this reason.

Even for recreational computer users, there is danger in the extended use of the keyboard and mouse. Researchers have found that Web surfing can be hazardous to your health particularly because it is a leisure activity and people are less aware of their posture and the way they use the mouse and keyboard. By leaning away from the keyboard, users put extra stress on wrists and elbows. They also tend to keep constant pressure on their mouse-click finger while scrolling through long Web pages and don't take advantage of natural waiting periods during downloads, instead keeping their hands on the mouse in a position called "mouse freeze."[9]

Ergonomics

The work motion and the equipment used by the worker necessitate considering the concept of **ergonomics,** or **human factors engineering.** Ergonomics is defined as the science of designing the workplace in such a way as to keep people healthy while they work, resulting in higher morale and more productivity. Ergonomics combines the knowledge of engineers, architects, physiologists, behavioral scientists, environmental scientists, physicians, and furniture designers and manufacturers to determine the best design of tools, tasks, and environments.

---

9. "Health Dangers Lurk for Internet Surfers," *The Atlanta Journal-Constitution,* August 1, 1999, p. F1.

The goal of ergonomics is to create optimum balance between productivity and well-being. An ergonomically designed workstation will allow the worker to work in a comfortable posture, thereby reducing the risk of developing a repetitive stress injury. This design would include consideration of the height and position of the monitor, the height and angle of the keyboard, the task chair, proper indirect and task lighting, proper ventilation, noise reduction paraphernalia, and a footrest if the user's feet are not resting squarely on the floor. Of these, the task chair or seat is probably the most important. It should have an adjustable back and arm supports and height capabilities. Figure 12-7 shows an ergonomically designed workstation.

Although the equipment may be ergonomically adjustable, the worker must be educated on how to make adjustments to the workstation and on the importance of using them. Many employers are approaching the injury problem as a team effort and find that including the information system manager as part of the team is beneficial. This team approach makes using the equipment properly as important as efficiency and productivity. The team approach also improves the working relationship between management and the worker. A positive mutual attitude has been shown to be far more productive both in work quality and injury reduction.

Because the keyboard is at the root of many repetitive stress injuries, several keyboard designs are on the market, each claiming that users may use it with their hands in a natural position. Figure 12-8 shows one of these ergonomic keyboards. High-speed scanners and bar code wands can also help by reducing repetitive key data entry.

Figure 12-7 Ergonomic Workstation

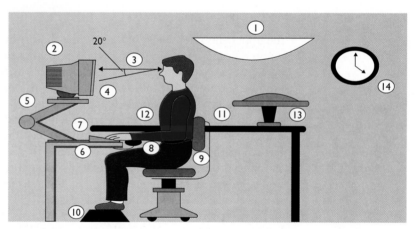

1. **Indirect Lighting:** Fixtures that bounce light off ceilings or walls provide a softer light that is less likely to reflect off monitor screens and create glare.
2. **Monitor Height:** The top of the monitor should be no higher than eye level.
3. **Monitor Distance:** Sixteen to twenty-two inches is recommended for visual acuity; twenty-eight inches or more is recommended if there are emission concerns.
4. **Monitor Display:** High-resolution, noninterlaced screen with dark letters on a light background with an antiglare screen coating or antiglare filter.
5. **Adjustable Monitor Support:** The monitor should move up and down, forward and back, and tilt on its axis.
6. **Keyboard Support:** Adjustable between twenty-three and twenty-eight inches in height. Operator's arm should hang straight down from the shoulder and bend ninety degrees at the elbow and enable the operator to type without flexing or hyperextending the wrist.
7. **Keyboard:** Adjustable tilt to enable typist to keep hands in a straight line with the wrists and forearms.
8. **Wrist Rest:** Rounded, padded, adjustable support for the heel of the hand or forearm without constricting the wrist.
9. **Seat Height:** Adjustable between sixteen and nineteen inches. Users should be able to bend their hips and knees at ninety degrees and sit with their feet flat on floor.
10. **Footrest:** Enables typists with shorter legs to rest feet flat while working.
11. **Back Support:** Backrest should adjust up, down, forward, and backward to support the lumbar portion of the spine in the small of the back.
12. **Work Surface Height:** A comfortable height for reading, handwriting, drawing, and other nonkeyboard work.
13. **Reading Light:** An independent light source for reading letters, reports, books, and so on.
14. **Clock:** Schedule regular breaks, preferably five minutes an hour.

Figure 12-8 Ergonomic Keyboard

Psychological Problems

The psychologically healthy person uses the computer in healthy ways but may also suffer some negative effects. As a tool, the computer extends the expectation of work productivity. When results fall short of expectations, and they frequently do, a slow process of frustration and anxiety may result in a gradual erosion of self-esteem, leading to feelings of inadequacy and depression. After all, self-esteem is enhanced by success, and when perceived failures, no matter how minor, occur, disappointments and depression may ensue. Pressures to produce may take from the worker time previously available to family. An interruption of this process may cause problems in relationships with both spouses, children, and significant others.

As with any other tool, the computer can exacerbate existing pathologies by presenting another avenue for expressing potentially negative behavior. Typical types of behavior that can be facilitated by the computer and the Internet include a type of "Web addiction," introversion, depression, and pedophilia. A widely quoted 1999 survey of Web use appeared to show that 6 percent of all Internet users were "addicted" and 10 percent were abusers whose Internet use was impinging on the rest of their lives. However, if one looks closely at the survey, which was answered by seventeen thousand users, the key caveat was: People who appear to be addicted to the Web have other problems as well. A previous study showed that the average Web "addict" had also experienced previous psychiatric disorders.

Health Problems at fareastfoods.com

Fareastfoods.com provides its employees, whether working in the office or telecommuting, the most ergonomic workstation it can find and encourages its employees to report any work-related health problems immediately. It also runs periodic educational programs that train its employees in the proper use of a keyboard.

Quick Review

1. What does *RSI* stand for? What are two other names for RSI?
2. List three features of an ergonomic workstation.

Web Content Issues

The Internet has brought a tremendous advance in the availability of information, resources, and activities. Unfortunately, issues are raised by the content of some Web sites. These issues involve three categories of Web sites:

- Adult-oriented material that should not be seen by children
- Material that can be used to harm others
- Gambling activities

In this section, we will discuss each of these categories of Web content and the ways in which they are being handled.

Adult-Oriented Web Sites

Although there is little argument that adult-oriented Web sites and chat rooms are inappropriate for children, there is a great deal of discussion about how to ensure that children don't visit these sites. Various approaches have been tried, including:

- Passing legislation restricting the content of Web sites
- Using filtering software
- Installing filters on material coming into a country

In the first approach, the United States has enacted several laws attempting to restrict Web content that is "indecent" or "patently offensive" from all online systems accessible to minors. The first of these laws was the **Communications Decency Act (CDA)** in 1996. It was struck down by the U.S. Supreme Court in 1998. Later that year the **Child Online Protection Act (COPA)** was passed but was also ruled unconstitutional by a federal judge in 1999. At this writing, this ruling is under appeal by the Justice Department. These two attempts to restrict online content and the corresponding legal rulings invalidating them point out the problems associated with censoring the Internet. In the United States, the First Amendment to the Constitution guarantees freedom of speech and has been interpreted by the courts to include the Internet.

Instead of depending on legislation to protect their families from inappropriate material on the Internet, many parents are adding **filtering software** to their browsers to restrict access to Web sites that contain objectionable material. Software like CyberSitter and Surfwatch uses various approaches to choose sites that are to be blocked. These approaches range from a simple system based on words found in the Web sites to more-complex systems that can determine the pictorial content. The word system has problems because sites such as that of the Girl Scouts of America could be restricted if "girl" is used as a keyword on which to base Web site blocking. In addition to filtering software, there is at least one national ISP (MayberryUSA: www.mbusa.net) that is dedicated to filtering pornographic and hate Web sites for its users.

The issue of using filtering software on computers in libraries connected to the Internet in the United States has been heavily debated, but such filtering has been ruled unconstitutional on the grounds of freedom of speech by a federal judge. There have been calls in favor of passing legislation to make library filtering legal.

Entire countries use filtering to keep objectionable material outside of their borders. For example, Australia has enacted legislation requiring its Internet service providers (ISPs) to prevent pornographic or other content deemed indecent from reaching their clients. ISPs will be required to remove objectionable content from their servers within twenty-four hours of being directed to do so by national authorities and to provide means to block access to objectionable overseas sites as well. Australia is well known for its liberal attitude toward freedom of speech and other civil rights, so restricting its citizens from freely surfing the Web will be difficult. In fact, a loophole in the law has already been found through which Australian citizens may be able to anonymously surf the Web.

The disintegration of borders means that a free country like Australia will have difficulties in monitoring what its citizens view online. In fact, many Australian adult Web site operators are moving their servers to other countries, asserting that this puts them beyond Australian law. Even if ways are found to filter all online content entering the country, many feel that doing so would devastate electronic commerce in Australia by putting such a heavy burden on ISPs there.

Terrorist-Oriented Web Sites

The existence of terrorist-oriented Web sites was widely discussed after the Columbine, Colorado, high school shootings in May of 1999 after it was discovered that the killers may have learned how to create pipe bombs on the Internet. There was an outcry against such Web sites, and one poll showed that 68 percent of American citizens wanted the FBI or other federal law enforcement agencies to monitor the Internet.[10] Legislation also has been submitted in the U.S. Congress to require registration of all sites that provide information about gun sales. On the other hand, free speech advocates feel that such monitoring or legislation would violate the freedom of speech guaranteed by the United States Constitution. (Other countries have constitutions that do not guarantee free speech.) Parents who wish to keep information on such sites out of their homes can use the same filtering software that is used to try to protect children from adult-oriented sites.

Web-Based Gambling Sites

In 1999, worldwide online gambling revenue was an estimated $1.2 billion and was expected to grow to $4.2 billion by 2001. Much of this growth may be located in Australia, where companies are obtaining Internet gambling licenses from various states.[11]

However, this growth may never occur; the U.S. Senate has indicated that it would ban online gambling. In addition, in 1999, a federal commission on gambling recommended banning Internet wagering not already approved in the United States,

Online gambling Web sites, like this one, may be ruled illegal.

---

10. Declan McCullagh, "Washington: The Net Must Pay," *Wired News,* May 1, 1999.
11. "Report: Global Net Gambling to Explode," http://www.news.com, July 16, 1999.

and a New York State Supreme Court judge ruled that even though a casino was located in the country of Antigua, it was still subject to New York laws. In this case, the judge ruled that the Internet site created a virtual casino in the user's computer and therefore broke state and federal gambling laws. Gambling proponents, on the other hand, argue that because the server was located in a foreign country, it should not be subject to U.S. laws.

At this writing, the future of Internet gambling in the United States is an open question, depending on the outcome of legislation at the federal level and rulings by various courts. Even if outlawed in the United States, the disintegration of borders may make it very difficult for authorities to prosecute off-shore gambling sites if there are no extradition treaties with the countries in which the sites are located.

The Future of the Networked Economy

Predicting the future of the networked economy is a risky business, at best. However, two safe predictions are that there will be a continuing movement toward ubiquitous computing and connectivity and that commerce will become increasingly electronic and global. As computers become smaller, cheaper, and faster and as bandwidth increases, the number of computers connected to the Internet will continue to grow in the United States and other developed countries. As a result, consumers will demand that goods and services be made available electronically causing commerce increasingly to be handled electronically on a global scale. For you as a college student, this means that you must find ways to become knowledgeable about these trends so that you can take advantage of them. Failure to do so will put you at a severe disadvantage. Remember that there will be many new jobs in the networked economy as well as old jobs in new forms. Understanding the networked economy will enable you to do this.

These two trends are being manifested in a number of ways, including:

- Consumer appliances being connected to the Internet, giving homeowners the capability to control them from a distance as well as enabling them to communicate with one another or, if necessary, a repair service
- Expanded wireless Internet connections giving people the capability to connect to the Internet from any location—car, boat, hiking trail, and so on
- Computer networks in the home enabling families to communicate via e-mail or Web site as their time becomes more fragmented
- Client computers in hotel rooms or on the backs of airline seats making it no longer necessary to lug around a laptop
- Time becoming the scarcest resource of all, leading to increased use of videoconferencing to avoid long business trips and to enable virtual meetings
- A continuing move to personal outsourcing as people seek ways to concentrate their time on the tasks and recreation that they wish to pursue instead of chores

A Day in the Life of Mary: 2005

To help you envision this future, consider the following day in the life of a college student named Mary in the year 2005. Mary attends the University of Georgia on a Hope Scholarship. Note that although we cannot guarantee that all of these changes will occur by that year, there is a high probability that many of them will—some long before 2005![12]

7:00 A.M. The day starts with Mary being awakened by her computer playing some new Celtic videos, which had been downloaded in compressed format

---

12. This scenario was originally created by Professor Richard Watson of the University of Georgia.

Ⓕocus on People

Steve Jobs

On April Fool's Day of 1976, Steve Jobs and Steve Wozniak founded the Apple Computer Company to sell the computers that they were building in their garage. For the next nine years, Jobs served in various positions with the company, includng president and chairman of the board, as it grew into a giant in the computer field. During this time, he was instrumental in developing the Apple II and Macintosh lines of computers. The Apple II enjoyed wide use in the education fields while the Macintosh pioneered the use of the graphical-user interface that is now the standard for virtually all computers. In 1985, Jobs lost a power struggle with John Sculley and left Apple to found a new company, NeXT Computers. When NeXT failed to be a success, Jobs sold it to Apple and became involved with Pixar, Inc., the company that gave us the *Toy Story* computer-animation movies, as its CEO and president.

Because Jobs sold NeXT to Apple, who at that point planned to make NeXT the foundation of its next generation operating system, he was then able to devote his attention to Pixar, Inc. In 1997, after a period of falling sales and stock prices, Apple chose to bring Steve Jobs back as the interim CEO, a title he still holds. Under his leadership, Apple has released the extremely popular iMac, G3, and iBook lines of computers, as well as releasing several much-needed upgrades to the operating system. Apple's stock rebounded from a low of $12 in October of 1997 to a high of over $70 in 1999. Another innovation from Apple, under Jobs, was the introduction of the extremely fast G4 computer utilizing the revolutionary PowerPC G4 chip. Even though its speed rating in MHz is no higher than competing chips, it achieves must faster processing speed by processing more data at a time. The PowerPC G4 chip has been able to perform over one *billion* operations per second (1 *gigaflop*)—fast enough for the U.S. Defense Department to classify it as a supercomputer and restrict it from being exported to certain countries.

As founder and current interim CEO of Apple Computers, Steve Jobs has been the driving force behind many of Apple's most successful products.

overnight. The videos are displayed on a flat-screen monitor hung on the wall (it doubles as a watercolor landscape when not in use). After five minutes, it switches to a Web page displaying news customized to Mary's interests. After a quick breakfast, Mary leaves for campus. As she drives in, her automobile connects to the Internet and reads her e-mail to her through its sound system. It also provides Mary with a reminder of the classes she is scheduled to attend that day.

8:00 A.M.–9:15 A.M. Mary's first class is Globalization, Regionalism, and Information Technology Systems (commonly known as GRITS), an elective course examining how IT influences globalization and regionalism. Today's class topic, "Singapore: The Wired Nation," features speakers from Singapore's National Computer Board and the National University of Singapore. As well as being seen by students in Georgia, the live broadcast is seen by students in Singapore, Norway, Brazil, and South Africa. All are taking the same course, which has to start at 8:00 A.M. because of the twelve-hour time difference between Athens and Singapore.

9:15 A.M.–10:30 A.M. After class, Mary heads off to the combination computer lab–coffee shop, where she can recharge her laptop at any table. The retractable charging cords plug straight into laptops, doing away with the need to carry around a bulky transformer. Before finding a seat, Mary purchases a bottle of water and a muffin. As she leaves the food area, she checks the wall-mounted LCD panel to verify that the correct amount had been deducted from the contactless smart card in her backpack. Cash had practically disappeared from her university two years ago with the introduction of contactless smart cards that do not require swiping; all you do is walk through the food area exit. You can program the cards to display selected information every time you pass through a reader. For her Finance class, Mary's team is managing a portfolio of mature Internet stocks, and she had programmed her smart card to display the portfolio's latest value. The bottom line of the LCD panel shows that the portfolio is down 1.5 percent for the day based on a number of stock exchanges around the world.

Upon opening her laptop, Mary is instantly connected to the wireless local area network. She checks her Web-based to-do list and is reminded she has to take a quiz for her Networked Economy class and finish a report on Mississippi.com for the Strategic Management course. Before working on her assignments, Mary checks her integrated mailbox and answers three e-mails and one voice mail and deletes video spam. The quiz takes about thirty minutes, and she is relieved to immediately find out that she scored 92 on the quiz. Next, Mary consults an online collection of databases—introduced at her university in the late 1990s—several times while doing the Mississippi.com assignment and checks a few Web sites. When she finishes the electronic report, she submits it via e-mail to the professor. Even though the professor is working with an MBA team on a consulting assignment in Portugal, she knew that he would grade the paper within a couple of days and return it with attached audio comments. She thinks this mix of classroom lectures and independent learning is good preparation for her business career because she is learning how to learn by herself.

10:30 A.M.–11:45 A.M.   Mary attends her Networked Economy class and, via the Web, participates in an interesting class discussion that includes the use of voice over the Internet. Whereas some of her fellow students are in her classroom, others are at home or in offices as many as five time zones away. However, all work from the same Web page and wear a special headset-microphone combination that allows them to hear and respond to other class members' comments.

1:00 P.M.–3:00 P.M.   After lunch, Mary's Data Management class team (Mary, Eduardo from Brazil, and Tore from Norway) meets to review its database design. The team did an audio conference with a shared screen, so the team members all see the same data model and can take turns amending it until they agree. It is a high-fidelity model of the timetable for the Saõ Paulo subway. The Data Management class is simultaneously taught with the partner business schools in Brazil and Norway, and students learn how to design and query databases at the same time they hone their skills in working in cross-cultural teams. After completing the project, Mary catches a bus to the recreation center to play racquetball.

5:00 P.M.–6:00 P.M.   Mary's team in her Corporate Consulting class meets at the video booth in another lab. An alumnus working in New York has agreed to critique the team's presentation prior to the team's final meeting with the client. It takes only a moment to set up the camera and check the video connection, and then the team presents its spiel with slides. As he watches the presentation on his network computer in New York, the alumnus makes electronic notes whenever he spots something of concern. The presentation analyst software tags the comment to the exact point in the presentation so that, during the playback, he is able to go directly to the portions of the presentation that needed some more work and point out the flaw. After a few retakes of portions of the presentation and some more comments by the alumnus, the team declares victory.

6:30 P.M.–7:30 P.M.   Mary's boyfriend comes over for a dinner, which she ordered earlier from an Atlanta-based company called CyberCusine that specializes in same-day shipments of custom meals. During dinner, her sound system stops playing the latest REM DVD and announces that a priority voice mail has arrived. Mary uses the remote to instruct the system to play it for her; it is the alumnus who viewed her team's presentation that afternoon. He was impressed by her role in the presentation and wondered if she could cut and paste her section of the presentation and mail it to the company's recruiter. It takes Mary about five minutes to locate the video on the college server, edit it, and e-mail it to the recruiter. After dinner, she celebrates her new job opportunity by ordering a digital copy of the old video *Something about Mary* from the Web-based video library. Her computer automatically pays for the video through her contactless smart card.

⊘ Summary

To summarize this chapter, let's answer the Learning Objectives questions posed at the beginning of the chapter.

How has the rise of ubiquitous computing and communications changed our concepts of time, distance, and borders? The most evident change is the number of people "living in Internet time," that is, living in a world that is moving faster and faster, a world in which we have to resort to personal outsourcing to handle many of our nonwork responsibilities. From a social issue point of view, the networked economy is built on three key elements: ubiquitous computing and communications (computer and communications technology everywhere), education, and freedom of ideas and trade. Ubiquitous computing has changed our concept of time and distance by introducing the death of distance, the homogenization to time, and the disintegration of borders. The death of distance means that we are no longer restricted by geography, making it possible for many workers to avoid long commutes to and from work by telecommuting using the Internet or private networks. The homogenization of time means that we live in a 24/7 world where business continues somewhere all of the time. This is causing the blurring of work and home as we find we can work around the clock if necessary. Finally, the disintegration of borders means that states and countries can no longer protect themselves from the import of ideas and goods without seriously hampering their entry into the networked economy.

What economic issues are we facing in the networked economy? The networked economy is affecting issues of productivity and the workplace, changing work requirements and economic dislocation, and taxation policies. In terms of productivity and workplace issues, the networked economy has led to lower inflation and higher productivity through the use of information technology. It has also created greater gender equity for executive positions and the opportunity for employees to use telecommuting. In terms of changing work requirements and economic dislocation, the networked economy is putting an increasing emphasis on education. No longer will a high school education be acceptable for working in information technology-related positions. Unfortunately, it appears that many of those with the lowest educational attainment will be the ones who do not use the Internet very much. In terms of taxation policies, there is a great deal of discussion regarding taxation of electronic commerce sales, with no resolution at this time.

How has telecommuting changed the lives of many employees in the networked economy? There are numerous advantages to telecommuting for the company, the employee, and the community. For the company, studies have shown that although the monetary benefits are difficult to measure, the company benefits from more-productive, happier workers. For the employee, telecommuting leads to a less-stressful job, a shorter (or no) commute to work, and a better family life. For the community, telecommuting leads to less traffic and air pollution. On the other hand, telecommuters require a different type of management because they are not in the traditional workplace. In addition, telecommuting is not for every worker because it requires a large degree of self-initiative. Finally, it can cause problems when the worker cannot separate their work life from home life—too much homogenization of time.

What health issues has the networked economy brought on? Working at the speed of the Internet can cause health problems associated with long-term use of the keyboard and mouse. These problems cost employers large sums of money in workers' compensation costs and lost productivity. The primary problem is repetitive stress injury (RSI) due to the overuse of a keyboard and a mouse in work and leisure activities involving the computer and the Internet. Carpal tunnel syndrome is the most common form of RSI. In this syndrome the median nerve becomes compressed as the result of swollen, inflamed tendons exerting pressure on a nerve. The work motion and the equipment used by the worker necessitate considering the concept of ergonomics. The goal of ergonomics is to create optimum balance between productivity and well-being. An ergonomically designed workstation allows the worker to work in a comfortable posture, thereby reducing the risk of repetitive stress injury.

How has Web content caused problems for society? Web content has caused problems in three ways: adult-oriented material that should not be seen by children, material that can be used to harm others, and gambling activities. A variety of ways have been used to protect children from adult-oriented material, including passing laws against such content, using filters on Web browsers to screen such content, and filtering all Web content coming into a country. Protecting against material that can cause harm, such as bomb-making instructions, follows the same methodology. At the same time that Australia is licensing online gambling, the United States at both the federal and state levels appears to be moving strongly against Internet gambling.

What kinds of changes in our society might we see in the future? There will be a continuing movement toward ubiquitous computing and connectivity as computers become smaller, cheaper, and faster and as bandwidth increases, and commerce will increasingly be handled electronically on a global scale. This will bring about both opportunities and problems for society as we learn to deal with these changes. Opportunities will be available to those who learn how to take advantage of these changes, whereas those who don't will be at a severe disadvantage in the networked economy.

⊙ Review Questions

1. What do ubiquitous computing and communications have to do with societal issues in the networked economy?

2. What is *reach creep*, and what does it have to do with living in Internet time?

3. What does the *death of distance* have to do with telecommuting?

4. How have educational requirements for working in the networked economy changed compared to those for the industrial economy?

5. What are some advantages and disadvantages of telecommuting?

6. What are the two points of view of companies and state/local governments regarding taxation of electronic commerce?

7. What does ergonomics have to do with RSI?

8. What are the three types of Web content problems? Which types can be handled by adding filtering software to browsers?

9. Why have laws against adult-oriented Web sites been struck down in the United States?

10. What two major changes are we fairly certain to see over the next few years?

⊙ **Discussion Questions**

1. Talk with your parents or adults who are at least twenty years older than you to compare your student lifestyle with theirs at the same age. What differences did you find? What similarities do you find?
2. Review the classified advertisements in the Sunday newspaper, and determine which jobs would be considered a part of the networked economy. Which jobs will allow telecommuting?
3. Discuss why computer health problems are no longer restricted to people working in computing-intensive positions.

⊙ **CASE**

WildOutfitters.com

Alex was pulling an extension cord out of the front window of the store to hook up the laptop when Claire pulled into the drive. The laptop was sitting on the collapsible camp table that he had set up on the front lawn of the store.

Claire greeted him with a kiss and asked, "Working outside to enjoy the nice weather?"

"That's only a fringe benefit," Alex replied. "Actually, I need to write some product reviews but Jill's at my desk doing some system upgrades. You might want to join me out here, Bob's working on some invoices at your desk."

"It seems that we need to do something about our lack of space. Things didn't seem so crowded in the old days," Claire sighed.

"I've been thinking that we might have an alternative to adding onto the store," said Alex. "One word—telecommuting."

The Campagnes have had to expand their staff because of the expansion of business they have experienced since starting their Web site. This success has brought on new problems, such as the lack of space in their original store to accommodate the new employees. They have been pondering an addition to the store to add more office space. As Alex mentioned, an addition might not be needed or may at least be delayed if they can provide a telecommuting option for their employees.

Several advantages of telecommuting make the idea attractive to the Campagnes. First, it would provide savings in terms of facility costs. In their case, a very real savings could be realized if they do not need to build additional space. Second, telecommuting programs have been known to produce increases in productivity from 10 percent to 40 percent. Third, remote access to important functions such as network maintenance and customer service would make them more resilient to disruptions. Fourth and possibly the most

attractive to the Campagnes is the improved quality of life that telecommuting might provide for their staff. This one is dear to their hearts because their major motivation for starting the Wild Outfitters store to begin with was to improve their own quality of life. Much like their business has given them more opportunity to do what they love, telecommuting might give this ability to their workers.

In order to set up a telecommuting program, they will have to consider additions to their information system. Information system resources for telecommuting will include home office equipment, central site equipment at Wild Outfitters, telecommunications access for both the home offices and the central site, and software for security and network management. The technology available for these components varies in expense, access speeds, bandwidth, and reliability.

Perhaps more importantly, they will also need to examine their management policies to understand how these should change for a telecommuting program. They will need to identify the qualities that make a good telecommuter and use these in their hiring and training. Other issues to examine include the hours of duty, pay and leave policies, and overtime guidelines. It will be important for them to establish clear work policies for the telecommuters and to ensure that these are well communicated to them. A program such as this will take a lot of thought and planning, but it seems to be a good next step in the evolution of Wild Outfitters.

"You know, if we do this telecommuting right," Claire said as she stirred sweetener into the coffee that she had prepared on the camp stove, "we could set up an office like this anywhere."

Alex leaned back against a pile of sleeping bags and smiled. "Only a little while ago it seemed that we were just a couple of small store owners. Now look at how far we've come," he said as he waved his hand over the make-shift office.

"I can see the headlines now: Campagnes Office-Less Due to Cyber-Success." Claire and Alex beamed with pride over the new challenges that their networked business had provided.

1. What benefits and costs could the Campagnes derive from starting a telecommuting program at Wild Outfitters?

2. What characteristics should a person have that would make them a good telecommuter? Explain.

3. *(Hands on)* A telecommuting program creates a nontraditional working environment. Old methods of management and evaluation may not work well in this new environment. Search the Web for suggestions about how to manage telecommuters. Use what you find to develop a telecommuting agreement that may be used to communicate the expectations between a supervisor and a telecommuting employee at Wild Outfitters.

4. *(Hands on)* Alex and Claire would like to analyze the costs versus benefits of developing a telecommuting program at Wild Outfitters. They have found that there are several options for providing the resources discussed in the case. A little research has allowed them to develop several equipment options. The information related to the costs and benefits of these options are stored in an Excel file at http://www.harcourtcollege.com/infosys/mckeown. Use this information to perform a cost–benefit analysis for each option. Based on your analysis, discuss the options that you think would work best for Wild Outfitters.

Glossary

Access control
Techniques for controlling access to stored data or computer resources (chapter 5)

Ad hoc analysis
Another name for data-based DSS (chapter 6)

Ad hoc decisions
Another name for unprogrammed decisions (chapter 6)

Adaptable Web site
A site that can be customized by the visitor (chapters 7 and 11)

Adaptive Web site
A site that learns from the visitor's behavior and determines what should be presented (chapters 7 and 11)

Analysis stage
The second step in the structured systems development process in which the analyst fills in the details of the system under study (chapter 8)

Anonymous FTP
An FTP site that does not require users to have a user ID and password (chapter 3)

Ansi X 12
An EDI protocol used in the United States (chapter 3)

Antivirus policies
Organizational policies that are enacted to protect the computer system from viruses and other destructive software (chapter 10)

Application software
Software that constitutes the greatest proportion of software used on computers and performs specialized tasks (chapter 2)

Artificial intelligence (AI)
Hardware and software systems that exhibit the same type of intelligence-related activities as humans—listening, reading, speaking, solving problems, and making inferences (chapters 6)

ASCII
(Pronounced "as-key") An acronym for *American Standard Code for Information Interchange* (chapter 2)

Attractor
A Web site that continually attracts a high number of visitors (chapter 7)

Attribute
The term used for the fields or columns in a relational database (chapter 5)

Backbone
In a computer network, the primary high-speed communications link to which other networks are connected (chapter 3)

Backup
A copy of software or data that is made by the user to guard against accidental loss of software or data (chapter 10)

Bandwidth
The term used as a measure of the capacity of a communication channel, expressed in bits per second (chapter 1)

Bar code reader
A device for converting a bar code into a price or other data (chapter 2)

Bar codes
Combinations of light and dark bars that are coded to contain information (chapter 2)

Baseband transmissions
A classification of transmission in which the full capacity of the transmission media is used and multiple sets of data are transmitted by mixing them on a single channel (chapter 3)

Batch processing system
Combining data from multiple users or time periods and submitting them to the computer for processing in a batch (chapter 4)

Benchmark
A test in which the competing products are compared using programs and data typical of the actual conditions under which the proposed system will operate (chapter 9)

Beta testing
Engaging the services of users to test prerelease versions of software (chapter 9)

Binary number system
Base 2 number system based on zero and one (chapter 2)

Bit
The basic unit of measure in a computer; contraction of *BI*nary and digi*T* (chapters 2 and 5)

Bots
Another name for intelligent agents (chapter 6)

Bridge
A combination of hardware and software that connects two similar networks (chapter 3)

Broad customization
A Web site attempts to communicate with a number of types of stakeholders or many of the people in one stakeholder category (chapter 7)

Broadband transmissions
Simultaneous transmission of large amounts and types of data, including audio, video, and other multimedia using different frequencies (chapter 3)

Browser
Client software used on the Web to fetch and read documents on-screen and print them, jump to other documents via hypertext, view images, and listen to audio files (chapters 2 and 3)

Bugs
Errors in the execution of a program (chapter 9)

Bus
A primary cable to which other network devices are connected (chapter 3)

Bus network
A computer network in which computers are tied into a main cable, or bus (chapter 3)

Business critical applications
A software application that is critical to the continued existence of the organization (chapter 2)

Business process improvement (BPI)
Taking advantage of the opportunities for improved operations offered by information technology by making changes to the way in which the organization operates (chapter 4)

Business process reengineering (BPR)
Creatively destroying the current way of doing business in favor of new ideas and new technology (chapter 4)

Business service infrastructure layer
The software layer of electronic commerce that handles services required to support business transactions (e.g., encryption) (chapter 7)

Byte
A group of eight bits—equivalent to a single character (chapters 2 and 5)

Carpal tunnel syndrome
A painful wrist condition that can result from excessive keyboarding (chapter 12)

CASE repository
A database of metadata about a systems development project (chapter 9)

CASE tools
Specific CASE software used in systems development (chapter 9)

CD-ROM
A form of read-only optical storage using compact disks (chapter 2)

Central processing unit (CPU)
The part of the computer that handles the actual processing of data into information (chapter 2)

Chatbots
Another name for natural language systems (chapter 6)

Child Online Protection Act (COPA) of 1998
Legislation aimed at protecting children from pornography and hate-related material on the Internet (chapter 12)

Chip
A tiny piece of silicon that can consist of over one million electronic elements (chapter 1)

Ciphertext
A coded, unreadable form of information (chapter 10)

Clear Air Act of 1990
Legislation aimed at reducing the amount of air pollution that included a recommendation for increased telecommuting (chapter 12)

Client
A computer running an application that can access and display information from a server (chapters 2 and 3)

Client/server computing
A combination of clients and servers that provides the framework for distributing files across a network (chapters 2 and 3)

Coaxial cable
A type of cable similar to that used to transmit cable television signals into your home (chapter 3)

Command-driven interface
The software responds when the user enters the appropriate command or data (chapter 2)

Communication flip-flop
A fundamental change in the nature of the relationship between buyers and servers caused by electronic commerce (chapter 7)

Communications Decency Act (CDA) of 1996
Legislation, since ruled unconstitutional, that aimed at protecting citizens from pornography on the Internet (chapter 12)

Computer
An electronic, automatic machine that manipulates and stores symbols based on instructions from the user (chapter 1)

Computer integrated manufacturing (CIM)
Computerizing the entire conversion operation (chapter 4)

Computer language
A language used by humans to give instructions to computers (chapter 2)

Computer matching
The process of matching records in two data banks to determine which records exist in both data banks (chapter 11)

Computer monitoring
Management's monitoring of an employee's use of a personal computer or computer terminal (chapter 10)

Computer network
A combination of two or more computers with a communications system that allows exchange of data, information, and resources between the computers (chapters 1 and 3)

Computer program
See Program

Computer Security Act of 1987
Legislation aimed at ensuring the security of U.S. government computers (chapter 11)

Computer-aided design (CAD)
A graphics software package that assists the user in developing engineering and architectural designs (chapter 4)

Computer-aided manufacturing (CAM)
The use of computers and robotics to automate the conversion process (chapter 4)

Computer-aided software engineering (CASE)
The use of software to help in all phases of system development, including analysis and design and writing programs (chapter 9)

Computer-based training (CBT)
Self-paced training programs presented on and controlled by a computer (chapter 9)

Connectivity
The availability of high-speed communications links that enable the transmission of data and information between computers and conversations between people (chapter 1)

Conversion process
Transactions associated with the production of goods and services (chapter 4)

Cookie
In Web terminology, a small data file with data about the user that is kept on their computer and read by the browser when a particular Web site is visited (chapter 7)

Cost/benefit analysis
A measurement of relative costs against projected benefits (chapter 8)

Creative destruction
A concept that emphasizes that the most important part of the change process for a

business is not what remains after the change but rather what has been destroyed (chapter 1)

Customer convergence
The Web marketing concept that firms must describe their products and services so that potential customers converge on the relevant Web pages (chapter 7)

Data communications software
Software that is necessary to direct the data or information flow (chapter 2)

Data dependence
The dependency between data and data storage (chapter 5)

Data encryption system
Combinations of software and hardware that convert data coming out of a computer into an unreadable form for transmittal over a network (chapter 10)

Data flow diagram (DFD)
A pictorial representation of the flow of data into and out of the system (chapter 8)

Data hierarchy
The order in which data or information is organized in the computer (chapter 5)

Data integrity
The correctness of data in a database (chapter 5)

Data management system
The part of a decision support system that retrieves information from a database as needed (chapter 6)

Data mining
A search for relationships within the data (chapter 6)

Data model
One of several models of the way data will be represented in a database management system (chapters 5 and 8)

Data redundancy
The repetition of data on multiple files (chapter 5)

Data security
The protection of a computer's software and data from unauthorized manipulation, destruction, or theft (chapter 10)

Data sharing
A function of a database query language that coordinates the sharing of database information by multiple end users (chapter 5)

Data surveillance
Computer matching of databases or profiling of individuals who fall into specific groups (chapter 11)

Data types
Specification of the type of data that will be stored in a database field (chapter 5)

Data warehouse
A subject-oriented snapshot of an organization at a particular point in time (chapter 5)

Data
Facts, numbers, or symbols that can be processed by humans or computers into information (chapters 1 and 5)

Databank
A store of information on people or organizations (chapters 11)

Database
A collection of information that is arranged for easy manipulation and retrieval (chapters 5 and 6)

Database management system (DBMS)
A database software system that can work with multiple files (chapters 5)

Database marketing
Advertisers using data mining and data warehouses to select a group of individuals who are most likely to buy their products (chapter 6)

Data-based DSS
A decision support system that is aimed at exploring data warehouses to analyze data found there to answer questions from decision makers (chapter 6)

Death of distance
A result of the networked economy in which people are no longer restricted by geography (chapter 12)

Decision making
Recognizing problems, generating alternative solutions to the problems, choosing among alternatives, and implementing the chosen alternative (chapter 6)

Decision support system (DSS)
Information systems aimed at helping an organization prepare for the future by making good decisions (chapters 1, 4, and 6)

Decryption
Conversion of encrypted text represented by characters into a readable form (chapter 7)

Dedicated server network
A network in which at least one of the computers linked to the network acts as a server (chapter 3)

Default HTML file
The Web page file that is accessed automatically at a Web site when no HTML file is shown as part of the URL (chapter 3)

Demand reports
Reports that are generated by the MIS upon a request by a manager (chapter 6)

Demand risk
The risk that changing demand or the collapse of markets significantly reduces demand for a firm's products or services (chapter 4)

Demonstration prototype
A version of an information system that "looks" like the final version but does not actually do anything (chapter 9)

Demonstration prototyping
Creating a prototype that will be used to demonstrate features of a potential system (chapter 9)

Design stage
The systems development stage in which the *how* questions are answered (i.e., How will the system be developed and how will it work?) (chapter 9)

Desktop publishing software
Combining word processing, graphics, and special page-definition software to create documents (chapter 12)

Digital cash
The storage of value in a digital format in one of two broad forms: card-based or computer-based (chapter 7)

Digital divide
A separation of the world population based on their knowledge of and access to the Internet (chapter 12)

Digital economy
See Networked economy

Digital form
Strings of zeros and ones in computers (chapter 1)

Direct conversion
A conversion from one system to another in

which the old system is discarded at the time that the new system is installed (chapter 9)

Direct Internet connection
Connecting an enterprise network directly to the Internet with no intervening ISP (chapter 10)

Disintegration of borders
A result of the networked economy in which countries cannot control the material entering over the Internet (chapter 12)

Disintermediation
The process of eliminating intermediaries (chapter 7)

Disk drive
A device that writes information onto or reads information from a magnetic or optical disk (chapters 2)

Document database
A database that, instead of storing tables, stores related documents (chapter 5)

Document-based groupware
Groupware used specifically for knowledge management through a document database (chapter 5)

Domain database
The part of an expert system knowledge base which contains the facts about the subject being considered by the expert system (chapter 5)

Domain name
Another name for the server computer address (chapter 3)

Dumb terminal
A low-cost device that consists of a keyboard, a monitor, and a connection to a server but no processing chip, internal memory, or secondary storage (chapter 2)

DVD
Digital versatile disks used for storage of data as well as audio and video programs (chapter 2)

Economic feasibility
An indication that solving the problem or developing a system is an economically wise decision (chapter 8)

EDIFACT
An EDI protocol commonly used in Europe (chapter 3)

Electronic commerce topology
The three types of communication networks used for electronic commerce: Internet, intranet, and extranet (chapter 7)

Electronic commerce
Carrying out business transactions over computer networks (chapters 1 and 7)

Electronic Communications Privacy Act of 1986
Legislation that extended wiretap laws protecting aural conversations to include communications between computers (chapter 11)

Electronic communities
Communities that are real in the sense that they are made of people, but electronic in the sense that all communication is in an electronic form (chapter 1)

Electronic data interchange (EDI)
Allows computers to exchange electronic transmissions of data and information, thus automating routine business between retail stores, distributors, and manufacturers (chapters 3 and 4)

Electronic funds transfer (EFT)
The transfer of payments between organizations engaged in business-to-business electronic commerce using the public banking system (chapter 7)

Electronic mail (e-mail)
An electronic technology that handles the sending and receiving of messages (chapters 1 and 3)

Electronic supervision
Organization managers monitoring the amount of work performed by employees on networked computers for entering data, making reservations, and so on (chapter 11)

Electronic wallets
A digital form of storage that enable the user to electronically store multiple credit cards in a combination of software and data (chapter 7)

Encryption
The conversion of readable text into characters that disguise the original meaning of the text (chapter 7)

End users
The people who will eventually use any information system (chapter 8)

End-user development
Development of an information system by an end user (chapter 8)

Enterprise information portal (EIP)
A Web site on an intranet that allows the individual seeking help with a decision to use all three types of information systems without having to worry about which one is being used (chapter 6)

Enterprise resource planning (ERP) systems
A large, integrated system handling business processes and data storage for a significant collection of business units and business functions (chapters 8 and 9)

Ergonomics
The study of the relationship between efficiency and comfort in a worker's use of machines (chapter 12)

Ethics
Value judgments on what is "good" and "bad" that have resulted from consensus in society (chapter 11)

Evolutionary prototype
A type of prototype that evolves through iterative interaction with the user (chapter 9)

Exception report
A report that is generated by the MIS only when an abnormal event occurs (chapter 6)

Executive information system (EIS)
A personalized, easy-to-use system for executives, providing data on the daily operations of an organization (chapters 6)

Expenditure process
The process that handles the transactions associated with the payment of expenses associated with running the organization (chapter 4)

Expert system
A computer system that makes the collective knowledge of various experts in a field available to the user (chapters 5)

Explicit knowledge
Knowledge that is codified and transferable (chapter 5)

Extensible markup language (XML)
An extension of HTML that allows companies to create their own tags to be used in sending data to trading partners (chapter 4)

Extranet
A wide area network using the TCP/IP protocol to connect trading partners (chapters 3 and 4)

Fair Credit Reporting Act of 1970
Legislation that regulates some actions of credit bureaus that collect credit information on individuals (chapter 11)

Fair Information Practice (FIP) Principles
Five widely accepted principles of privacy protection (chapter 11)

Family and Medical Leave Act of 1992
Legislation that encouraged telecommuting as a way of employees remaining at home to care for family members (chapter 12)

Fat client
A client computer, usually a PC, that can also be used as a stand-alone computer (chapter 2)

Fax conversion
The use of optical character recognition to convert incoming fax documents into ASCII format (chapter 5)

Fax modem
A hardware component that combines the capabilities of a modem and a facsimile machine (chapter 5)

Feasibility study
The part of the planning process in which the analyst determines whether or not an acceptable solution to the problem exists (chapter 8)

Feature creep
The tendency for users to repeatedly request additional features in a development project (chapter 9)

Fiber optic cable
The newest type of media that consists of thousands of glass fiber strands that transmit information over networks (chapter 3)

Field
A single piece of information such as a name, a Social Security number, or a profit value (chapter 5)

Field name
An identifier given to a field in a database file (chapter 5)

Field type
The type of information—character, numeric, date, or logical—that will be stored in a field (chapter 5)

Field width
The number of positions set aside for data in a particular field (chapter 5)

File
Any collection of data, information, or programs to which the user can attach a name (chapter 2)

File management system (FMS)
Database management software that can work with only one file at a time (chapter 5)

File server
A server computer with a large amount of secondary storage that provides users of a network access to files (chapter 2)

File transfer protocol (FTP)
A protocol that supports file transfers over the Internet (chapter 3)

Filtering software
Software that restricts access to Web sites that contain objectionable material (chapter 12)

Financial process
The business process that summarizes all

transactions in accounting terms (chapter 4)

Firewall
A device placed between an organization's network and the Internet to control data access (chapters 4 and 10)

Firmware
Instructions on a ROM chip (chapters 1 and 2)

Fixed-price contract
A type of outsourcing contract in which a fixed price for the project is negotiated (chapter 9)

Forecasting model
A process that uses currently available information to predict future occurrences (chapter 6)

Foreign key
A primary key for another table placed in the current table (chapter 5)

Frequently asked questions (FAQs)
A list of frequently asked questions about software or Web topics along with answers to the questions (chapter 3)

Frictionless economy
An Internet-based economy in which goods and services are bought and sold without the need of intermediaries, resulting in lower cost (chapter 12)

FTP server
A server that is running an FTP application (chapter 3)

Gateway
A combination of hardware and software that connects two dissimilar computer networks; it allows a LAN user to access a mainframe network without leaving his or her PC (chapters 2 and 4)

Gbyte (gigabyte)
The largest commonly used measure of computer storage, equal to 230 (approximately 1 billion) bytes of storage (chapter 2)

Graphical applications developer
A software package that allows end users to create menus, boxes, and so on and then to write just the instructions needed for the specific menu or box (chapter 8)

Graphical user interface (GUI)
An interface that uses pictures and graphic symbols to represent commands, choices, or actions (chapters 2 and 3)

Group support system
An information system that is developed to facilitate group problem solving (chapter 5)

Groupware
Software aimed at helping groups of people structure, focus, and facilitate the transfer of information and knowledge among themselves (chapter 5)

Hackers
Individuals who gain unauthorized access to a computer for fun or challenge (chapter 10)

Hard disk
A type of magnetic disk that is fixed in the computer (chapter 2)

Hardware
The electronic part of the computer that stores and manipulates symbols under the direction of the computer software (chapters 1 and 2)

Homogenization of time
A result of the networked economy in which citizens live in a 24/7 world where business continues somewhere all of the time (chapter 12)

Host computer
A computer to which other computers are connected; also, a computer in a network

that is connected to the Internet (chapters 2 and 3)

Hoteling
A type of telecommuting in which temporary office space is created for drop-in use by employees (chapter 12)

Hub
A device for concentrating connections to multiple network devices (chapter 3)

Human capital
Those individuals in an organization who have knowledge about the social networks and problem solving (chapter 5)

Human factors engineering
See Ergonomics

Hypertext markup language (HTML)
A markup language used to create Web pages consisting of text, hypertext links, and multimedia elements (chapter 3)

Hypertext transfer protocol (HTTP)
The protocol for moving hypertext files across the Internet (chapter 3)

Hypertext
A method of linking related information in which there is no hierarchy or menu system (chapter 3)

Icons
Graphical figures that represent operations in a GUI (chapter 2)

Identity theft
The process of stealing a person's credit rating or other information specific to that person (chapter 11)

If–then rule
The rule used in an expert system that, together with facts, create the knowledge base (chapter 5)

Imaging
The process of converting paper versions of documents to a digital form using some type of scanner and saving them to optical or magnetic secondary storage (chapter 5)

Implementation stage
The process of installing the information system that has been designed and developed, acquired, or outsourced (chapter 9)

Indexing
The process of using data values or descriptors to search through documents (chapter 5)

Indirect Internet connection
Connecting the enterprise network to the Internet through an ISP (chapter 10)

Inefficiency risk
The risk that a firm loses market share because it fails to match competitors' unit costs (chapter 4)

Inference engine
The deductive part of an expert system that uses the information in the knowledge base to make suggestions or ask additional questions (chapter 5)

Influence filter
A Web site feature that makes the site more attractive to a specific stakeholder group and less attractive to others (chapter 7)

Information brokers
A new group of individuals who are using databanks to buy and sell information (chapter 11)

Information
Data that have been processed into a form that is useful to the user (chapters 1 and 5)

Information system cycle
Information systems for handling the present,

remembering the past, and preparing for the future (chapters 1 and 4)

Information system life cycle
The three phases in the life cycle of an information system: development, effective operation, and decline in effectiveness (chapter 8)

Information system
Within an organization, a system that converts raw data into information that is useful to managers and other interested parties (chapters 1 and 4)

Information technology (IT)
All forms of technology used to create, store, exchange, and use data, information, and knowledge; also, the infrastructure of the networked economy (chapters 1, 2, and 4)

Information-based DSS
A generic name for many types of information systems that have the same goal: to provide decision-makers with the information they need in a form that is appropriate for them (chapter 6)

Infrastructure
The underlying foundation or basic framework of a system or organization (chapter 1)

Ink-jet printer
A printer that sprays tiny droplets of ink to create letters and graphic images (chapter 2)

Innovation risk
The risk that a firm faces when it fails to continually improve its products and services and loses market share to more innovative competitors (chapter 4)

Input
Receiving the data to be manipulated and the instructions for performing that manipulation (chapters 1 and 2)

Input/process/output (IPO) table
A table for each module of a software package showing the input to the module, the processing that takes place in the module, and the output from the module (chapter 9)

Integrated data management
The storage of all data for an organization in a single database (chapter 5)

Intelligent agents
Computer programs that can be trained to carry out a search over the Internet for needed information (chapter 1 and 8)

Interactivity
The capability of the Web site to interact with the user in some way (chapter 7)

Interface
The format of the viewable screen (chapter 9)

Intermediaries
Individuals and companies that act as *middlemen* or *brokers* between the consumer and the company providing the good or service (chapter 7)

Internet communications data
Non-Web data about individuals transmitted over the Internet including mail messages, "conversations" in chat rooms, postings to bulletin boards, and messages to newsgroups (chapter 11)

Internet economy
See Networked economy

Internet newsgroups
See Newsgroups

Internet operations
A variety of operations that can be carried out on the Internet including FTP, e-mail, telnet, newsgroups, and the World Wide Web (chapter 3)

Internet security
Policies and procedures aimed at protecting the enterprise network from intrusion over the Internet (chapter 10)

Internet service providers (ISP)
Companies that specialize in linking organizations and individuals to the Internet as well as providing services to them (chapters 2 and 3)

Internet Tax Freedom Act of 1998
Legislation that placed a three-year waiting period on state and local Internet taxes in the United States and created the Advisory Commission on Electronic Commerce to study this issue (chapter 12)

Internet
A worldwide network of computers and computer networks in private organizations, government institutions, and universities, over which people share files, send electronic messages, and have access to vast quantities of information (chapters 1, 2, and 3)

Interorganizational system (IOS)
A system that connects the value chains of two or more organizations (chapter 4)

Intranet
An intraorganizational network based on using Internet technology; it enables people within the organization to communicate and cooperate with each other (chapters 3 and 4)

IP address
A numeric address for a server on the Internet consisting of four groups of four digits (chapter 3)

IP-spoofing
A form of Internet intrusion in which an internal IP address is used to fool the server into believing it is in contact with a trusted computer (chapter 10)

IT crime
An illegal act that requires the use of information technology (chapter 10)

IT security
The methods used to protect the hardware, software, data, and user from both natural and criminal forces (chapter 10)

Iterative development
A development process in which there are repeated cycles of prototype creation and testing by the user until an acceptable version is completed (chapter 9)

Kbytes
One kbyte equals 210 (1,024 or approximately one thousand) bytes (chapter 2)

Keyboard
An input device made up of keys that allow input of alphanumeric and punctuation characters (chapter 2)

Knowledge
A human capacity to request, structure, and use information (chapters 1 and 5)

Knowledge base
In an expert system, the facts, judgments, rules, intuition, and experience provided by the group of experts (chapter 5)

Knowledge workers
Workers in organizations who use their knowledge to work with information (chapters 1 and 12)

Laser printer
A nonimpact printer that uses a laser beam to write dots on a drum coated with light-sensitive material that transfers ink to the paper (chapter 2)

Legacy systems
Another name for large, centrally located mainframe computers (chapter 5)

Listserv
A group e-mail function available on the Internet; it enables end users to subscribe to special-interest mailing lists (chapter 3)

Local area network (LAN)
A computer network that is restricted to one geographical area (chapters 2 and 3)

Logic bomb
A computer crime in which a disruptive program executes whenever a certain command is given (chapter 10)

Logic trace
A trace of the line of reasoning used by an expert system to reach a conclusion (chapter 5)

Macros
Programs written as a part of application software that enables it to carry out specific tasks (chapter 8)

Mainframe
A very large and fast computer that requires a special support staff and a special physical environment (chapters 1 and 2)

Maintenance
For an existing program, the process of fixing bugs, adding features, altering parts of the program, and performing other activities to keep the program current (chapter 9)

Management information system (MIS)
An integrated user-machine system for providing information to support operations, management, and decision-making functions in an organization (chapters 6)

Many-to-many communication
A form of communication in which many people can communicate with many other people (chapter 1)

Many-to-many relationship
In a data model, the situation in which multiple fields are related to one another (chapter 5)

Mass customization
The process of making each visitor to a Web site feel that the site has been customized to their needs (chapters 7 and 11)

Mbytes (megabyte)
Measure of computer equal to 220 (approximately 1 million) bytes of storage (chapter 2)

Message distribution infrastructure layer
The software layer of electronic commerce that sends and receives messages (chapter 7)

Meta tag
An invisible HTML tag that is supposed to describe the contents of the Web page (chapter 6)

Metadata
Data about the data fields in a database (chapter 9)

Microwaves
High-frequency radio transmissions that can be transmitted between two earth stations or between earth stations and communications satellites, which are commonly used to transmit such things as television signals (chapter 3)

Mobile computing
A trend in making computing more mobile made possible by the use of laptop computers, wireless fax-modems, cellular phones, and pagers (chapter 3)

Model
A simplified version of the system that allows the analyst to understand the system's important parts (chapters 6 and 8)

Model base
A collection of a variety of types of models that can be used to analyze the data from the database (chapter 6)

Model management system
The part of a decision support system that is used to select a model that can be used to help find a solution to a problem (chapter 6)

Model-based DSS
A decision support system that combines data from the database or data warehouse with mathematical models to answer questions asked by management (chapter 6)

Modem
A communications device that modulates computer signals into outgoing audio signals and demodulates incoming audio signals into computer signals (chapter 2)

Module
A separate program that performs a specific task and shares data with the other modules to lead to an integrated system (chapter 8)

Monitor
A cathode ray tube or flat screen output device that displays output (chapter 2)

Mouse
An input device—about the size of a mouse and connected to the computer by a long cord—that allows input through movement over a flat surface (chapter 2)

Multidimensional databases
A database with two or more dimensions in which each dimension represents one of the parameters that can be varied to determine the effect on the variable (chapter 6)

Multimedia files
Digitized images, videos, and sound that can be retrieved and converted into appropriate human recognizable information by a client (chapter 3)

Multimedia
An interactive combination of text, graphics, animation, images, audio, and video displayed by and under the control of a personal computer (chapter 3)

Music piracy
Illegally downloading music files over the Internet (chapter 10)

National information infrastructure
A nation's communication networks, including the TV and radio broadcast industries, cable TV, telephone networks, cellular communication systems, computer networks, and the Internet (chapter 7)

Natural language processing (NLP)
The use of natural languages to process data into information (chapter 6)

Network
A combination of two or more computers with a communications system that allows exchange of information between the computers (chapters 1, 2 and 3)

Network computer (NC)
A computer that can only be used when connected to a client/server network (chapter 2)

Network externalities
The relationship that states that as the number of devices added to a network goes up linearly the power (or value) of the network goes up as the square of the number of devices on the network (chapter 1)

Network interface card (NIC)
A card in a PC that connects the PC to the network and handles all the electronic functions of network access (chapter 3)

Network news transfer protocol (NNTP)
The protocol used for newgroups (chapter 3)

Network operating system
The software that controls a computer network (chapter 3)

Networked economy
Enhanced, transformed, or new economic relationships based on computer networks and human knowledge (chapter 1)

Neural networks
Computer processing using multiple processors that are "trained" through repetition to handle some task without an extensive, highly specific program (chapter 6)

Newsgroups
A vast set of discussion lists that can be accessed through the Internet (chapter 3)

Object-oriented database
A form of database that is based on a data type called an object; an object contains both the data and the rules for processing the data (chapter 5)

Object-oriented languages
Languages that use objects (self-contained items that combine data and algorithms) that cooperate in the program by passing strictly defined messages to one another (chapter 9)

One-to-many relationships
In a data model, the situation in which one field is related to multiple other fields (chapter 5)

One-to-one relationships
In a data model, the situation in which one field is related to only one other field (chapter 5)

Online analytical processing (OLAP)
A software tool that enables an analyst to extract and view data from a variety of points of view (chapter 6)

Online transaction processing (OLTP)
Each transaction is processed at time of entry rather than being held for later processing (chapters 4 and 6)

Operating system
The primary component of systems software; manages the many tasks that are going on concurrently within a computer (chapter 2)

Operational decisions
Operations that control the day-to-day operation of the organization (chapter 6)

Optical character recognition (OCR)
The use of a scanner to convert a document to digital form and then using software to determine the letters and symbols present (chapter 5)

Optimization
The use of a mathematical technique to find the best solution to a model (chapter 6)

Organizational feasibility
An indication that the problem can be solved or system developed within the limits of the current organization (chapter 8)

Organizational memory
Remembering the past through data, information, and knowledge management (chapters 1, 4, and 5)

Organizational productivity
Making an organization more productive through shared data, information, and resources (chapter 1)

Output
The result of the processing as displayed or printed for the user (chapters 1 and 2)

Outsourcing
A process that involves turning over some or all of the responsibility for the development or maintenance of an information system to an outside group (chapters 9)

Packet switching
In a wide area network, dividing long messages into smaller data units to be transmitted more easily through a network (chapter 3)

Packets
Data that has been grouped for sending over a network (chapter 2)

Page
An electronic document on the Web that contains text and hypertext links to multimedia elements and other pages that are stored on server computers (chapter 3)

Parallel conversion
The conversion of one system to another in which both systems run in parallel before the conversion is completed (chapter 9)

Password
A secret combination of letters, numbers, and/or symbols that is used to ensure that only the legitimate user can access a computer with the given user number (chapter 10)

Password policies
Specific company policies designed to protect data and software through responsible use of passwords (chapter 10)

Path
A portion of the URL that includes the name of the home page file plus any directories or folders in which it is located (chapter 3)

Peer-to-peer configuration
A LAN configuration in smaller networks in which the emphasis is on users sharing files; each computer can function as both a server and a workstation instead of as a single dedicated file server (chapter 3)

Personal computer
Small, one-user computers that are relatively inexpensive to own and do not require a special environment or special knowledge to use them (chapter 2)

Personal identification number (PIN)
A secret numerical password used to access a bank account from an automatic teller machine (chapter 10)

Personal outsourcing
The practice of individuals outsourcing as many of their nonprofessional responsibilities as possible (chapter 12)

Personal productivity software
PC application software, so-called because it allows individuals to increase their productivity (chapter 1)

Phased conversion
An approach to the implementation of an information system where the new system is implemented in phases or modules (chapter 9)

Physical security
The protection of the computer hardware from natural and human damage (chapter 10)

Pilot conversion
An approach to the implementation of an information system where the new system is "tried out" in one of the areas of the organization in which it will ultimately be implemented (chapter 9)

Plain text
The readable form of a message (chapter 10)

Planning stage
The systems development stage in which the problem is identified, a feasibility study is run, and plans are made to begin development (chapter 8)

Platform for Privacy Preferences (P3P)
Proposed technology that would give consumers control over their own personal data by building the necessary mechanism into Web browsers such as Netscape and Internet Explorer (chapter 11)

Point-and-click operations
A method that involves using a mouse or other pointing device to position the pointer over a hypertext link or the menu bar, tool bar, location window, or directory buttons and clicking a button to retrieve a Web page or execute a corresponding command (chapter 3)

Point-of-sale (POS) transaction processing
An input system that is used to store and process important information that is obtained at the time a sale is made (chapter 11)

Port number
An internal address within a Web server (chapter 3)

Portable document format (PDF)
A form of electronic document created with Adobe's Acrobat Exchange that can be easily shared with anyone who has an Acrobat reader (chapters 5 and 12)

Postscript files
A type of file created by desktop publishing software that can be sent to a commercial print shop to be used to publish a document (chapter 12)

Pretty Good Privacy (PGP)
A popular form of public-key encryption, readily available to Internet users (chapter 7)

Primary key
A field or combination of fields that uniquely identifies each record in a table (chapter 5)

Printer
An output device that places words and symbols on paper (chapter 2)

Privacy Act of 1974
Legislation that attempted to correct most of the recordkeeping practices of the federal government (chapter 11)

Privacy
An ethical concern related to the information about one's self that a person wishes to control (chapter 11)

Privacy seal of approval
An icon that a Web site can display if it has agreed to follow the FIP principles as defined by the seal-granting organization (chapter 11)

Private key encryption
A form of encryption in which the key is known only by the person sending and receiving encrypted messages (chapter 7)

Private key
In a public key encryption system, the only key that can decrypt the message (chapter 7)

Procedures
Groups of instructions in a computer program (chapter 9)

Processing
Converting data into information (chapter 1)

Profiling
The use of past experience to infer character-

istics about groups of individuals and then searching databases for individuals with a close fit to those characteristics (chapter 11)

Program
A series of instructions to the computer (chapters 1 and 2)

Programmed decisions
Day-to-day operational decisions based on basic rules and policies set at higher management levels (chapter 6)

Programming
The process of writing a series of instructions for the computer to follow in performing some specific task (chapters 2 and 9)

Project manager
The person who ensures that the project is completed on time and within budget and who is responsible for bringing other people onto the team (chapter 8)

Project plan
The document that provides a description of the desired information system including a clear statement of the scope of the desired project (chapter 8)

Project sponsor
The person who has an interest in seeing the system succeed and who will provide the business expertise to the project (chapter 8)

Prompt
An indicator on the computer screen that data or commands should be entered (chapter 2)

Protocol
A formal set of rules for specifying the format and relationships when exchanging information between communicating devices (chapter 3)

Prototype
A version of the system that contains the bare essentials and that can be used on a trial basis (chapter 8)

Prototyping
Creating a "quick and dirty" prototype of software to get around the lengthy systems analysis and design process (chapter 9)

Pseudocode
A written form of an algorithm that can easily be converted into a computer program (chapter 9)

Public key
In a public-key encryption system, the key can be freely distributed (chapter 7)

Public-key encryption
An encryption system with two keys: one private and the other public (chapter 7)

Push technology
Technology that sends or "pushes" Web pages to the user's desktop rather than being pulled by the user (chapter 6)

Queries
The steps used by a user to retrieve information from a database (chapter 5)

Random-access memory (RAM)
The section of memory that is available for storing the instructions to the computer and the symbols to be manipulated (chapter 2)

Rapid applications development (RAD)
Methods and tools such as CASE tools, prototyping, and end-user computing that allow for faster development of application software (chapter 8)

Reach creep
A by-product of the networked economy in which individuals take on more and more work because technology allows it (chapter 12)

Read-only memory (ROM)
The section of memory that is placed in the computer during the manufacturing process and remains there even after the computer is turned off (chapter 2)

Real time
At the same time, as opposed to being delayed (chapter 2)

Record
A collection of fields with information that usually pertains to only one subject (e.g., person, place, event, etc.) (chapter 5)

Reintermediation
The process of creating new intermediaries in electronic commerce (chapter 7)

Relational database management system (RDBMS)
A database system in which elements are represented as being parts of tables, which are then related through common elements (chapter 5)

Relations
Data organized as a table and used in a relational database (chapter 5)

Repetitive stress injury (RSI)
A condition in which workers suffer from moderate to severe muscle and joint problems in the hand, wrist, arm, and shoulder (chapter 12)

Request for proposal (RFP)
The process of requesting that vendors submit a proposal on a hardware or software job (chapter 9)

Revenue process
Receiving revenue for the sale of goods and services (chapter 4)

Router
A computer that determines the path a message will take from the sending to the receiving computer (chapter 3)

Rule database
The part of an expert system knowledge base that contains the rules to be used by the reasoning element of the expert system (chapter 5)

Satellite office
A fully equipped office where employees can reserve space and work one or more days a week closer to their homes (chapter 12)

Scanner
A device used to translate a page of a document into an electronic form that OCR software can understand (chapter 5)

Scheduled reports
A report generated by the information-based DSS on a regular basis, containing summary reports of the results of the data processing operation (chapter 5)

Secure Electronic Transaction (SET)
A security system used to protect merchants from credit card fraud (chapter 10)

Server address
The address of the computer on which the Web resource is stored (chapter 3)

Server
A computer on a network running an application that provides services to client computers (chapters 2 and 3)

Service resource
Another name for a protocol on the Web (chapter 3)

Shareware
Software that is made available to users for a nominal fee or donation (chapter 11)

Shrink-wrapped software
Software on disk(s), instructions, and documentation all wrapped together (chapter 2)

Siftware
Software used in data mining to "sift" through the data looking for elements that matches the search criteria (chapter 6)

Signed message
A message that can be authenticated as being from a particular person (chapter 7)

Simple mail transfer protocol (SMTP)
A protocol for transferring mail messages over the Internet (chapter 3)

Simulation
The process of exercising a model using multiple values to determine the outcome under different circumstances (chapter 6)

Smart card
A card, containing memory and a microprocessor, that can serve as personal identification, credit card, ATM card, telephone credit card, critical medical information record, and as cash for small transactions (chapter 7)

Sniffer
A type of computer program on an intermediate Internet computer that will briefly intercept and read a message (chapter 7)

Software piracy
The unauthorized copying of software for either personal use or financial gain (chapter 10)

Software
Programs that direct the activity of the computer (chapters 1 and 2)

Spam
A commonly used term for junk e-mail (chapter 11)

Speaker
A device designed to generate sounds (chapter 2)

Spike
A voltage surge, such as lightning or some other electrical disturbance, that causes a sudden increase in the electrical supply; delicate chips and other electrical parts can be destroyed (chapter 10)

Stakeholder analysis
An analysis to determine the effect of the change in the existing system on any person or group that will affect or be affected by the new or revised system (chapter 8)

Stakeholders
The people who determine the future of the organization (e.g., stockholders, employees, customers, etc.) (chapter 7)

Statistical model
A model in which the objective is to learn about tendencies within the data set or to prove that differences exist between parts of the data (chapter 6)

Strategic decisions
Decisions that determine the long-term direction of the organization by creating policies (chapter 6)

Structured approach
An approach to systems development in which each stage must be completed in a specific order after certain objectives are achieved in the previous stage, including a specified set of deliverables and management approval (chapter 8)

Structured decisions
Decisions that can be programmed in advance (chapter 6)

Structured query language (SQL)
A popular language that is used for retrieving information from a relational database (chapter 5)

Supply chain
A name for the inbound logistics part of an organization's value chain (chapter 4)

Surge protector
A device that protects the computer's hardware and memory from a voltage surge (chapter 10)

Switching costs
Costs associated with an individual or an organization switching suppliers (chapter 4)

System administrators
People who manage security and user access to an intranet or LAN (chapter 10)

System degradations
The point in the IS life cycle in which the performance of the system drops off markedly and the quality of information provided by the system suffers (chapter 8)

System proposal
A document that describes what the new system should look like (chapter 8)

System request
A document that lists the business need for the project, its expected functionality, and the benefits that would likely result from its completion (chapter 8)

System specification
A document that is used in the implementation stage to program the new system, outsource it, or acquire it, depending on the decision made at the beginning of the design stage (chapters 8 and 9)

System unit box
The main case of the PC in which the CPU and internal memory are housed (chapter 2)

System
A group of elements (people, machines, cells, etc.) organized for the purpose of achieving a particular goal (chapter 1)

Systems analysis and design process
See Structured development

Systems analyst
A person who carries out the systems analysis and design process (chapters 8)

Systems audit software
Security software that keeps track of all attempts, especially unsuccessful ones, to log on to the company's computer system (chapter 10)

Systems development
The process of developing a system design to meet a new need or to solve a problem in an existing system (chapter 8)

Systems development life cycle (SDLC)
See Systems analysis and design process

Systems life cycle
See Systems development

Table
A type of HTML tag that supports the presentation of a table containing a caption, column, row headers, and cell elements (chapter 5)

Tacit knowledge
Personal knowledge, experience, and judgment that is difficult to codify (chapter 5)

Tactical decisions
Decisions that are made to implement the policies created by strategic decisions (chapter 6)

Target marketing
The process by which advertisers use data banks to select a group of individuals who are most likely to buy their products, thereby allowing advertisers to spend more time and money on fewer prospects (chapter 11)

Target refractor
A method for customizing a Web site to meet the needs of stakeholders (chapter 7)

Technical feasibility
An indication that the technology exists to solve the problem or develop the system (chapter 8)

Telecommuting
A work arrangement in which employees work at any time or place that allows them to accomplish their work in an effective and efficient manner (chapter 12)

Telnet
The capability to use the Internet to log onto a computer other than your local computer (chapter 3)

Telework center
Office space that is utilized by employees from different organizations, with employers being charged for the space and services utilized by each employee per day (chapter 12)

Tendonitis
A general inflammation and swelling of the tendons in the hands, wrists, or arms (chapter 12)

Thin client
Client computers on a network that cannot be used in a stand-alone mode (chapter 2)

Threaded
An organization of questions and answers in which answers or comments that relate to a previous question or comment are linked to it (chapter 5)

Three-tiered client/server architecture
A client/server architecture in which there is an intermediate computer between the server and client (chapter 2)

Throw-away prototype
A prototype that is not meant to be kept but is used to do exploratory work on critical factors in the system rather than being used just for interface designing or for demonstrating an idea to a client (chapters 8 and 9)

Time bomb
A computer crime in which a disruptive program is timed to execute itself on a certain date (chapter 10)

Time-and-materials contract
An outsourcing contract in which the client is charged for the time and materials required to complete the project (chapter 9)

Transaction processing system (TPS)
Converting raw data into a usable, electronic form (chapters 2 and 4)

Transaction
The exchange between customer and merchant (chapter 3)

Transactional data
Data that are created when a transaction takes place that requires the customer to reveal his or her identity (chapter 11)

Transmission control protocol/Internet protocol (TCP/IP)
The communication protocol of the Internet (chapter 3)

Trapdoor
A part of the operating system that will allow knowledgeable users unauthorized access (chapter 10)

Trojan horse
A computer program that sabotages the original program or modifies it to perform illegal activities (chapter 10)

Tuple
The term for a row in a relation used in a relational database (chapter 5)

Twisted pairs
A media for information transfer that is made of pairs of copper wire twisted together (chapter 3)

Uniform resource locator (URL)
A standard means of consistently locating Web pages or other resources no matter where they are stored on the Internet (chapter 3)

Uninterruptible power supplies (UPS)
A device that continues power to a personal computer if the electrical current is disrupted (chapter 10)

Unprogrammed decisions
Decisions that cannot be programmed in advance (chapter 6)

Unstructured decisions
See Unprogrammed decisions

Update
In a database, to make changes to one or more columns for a particular row (chapter 5)

User
In a model-based DSS, the person using the models and data to generate alternative solutions to a problem (chapter 6)

User interface
Viewable information on a screen (chapter 2)

User interface system
In a model-based DSS, the system with which the user works (chapter 6)

User interface prototype
A version of an information system used for testing that "looks" like the final version of a system and allows prospective users to interact with the screens (chapter 9)

User interface prototyping
A type of prototyping in which the user interface is created to show the user how the final system might appear (chapter 9)

Value chain
The chain of business activities in which each activity adds value to the end product or service (chapter 4)

Value system
The linkage of the value chains of two organizations (chapter 4)

Value-added contract
A type of outsourcing contract in which the client is charged for the additional benefits accruing from the project (chapter 9)

Value-added network (VAN)
Public networks, available by subscription, to provide data communications facilities beyond standard services; often used to support EDI (chapters 3 and 5)

Videoconferencing
A way of enabling groups or individuals in different locations to meet at the same time through real-time transmission of audio and video signals between the different locations (chapter 5)

Virtual company
A company that has no physical presence other than a small marketing staff (chapter 2)

Virtual/mobile office
A form of telecommuting in which employees are equipped with the communications tools and technology needed to perform job duties from wherever they need to be—home, office, customer location, airport, and so on (chapter 12)

Virus
A computer program whose purpose is to replicate itself, with mischievous or malicious intent, within the computer's memory (chapter 10)

Voltage surge
A surge of electricity that can destroy a computer's hardware or memory (chapter 10)

Waterfall approach
Another name for the *structured approach* (chapter 8)

Web browser
See Browser

Web page
A special type of document that contains hypertext links to other documents or to various multimedia elements (chapter 3)

Web site
An Internet server on which Web pages are stored (chapters 3 and 5)

Web topologies
The three network topologies used in electronic commerce; Internet, intranet, and extranet (chapter 7)

Web-visit data
Data generated about a user's computer whenever a visit is made to a Web site (chapter 11)

Wide area network (WAN)
A network covering more than a single building (chapter 3)

Wintel
A combination of Windows and Intel indicating a PC with a Intel chip running a version of the Windows operating system (chapter 2)

Wireless LANs (WLANs)
Local area networks that use radio waves rather than wires for transmission of data (chapter 3)

Workplan
A document that lists the tasks that must be accomplished to complete the project, along with information about each task, the number of persons required, and an estimated time to complete each task (chapter 8)

Workstation
A specialized client computer that allows the use of specialized applications requiring high-speed processing of data into information; also, any combination of computer and associated furniture (chapters 2 and 12)

World Wide Web (WWW)
A body of software, a set of protocols, and conventions based on hypertext and multimedia techniques that make the Internet easy for anyone to browse and add contributions (chapters 1, 2, and 3)

World Wide Web Consortium (W3C)
A nonprofit group directed by the inventor of the World Wide Web, Tim Berners-Lee, that seeks to promote standards for the evolution of the Web (chapter 11)

Worm
A disruptive program that travels through the computer's memory, wiping out information in the process (chapter 10)

Credits

p. 4 Courtesy of AirTran Airways

p. 9 © 1999 B&H Photo-Video

p. 13 (left) © Michael S. Yamashita/Corbis Images

p. 13 (right) © Tony Cordoza/Liaison International

p. 17 Courtesy of Intel Corporation

p. 20 (left) © Charles E. Rotkin/Corbis Images

p. 20 (right) Courtesy of International Business Machines Corporation

p. 27 Permission granted by Lands' End, Inc.

p. 32 These materials have been reproduced by Harcourt College Publishers with the permission of eBay Inc. Copyright © eBay, Inc. All Rights Reserved.

p. 35 Pentium® III processor-photo courtesy of Intel Corporation

p. 40 AP Wide World Photos/Paul Sakuma

p. 42 (bottom) © James D. Wilson/Liaison International

p. 44 Courtesy of International Business Machines Corporation

p. 49 Courtesy of Sun Microcomputers

p. 57 © Mary Kate Denney/PhotoEdit

p. 64 Courtesy of Square D Company

p. 67 © Spencer Grant/PhotoEdit

p. 73 Cisco 2600 Multiservice router courtesy of Cisco Systems

p. 76 Courtesy of 3Com Corporation

p. 91 (left) © Reuters/Corbis Images

p. 91 (right) Courtesy of 3Com Corporation

p. 98 Courtesy of Manheim Online

p. 104 Courtesy of Johnson Technologies, Oak Park, Illinois

p. 108 © Bob Rowan/Corbis Images

p. 110 Courtesy of International Business Machines Corporation

p. 126 © Copyright Kompass International Neuenschwander SA 1999

p. 141 © Owen Franken/Stock, Boston

p. 147 © Mark Richards/PhotoEdit

p. 148 Lotus and Lotus Notes are registered trademarks of Lotus Development Corporation.

p. 150 Courtesy of Brightware, Inc.

p. 155 Courtesy of Bell Atlantic

p. 159 © Copyright Sterling Software, Inc.

p. 166 Courtesy of Microsoft Corporation

p. 170 Courtesy of Excite, Inc.

p. 176 Photo courtesy of Pine Cone Systems, Inc.

p. 185 © Jonathan Elderfield/Liaison International

p. 187 Courtesy of Edmund Publications Corporation

p. 188 Permission granted by Lands' End, Inc.

p. 189 Courtesy of International Business Machines Corporation

p. 191 Courtesy of W3C-World Wide Web Consortium/Donna Coveney/MIT

p. 197 © Randy LaVoy/Photographic Group

p. 201 Courtesy of America Online Inc.

p. 210 © Michael A. Dwyer/Stock, Boston

p. 220 Photo courtesy of Mannheim Auctions

p. 230 Courtesy of AutoNation, Inc.

p. 234 © AP Wide World Photos/Adam Nadel

p. 248 Courtesy of Merrill Lynch Online

p. 254 Courtesy of Ed Yourdan

p. 268 © Copyright 1999 Compaq Computer Corporation

Fig. 9.10 © Copyright by SAP AG

p. 286 © Jim Bounds/SYGMA

p. 287 Courtesy of National Computer Registry

p. 293 © AP Wide World Photos/Saurabh Das

p. 296 © AP Wide World Photos/Daniel Hulshizer

p. 300 Courtesy of EyeDentify Inc.

p. 301 Courtesy of American Power Conversion Corporation.

p. 303 Courtesy of Phil Zimmerman

p. 305 Special permission to reproduce a screen shot of the Web page found at http://www.cert.org, © 1999 by Carnegie Mellon University, is granted by the Software Engineering Institute.

p. 308 © AP Wide World Photos/Alexander Zemlianichenko

p. 314 Courtesy of Bigfoot International

p. 319 Courtesy of Roger Clarke

Fig. 11.01 Courtesy of Privacy.net

p. 324 Courtesy of Northern Light Technology, Inc.

p. 336 Courtesy of Webvan

p. 338 Courtesy of The Brookings Institute

p. 344 © Brad Mangin

p. 350 © Jim Sulley/The Image Works

p. 351 © Spencer Grant/PhotoEdit

p. 357 © Matthew Borkoski/Stock, Boston

p. 358 © AP Wide World Photos/Douglas Pizac

p. 361 © Ed Young/Corbis Images

p. 367 © AP Wide World Photos/Stuart Ramson